Social Policy in a Developn

Social Policy in a Development Context

Social Policy in a Development Context is a new series which places social policy at the centre of research while maintaining The United Nations Research Institute for Social Development's (UNRISD) unified approach to social development. The series provides a new and exciting contribution to the literature in economic development and social policy. In economic development, social policy has been recognized as an integral part of development, but the literature often falls short of elaborating social policy for a unified approach to economic and social development. In social policy, analysis has concentrated mainly on European and North American countries, and studies on developing countries often lack comparative rigour. The bridge between economic development and social policy will not only contribute to the academic research but also inform the policy debate at the international and national levels.

Titles include:

Huck-ju Kwon
TRANSFORMING THE DEVELOPMENTAL WELFARE STATE IN EAST ASIA

Thandika Mkandawire (*editor*)
SOCIAL POLICY IN A DEVELOPMENT CONTEXT

Social Policy in a Development Context
Series Standing Order ISBN 1–4039–4295–1 (hardback); 1–4039–4296–X (paperback)
(*outside North America only*)

You can receive future titles in this series as they are published by placing a standing order. Please contact your bookseller or, in case of difficulty, write to us at the address below with your name and address, the title of the series and the ISBN quoted above.

Customer Services Department, Macmillan Distribution Ltd, Houndmills, Basingstoke, Hampshire RG21 6XS, England

Social Policy in a Development Context

Edited by

Thandika Mkandawire

UNITED NATIONS
RESEARCH INSTITUTE
FOR SOCIAL DEVELOPMENT

First published 2004 by
PALGRAVE MACMILLAN
Houndmills, Basingstoke, Hampshire RG21 6XS and
175 Fifth Avenue, New York, N.Y. 10010
Companies and representatives throughout the world

PALGRAVE MACMILLAN is the global academic imprint of the Palgrave
Macmillan division of St. Martin's Press, LLC and of Palgrave Macmillan Ltd.
Macmillan® is a registered trademark in the United States, United Kingdom
and other countries. Palgrave is a registered trademark in the European
Union and other countries.

ISBN 1–4039–3660–9 hardback
ISBN 1–4039–3661–7 paperback

This book is printed on paper suitable for recycling and made from fully
managed and sustained forest sources.

A catalogue record for this book is available from the British Library.

Library of Congress Cataloging-in-Publication Data
Social policy in a development context / edited by Thandika Mkandawire.
    p.   cm. — (Social policy in a development context)
    Includes bibliographical references and index.
    ISBN 1–4039–3660–9 — ISBN 1–4039–3661–7 (pbk.)
    1. Social policy.   2. Economic development.   3. Economic policy.
    I. Mkandawire, P. Thandika.   II. Series.
    HN17.5.S5987 2004
    361.6'1—dc22   2004052594

10   9   8   7   6   5   4   3   2   1
13   12   11   10   09   08   07   06   05   04

Printed and bound in Great Britain by
Antony Rowe Ltd, Chippenham and Eastbourne

Contents

v

List of Tables

List of Figures

Preface

All but one of the papers in this volume were presented at an international conference in Tammsvik, Sweden in September 2000. The conference marked the beginning of a major project on 'Social Policy in a Development Context'. The main problem addressed by the project is: *How can social policies be used to enhance social capabilities for economic development without, in the process, eroding the intrinsic value of the social ends that social policies claim to address?*

To address this question UNRISD launched a research programme which currently consists of nine networks involving more than 100 researchers from different disciplines and parts of the world. The immediate task of the project was to shift social policy thinking away from the rather static and residual category of 'safety nets' towards a conception in which social policy worked in tandem with economic policy to ensure equitable development. A series of volumes is anticipated from the project.

UNRISD would like to take this opportunity to thank the Olof Palme Institute for hosting the conference in Sweden and for the active participation of its staff in the conference. We would also like to thank the Swedish International Development Cooperation Agency (SIDA) for the financial support of the conference and the publication of these papers.

Many people at UNRISD have been involved in this project. I would like to express thanks especially to Cynthia Hewitt Alcántara and Shahra Razavi for useful discussions in the early phases of the project. I would also like to thank Virginia Rodriguez and Nina Torm for their support in the preparation of the manuscript. Thanks are also due to Huck-ju Kwon who is coordinating the project.

As is the case with all UNRISD projects, work on this project would have not been possible without the core funding of the governments of Denmark, Finland, Mexico, the Netherlands, Norway, Sweden, Switzerland and the United Kingdom. Let me once again take this opportunity to express our gratitude.

THANDIKA MKANDAWIRE
Director, UNRISD

Notes on the Contributors

Ha-joon Chang is Assistant Director of Development Studies at the University of Cambridge. His research interests are the role of the state in economic change; industrial policy, privatization and regulation; theories of institutions and morality; the East Asian economies; globalization; and economic development in historical perspective.

Diane Elson is Professor of Sociology at the University of Essex, UK. Previously, she worked for the United Nations Development Fund for Women (UNIFEM) and for Manchester University where she was Chair in Development Studies. Her current research and teaching interests are in global social change and the realization of human rights with a particular focus on gender inequality. She edited *Male Bias in the Development Process* (1995); co-edited *Special Issues of World Development on Gender, Adjustment and Macroeconomics* (1995); *Growth, Trade, Finance and Gender Inequality* (2000) and the *UNIFEM Report on Progress of the World's Women* (2000).

Ben Fine is Professor of Economics at the School of Oriental and African Studies. He teaches economic history of South Africa in the twentieth century; South African minerals-energy complex; economic assessment of, and policy for, South Africa and economics training and capacity building. Some of his recent publications are *Women's Work and the Capitalist Family* (1992); *Making Democracy Work: A Framework for Macroeconomic Policy in South Africa* (joint contributing ed., 1994) and *South Africa's Political Economy: From Minerals-Energy Complex to Industrialisation?* (with Z. Rustomjee, 1997).

Jayati Ghosh is Associate Professor at the Centre for Economic Studies and Planning, Jawaharlal Nehru University, New Delhi and a collaborating researcher for the UNRISD Project on Globalization, Export-Oriented Employment for Women and Social Policy.

Huck-ju Kwon is Research Coordinator at the United Nations Research Institute for Social Development (UNRISD), while on leave from the Sung Kyun Kwan University, Korea. He has worked on issues of comparative social policy in East Asia, social policy and democracy, and politics of public policy. His publications include *The East Asian Welfare Model: the State and Welfare Orientalism* (1998) and 'Beyond European Welfare Regimes: comparative perspectives on East Asian welfare systems' (*Journal of Social Policy*, 1997). He is also co-editor of the *International Encyclopaedia of Social Policy* (2005).

Maureen Mackintosh is the External Research Co-ordinator for the UNRISD subproject on *Commercialization of Health Care: Global and Local Dynamics and Policy Responses* within the project entitled 'Social Policy in a Development Context'. She is Professor of Economics at the Open University in London. Her specialization covers economics of public services and social sector markets, and development economics. She has published numerous articles in journals and written books on health care and social provision. Her latest publications include 'Flexible contracting? Economic cultures and implicit contracts in social care' *Journal of Social Policy*, (2000) and 'Inclusion by design: Rethinking health care market regulation in the Tanzanian context' (*Journal of Development Studies*, with P. Tibandebage, 2002).

Carmelo Mesa-Lago is Distinguished Service Professor Emeritus of Economics and Latin America at the University of Pittsburgh. He is the author of 58 books and more than 200 articles and chapters in books on social security and health care, and comparative economic systems, published in 8 languages in 33 countries, including *Market, Socialist and Mixed Economies: Comparative Policy and Performance – Chile, Cuba and Costa Rica* (2000).

Guy Mhone is the Head of the Graduate School of Public and Graduate Management, Wits University, Johannesburg. His books include a study of the Zambian copper industry, co-authored books on environment and development in Zimbabwe and Southern Africa, and edited collections on the informal sector and Malawian political economy. He has published numerous academic and journalistic articles and essays on structural adjustment, employment and development in Southern Africa. His research interests are the development implications of enclave legacies, alternatives to structural adjustment and stabilization reform, the informal sector and labour market issues (discrimination, migration, equity and efficiency balances).

Thandika Mkandawire is Director of the United Nations Research Institute for Social Development (UNRISD). He is an economist with long experience in the promotion of comparative research on development issues. From 1986 until 1996, he was Executive Secretary of the Council for the Development of Social Science Research in Africa (CODESRIA), based in Dakar.

Christopher Pierson is Professor in Politics at the University of Nottingham. He is the author of *Beyond the Welfare State?* (1992) and *Marxist Theory and Democratic Politics* (1986).

Judith Tendler is Professor of Political Economy with an institutional focus and her research interests lie in the study of better-performing government and NGO programmes, and in grounding theory and policy advice in the actual experiences of developing countries. Her most recent book, *Good Government in the Tropics* (1997), was named one of the top ten economics books of the year (1998) by The Boston Globe. Other recent publications are three lead articles in the *World Development Journal*: 'Tales of Dissemination in Agriculture' (1993); 'Trust in a Rent-seeking World: Health and Government Transformed in Northeast Brazil' (1994) and 'Small Firms and Their Helpers: Lessons on Demand' (1996). In addition, she has written *New Lessons From Old Projects: The Workings of Rural Development in Northeast Brazil* (1993) and 'Why Are Social Funds So Popular?' *Local Dynamics in the Era of Globalization* (edited by Shahid Yusuf *et al.*, 2000).

Paula Tibandebage is a former Senior Research Fellow at the Economic and Social Research Foundation, a not-for-profit, non-government policy research institute in Tanzania, and thereafter an independent researcher. She currently works as Deputy Course Convener/Course Manager for a collaborative (Economic and Social Research Foundation, Research on Poverty Alleviation and Institute of Social Studies) Postgraduate Diploma Programme in policy analysis. She is a political economist specializing in social policy issues. Her recent work includes two co-authored articles: 'Inclusion by design: rethinking regulatory intervention in Tanzanian health care' *Journal of Development Studies* 2002, and 'The market shaping of charges, trust and abuse: health care transactions in Tanzania' *Social Science and Medicine*.

Peter Townsend is Centennial Professor of International Social Policy in the London School of Economics and Political Science (LSE) and Emeritus Professor of Social Policy in the University of Bristol. He has Honorary Doctorates from the University of Essex (1991), the University of Teesside (1994), the Open University (1995), the University of Edinburgh (1996), the University of Lincolnshire and Humberside (1997), and the University of York (2000). In 1999 he was elected a founder Academician of the new Academy of Learned Societies for the Social Sciences. He has investigated and written extensively on poverty, health, social policy and old age. His work in the 1990s has sought to carry forward the early work for which he is best known: a major national analytical survey *Poverty in the United Kingdom* (1979) and a national review of health *The Black Report on Inequalities in Health* (1980, 1992). His first co-authored book on European poverty was *Responses to Poverty: Lessons from Europe* (1984).

Juhana Vartiainen was the Head of Labour Market Studies at the Labour Institute for Economic Research, Finland. He is also Senior Research economist at FIEF (Trade Union Institute för Ekonomisk Forskning). He has a Ph.D. in Economics and his research interest is in Labour Economics. His latest publications (in English) are: *Gender differences in job assignment and promotion in a complexity ladder of jobs* (together with Thomas Pekkarinen) a paper presented at the 14th annual conference of the European Association for Labour Economics, Paris, 2002; 'The labour contract in Japan and Asia – what can we learn about Europe and the US?' to be published in *Neoliberalism and Institutional Reform in East Asia*, edited by Meredith Woo-Cumings (forthcoming); 'The Nordic Countries' *Where are National Capitalisms Now?* edited by Jonathan Perraton and Ben Clift, (2004); and *Gender wage differentials in the Finnish Labour Market* (2002).

Laurence Whitehead is Official Fellow in Politics at Nuffield College, Director of the Mexican Studies Centre and Chairman of the Area and Development Studies Committee. Among his special interests are US relations and European relations with Latin America and current processes of democratization. He recently occupied the Alfonso Reyes Visiting Professorship at the Institute des Hautes Etudes d'Amerique Latine in Paris. He also teaches the options on Mexican politics, and on comparative social revolutions at the Centre. His most recent publications are *Democratization: Theory and Experience* (2002) and an edited volume *Emerging Market Democracies: East Asia and Latin America* (2002).

1

Social Policy in a Development Context: Introduction

Thandika Mkandawire

Background

Both the contemporary normative discourse and the emerging consensus on development insists on putting in place social institutions (including states) that are developmental (in that they sustain high rates of growth and the structural transformation of economies), that are socially inclusive and that are sanctioned by democratic processes that fully respect the human rights of all citizens. Such an understanding can be surmised from the many resolutions of major international conferences of the 1990s and is reflected at the national level in struggles for democracy, equity and the clamour for bringing development back onto the economic policy agenda. On a more theoretical level, this understanding of development has been succinctly stated by Amartya Sen (1999) in his *Development as Freedom* in which he argues that economic development, equity and democracy are mutually constitutive.

Social policy is collective interventions in the economy to influence the access to and the incidence of adequate and secure livelihoods and income. As such, social policy has always played redistributive, protective and transformative or developmental roles. Although these different roles always work in tandem and synergistically, the weight given to each of these elements of social policies has varied widely across countries and, within countries, over time. In the context of development, there can be no doubt that the transformative role of social policy needs to receive greater attention than it is usually accorded in the developed countries and much more than it does in the current focus on 'safety nets'. The leitmotif of this volume is the following problem: How can social policies be used to enhance social capacities for economic development without, in the process, eroding the intrinsic values of the social ends that policy makers purport to address? This problem of the relationship between social welfare and economic performance has a long

1

pedigree, having occupied the minds of some of the luminaries of classical political economy – Smith, Turgot, Condorcet – who were acutely aware of the positive link between social welfare and economic progress, the reputation of economics as a 'dismal science' notwithstanding. The economic historian Emma Rothschild argues that the 'cruel reputation' of political economy is quite undeserved:

> The political economy of the late Enlightenment provides no support for the view of many contemporary proponents of *laissez faire* that social security is inimical to economic development, or that social equality is a form of luxury, to be promoted only in countries which are already rich. The characteristic presumption of Smith's early friends and follow-ers in France was rather that political liberty, and the social integration of the poor, were causes (as well consequences) of economic development. (p. 121)

In opposition to this view was the argument of a trade-off between social and economic development, and between equity and efficiency. And it is the latter view that took precedence, as that of Smith, Turgot and Condorcet (which Rothschild describes as 'the road not taken') lost out.

Although much contemporary criticism of economic development is directed at the absence of 'social dimensions' among its core concerns, most of the 'pioneers' of economic development were drawn to the subject because it addressed issues of poverty. They considered elimination of poverty the central preoccupation of development, and economic growth an import-ant instrument for achieving that goal. Various social policy measures were to be adopted in tandem with economic growth as instruments for the elim-ination of poverty. Gunnar Myrdal, one of the 'pioneers in development' (Meier and Seers 1984), was probably the most articulate advocate of this 'road not taken'. In the 1930s, Myrdal pointed out that social expenditure was not merely public consumption, but constituted an important instrument for development. He was quite adamant about this position, and in a reflective, biographical article he insisted:

> The productivity of higher consumption levels stands as a major motivation for the direction of development policy in underdeveloped countries. Higher consumption levels are a condition for a more rapid and stable growth. (Myrdal 1984: 154)

Thus 'human resource' development and social progress were seen as an important aspect of the economic developmental process. This view was not exclusive to development studies, but was actually derived from the Keynesian macroeconomics whose understanding was that the relation between macroeconomic policy and social policy was a positive one, a point stressed by Peter Townsend in this volume.

Over the years, these insights on the mutually constitutive nature of social and economic development have been rejected, downplayed or ignored for a wide range of reasons. For some, social welfare may be an end of development, but it is a poor instrument because it is seen as essentially obstructive largely because of postulated 'equity–efficiency' or 'equity–growth' trade-offs. Attempts to address social needs in the process of development are thus seen as premature because they fail to address the issue of resource constraints and are, therefore, ultimately self-defeating since they can only induce the unsustainable and inefficient deployment of resources (for example, through 'macroeconomic-populist'[1] fiscal policies, which lead to cumulative deficits, and through perverse incentive effects). Social expenditure is seen as merely paying for social consumption. As such it is considered to have a negative impact on economic development because it reduces savings and, therefore, investment. And if social policy is introduced at all, it is often as a way of 'correcting' the pathologies of economic development.

The opposing point of view restates the trade-off thesis in favour of equity. Here the use of social policy as an instrument is unacceptable on principle, because it downplays the importance of social goals. Advocates of this position caution that such 'instrumentalization' of important ends may erode or dilute their intrinsic value. Usually, critics of instrumentalization are engaged in project or micro-level activities to empower social groups or directly address problems of poverty. With their attention thus fixed on the livelihood strategies of individual households or communities, however, many critics of instrumentalization fail to relate these micro-level strategies to macro-level social polices or economic performance. More specifically, as a consequence of this 'projectizing and micro-izing', to borrow Judith Tendler's apt characterization (in this volume), they tend not to address the impact of their activities on efficiency in the allocation of scarce resources, their incentive compatibility in largely market economies, or their effects on long-term economic growth. While the aversion to the 'handmaiden model' of social policy that relegates social services to an adjunct of economic policies is a healthy reminder of what the purpose of economic development is, it has tended to give social policy a passive role with respect to resource mobilization and generation and unnecessarily inhibited study of the contribution of social policy to economic development. The result has been that less attention has been paid to social development as involving enhancement and deployment of 'social capacities' on the supply side for further social progress.

A starting point is to re-think social policy and move it away from its conception as a residual category of 'safety nets' that merely counteract policy failures or developmental disasters. Social policy should be conceived as involving overall and prior concerns with social development, and as a key instrument that works in tandem with economic policy to ensure equitable and socially sustainable development. Social policy must be designed not only residually, to cater for social casualties, but also integrated as a central component of policies, to ensure the wherewithal for their sustainability. More specifically, social policy must not confine itself to only the 'social inclusion' part but must also directly address the issues of economic development and the consolidation of the democratic order. It definitely must not be conceived so as to undermine either of them. In this context it must also be among other social constraints that set limits to what instruments can be used in macroeconomic policy. Much of the new social policy consists of attempts to find *ad hoc* solutions to the social consequences of both economic decline and economic policy. In this reactive role, social policy does not constitute a fundamental interrogation of the macroeconomic models that may be partly responsible for the social crisis.

Structure of the book

Although, given the cross-cutting nature of the themes, it is difficult to group the essays in this book in distinct categories, the book is divided into three parts. The first part deals with more conceptual issues. The focus is on the relationship between economic policy and social policy. The chapters in this section also cover issues of the political and ideological contexts of social policy and the reason behind the new interest in social policy. In the second part, the book considers meso- and micro-level arguments for social policy, taking up issues of income distribution and social protection. The third part is more historical, drawing lessons from experiences of 'late industrializers' and looking at some contemporary experiences. The essays consider at the role of social policy in late industralization. Part III contains one chapter that makes a theoretical case for social policy in late industralization. It is followed by a comparative study on social policy in late industralization. Case studies of South Korea, India and Zambia provide further material on social policy.

Conceptual underpinnings of social policy

One remarkable feature of writing on social policy is its lack of theoretical and conceptual underpinnings – beyond the general suggestions that social policy must be somehow holistic and integrated with economic policy. There is little in social policy studies in developing countries that is as heuristically potent as Esping-Andersen's work on welfare regimes. Studies on social policy in the developing countries have tended to be excessively descriptive. Maureen Mackintosh and Paula Tibandebage (Chapter 7) highlight this absence of theoretical underpinning which has led to what they call 'thick descriptions, thin explanation' syndrome. They observe that in the development context, the health policy literature, for example, is strongly characterized by an emphasis on egalitarian objectives and by repeated demonstration of redistributive failure, but that there is remarkably little expended in researching explanations of the observed regressive distributional behaviour. One immediate consequence of this is the privileging of pre-scription and evaluation over explanation. Prescriptions are made for greater equality without any tackling of the problem of the persistent redistributive failure. This methodological 'thinness' of the literature on social policy is contrasted to the situation in Europe, where social policy debates are embedded in theoretical discourses on the welfare state. Para-doxically, one says this while recognizing the seminal work of researchers like Amartya Sen, Partha Dasgupta and Jean Dreze, whose theorizing of social conditions of poverty is now influencing work on social policy in the developed countries. Part of this gap can be explained by the mistaken view of social policy in the developed countries as being largely an aspect of the end-state of development – the welfare state – and therefore not relevant to developing countries. And so little of the theoretical insights from the study of welfare regimes has found its way in the field of social policy in developmental contexts. However, as the essays in the volume underscore, both the history and the current use of social policy in the developed countries can provide useful insights and lessons for developing countries. It has definite value in aiding the conceptual understanding of the relationship between economic and social policy in market economies, and can lend depth to analysis as a result of the diverse historical paths taken and the wide range of current practices.[2]

One point that is emphasized in most of the chapters in this collection is the fact that the 'social' and 'economic' are inherently inseparably inter-twined so that economic policy is social policy and social policy is economic policy. However, for both ideological and institutional reasons, the two are often separated with the 'economic' often treated as more fundamental than the 'social'. Indeed, in the current policy discourse social policy assumes a residual category. Exigencies of 'good social policy' impose no constraints on macroeconomic policy instruments. Ha-joon Chang reminds us of Karl Polanyi's (1946) message, when he notes that the 'economic is inseparably linked to the social' which legitimizes the market and defines its bound-aries on the basis of the complex interaction between political bargaining, moral values and technical considerations of the markets. And Diane Elson points out that the separation of social policy from economic policy is more a reflection of institutional division of labour than how people live the 'economic' and 'social'. The separation of the social from the economic has led, in the extreme, to an economic theorizing that has sought to expunge from its purview the 'social' – values, conflicts, employment, poverty and so on.

The macroeconomic problem and social policy

Keynesian economics insisted on: (a) the autonomous existence of macroeconomics as a policy domain not reducible to 'micro-foundations' and; (b) that government was a necessary condition and determinant of operating markets and consequently economics must incorporate governments as a 'structural assumption' of political economies. It also directly took on board issues of distribution which impacted on growth through aggregate demand and propensities to save and invest. Peter Townsend's contribution (chapter 2) reminds us of the deep social and economic imagination that gave the world Keynesian economics. Keynes was preoccupied with the social misery that the Depression of the 1930s had caused, the devastating economic and social consequences of war and the need for social ease in a capitalist world whose foundations had been rudely shaken by social revolutions, depressions and war. The message from Keynes was that macroeconomic policy had to be sensitive to its social impact and that social expenditures could be one of the instruments for addressing macroeconomic problems. The social objective could not only set constraints on what macroeconomic policy instruments can be used but could also serve as an important policy instrument for eventually broadening macroeconomic options (through economic recovery and growth).

Once macroeconomics is understood as being embedded in society, the main challenge then is not 'adding-on' the social to the macroeconomic but 'mainstreaming social issues into macroeconomic', as has been suggested in the context of 'engendering' macroeconomics. Such mainstreaming touches on the core of the dominant paradigms and has far-reaching implications on 'the rethinking of macroeconomics *and* of the organization of macroeconomic policy processes in order to recognize the salience of social issues and social policy'.

This, however, has not been the view informing macroeconomics during the last two decades. For much of the 1980s and 1990s, two views characterized macroeconomic understanding. The first was its self-limitation to stabilization and its neglect of economic growth and equity The second was a return to a pre-Keynesian view of the micro-foundations of macroeconomics in which macroeconomics was a simple aggregation of individual decision making or only necessary because there are market distortions. Such a view has had a profound effect on both the diagnosis of the causes of the economic malaise and the solutions advanced. And, more pertinent to social policy, it has also contributed to the failure to find room for social policy at the macro-level and to tend to treat it as a source of 'distortions' at the micro-level that somehow added up to the macroeconomic crisis. Significantly, the general understanding is that social arrangements must be made to conform to the exigencies of sacrosanct economic fundamentals while no social constraints are imposed on both the instruments and scale of macroeconomic policies.

They are not considered to be part of the 'fundamentals' that must be got right if development is to take place.

By the mid-1980s, in the new ideological dispensation of stabilization and structural adjustment, social policy was associated with the fiscal crisis of the state and was thus treated as one more source of economic instability and inflation. Moreover, the association of social policy with state intervention opened it to neo-liberal attack as one of the sources of economic failure. Social expenditures were seen to detract from stabilization and would have to be curtailed if fiscal deficits were to be checked. This policy shift led to cutbacks in social investment, the privatization of social programmes and the abandonment of social planning as an integral part of policy making. It should be added at this point that pressures from non-governmental organizations (NGOs) for popular participation have also contributed to a growing sense of marginalization of social policy as a state preoccupation, let alone responsibility. Pressures for cutting public social expenditures have thus been unrelenting, with the result that the long-run effects on growth of such cutbacks have been obscured. And when social expenditure has been condoned at all, it has been as a remedial measure, limited to 'safety nets' for vulnerable groups, with no consideration of the implications for future growth.

It should be noted that these arguments were buttressed by the general critique of the welfare state, which is often accused of inefficiency for: (i) 'crowding out' the more efficient private sector; (ii) distorting labour markets by introducing all kinds of rigidities; and (iii) blunting incentives for unemployed workers to seek employment.[3] In the developing countries, moral and ideological premises of social policies were impugned by associating such policies with rent-seeking, urban bias and clientelism. This followed from the neo-liberal scepticism about social solidarity, given its view of human action as motivated by self-interest and devoid of any moral basis.

Social biases of macroeconomics

Although macroeconomic policy is often given an aura of technocratic neutrality, implicit in any economic policies are policies about gender, about full employment and about equity. Diane Elson (chapter 3) argues that conventional macroeconomics contains biases that not only reflect its social project but that also have far-reaching social consequences. Elson lists three such biases: (i) deflationary bias; (ii) male breadwinner bias; and (iii) the commodification bias. The deflationary bias shows up in the fact that the era of liberalization has been generally associated with lower rates of investment and growth. The 'fundamentals' insisted upon by orthodox macroeconomics may have been adequate for stabilization (a highly questionable proposition in itself), but they have clearly worked against growth and development, a fact grudgingly acknowledged in appeals for a 'post-Washington Consensus'. The 'male breadwinner bias' comes from the assumption that articulation of the unpaid care economy to the market economy is mediated by a male breadwinner whose income is large enough to provide for the cash needs of a set of dependents. These biases shape what is considered as viable or sound social policy by defining targets of social policy, possible instruments to be used and the economic resources and fiscal envelope available. Implicit in any social policy is a structure of distribution which spells out the incidence of both costs and benefits.

And yet despite such socially salient biases, macroeconomics is often treated as merely a technocratic framework which establishes the economic framework to which social policy must conform. Much macroeconomic policy making is totally oblivious of the normative discourse on social and human rights. A more holistic approach would simultaneously consider the 'social' as posing political and social limits on what values macroeconomic variables can assume. In addition, a whole range of macroeconomic goals can be achieved by different combinations of instruments and under varying welfare regimes. The choice of these instruments is highly political, since each instrument contains within it certain implications for a specific allocation of costs and benefits of adjustment which in turn are reflections of biases, social arrangements and ideological predispositions that must be squarely addressed. The recognition of the social nature of macroeconomic policy making, the 'biases' that go along with it and the political nature of choice of policy instruments and goals highlight the need for social dialogue which rejects the view that 'sound' macroeconomic policies are beyond social scrutiny, to be taken as an immutable given to which social actors must simply adjust. Elson suggests that this social dialogue can be facilitated by more heterodox economics that goes beyond the neo-Keynesian economics to include insights from feminist economics, which has insisted on the articulation between economic production and social reproduction.

The rediscovery of poverty and development

One factor accounting for the increasing recognition of the important role of social policy has been the persistence of poverty even in situations of economic 'success'. The introduction of metrics of development other than gross domestic product (such as the Human Development Indices) has underscored the essentially *social* nature of development. Such metrics have problematized the link between growth and welfare by stressing that growth should be part of a whole series of measures intended to widen the scope of choice of individuals and communities. It is now widely accepted that sustainable attacks on poverty will demand fairly high levels of economic growth even in situations of significant redistribution of existing resources. While some countries or regions have achieved laudable social progress even in times of poor economic performance (Ghai 2000), such achievements have generally proved unsustainable in the long run in the absence of good overall economic performance. Social development arguably occurs faster and in a more sustainable way in situations of economic progress, which itself is facilitated by social development and provides the wherewithal for further social development.[4]

As Diane Elson notes, the adjustment programmes adopted by many countries in the 1980s and 1990s undermined economic growth because of their 'deflationary bias'. While these policies, with their anti-growth biases, dominated policy making, there was revived interest in academic circles in growth economics – the 'catch-up hypothesis' and so-called 'new growth theories' or 'endogenous growth' models – which now recognizes that social development contains crucial instruments for economic development. The catch-up hypothesis states that 'being backward in level of productivity carries a *potential* for rapid advance' (Abramovitz 1995: 386). However, this is conditional on the 'social capability' of the countries in the less techno-logically advanced group. Although the definition of such capability remains elusive, several of its components have been identified. They include educa-tional levels, physical infrastructure, corporate governance, competitive con-ditions (including openness to foreign competition), political stability, labour market structure, and 'social capital' (understood to include, among other things, institutions, inter-personal trust, national or social cohesion, norms of civic co-operation, associational activities and formal institutions). A broader argument is stated by Frances Stewart, Gustav Ranis and Alejandro Ramirez who consider the two-way influence of economic growth and human devel-opment (Stewart *et al.* 2000). They argue that those countries which have leaned towards human development through a whole range of social policies affecting education, health and equity tend eventually to enjoy higher rates of growth. Macro-level studies also provide robust evidence that initial income inequality and subsequent growth are inversely related, and that better income and wealth distribution helps growth (Alesina and Perotti 1994; Birdsall 1997; Woojin Lee and Roemer 1998).

The important message in 'New Growth Theory models' is that social policy constitutes one of the most important determinants of economic growth. For a while there was the hope that recognition of the 'social' might lead to increased interest in social policy, and 'fill out the analytical space in which to construct the social as a complement to economic policy' (Ben Fine, this volume). However, recognition of the transformative and productivity-enhancing quality of measures that contribute to social development does not necessarily lead to their adoption, not even in democratic political settings where numbers would tend to favour the poor. Even the widespread recognition of 'social capital' has not been sufficient to place social policy at the core of development policies. There are many impediments to the translation of new insights into policy measures. The first of these impediments is the persistence of economic policy making based on a 'leader/follower' model, where macroeconomic policy (stability and growth) is determined first and social policy is left to address the social consequences (Atkinson

1999). Such an approach clearly goes against the insights of the literature, which argues that the exploitation of synergies between welfare-enhancing measures and economic growth requires a holistic approach to development policies. In addition, there is the tendency to treat the many variables identified by 'growth accounting' separately, although the fact that these are complementary and synergic indicates that they must be harnessed simultaneously. Ultimately the issue is not just 'health policy' or 'education policy', but 'social policy' within which these measures are coherently embedded. In the absence of such a holistic understanding of social policies, there is the distinct danger that various specialized agencies, ministries or NGOs will pick up their own 'variable', completely oblivious of its crucial relationships with others.

The second impediment is the uncertainty over the exact nature of these relations and the many reservations about the robustness of empirical results. Much research on growth and elements of social policy is still dominated by cross-section and panel data regression analysis. There are few time-series analyses using institutional or historical information to trace the interactions among the variables in specific contexts. One difficulty with drawing lessons from simple cross-country comparative studies is that social policy is context-specific and is often explicitly or implicitly embedded in the overall macro-policy model, so that its separate influence on economic development is not easily decipherable, let alone quantifiable. And even among those countries that have done well in both economic and social indicators, and reached similar endpoints, over the years the sequencing and weight attached to these indicators have varied between countries and within each country, making the drawing of lessons for policy singularly treacherous. In addition, what may appear as social policy *ex post* may be an unintended consequence of a set of policies intended to address entirely different issues. For instance, education programmes to address gender or ethnic differences may lead to an overall improvement in human capital that may not have been the explicit objective of the policy. It is also clear that measures that are apparently similar may have entirely different implications for development, depending upon a country's political and institutional arrangements, and the historical trajectories traversed by its institutions. This points to the need for in-depth historical and time-series studies of the experiences of individual countries with social policy and development.

The third impediment arises partly as a result of ambiguities of concepts such as 'social capital' (succinctly discussed by Ben Fine in this volume) and the complexity and ambiguity of the policy implications of both the new growth theories and the institutionalist growth paths. Neither of these analyses points to a particular form of social organization, let alone social policy proposals. One reason for the tentativeness and weak articulation of these ideas in the policy realm is the possibility of multiple trajectories – equilibria – which are often 'path-dependent'. The economy and the variables that account for its transformation are permeated by social relations and are embedded in social institutions, the improvement of both of which constitutes a cornerstone of social development. This, of course, opens the route to the study of a whole range of variables that affect long-run growth and that are amenable to or reflective of social polices. However, there is no clear theory of how social policy acts on development-enhancing social factors so as to induce growth, nor is there agreement on the patterns of growth that are most appropriate to meeting the spectrum of social goals that are now on both national and international agendas. In addition there is the ahistorical nature of the concept of social capital. There are no accounts of how societies have deliberately accumulated 'social capital'. Indeed, the 'social' is defined so as to exclude socioeconomic forces and conflicts that are known to have underpinned the emergence and evolution of the welfare state. As both Ben Fine and Jayati Ghosh argue, social policy has not simply emerged to correct market failures; rather, it has emerged from responses to the contradictory economic and social reproduction of capitalist societies.

And, finally, there are political and ideological impediments. Social policy is a highly political process, touching upon power relations, access to resources and ideological predilections about the role of state and markets. We still need to know what societal variables facilitate the placement of these items on national policy agendas. Economics is usually murky as to how issues are placed on the political agenda or how certain institutions emerge. Yet macroeconomists increasingly recognize that political variables and institutions are important determinants of policy choices and outcomes. However, for ideological reasons, there is aversion to drawing out the full policy implications toward which empirical analysis points.

Partly in response to both the criticisms of their deflationary bias, the growing political salience of poverty and inequality and the growing literature on the dynamics of growth and development that points to the failure of adjustment to address problems of poverty and to place economies on a long-term growth path, the Bretton Woods institutions have signalled something tantamount to a paradigmatic shift. The World Bank has begun to shift its focus toward poverty alleviation and to argue for support to social sectors on developmental grounds. Even the IMF has been compelled to give explicit recognition to the importance of social policy. And has accordingly relabelled the extended structural adjustment facility as 'Poverty Reduction Strategy Papers' and 'Poverty Reduction and Growth Facility'. The stated aim of these changes is a 'coherent strategy to help poor countries move on to a sustainable faster growth path, bringing a substantial reduction in poverty' (IMF, 2000). The new strategy is intended to ensure consistency between a country's macroeconomic, structural and social policies, and the goals of poverty reduction and social development. The leverage of the BWIs with respect to all these is assured by the close link between the PRSPs and debt relief under the HIPC initiative.

The political contexts of social policy

Which social policies are adopted does not entirely depend upon their perceived instrumental efficacy in improving economic growth. No amount of evidence of the instrumental efficacy or of the intrinsic value of particular social policies will lead to their adoption if they are not deemed to be politically feasible. To the extent that such policies are driven by the values of different social actors with different ideological positions, and to the extent that they invariably entail intra- and inter-generational redistribution issues, they are the outcomes of political bargains and conflicts since they touch upon power in society – its distribution and accessibility to different political actors. In any society, it is obvious that the state will not institutionalize social policies that conflict fundamentally and consistently with principles of the dominant economic system and power relations. Consequently, the study of social policies in *developmental* contexts must be sensitive to the *political* contexts within which they are formulated and implemented.

Different political institutions and arrangements tend to favour particular social policy regimes. They also tend to produce different political capacities for extraction of the resources necessary for financing social programmes. Thus, the type of political regime has enormous implications for social policy. It is therefore necessary for research to take on board the *politics of social policy*. Comparative research on history and the 'path dependence' it induces, as well as how current political arrangements impinge on social policy regimes, is required.

Social policy has been formulated under the aegis of a wide range of political regimes – elitist/populist, democratic/authoritarian, right fascist/Stalinist, colonialist/*nationalist*, etc. The scope for popular pressure for the institution of social welfare has varied widely in these arrangements. In some societies, social welfare has been an essentially elite project to achieve goals determined by the ruling elite. Such goals have usually included nation-building, development or co-optation of subordinate classes. In some cases, social welfare has been the result of popular pressures for equity and inclusion. Cultural values have also played an important role in conceiving or rationalizing social policies. In East Asia, for example, the limited role of the state in providing social welfare services was justified on the grounds of 'oriental' family values.

Problems of the legitimacy of the state, 'ownership' of policies and political stability highlight the importance of the social regimes within which growth is presumed to take place. It is notable that this realization has been reinforced by the current wave of democratization, and by popular pressures to place social issues on national policy agendas. In early 'modernization' theories, the establishment of political stability as a prerequisite for development was one of the intractable problems of rapid social change. Operating on the assumption of a trade-off between equity and growth, much of the writing of the time tended to advocate 'political order' of an authoritarian nature, which would not be encumbered by the clamour for social welfare (Huntington 1968). Redistributive social policy, being inimical to accumulation, was not considered possible as an instrument for ensuring the stability necessary for accumulation. Indeed, it was often dreaded for leading to 'revolutions of rising expectations', which would stifle economic growth. In reality, states, including the most authoritarian, have had to be concerned with reconciling the exigencies of accumulation with those of legitimacy and national cohesion. Consequently, the pursuit of social policies that enhance accumulation while securing the state the necessary legitimacy for political stability has constituted the cornerstone of developmental management. Indeed, there have been cases in which unelected regimes in 'developmental states', lacking political legitimacy or facing 'democratic deficits', have sought legitimacy through social and economic 'performance', with the result that some of the most dramatic improvements in welfare have taken place in undemocratic contexts.

It is important to recall that the successful developmental states of East Asia were largely authoritarian. The power of the state was used to suppress popular claims over a long period of time, and those public welfare measures that were introduced were largely unaccountable to the public and reflected the political logic of authoritarian rule and its understanding of developmental imperatives (Goodman *et al.* 1998). In the current normative discourse, the growing consensus is that the developmental model chosen must respect both human rights and rights to development. This can be construed as a case for development under political regimes that are democratic. Thus the developmental and redistributive policies of states will be shaped to some extent by this new democratic dispensation, which is politically more inclusive and, consequently, broadens the constituency likely to call for more wide-ranging social policy. What will be the type of social policy compatible with the 'democratic developmental model' pursued by such states?

One of the posited trade-offs in the process of development has been that between 'development' and 'democracy'. In the current normative discourse democracy and development are not considered as mutually constitutive components of the 'good society'. However, the historical record is that such an association is contingent on a number of factors including significantly *social policy*. Laurence Whitehead examines the lines of interaction between democracy and development, their 'connectedness' and 'elective affinity'. Although both democracy and development have a long genealogy, both their substantive content and relationships have varied over time. The post-Second World War context of the 'Cold War' has had an enormous impact upon the fortunes of the relationship. Significantly, a common understanding of development led to its apoliticization and the belief that it could be achieved through technical means. In some accounts, the encumbrances of democratic policies were considered as decidedly inimical to the development project. It is only with the end of the Cold War and the emergence of a generation not beholden to the 'developmentalist' ideologies which down-played democracy that we see a renewed interest in the 'democratization of development'. Whitehead argues that if the new view that democracy and development are inseparably intertwined and mutually constitutive is to hold, then it will be necessary to reconceptualize both of them. This could very well entail incorporating some very considerable elements drawn from democratic theory into economic development. Likewise, future conceptions of 'democracy', appropriately understood and updated, could quite properly include much that has recently been studied within the limiting confines of the sub-discipline of 'economic development':

> When the application of knowledge, rather than mechanical power, pro-vides the main key to economic prosperity the most effective producers can be expected to set a high standard of demand for citizenship rights and governmental accountability. When a central task of modern demo-cratic government is to secure informed assent to complex public choices in the era of economic management, our conception of 'development' can hardly continue to omit consideration of the social acceptability and legitimacy of the policies to be selected. It is in this area of convergence between notions of 'democracy' and 'development' that the best future of development studies lies.   (Whitehead, Chapter 5, p. 103)

However, the conventional definitions of democracy (as no more than holding competitive elections) and development (consisting of high rates of growth) and their compartmentalization in both theory and practice does not suggest that either of these conceptions is in need of the other. Whitehead suggests that social development provides a key point of intersection between the separate discourses of democratisation and economic development: 'To the extent that these discourses converge social policies and citizenship entitlements will move from the margins to the centre of attention in these scholarly communities.' However, the convergence of the discourses is still at a rhetorical level.

Although the current normative discourse insists that social policy must obtain its legitimacy from democratic and participatory processes, a number of factors tend to militate against such an outcome. One is the technocratic nature of policy making. The other is an exclusionary process of identification of worthy partners that often deliberately seeks to isolate the most organized and most articulate groups that have historically pushed for progressive social policies. Judith Tendler points to the often-ignored question of what coalitions can be built at the national level in support of social programmes. Largely because much of the discussion on poverty alleviation is tethered to debt relief, it tends to be oblivious of the political basis for such programmes. Where the finance is external, there seems to be no need for building or identifying coalitions to sustain such programmes. Indeed the new formulation of anti-poverty programmes tends to be opposed to existing social movements, especially labour movements, being content with the participation of a few NGOs who end up being beneficiaries as service providers. Tendler points to the inadvertent translation of an anti-poverty agenda into an anti-labour agenda. When critical social organizations such as labour movements are sidelined, the programme becomes donor driven and lacking national anchoring.

The anti-labour argument is often couched in populist terms in which organized labour is seen as a kind of 'labour aristocracy' whose defence of labour standards undermines employment creation and the competitiveness of the economy in the global market. In this era of globalization, many developing countries fear that labour and environmental standards will undermine their competitiveness. This is an understandable reaction to the protectionism parading as social concerns, but it should not be used to distract from national demands for socially acceptable labour standards and the real possibility for participation in the global market without violations of fundamental workers' rights. If countries are to avoid the 'race to the bottom' or being trapped in a low productivity-low wage 'sweatshop equilibrium' they will have to introduce social policies that address both the equity and productivity considerations.

Sectoral and micro-level issues

Ben Fine, Judith Tendler and Diane Elson remind us that the 'social' has been easier to absorb at the micro level than at the macro level through concepts such as 'participation' and 'social capital' and that the revalidation of the 'social' as having more than a residual status has been accepted more at the micro level than at the macro where the 'social' is still seen as an afterthought. Such a narrowing of the role of social policy – ignoring its overall redistributive and developmental roles – can be attributed to a number of factors. Ben Fine suggests that the acceptance of the 'social' at the micro level comes from interpreting the macroeconomic crisis as emanating from micro-level failures, and assuming that the orthodox policies are fundamentally sound, there have been attempts to find faults at the level of state failure, market failure or societal failure. The realization of the pervasiveness of these failures has led to a recognition of the 'social' as an essential means to correct them. And thus 'social capital' is fully embraced as the 'missing link'. In the process the concept of social capital has assumed a protean character consisting not only of the positive side, but revealing a dark side as its definition includes virtually any social arrangement. Although 'social capital' relates to both the macro and micro levels, it has tended to be used in relationship to the latter often in isolation from the economy, formal politics and social conflicts. Within the Bretton Woods institutions (BWIs) 'social capital' is conceptually and administratively separated from debates on macroeconomic policy with the consequence that while sections of the BWIs claim to be constructing 'social capital' at the micro level, macroeconomic policies are dismantling the social contracts that may have sustained past political stability.

In her contribution to this volume, Judith Tendler identifies four such factors. The first of these is what she calls 'projectization' whereby all initiatives in the realm of social policy are to be conducted at the micro level. This has tended to distract attention from broader social reforms. Such a position has been encouraged both by the onslaught on central government authorities and by the rise of NGOs in social provision. The second is the demise of development policy within which social policies were embedded. The salience of concerns on employment and labour market conditions gave social policy a prominent role in the development process. Such policies as those on local procurement were not merely aimed at technological acquisition or mastery but were intended also to address issues of employment and redistribution. Thirdly, there is the focus on the informal sector and small enterprises and the belief that social policy, because of its insistence on certain standards, constitutes one of the 'distortions' that have hurt this sector. State legislation of standards in labour markets is anathema in the current orthodoxy. And, finally, there is the downplaying or neglect of some of the central preoccupations of nation-building for which social cohesion and the role of social policy in that was important especially, the conception of development as a national project requiring adhesion of many actors.

In addition, there has been a tendency to downplay the redistributive content of both sectoral and micro-level interventions, partly by simply assuming that market forces will handle such issues. Thus, Maureen Macintosh and Paula Tibandebage argue that in the area of health, the egalitarian thrust of health policy has led to the conclusion that public expenditure ought to be targeted towards the poor. The point of departure has been the view that curative care is nearly a pure private good and thus quite appropriate for allocation by the market. Public support should therefore be targeted towards those who do not have any means to purchase health services. This reliance on market for providing much of the health services is based on a leap of faith attributable to ideological predisposition or a conflation of textbook markets with real markets. It also assumes away the redistributive function of health provision itself by relegating such a role to the government budget to 'target' those unable to pay for health services. Such a view sharply diverges from the health care system approach which takes into account the redistributive role and considers cross-subsidization and risk-pooling as the primary functional method for tacking distribution and equity outcomes.

Microeconomic concerns need not obviate social policy. New trends in microeconomics, whether informed by the transaction cost school or theories of imperfect knowledge, have challenged some of the principal results of mainstream economics – for instance the Walrasian neo-classical view of the separability of equity and efficiency – because the terms and conditions of contracts that directly affect the efficiency of resource allocation now crucially depend upon ownership structures and property and social relations. This research argues that inequality can lead to the perpetuation of dysfunctional arrangements at the community, firm and national levels.

Gender studies have provided another important micro-level argument for rethinking social policy in the context of development. The work on gender and economics clearly suggests the potency of socially-sensitive analysis in incorporating social divisions of labour, power and choice in the analysis of growth and structural adjustment and of overcoming the dichotomization between 'economic analysis' and 'social analysis' without dissolving the difference and tension between the two aspects of life. An argument for a wide range of policies subsumed under the heading 'social welfare' is that they contribute to labour productivity.[5] Researchers working on gender and development hold that labour is a 'reproduced means of production' – in other words, that effective labour is not an exogenous or biological given, but a socially constructed capacity or potential resulting from deliberate investment in human capital or institutional arrangements that determine the participation of individuals from different social groups in labour markets. In this, the reproductive and nurturing roles of women are central to understanding the well-being of individuals, households, communities and indeed nations (Elson 1991; Folbre 1994). Conventional theory, which treats the supply of labour as infinitely elastic, pays little attention to the well-being, efficiency and needs of the 'unpaid care economy'. And yet its operations have a far-reaching implication for the quantity and quality of labour and the stability of the social arrangements within which the market is embedded. Significant investments in human capital take place in the household sector, in the form of women investing long hours of 'unpaid' work (also referred to in the literature as reproductive labour) in the care and socialization of children who will become the next generation of adults/workers. While household technology has altered the way physical tasks are performed (reducing the amount of time women spend on routine domestic work), it cannot replace the important emotional, inter-personal and educational aspects of parenting that take place in the home (many of which are still feminized, as time allocation studies have shown). Thus feminists have produced a valuable analysis of the supply side of the labour market and the role of domestic labour in reproducing labour. In this respect, acknowledging the creation of human capital in the household complements parallel contemporary debates about community networks and 'social capital'.

This understanding of human capital has been used by feminists as an analytical tool for improving understanding of the interface between the market and household sectors, and as a political (policy advocacy) tool for improving women's economic and social position within households and labour markets. They have argued (especially during the decade of adjustment marked by drastic social sector cutbacks) that there is nothing 'natural' about the household sector continuing to create human capital if there are no supportive social policies. In other words, it cannot be assumed that women will continue to supply all the labour and care that is needed to ensure the satisfactory reproduction of human beings, compensating for all the short-falls in purchased inputs and state support to sustain human resources. A breaking point can be reached when the household is no longer able to reproduce itself. Investments in infrastructure (including child care facilities, water supply, electricity, labour-saving domestic technologies), parental and family leave, and workplace flexibility have all been cited as ways of making the dynamic relations between the household and market sectors work more effectively.

And finally, social expenditure can also be considered a 'social wage', raising social efficiency wages due to their felicitous effects on effort and educational investment choices among the poor. Social expenditure that lowers the cost of labour by increasing its productivity tends to increase profits and, assuming a propensity to invest profits, will lead to higher levels of investment and growth. Studies of other social welfare policies point in the same direction.[6] Health improvements are also found to play a role in economic growth through their impact upon productivity and demography. In addition, Tendler reminds us that not only are such expenditures significant invest-ment in enhancing a country's competitiveness, but the exigencies of social inclusiveness and equity can themselves spur economies to more efficient deployment of resources and creation of social harmony essential to an economy's weathering of the increasingly volatile global environment. Com-panies adopt more efficient methods in response not only to competition but also to social and political pressures to meet certain social standards.

The chapters in this section clearly suggest the need for a better under-standing of the link between the micro-level benefits of social policy and their implications for the macroeconomy, and vice versa. The importance of such an approach is that what happens at the micro level – at the level of individuals and households – provides us with a measuring rod for macro-economic policies. In the words of Atkinson (1999:21):

> Where economic and social policies are in conflict, the conflict can only be resolved by assessing their impact on human welfare. We need to build links between macroeconomic variables and household incomes and this cannot be done if the macroeconomic and social are kept rigidly separate.

Redistribution, social policy and development

One major purpose of social policy is the redistribution of income (often) in order to move toward equity. It is this objective that has been subject to sustained attack by those who think 'the social' poses a serious threat to development. Development, according to such arguments, demands that societies traverse the 'vale of tears' before they have the wherewithal to address social problems. For proponents of this view, growth has gained ascendancy to such an extent that it sometimes assumes the status of an end in itself, with other long-term objectives such as welfare and equity achieved when the effects of growth 'trickle down'. Kuznets' hypothesis – that income inequality first increases with economic growth, but later decreases as societies become more developed – has been used to sanction tolerance for growing inequality in poor countries.

The case for redistributive social policy has been made along a number of lines. The first of these was of Keynesian and 'underconsumptionist' inspiration.[7] More egalitarian income distribution, it was posited, would broaden domestic markets, encourage better capacity utilization and encourage new investment.[8] It was argued that the level and structure of demand are important not only to patterns of growth, but also to its pace, because they affect both patterns and levels of savings and investment.[9] To the extent, therefore, that social policy inevitably impacts on the demand side it immediately emerges as one of the instruments of economic development. One persistent argument has been that skewed income distribution tends to limit the domestic market, and that redistribution would provide an impetus to consumption, increasing aggregate demand, doing away with excess capacity and encouraging further investment in capital. Income redistribution would also induce structures of demand that favoured more labour-intensive technologies, saved foreign exchange by being less import intensive and exploited a country's comparative advantage (Stewart 1978). This view of demand-driven growth and the consequent argument for redistribution on the grounds of demand were severely tested by supply-side limits to growth over the last two decades. These challenged egalitarian arguments by shifting attention to the effects of egalitarian policy on the supply side: 'competitiveness', which is to say on costs and incentives to investors and workers.

A second argument has had to do with political instability. Simply stated, high income inequality can lead to political conflict, which can undermine development. In addition, societies with high levels of inequality may be inflexible when faced with external shocks. Societies that are highly polarized socially and economically are unlikely to pursue policies that have long-term benefits for all, since each social group will be reluctant to make long-term commitments.[10] Jayati Ghosh reminds us of the importance of social policy in managing modernisation, and the economic and social shocks that go along with it. All capitalist societies have to address issues of accumulation and legitimation of the accumulation process and outcomes and of the state itself. Redistributive social expenditures can contribute to political stability by enhancing the legitimacy of the state. Social policy, as an instrument for ensuring a sense of citizenship, is thus an important instrument of conflict management, which is in turn a prerequisite for sustained economic development. With respect to accumulation social policy takes the form of social investments that enhance the social productivity of labour (through better health and education) and by setting minimum labour standards. As an instrument of legitimation, social policy can be used both for the management of social pressures that are engendered by rapid economic transformation and also as a corrective to the inherently volatile process of capitalist accumulation. Social policies have sought to enhance a notion of citizenship or to ensure a minimum degree of inclusion for social cohesion. Here policies relating to equity among households, classes and even regions immediately come to mind. Of course, not all policies can be neatly assigned to either of these functions, education can serve both the accumulation imperatives (human capital) and the legitimation imperative (equity or socialisation). The point here is that social policies tend to serve both these functions. There is often tension between these separate functions of social policy that is not easily resolved. The solutions ultimately reached depend on politics.

A third argument has to do with challenges to the 'equity–growth/ efficiency' trade-off. Bowles and Gintis argue, for instance, that 'egalitarian redistribution, if properly designed, can attenuate many of the costly incentive problems facing modern economies and hence can be productivity enhancing' because it facilitates the evolution of productivity enhancing governance structures (Bowles and Gintis 1995: 409). This it does by reducing the need for costly enforcement expenditures (in terms of policing, security, etc.) because equality enhances co-operation and trust, which are essential to economic performance, particularly where limited, asymmetric information makes both state intervention and market allocation inefficient, and because equality may impact on politics and culture in a way that fosters solidarity. It can also be used to underwrite the accumulation process by subsidizing labour costs. It has to achieve this in a manner compatible with the incentives for capital accumulation by the private sector. In addition social policy has directly contributed to accumulation through its provision of funds for investment (through pension schemes).

Income distribution is, of course, at the core of political economy. Drawing on a wide range of empirical material, Maureen Macintosh and Paula Tibandebage argue that redistribution commitment within a health care system is deeply influenced by the general pattern of social class and inequality in society and also by the particular institutions of the system and norms of behaviour established within them. They stress the ideological and political underpinnings of redistributive health policies. It is interactive or endogenous in the sense that it is influenced and influences other variables in the system and is path-dependent. It is often part of the 'welfare settlements', 'social pacts' or 'social contracts' that have been arrived at through political arrangements and that have provided the explanatory framework for social claims and the political receptivity to such claims. Whether evoked in the context of nation-building or the construction of full citizenship, health systems are deeply imbricated in the ethical and political contestations of society. For a health care system to operate redistributively requires not only government commitment to redistributive behaviour in allocation of funds but commitment at the institutional level to operate in an inclusionary manner, and within communities, to sustain inclusion of the poor.

Social insurance and development

Another set of social welfare policies with an important bearing on economic development – through both political and economic channels – relate to social protection. One prominent form of social insurance is pensions. The structure of pensions reflects attitudes towards efficiency and equity. On the ideological level, it reveals attitudes towards solidarity and citizenship. Consequently, there are often sharp differences among different actors on how such schemes should be designed.

An important development aspect of pension schemes is their effect on capital accumulation since they impinge on savings and the functioning of financial markets through effects on demographics, distribution and incentives. Their effect on savings can be through forced savings or through their impact on the development of financial markets. The latter argument has been advanced by advocates of neo-liberalism who argue that the privatization of pension funds can help by jump starting financial institutions such as the stock exchange and by 'deepening' financial markets – processes which are supposed not only to increase savings but also to lead to a better allocation. In the era of adjustment when equity considerations have been given lower priority relative to efficiency considerations, privatization of pensions funds has been advanced as a means for ensuring not only the financial viability of the pension systems themselves, but also their efficiency as well as a result of competition. The high yields of this more efficient market would encourage individual savings and investments (and therefore growth) through contributions to development of financial markets and through financial deepening. It is also argued that the existence of private accounts would extend coverage of pension schemes. Chile was the ultimate testing ground for the kinds of extreme privatization of pensions to an extent that no modern democracy had dared embark upon. Many countries – first in Latin America and later in the developed countries – borrowed heavily from this model, often under pressures from the BWI institutions and despite strong protests by labour.

Many of these claims are derived from first principles about how unregulated markets function. The paper by Mesa-Lago (in this volume) suggests that these claims do not stand up to close empirical inspections. The case of Chile shows that the much-touted efficiency that might be derived from competition has been undermined by the very high levels of concentration so that the three largest pension funds administer 70 per cent of the insured.

In addition, the rate of return has been low and the high fees and commission charged have turned out to be regressive. Coverage has remained virtually constant while contributions to the development of financial markets have been marginal. Significantly, for developing countries, reforms have been negative on national savings. There are many issues to consider about pension schemes. These include their coverage, the effect on different individuals depending upon the nature of the activity and gender, and their effect on income distribution. While it is admitted that the experiment with private management of pensions in Chile may have led to financial deepening, which may, in its own right, contribute to economic growth, available evidence suggests it has failed to raise savings rates, partly due to high transaction and fiscal costs (Cruz-Saco and Mesa-Lago 1998; Huber and Stephens 2000).

Significantly, not all Latin American countries adopted the much-touted Chilean model. In half of the systems in the ten pension reforms, privatization was limited. Significantly, in all cases the proper function and sustainability of the 'private' system the state proved absolutely necessary through (a) mandatory affiliation, (b) strong and detailed public regulation of the system and (c) control.

Social policy and the late industrializers

Another argument for the need to re-think social policy comes from the literature on 'late industrializers'. In a seminal paper, Alexander Gerschenkron (1962) argued that late industrializers were likely to evolve different institutional forms in order to exploit their lateness or to 'catch up'. More specifically, the state was bound to play a much more active role than in the pioneer countries. The 'late industrialisers' were likely to make use of the joint-stock form of enterprise, and to depend more heavily on bank finance than on financial equity markets for financing industrialization. What has rarely been explicitly theorized, however, is that among the institutions adapted for such late industrialization were those dealing with social policy: these same latecomers were among the pioneers of the modern welfare state.

The role of social policy in the late industrializers is spelled out more explicitly by Vartiainen (in this volume), who argues that late industrializers have to deal with two groups of externalities: human capital, technology and financial externalities recognized by Gerschenkron; and also the strategic action and distribution issues addressed by social policy. With respect to the latter, Vartiainen highlights two issues concerning development in which social policy can play a significant role. The first of these is the relationship of the intertemporal decisions about investment, consumption and accumulation. An important argument on the relationship between invest-ment/consumption decisions and growth has been premised on assumptions on how different patterns of distribution affect accumulation. As he notes, 'economic growth and development are about deferring consumption of resources today in order to create more resources in the future'. The question that arises then is what factors account for the sharp differences in investments (or deferment of immediate gratification). Vartiainen identifies three kinds of economic mechanisms that can lead to a situation in which investments is discouraged, even though the overall benefits of investment to the economy as a whole are widely acknowledged:

1. Discrepancy between social return and private returns of growth-enhancing investment;
2. Dynamic externality associated with the discrepancy of *ex ante* and *ex post* bargaining over distribution;
3. The individual and idiosyncratic uncertainty of investment returns.

The first refers to positive externalities and has been a major argument for public intervention in investment. This is particularly the case with social investments in health and education which government must undertake if the economy is not to be stuck in a 'low-development' trap. The second point concerns dynamic externality associated with the division of returns of productive investment. Even if a society agreed that sacrifices be made in terms of forgone consumption in order to enhance accumulation, there might still be opposition to any such 'sacrifices' being made if there are no guarantees that the gains from such 'sacrifices' will be fairly distributed. If, for instance, workers accept a lower wage in order to encourage high levels of profits, the 'sacrifice' will have been in vain, if the resultant profits are expatriated or allocated to conspicuous consumption. Vartiainen argues that 'the state can be seen as a kind of broker that ensures that the *ex post* distribution of resources is such that it corresponds to those incentives that were *ex ante* necessary to induce the necessary investments'. It can intervene in the economy to make high re-investment of profits the preferred behaviour of capital owners. Here 'social pacts' can play an important role.

The third aspect arises from the inevitable *individual* uncertainty associated with innovation and new investment projects as well as economic restructuring. This raises the important issue of social insurance in economic development. A number of investments that could be undertaken for the benefit of the economy may be hampered by the high risks involved in undertaking them. Significantly, this also applies to many investments that the poor might wish to make in terms of education and investments in innovations. 'Safety nets' may be important in reducing the costs of failure.

The second issue raised by uncertainty has to do with people's readiness to accept policy changes. Economic development involves major structural changes with 'winners and losers'. In most cases, individuals may not know what category they will fall into, and, given risk aversion, they may oppose change which is likely to benefit many. Here again, the state, with its many instruments, including social insurance, can ensure that the final outcome is not so disadvantageous for any particular group as to induce paralysis or political opposition. In a situation of rapid technological change, the best way to contain 'luddite' tendencies is to provide sufficient guarantees to everybody that they will share in the ensuing benefits of such changes. This 'risk-pooling' is vital not only for political stability, but also in making individuals take risks and accept changes that are inherently fraught with risk and uncertainty.

Insurance aspects of social welfare systems, like all insurance systems inhere in them the potential for 'free riding', 'moral hazards', rent-seeking and capture and overshooting. This opens up room for conflicts over distribution, which, in turn, points to the potential role of the state as a mediator or as a partner in social concertation to strike acceptable bargains on income distribution. But as Vartiainen (1999) states:

> To get industrialisation under way, the state must mobilise and organise the economy, and act to build a coherent corporatist structure with which it can work and design growth-promoting policies. This means that it must also be able to deal with the inevitable distributional conflicts. The state must cope with the inherent paradox that rapid structural change requires more social organisation and political co-ordination of resources, which, at the same time, may aggravate problems of inefficient corporatism and unilateral interest group action at redistributive rent-seeking. (p. 142)

A more historically grounded account is provided by Pierson (chapter 10). Pierson starts off with the observation that there is no straightforward association between the *level* and duration of industrialization and the *extent* of welfare state development. Indeed in the case of Western Europe, the very first welfare states did not emerge among the pioneers of industrialization. It was Europe's 'late industrialisers' which led the process of welfare state innovation. Significantly, after 1923, 'there has been a tendency for countries to adopt welfare state measures at a lower level in their own economic development and "late starters" have tended to develop welfare state institution earlier in their own individual development and under more comprehensive terms of coverage'.

One suggested explanation for this trend is reminiscent of Gerschenkron's thesis, that 'late industrializers' would tend to adopt a number of institutional arrangements to speed up their industrialization process. Pierson observes that there is nothing automatic about the thesis, especially when it is extended beyond Europe. In the case of Latin America, while, within the region, later developers have learned some lessons from the region's pioneers, overall social spending is lower than might be predicted upon the basis of the level of development. This suggests that (a) 'lateness' is attended by as many disadvantages and advantages; (b) the exploitation of the advantages of 'lateness' is far from automatic.

At first sight, the experiences of the Asian late industrializers would seem to diverge from Vartiainen's model tying up the two types of externalities. This is partly because of the mystification of the 'Asian model' by both governments and admirers. By comparison with western countries, East Asian governments are relatively low spenders on welfare, and non-state agents – community, firm and family – have been expected to play a major role in providing welfare within the ideological context in which self/mutual help is encouraged and dependence upon the state is discouraged (indeed stigmatized). However as Chang, Kwon and Pierson argue in this volume, states in Asian NICs play an important role as a regulator, enforcing welfare programmes without providing direct finance. Moreover, to a significant extent, what would be considered social welfare activities were embedded in the corporate structure that emerged in these countries (following what has been referred to as the 'Japanese' model). The Asian experience seems to suggest that the composition of social policies in later industrializers may tend to pay greater attention to production-enhancing elements of social policy (health and education) and much less on the redistributive and protective aspects of social policy. In other words, implicit in late industrialization was social policy that served not only to ensure national cohesion (as is often asserted of Bismarck's innovative welfare legislation), but also to produce the social pacts and the human capital that facilitated industrialization.

In their contributions to this volume Chang and Huck-ju Kwon underscore the importance of 'social policy' in the economic 'Asian Miracle' and argue against a common misunderstanding of social policy in these societies. The usual view is that because of their ethnic homogeneity or Confucian respect for authority these countries have enjoyed political stability and social peace without having to introduce social policies to co-opt militant labour or to manage ethnic divisions. And yet until quite recently, East Asia was one of the most conflict-ridden places in the world. Revolutions, wars of national liberation, ethnic conflicts, and labour unrest are not alien to this part of the world. The social cohesion that these countries have enjoyed during the last three decades has been deliberately crafted through the active use of social policy – land reform in Taiwan and South Korea, 'affirmative action' in Malaysia, labour protection through lifetime employment in Japan, forced savings, comprehensive insurance and pension schemes in Singapore, restriction on luxury consumption notably in Japan and South Korea, and so on. These social policy measures may not have had the classical welfare state characteristics, but their influence on the development of these countries was far reaching. In a number of cases these policies encouraged human capital formation and made workers more open to technological change without the 'defensive obstructionism' that characterised responses to new technologies in some industrialized countries.

Prior to the East Asian crisis, it was suggested that such features made these countries exemplary, partly because they were linked to a developmental ideology and practice that subordinated welfare – particularly in the form of progressive redistribution – to the overarching priority of economic development and productivity. In addition, the model imposed a low fiscal burden, allowing public investment to go to directly 'productive' uses. By discouraging dependency upon the state, it provided positive work incentives and pressures for work discipline. And finally, funded insurance schemes provided substantial financial resources that could be used for developmental purposes under state direction. In right-wing circles the combination of high economic growth with a putatively anti-social policy regime was used as an argument against welfare policies in general.

The East Asian crisis brought out the negative aspects of this model. First, it demonstrated that the model's viability depended upon high growth and that, in times of crisis, the system could not provide the social protection that welfare systems are supposed to. The regressive nature of its redistributive measures has highlighted the inequalities in the model. Reliance on the non-state sector meant that women bore most of the burden, and this reinforced male dominance and female dependency. Built upon successful integration into global markets, the model was vulnerable to external conjuncture. Finally, it is important to note that the model thrived in essentially authoritarian contexts and would thus be unlikely to survive the wave of democratization that is likely to push for more progressive welfare policies. Can this 'developmental welfarism' be revamped to be able to function in a more democratic environment? This problem is addressed by Huck-ju Kwon in his contribution to this volume. South Korea possesses a conundrum by increasing its welfare programmes precisely at a time when they are being trimmed everywhere, when the 'developmental model' is under severe pressure and in conjunction with the democratization process. The question that immediately arises is: Why has Korea extended its welfare state, at a time when neo-liberal ideology has been predominant in public policy discourse in Korea and abroad? A prima facie account would be that in response to the Asian Financial crisis, the state had to introduce safety nets and ameliorative measures to deal with the crisis since its corporate-based welfare system could not cope.

Huck-ju Kwon challenges this argument by showing that the reforms that have been carried out have gone beyond the functional minima required by the economic crisis. He argues that the answer lies in the politics of welfare reform in South Korea. He points to the importance of understanding how social coalitions for different types of social policies are created and what capacities they have for exploiting opportunities that present themselves in the course of a country's history. He also points to the importance of ideological shifts in the population at large in facilitating changes in social policy. With the end of the authoritarian development states, a new 'social pact' premised on a more participatory political process had to be crafted. The 'social compact' created among employers, employees and politicians facilitated the process of labour marker reforms. In return for such reforms, which led to increased unemployment, the government introduced a package of social policy – 'the Master Plan for Tackling Unemployment' – which included, among other things, the extension of the Employment Insurance Programme, a public works programme. The total outlay of the government in the social policy area rose by 22.1 per cent from 1997 to 1998 and 28.3 per cent from 1998 to 1999.

Latin America is a region which has experimented with a wide range of economic policies under a wide range of political regimes. It is therefore an appropriate region for examining the question of the relationship between developmental goals (equity versus growth) and means (market versus state). In his contribution to this volume, Mesa-Lago takes three countries as prototypical of the three models that have appeared in Latin America: Chile as an example of the neo-liberal model; Cuba as the centrally planned socialist model; and Costa Rica as the mixed economy model. These countries are important examples in Latin America of a relatively early emphasis on social policies.

We suggested earlier that the challenge of development is the edification of a social order that was developmental, democratic and socially inclusive. Few societies have achieved all these objectives at once. Taking development (growth) and social inclusiveness, Mesa-Lago notes that Costa Rica had a fair performance with respect to economic indicators and the best results in social indicators; Chile performed well on economic indicators, but poorly on social indicators; in the 1980s Cuba led the region with respect to social indicators, but performed poorly in terms of economic indicators. Of the three only Costa Rica was a democracy, suggesting the possibility of developmental strategies that were developmental, democratic and socially inclusive.

India is a democracy where the inadequacy of social policy has clearly impacted negatively upon the country's development project. Not surprisingly, the case of India has always featured in debates about democracy, social policy and equity in developing countries. Jayati Ghosh addresses the question of the political underpinnings and the social contractual character of social policy in the management of the development project. In India, social policy has included the following elements: agrarian reform, food procurement and distribution, education, employment creation through public works, affirmative action in the form of reservation for public services employment and educational institutions, anti-poverty programmes directed towards small asset creation or micro credit, changes in forms and structures of governance through decentralization, and some devolution of resources.

However, as Jayati Ghosh argues, while social policy may be both a desirable and necessary concomitant of the development process, its adoption cannot be taken for granted: it depends upon the constellation of political forces and the development strategies pursued. She argues that social policy has not been a basic instrument of development. Rather, it has emerged essentially in the form of ad hoc responses to particular demands emanating from groups that (at least temporarily) have acquired some degree of political voice. Indeed in the case of India the relative inadequacy of social policy over the post-independence period 'is one important reason why the development project itself has remained incomplete and unsatisfactory in terms of fulfilling the basic requirements of the majority of citizens'. This immediately raises the question why, in the case of India as the world largest liberal democracy, democracy itself has not resulted in greater attention being paid to the provision of basic goods and minimally acceptable level of public services to all citizens? Ghosh advances a number of possible explanations. One is the federal character of India. The second is the failure to introduce land reform and reduce asset and income inequality. Linked to this is a high level of tolerance for high levels of inequality. Inequality has contributed to the limits on the expansion of the domestic market for mass consumption goods most apparent in the 1960s with the exhaustion of import-substitution-driven industrialization. It also compelled the state to subsidize industry on the basis of limited revenue. This subsidization of the private sector and the failure of the state to impose minimum discipline on those receiving its favours led to a fiscal crisis that eventually led to adhesion to neo-liberal policies that would curtail subsidies and lead to the privatization of state enterprises. Liberalization has undermined some of the initial gains in social policy. Growing inequality and the conspicuous consumption of the elite induced by 'the demonstration effect' of opening up is increasing social tensions, some of which show up in the form of violence against minorities.

Guy Mhone's account of the case of Zambia clearly testifies to the importance of path dependence and initial conditions matter in determining appropriate policies and their effectiveness. Zambia emerged at independence as a monocultural dualistic economy in which the 'modern' sector was only tenuously linked to the 'traditional sector' largely through the importation of labour to the mines. Superimposed on this dualistic model was a racialized formal labour market in which, over the years, the white working class had won for themselves a fairly extensive set of welfare rights. In the initial years, the colonial government treated the African workers as essentially 'target workers' on a brief sojourn through the urban areas. Consequently, no provisions were made for the social welfare. However, it soon became clear that the disruptive effects of 'modernization' on rural societies stoked rural-to-urban migration. Growing militancy of the black labour force also drew attention to the plight of black labour and to their disruptive potential. In addition, stabilization of the labour force required improved living conditions in the urban areas. 'Native welfare' therefore entered the policy agenda.

The post-colonial regime was faced with: (a) the problem of deracializing the labour market; (b) creating more employment opportunities; and (c) bridging the urban–rural divide. For a while, high copper prices gave the state the resources to address some of these problems. However, the policies eventually ran into a fiscal crunch. Mhone argues that no conscious attempts were made to define comprehensive social policy in a developmental context. There has been little attempt to align social policy and economic policy and policies did not pay much attention to the developmental side, partly because of the belief that the rents from mining could underwrite the social programmes.

Mhone points out the failure of social policy in both colonial and post-colonial Zambia to 'seize upon traditional social systems as stepping stones for the developing of new support systems'. This is a poorly researched area that deserves attention in societies where non-wage labour will continue to constitute a significant source of the livelihoods for large numbers of people.

Globalization and social policy

One recurring theme in the essays in this volume is the impact of globalization on social policy. Globalization affects social policy both at the normative level and in a more practical way, by setting constraints that social policy must be attentive to. Adhesion to international conventions, adjustment to fiscal pressures and responses to an international discourse on 'social rights' permeate domestic politics and affect social policy – or at least the thinking about it.

In the more practical sphere, it is often feared that globalization is not only reversing the social gains made in the developed countries in the 'golden era' of capitalism and the welfare state, but that it makes it highly improbable that developing countries will have the policy autonomy to nurture policies that would lead to 'distortions' in the labour market without losing international competitiveness and scaring away domestic and foreign investors. Furthermore, the erosion of the fiscal capacity of the state (partly due to great 'exit' possibilities for capital) is likely to undermine the domestic capacity to finance social policy. In sharp contrast to this view is the argument that there is no simple relationship between globalization and social policies or social indicators. National political arrangements and resolution of social conflicts mediate the pressures of globalization. As Pierson notes, 'openness' to trade has often been associated with increased social expenditure, and there is no uniform pattern of response among the developed countries to globalization. Jayati Ghosh also argues that social policy has played a 'very important but largely unsung role' in terms of underwriting a significant part of labour costs for private capital, therefore providing employers with greater flexibility and contributing to their external competitiveness. In addition, social polices have cushioned some key social groups against the volatility that globalization brings along. As Dani Rodrik has argued, the economic costs of external shocks are magnified by the distributional conflicts they trigger, and this diminishes the productivity with which a society's resources are utilized. This is largely because social polarization makes it more difficult to build consensus about policy changes in response to crisis.[11] As a consequence, policy makers in developing countries find themselves torn between the exigencies of global competition and the growing global and domestic demands for equity and justice. For developing countries, the exigencies of globalization are expressed not only through the spontaneous workings of the market but also (and sometimes largely) through the policies imposed or authorized by international financial institutions and the demands by trading partners that developing countries meet certain social standards.

Closely related to this is the possibility of developmental states in the context of globalization. One outstanding feature of developmental states has been the 'governing' of markets through import-substitution policies: export promotion, credit rationing, industrial policy and a whole gamut of interventionist policies. Many of these instruments are now either ruled out, in structural adjustment programmes, or are illegal under the new world trade dispensation. One conjecture is that developmental states will resort to more direct interventions through social policy or even ownership structure. One important feature of Keynesian economics was its contribution to the liberal embeddedness of policy in which open international trade and investment went side by side with unilateral interventionism at the national level, permitting nation-states to pursue national goals such as growth, full employment and social equity. Peter Townsend reminds us of how Keynes recognized the significance of the global financial architecture and the fact that such architecture had to be constructed as if employment and welfare mattered. This point, which has been forcefully made by Dani Rodrik, is most pertinent in the context of globalization. 'Open economies' are subject to the volatile functionings of the global market and therefore need social policies that reassure citizens that adjustments to the exigencies of globalization will be equitably shared. Pierson suggests that today's global order will tend to push social policies (including those of welfare states in the developed countries) towards the East Asian 'regulatory' welfare regimes in which the state regulates social provision by the private sector, voluntary organization or household. In addition, for developing countries, the changes in policy stances of the IMF and the World Bank and other donors will have significant impacts on the nature of social policy in the developing countries.

A globalization process that takes development seriously should seek to increase the instruments available to developing countries, not only to enable them to 'catch up' but also to permit them to manage the vagaries and social consequences of an increasingly volatile system. The boldness of Keynes' thinking in this respect is yet to be matched in thinking of a new global economic architecture, which functions as if development mattered.

Concluding remarks: the missing policy link

The triumph in the 1970s of what Albert O. Hirschman termed 'monoeconomics' or what Krugman (1992) called the 'counter-revolution' against development economics detached economics from development studies in general, and from social development in particular. The chapters in this volume clearly elaborate the case that social policy can work in tandem with economic policy to lead to socioeconomic development and argue strongly for the inseparability of the economic and social. They therefore point to new approaches in social policy in which it serves both as an end and as an instrument of social development. Both the theoretical and historical essays in this volume underscore the need for context-sensitive research on the links between macroeconomic performance and the fundamental goal of raising human welfare. There is also a clear need to bridge the hiatus between theoretical and empirical findings and social policy making, and between means and ends. This argues for the necessity of research that brings together the diverse strands of analysis and encourages more explicit consideration of policy implications in different political, economic, and social settings.

Finally, social policy addresses fundamental values of social inclusion, equity, human rights and widening of human capabilities: It is important that these intrinsic values are always at the forefront of thinking about social policy. However, in situations of extreme scarcity, any strategy that aims at sustainable improvement in the conditions of life of the majority must address both the problems of accumulation and the efficient allocation of scarce resources. The failure to do so can be self-defeating and can lead to a severe curtailment of people's capabilities. The pursuit of things of intrinsic value has to be seen in the context of the contending claims of efficiency, and in general of aggregative concerns (Sen 1999). This is the challenge of social policy in the development context.

Notes

1. On macroeconomic populism, see Dornbusch and Edwards (1990).
2. Ian Gough (2000) makes this case for the seminal work of Gøsta Esping-Andersen on welfare regimes in OECD countries as ways of conceptualizing the programmes, outcomes and effects of those capitalist countries that have been transformed into welfare states.

3. For a succinct review of this literature, see Atkinson (1999).
4. This is a central message of the studies in Mehrotra and Jolly (1997).
5. UNRISD's interest in these issues clearly emerges in some of the studies it has commissioned. See, especially, Cassen and Wignaraja (1997), which reports some of the micro-level evidence on the importance of social expenditure for human development and the ability of the poor to improve their capacities. The paper also considers studies of the effect of human capital on comparative advantage.
6. For a review of the literature on the relationship between health, nutrition and development, see Strauss and Thomas (1998).
7. This view was quite prevalent in Latin American 'structuralism' writing.
8. For a rigorous exposition of this position, see Taylor (1983, 1991).
9. Among the 'pioneers' of development economics, Nurkse's preoccupation with the need for 'balanced growth' raised the problem of the demand for goods produced by new industries in the absence of mechanisms that co-ordinated such supply with demand.
10. The importance of long-term 'trust' as social capital is tested by Knack and Keefer (1997).
11. The high profile given to safety-net programmes during adjustment is partly based on this argument. Such social programmes putatively make the adjustment process undermine the core logic of the adjustment model itself.

Bibliography

Abramovitz, M. (1995) 'Elements of Social Capability'. In B. H. Koo and D. H. Perkins (eds), *Social Capability and Long-Term Economic Growth*. London: Macmillan.

Alesina, A. and Perotti, R. (1994) 'The Political Economy of Growth: A Critical Survey of the Recent Literature', *World Bank Economic Review*, 8(3): 351–71.

Atkinson, A. B. (1999) *The Economic Consequences of Rolling Back the Welfare State*. Cambridge (Mass): MIT Press.

Birdsall, N. (1997) *Asset Inequality Does Matter: Lessons from Latin America*. Washington, DC: Inter-American Development Bank.

Bowles, S. and Gintis, H. (1995) 'Escaping the Efficiency–Equity Trade Off: Productivity-enhancing Asset Redistributions'. In G. Epstein and H. Gintis (eds), *Macroeconomic. Policy After the Conservative Era*. New York: Cambridge University Press.

Cassen, R. and G. Wignaraja (1997) *Social Investment, Productivity and Poverty: A Survey*. Geneva: UNRISD.

Cruz-Saco, M. A. and Mesa-Lago, C. (1998) 'Conclusions: Conditioning Factors, Cross Country Comparisons and Recommendations' in Cruz-Saco M. A. and Mesa-Lago C. (eds) *Do Options Exist: The Reform of Pension and Health care Systems in Latin America*. Pittsburgh: University of Pittsburgh.

Dornbusch, R. and Edwards, S. (1990) 'Macroeconomic Populism'. *Journal of Development Economics* 32(2): 247–78.

Elson, D. (1991) 'Male Bias in Macro-Economics: the Case of Structural Adjustment'. In D. Elson (ed.), *Male Bias in the Development Process*. Manchester: Manchester University Press.

Folbre, N. (1994) *Who Pays for the Kid? Gender and the Structures of Constraint*. London: Routledge.

Gershenkron, A. (1962) *Economic Backwardness in Historical Perspective*. Cambridge (Mass): Harvard University Press.

Ghai, D. (ed.) (2000) *Social Development and Public Policy*. In 'A Study of Some Successful Experiences'. Geneva: UNRISD/Macmillan.

Goodman, R. and White, G. *et al.* (eds) (1998) *The East Asian Welfare Model: Welfare Orientalism and the State*. London: Routledge.

Gough, I. (2000) *Globalisation and Regional Welfare Regimes: The East Asian Case*. Department of Social and Policy Sciences, University of Bath. (WWW) http://www.bath.ac.uk/ifipa/GSP/wp8.pdf (12.05.04)

Huber, E. and Stephens, J. D. (2000) *The Political Economy of Pension Reform: Latin America in Comparative Perspective*. Geneva: UNRISD.

Huntington, S. P. (1968) *Political Order in Changing Societies*. New Haven: Yale University Press.

Knack, S. and P. Keefer (1997) 'Does Social Capital Have an Economic Payoff: A Cross Country Investigation', *Quarterly Journal of Economics* CXII (4): 1251–89.

Krugman, P. (1993). *Toward a Counter-Counterrevolution in Development Theory*. Proceedings of the World Bank Annual Conference on Development Economics 1992, (Supplement to the World Bank Economic Review and the World Bank Observer) pp. 15–38.

Mehrotra, S. and Jolly, R. (eds) (1997) *Social Development in High Achieving Countries: Common Elements and Diversities*. Oxford: Clarendon Press.

Meier, G. and Seers, D. (1984) *Pioneers in Development*. New York: Oxford University Press/World Bank.

Myrdal, G. (1984) 'International Inequality and Foreign Aid in Retrospect'. In G. Meier and D. Seers (eds), *Pioneers in Development*. Washington, DC: Oxford University Press.

Polanyi, K. (1946) *The Great Transformation: the Political and Economic Origins of Our Time*. Boston: Beacon Press.

Rothschild, E. (2001) *Economic Sentiments: Adam Smith Condorcet, and the Enlightenment*. Boston: Harvard University Press.

Sen, A. (1999) *Development as Freedom*. Oxford: Oxford University Press.

Stewart, F. (1978) *Technology and Underdevelopment*. London: Macmillan Press.

Stewart, F., Ranis, G. and Ramirez, A. (2000) 'Economic Growth and Human Development', *World Development*, 28, 197–219.

Strauss, J. and Thomas, D. (1998) 'Health, Nutrition and Economic Development', *Journal of Economic Literature* 36(2): 766–817.

Taylor, L. (1983) *Structuralist Macroeconomics*. New York: Basic Books.

Taylor, L. (1991) *Income Distribution, Inflation, and Growth: Lectures on Structuralist Macroeconomic Theory*. Cambridge (Mass): M.I.T.

Vartiainen, J. (1999) 'The State and Structural Change: What Can be Learnt from the Successful Later Industrializers'. In Chang H.-J. and Rowthorn, R. (eds) *The Role of the State in Economic Change*. Oxford: Clarendon Press.

Woojin Lee and Roemer, J. E. (1998) 'Income Distribution, Redistributive Politics, and Economic Growth', *Journal of Economic Growth*, 3, 217–40.

Part I
Conceptual Issues

2

From Universalism to Safety Nets: The Rise and Fall of Keynesian Influence on Social Development

Peter Townsend

Introduction

The history of social policy during the last hundred years would be seriously incomplete without giving a full account of the dramatic influence of John Maynard Keynes. He was instrumental in helping Europe recover from the Second World War of 1939–45 – in contrast to the failures after the First – and in establishing the Bretton Woods institutions and the welfare state. Social development lay at the heart of his concern – in the construction of practical policies as much as in his astute handling of economic theory. He cut the ground from beneath the feet of classical and neo-classical economic theorists, and the policies he recommended were found to work in practice. Certainly the early postwar years represent an acknowledged watershed in world history. If not exactly a thing of the past mass unemployment was no longer an immediate threat. Recovery and economic progress were real. Inequality had been reduced. Colonial powers were in retreat.

Yet by the 1970s Keynes' steadying influence on world social development and the global market had faded, and monetarism and conservative political forces were in the ascendant. For more than three decades disciples of the free market have dismissed his ideas and successfully changed, but also shaped, the institutions of trade, communication and government as well as those of the market itself. Keynes was reduced to legendary status. Neo-liberal economists could safely honour the legend without absorbing its substance into their advice and action. However, it has become increasingly clear that Keynes' legacy has turned out to be larger than many had bargained for. After being relatively dormant for more than a generation Keynesian thought is suddenly alive and well. There are accumulating signs of the resurfacing of his ideas: The legend has become a strategy-in-waiting. Keynes' internationalism and sense of planning is one thing. His universalism in constructing a socially viable economy – to deliver decent minimal living standards and public services – is quite another. While pale pretences of the former certainly exist, the latter is still largely denied. In 2004, both offer solutions to some of the world's most intractable problems.

In this chapter I will offer reminders of Keynes' contribution to social policy – in the best sense of the term – in establishing the welfare state and fomenting international collaboration and development. I will go on to trace current examples of ideas that are springing back to life in forms that are as compelling as they are necessary.

The rise of Keynes in the 1930s and 1940s

There are many helpful strands of analysis. Keynes had established himself as the most prominent critic of interwar economic theories. The mass unemployment and poverty of the 1920s and 1930s had led to the emergence of Nazism and the outbreak of the Second World War. In 1936 his *General Theory of Employment, Interest and Money* was published. Neo-classical theory had insisted that recession had to be countered by reductions in wages and in public expenditure. Keynes took a different course, being the first to make a clear distinction between macro- and microeconomic theories.

There were questions affecting the management of the economy as a whole – what factors determined how many people were employed or the total amount a country produces or the divisions between wages and salaries or profits and rents. This was macroeconomics. Then there were more specific questions affecting the individual firms, other organizations and individuals within the economy – what factors determined the price charged for a firm's product, the level of profitability or productivity, and the wage received by employees. This was microeconomics. The significance of making the distinction lay in Keynes' argument that the factors determining the behaviour of the economy as a whole are not the aggregation of the forces determining the individual elements. For Keynes, mass unemployment was not a problem of supply – and of the prices that had to be charged by individual businesses; rather, it was one of demand. The remedy was therefore maximum feasible employment through unemployment benefits and government investment in jobs. He had rehearsed some of the principal arguments since the early 1920s and in preceding books, including his testimony of the value of investment in public works during a recession – *A Treatise on Money* – in 1930.

Keynes' macroeconomics was linked to his insistence on planning and social development. This put economics back in the big league – re-establishing the broad scope of thinking about economics that is embodied in the work of eighteenth- and nineteenth-century writers such as Adam Smith, Ricardo and even Malthus. Governments contributed, and were bound to contribute, to the elaborate institutional framework of demand. Consumers did not, and could not, act in the national interest, especially at times of crisis. Neither could governments disclaim their responsibility for the shaping of market demand, or indeed the developing structure of the market system itself. Since time immemorial they had been active participants – indeed dominant participants – in the evolution of economies; they could not pretend to be aloof or detached. Nor could complex economics be conceived or pursued without governments being incorporated as a structural assumption. They were – and are – a necessary condition and determinant of operating markets.

For Keynes economics was more an empirical science conditioned by the economic and social constructs of many generations to explain developments and predict improvements than it was a mechanical application of deductive logic to produce ideal models for application and action.[1] In his thinking evidence of condition and cause had to be paramount. It was the key to penetration and success. It permitted conventional wisdom to be overthrown, new ideas to flourish and not merely register, and scientific authority to enhance political negotiation.

These were years when the influence of the ideas that Keynes advanced began to shape hearts and minds everywhere. By 1936, the year which saw the publication of his *General Theory*, his star had entered the firmament. Voices raised against the appeasement politics of powerful Conservatives and the drawing together of a political coalition for war made him a key national – and international – figure. His advice was sought in all quarters. He went to the United States in the early 1930s and was made acutely aware of the effects of the slump and restorative effects of New Deal policies – actions which his own work had substantially influenced. His work on unemployment and the need for greater public expenditure during the interwar years had exerted influence in the US, even if it had encountered obstruction in the UK, despite strenuous advocacy and some professional support, throughout the early 1930s.[2] He praised some of the measures adopted in the New Deal, but was severely critical of others and received considerable publicity when he wrote an open letter to Roosevelt in 1933 (Skidelsky 1993: 489–495).

The New Deal was much more than a programme of public works, and recovery of employment. For example, the US introduced its Social Security Act in 1935, in which the provision of unemployment benefit was a core feature. A report prepared for the Committee on Economic Security, justifying the new law and explaining how it had come into being, declared: 'The unprecedented extent and duration of unemployment in the United States since 1930 has left no one who is dependent upon a wage or salary untouched by the dread of loss of work.' Relief was 'expensive to distribute and demoralising to both donor and recipient. A device is needed which will assure those who are involuntarily unemployed a small steady income for a limited period'[3]. Keynes had clearly left his mark. Unemployment insurance was the vehicle that was chosen in the US. Benefit had to be as of right. Risks had to be pooled. European countries provided the model. And provision of income in unemployment could not be separated from provision of income in old age, disability and raising children. The 1935 Social Security Act represented a key reversal in US strategy and despite the predatory incursions and threats of the Reagan and Bush years continues to represent a remarkable blip in the traditional grudging American approaches to welfare.

Keynes and the British Welfare State

Given an acknowledgement of Keynes' influence on the US during the early 1930s and the following New Deal it is unsurprising that during the war he had a powerful influence behind the scenes as well as directly on social developments in the UK. His backing of Beveridge at a critical juncture in the preparation of the 1942 plan for national insurance was probably the crucial difference between failure and acceptance by the British Coalition Government of the recommendations of the Beveridge Report. Beveridge himself was too self-important to acknowledge Keynes' role, and Keynes too absorbed in other national and international issues to want to seek credit.[4] Nonetheless, Keynes had prepared the way for comprehensive government planning and massive public investment or expenditure. He was aware of the grave limitations of private insurance and the needs of the poor – whether employed or unemployed. Most important of all – he was at the time of central importance to the British Treasury.

The Beveridge plan had a knock-on effect throughout Europe. It was not simply that the pooling of risks through compulsory social insurance contributions ensured a minimal income for the unemployed, but the message influenced many governments and also influenced those wanting to meet the needs of the elderly, disabled and families with children.

Keynes' work on behalf of national reconstruction and the reduction of unemployment was fundamentally social in character – observing the psychology of social renewal and inclusion as well as establishing minimally adequate living standards for all. This feature of his theories has not been properly recognized – even by sympathetic economists and biographers (for example Harrod 1951; Skidelsky 2000; and Stewart, 1967, 1972).

The internationalism of the 1940s: Bretton Woods

The fact that Keynes' ideas carried so much weight at this time needs some explanation. His theoretical work long before the war anticipated the need for the reorganization of international institutions. Thus, his 1930 book *A Treatise on Money* proposed a Super-national Authority or Central Bank (see Harrod

1951: 411–13). His chance came during the war, and in an attempt to reconcile American and British thinking in April 1943 he produced an international plan. This stated that there was a need to buttress economic recovery. 'We need a central institution, of a purely technical and non-political character, to aid and support other international institutions concerned with the planning and regulation of the world's economic life' (Harrod 1951: 527). At the time the plan was thought to be Utopian. Certainly there were dozens of exchanges with leading officials and ministers and new drafts. Inevitably Keynes was forced to concede ground but eventually, in late 1944, the International Monetary Fund and the International Bank for Reconstruction and Development were established. Of course, these institutions cannot be separated from the motives for setting them up and the objectives written into their policies and practices. Keynes had wanted the institutions to be both more democratic and more accountable than in fact they became. He was also an advocate of writing-off loans, and reducing the high interest rates on remaining loans, which crippled the poorest countries. He backed gifts as well as low-interest loans for these countries that were recovering from war or were otherwise impoverished.

Keynesian strategy re-born

Because Keynes was supposed to be relevant only to a special period of European history his influence has been allowed to wane (though there are powerful contemporary voices renewing his arguments, for example Hutton 1996: 239–47; Skidelsky 1993, 2000). The exigencies of mid-twentieth century war were certainly special – in some respects unique – and produced extreme demands. The Keynesian remedies of lend-lease, public ownership and public services, and state planning, had immense public appeal. After 1945, they certainly secured peacetime stability and a measure of security for all populations in many of the industrializing countries.

Both the international and domestic influence mattered. *The General Theory*, published in 1936, confirmed the influence that Keynes already exerted on international as well as national thinking about both economic and social policy through his other work – especially *A Treatise on Money* (1930). The 'uncertain prophet in the wilderness of the early 1930s' had, in Nick Timmins' words, become the fount of Keynesianism (Timmins 1995: 35).

Yet the general case for Keynes is stronger than is generally suggested. Because his macroeconomics was rooted in economic and social realities his policies linked market 'efficiency' with social justice. The scope of his work for both international social development is considerable. What he advocated had ramifying effects on social development in all of its forms and not just in establishing new international economic institutions to smooth the evolution of global capitalism. Some economists have argued that Keynesian employment policies are relevant only in circumstances in which the means of production exist, but goods are not being produced because there is too little effective demand. This seems to eliminate the situation in much of the Third World. These economists suggest that Third World governments have to adopt different policies. For example, 'More expenditure by government or consumers would not raise output and employment – it would merely raise prices and imports. For it is not effective demand that is lacking, but factors on the supply side' (Stewart 1972: 308). People are idle because 'there are no machines for them to work with, few managers to organise them and few skills or basic educational qualifications to be employed'. It is suggested that what is needed is techniques and equipment to raise productivity, education and investment in machinery, railways, power stations and irrigation systems (Stewart 1972: 308).

I believe this to be a misreading of Keynes as well as a misunderstanding of Third World economies. Economic and social rights were key objectives prioritized in the UN Charter and Keynes believed that three bodies – the IMF, the World Bank and an international trade organization – had to work together as part of the whole UN system to promote 'higher standards of living, full employment, and conditions of economic and social progress and development'. Full employment was viewed as a central goal, to be supported in all international economic operations. The international trade organization envisaged by Keynes had far wider functions than those that have been embodied in the WTO – not only to maintain free trade but also to help to stabilize world commodity prices, essentially through buffer stock arrangements:

> He recognised that the long-term international prices for commodities must be fixed in relation to both the economic conditions for efficient production and the human conditions for proper nutritional and other requirements to ensure a decent standard of living among primary producers ... Direct concern for nutrition and decent living standards has yet to be incorporated into the principles of international trade. (UNDP 1999: 98 and see also Keynes 1980)

However, many western economists persuaded themselves that the policies advocated by Keynes were relevant only to the developed western economies and were not open to comprehensive cross-national interpretation. The idea that his theories just happened to coincide with the particular needs of industrial countries at one stage of history has been used to minimize them but also to re-assert neo-classical and monetarist influence. Powerful counterarguments have had to be mobilized in Keynes' support. Loss of faith in monetary policy occurred before Keynes. It had been 'ineffective in pulling the economy out of the Depression' (Desai 1981: 35). But Keynes was the person who produced the most telling arguments about its failure in the 1930s and 1940s and these arguments applied to social development in poor as well as rich countries. Public investment, state planning, public services and the redistribution of income had to play a major role in both groups of countries.

The case for Keynes' social policy is also stronger than generally made out. Keynes is remembered best for his ideas about investment in jobs and benefits for the unemployed. But the reconstruction of social security (indirectly and directly he helped shape the Beveridge Report of 1942) and the expansion of public services also fell within the scope of his argument. His contribution to the emergence of the postwar welfare state was considerable.

Macroeconomics, social development and social policy

Keynesianism therefore had two particular effects. One was to redirect international economic development within a more disciplined relationship between market and state – including the establishment of the Bretton Woods institutions.

The second effect of Keynesianism was in increasing the momentum in favour of establishing welfare states in Europe.

Universalism: approaches to the welfare state

What Keynes did was to link international social development with the arguments for national welfare states. In comparing welfare states within Europe or within the wider OECD grouping the evidence can be framed in Keynesian terms.

For example, countries are usually grouped by social scientists into three or four sets. Esping-Andersen, for example, uses the principle of the commodification or decommodification of labour to identify those countries that characterize a liberal welfare state, a conservative-corporatist welfare state and a social democratic welfare state (Esping-Andersen 1990).

Critics of this categorization of welfare states include C. Pierson and S. Leibfried, who argue that countries like Germany, France and the Netherlands have deep regional divisions, socially heterogeneous populations and fragmented institutions, where 'centralized' policies are strongly influenced by 'territorial' politics. Europe, they say, is already a 'multi-tiered polity', and the integration of future social policy through different strategies of harmonization and integration is highly unlikely to succeed.

Their arguments deserve close examination. I believe they are subsidiary rather than contradictory. They represent fine-tuning rather than the central thrust of the argument. The typology has explanatory power, which has been borne out most recently in a study of the US, Germany and the Netherlands (Goodin *et al.* 1999). The authors admit that they would have wished to include Sweden because it best represented the active labour market policies and high levels of public employment and public consumption that characterize the social democratic welfare state. But with some corporatist characteristics they argue that the Netherlands deserves inclusion in the ranks of the 'social-democratic' welfare regime, especially as regards the tax-transfer side of social policy. The governing reason for the choice of these three countries was that they were the only ones for which ten-year socioeconomic data were available.

The study is devoted to exploring what differences alternative welfare regimes make to people's lives.

> The upshot of our analyses... has been to single out the social democratic welfare strategy as strictly dominant over both the others... [It] is at least as good as (and usually better than) either of the other welfare regimes in respect of all the social objectives we traditionally set for out welfare regimes... and at least as good as any other on economic objectives as well [including] economic growth rates.   (Goodin *et al.* 1999: 261–2)

The typology helps to direct attention away from a preoccupation with factors internal to a country. This prevents internal variations in culture and politics from taking up an exaggerated part of explanation and of the mobilization of future policy.

In some respects the UK model compares well, but in too many respects badly, with the corporatist and Scandinavian models. It also compares badly with the 'ideal' model put forward 30 years ago by Richard Titmuss. He also adopted three models of welfare (Abel-Smith and Titmuss 1974: 30–1). One, which was broadly similar to the 'liberal welfare state', was entitled 'the residual welfare model of social policy'. The second corresponded to the 'conservative-corporatist' model and was entitled 'the industrial achievement-performance model of social policy'.

But the third went much further than the 'social democratic model' established in the welfare states of Scandinavian and other countries. This was the 'institutional redistributive model of social policy'. This model conceived of 'universalist services outside the market on the principle of need'. But the principle of equality is applied in an increasing number of ways and 'systems of redistribution in command-over-resources-through-time' are incorporated. The ramifying problems of acquisitiveness and conspicuous wealth across the world were clearly forecast.

This analysis can, of course, be traced back to Keynes and deserves extension to middle-income and low-income countries. The constraint of 'industrialized' versus 'non-industrialized' countries is no longer justifiable, if it ever was. There is more of a continuum because of globalization and growing inequality within rather than only between countries that makes global analysis and planning inevitable.

Universalism: the shortcomings of targeting and safety nets

The speed of social polarization across much of the world in the final decades of the twentieth century (Atkinson 1996, 1999; Cornia 1999; Townsend 1991, 1993, 1999) seems to have been faster than at any previous era in recorded history, because wages and the labour market were deregulated, progressive taxation was reduced, means-testing of benefits was extended, social insurance was weakened, and publicly owned industries and services were substantially privatized. Such developments have been common across Europe. This recent trend has to be related to the analysis of welfare regimes. Its counterpart is a revival of Keynesian planning for modernized social insurance, more jobs in the public services, and more redistribution and less privatization in the economy.

When structural adjustment programmes began to be applied throughout Eastern Europe and the former Soviet Union in the early 1990s, they compounded the problems of poverty, following liberalization. Evidence now available for the trends in that region in the last decade provides an object-lesson in global strategy (see, for example, chapters by S. Clarke, Z. Ferge and L. Dziewiecka-Bokun in Gordon and Townsend (2001)). Prior to 1989 social security constituted a large part of the institutional infrastructures of these states. The collapse of the command economy and of industry might have led to external efforts to maintain at least a residual form of protection for vulnerable people – especially children, the disabled and the elderly. World Bank and IMF teams seem to have lacked both the necessary expertise and any appreciation of comparative history. The possibility that structural adjustment programmes might not be as applicable to the former industrial economies of different regions of the former Soviet Union as they were supposed to be to the poorest developing countries seems not to have occurred to them.

Keynesian analysis has become pertinent to the development strategies of the international agencies today. When introducing their structural adjustment programmes, first in Latin America and Africa, and then in the 'transition' countries of Eastern Europe and the former Soviet Union, the IMF and the World Bank tried to balance the unequal social consequences of liberalization, privatization and cuts in public expenditure with proposals to target help on the most vulnerable groups in the population. For some years, and still to a large extent today, this has been presented in terms of applying the principle of test of means. Even if coverage was poor, large sums of money would be saved, it was argued, if the near-to-poor were no longer subsidized by public funds.

A stream of reports on the transitional economies has also been influential. The international financial agencies have been trying to suggest that in many of the post-Soviet republics it is government that is resisting effective policies. But the agencies have ignored the history establishing public services and social security in those countries in looking for the development of appropriate national institutions (see, for example, Chu and Gupta (1998: 90–2 and 111–12). They did not consider how former universal provisions might have been modified to allow market competition to grow but not create penury amongst one-third or more of the population.

The loan conditions demanding lower government expenditures in the poorest countries that were imposed have led to sharp reductions in general social spending and the denial of access to basic health services and education on the part of the poorest people. Evidence from the IMF's own work shows that 'the poorest three-fifths of these nations are being excluded from whatever social "safety net" exists for education, health, housing and social security and welfare' (Kolko 1999: 56).

The loan conditionalities have had more widespread social effects. For example, not only has the number of government employees been cut, but salaries have been reduced and in many cases paid belatedly, thereby seriously weakening administration in general and protective welfare in particular. The intention of administering a short, sharp economic shock has turned into protracted economic misery for large proportions of the population. Price subsidies for commodities such as bread and cooking oil have been reduced, and high value added taxes have deepened the problem by taking a regressive form. The IMF's own studies provided 'a devastating assessment of the social and economic consequences of its guidance of dozens of poor nations' (Kolko 1999: 53).

Safety nets and targeting are now being assessed for both rich and poor countries. Those who have assembled evidence for different European countries over many years (for example Oorschot (1999)) point out that such means-test policies have a number of negative outcomes, being poor in coverage, administratively expensive and complex, provoking social divisions, being difficult to square with incentives into work, and tending to discourage forms of saving.

There are signs on the part of some international organizations that targeting can include 'categorical' policies affecting vulnerable or disadvantaged *groups* in the population – especially in Eastern Europe and the former Soviet Union. The objectives of ensuring a minimum standard of living for all citizens and a 'relatively flat income distribution' were reported sympathetically in this study, and there was a lively appreciation of the arguments in favour of social insurance and against 'the inefficiency and high administrative costs associated with means-testing programmes' (UNDP 1998: 90–2). The 'socially inclusive' strength of social insurance schemes was also acknowledged

> as a kind of contract between generations, whereby people invested their efforts in the collective welfare and were rewarded by a guarantee of supplemental income. Because social assistance allowances are very low

in all transition countries, moving pensions towards means-tested social assistance programmes would push practically all pensioners into poverty. (UNDP 1998: 108–9)

However, the World Bank has continued to avoid serious discussion of the subject (World Bank 1997: 2–3) and has sought instead to promote a programme successor to structural adjustment built on a conceptual framework of 'social risk management' (for example, World Bank 2000).

What are the lessons of the new approach recommended by UNDP? It is clear that funding should adopt public and private forms of Pay-As-You-Go. 'Categorical benefits should be offered to all in need, or at least to all those near or below the poverty line. It is very important to avoid providing support only to the "poorest of the poor" while neglecting the relatively poor.' This plea for group or 'categorical' benefits in place of means-tested benefits was qualified by a recognition that some such benefits could be conditional in different ways (World Bank 2000: 105).

One of the strategic choices lies between redistribution and privatization. The practical arguments for reducing an over-extended private sector have grown. They reinforce some of the theoretical arguments expressed over many years. Privatization has reached its peak in some countries – as some of the major international agencies are beginning to admit. The debate in Europe about the respective roles of the public and private sectors has been reopened. This means that new as well as revived arguments for more extensive public service can be developed. The regeneration of the public sector lies at the core of anti-poverty planning and future plans for the welfare state in general.

Whose policy? Theoretical problems

The resurgence of social policy at the heart of economic development depends not only upon demonstrating which policies actually work in fulfilling expressed objectives, and invoking historical examples from Keynes. It is also important that the conventional categorization of knowledge is shaken up. Sociological theory may gain from the same kind of distinction used by Keynes to separate the study of world society as a whole from the study of particular groups, classes, populations, and cultures – while accepting the relevance of policy analysis to both. In some quarters 'social policy' has been interpreted as taking an evolutionary course in theory and practice – as if its place in the world was natural rather than socially constructed.

Thus, the idea that it is an 'applied' social science has been instilled, and has to be disinterred. It was instilled unconsciously as a means of maintaining the primacy of the physical over the social sciences. The former were 'pure' and therefore more prestigious. Laboratory experiments with rats and mice to measure reactions, and the distillation of hydrogen and oxygen from air and water in different degrees to assess effects, were supposed to be much more important in advancing knowledge than measuring the effects of the submission of groups and societies to the policies imposed by governments. Government policies were not supposed in any way to be the determinants of societal problems and of structural and social change. They were benign instruments of remedial action.

Many social scientists have allowed this distinction between the pure and the applied to be maintained, partly by interpreting processes of adaptation or evolution in a more restricted manner than has subsequently been shown to be appropriate. Physical and material developments were understood to condition social circumstance and opportunity. Social structure and behaviour were believed to depend upon the physical given. One of the problems for social development is for social scientists to break free from this largely self-imposed mindset of intellectual subservience.

Many social scientists continue to accept the work they do as 'secondary' by virtue of precedents that have been institutionalized – an unsought inheritance that is not challenged. Professionals have mechanically accepted this subordinate status. Not for them to expose wrong-doing – only dutifully to pose bland alternatives. Theirs is not so much to reason why as to comprehend descriptive realities and carry out the government's bidding. Too often governments are left to set the research agendas and blame the messengers if they are not considered to have got the message right.

Examples of passive acceptance of this hierarchy of power are to be found in different forms of political and intellectual dependence. Political recognition of what is and what is not important in the work of social scientists can shape the career path of professionals. Orthodoxy can be cultivated by vice-chancellors, heads of government research departments and politicians alike. Intellectual activity that questions the conventional wisdom can be ignored or derided. Certainly deliberate action to assert equitable status with the physical sciences is hard to find.

Social policy is also too often interpreted as government policy – without regard to the pervading and sometimes critical influence of church, family, community, transnational corporation, regional authority and voluntary organization – to name but a few. It would be appropriate to give an answer to the question: 'Whose social policy?' The church has policies distinguishable from the state and which exert different effects on their adherents and non-adherents. Transnational corporations uphold policies for customers, employees and governments or states, which are also distinguishable. That some have better effects than others, or are viewed more enthusiastically than others by sections of the public, is obvious. But gestation, influence, and comparative effect are rarely investigated.

Elements of a strategy

Reorganization of the Bretton Woods institutions

Keynes was a central figure in the creation of the Bretton Woods institutions in 1944, but the structures that emerged were not what he wanted. In the 1930s, he had advocated the creation of an international credit-creating institution and in the early years of war he drew attention to the serious financial liquidity problems that would arise at its end. He saw that concerted action would be required if dangerous forms of instability were to be avoided. If the devastated countries of Western Europe had to restrict imports, devalue currencies, maintain tight price controls and cut public expenditure because they had insufficient resources combined with high levels of debt, then their recovery from the ravages of war would be long-delayed and economic growth would remain low. On top of the need for major postwar reconstruction was the problem of ensuring enough liquidity to finance the growth of world trade. Governments should not be forced by fluctuating balance of payments problems into cycles of deflation and competitive devaluation. That would depress employment and living standards in economically strong and not only weak countries.

Keynes then argued for a kind of world central bank, or 'Clearing Union', that created a deposit of new currency for every country in the world, which it could count on in times of difficulty to pay credit to governments. The total amount of currency deposited would rise steadily in rough proportion to world trade. In fact what materialized was a pale image of Keynes' intentions. The total resources made available turned out to be less than one-third of what he had advised. Countries were not awarded an allocation. They had to contribute to the Fund to be eligible for membership and hence opportunity to apply for loans – to which stringent conditions could be attached.

Today the case for a new Bretton Woods, especially a more convincing development plan, is moving to the top of the international agenda. For example, the UK Chancellor of the Exchequer has called for a new Marshall Plan for the Developing World (HM Treasury 2002). 'After 1945, George Marshall's plan for the reconstruction of Europe played a vital part in winning the peace. As a result both Europe and America flourished, with increased prosperity and employment helping to create a more stable peace' (HM Treasury 2002: 42). Another $44 billion needed to be added to debt relief, another $50 billion a year in official development assistance – through a Tobin tax, arms tax or by issuing Special Drawing Rights. Optimists hoped that the means would be approved and the necessary decisions reached at Monterrey in March 2002. But the recommendations came to nothing and at the time of writing the modest proposal of Chancellor Brown remains in limbo.

An international financial transactions tax

The principle of international taxation to finance development and not merely postwar reconstruction was implicit in Keynes' approach to Bretton Woods. The quota that governments were urged to contribute in overseas aid (0.7 per cent of GDP) was a poor substitute because it was optional. By 2004 only three or four (small) countries have achieved that target. During the 1990s there have been increasingly frequent references to the possibility of raising huge sums for the poorest countries by means of a tiny percentage tax on financial transactions across the world – given the difficulties of raising sufficient resources from overseas development assistance. James Tobin put forward the idea of a tax varying from 0.1 to 0.5 per cent of international financial transactions. A tax of only 0.1 per cent has been estimated to raise $400 billion a year. It would also dampen speculative operations in international markets.

Critics have said that the Tobin tax would be too complex, the economic effects would be ambiguous, and avoidance would be practised – for example traders would bypass foreign exchange markets and use derivative instruments – notably the futures and options markets.

James Tobin put forward his proposal to tax international currency transactions in a Princeton lecture in 1972. It was intended to enhance macroeconomic policy. Only subsequently did he appreciate the revenue potential of the tax – but even then he regarded this as a by-product of the policy. The proposal went largely unheeded – but he contributed a revised version to UNDP's Human Development Report in 1994. Following discussion with UNDP connections, a book about the idea was published in 1996 (ul Haq *et al.* 1996).

The political censors stepped in. Ordinarily, the ideas of great economists, especially those in the monetarist tradition, are not ruled out by legislators. This was a famous exception. Senator Bob Dole and three other senators introduced a bill to prohibit UN officials and UN agencies from developing or promoting Tobin's proposal, or any other scheme for international taxation. The title of the piece of legislation was the 'Prohibition on United Nations Taxation Act of 1996'. The bill was remarkable in limiting freedom of thought and research by government action – hardly the stuff of democracy.

Tobin had explicitly advocated the tax to 'preserve some autonomy in national and continental monetary policies and to defend them against the growing internationalisation of money markets' (Tobin 1974: 87). In 1994 Tobin recalled that no less a figure than Keynes had 'pointed out that a transaction tax could strengthen the weight of long-range fundamentals' (UNDP 1994). Subsequently, voices in favour grew in number (see, for example, Raffer 1998). Strong support has come recently from members of the European Union, and particularly from the French government.

In 2002, the General Assembly of the UN considered a report prepared at the instigation of Kofi Annan, the UN Secretary-General to the President of the General Assembly. This, the Zedillo Report, had been published on 25 June 2001. Its object was to 'recommend strategies for the mobilisation of resources required to accelerate equitable and sustainable growth in developing countries as well as economies in transition, and to fulfil the poverty and development commitments enshrined in the UN Millennium Declaration'. The report disengaged from the Tobin tax. Instead it conveyed lukewarm support for the alternative carbon tax. The Zedillo panel claimed that this was politically more realistic – since its objective of 'making polluters pay' was widely accepted.

Surprisingly, the Zedillo panel made no attempt to consider alternative practicable models of the Tobin tax, or to deal with the difficulties said to be involved in implementing it. They did not compare its merits with other methods of raising funds for overseas development. Their reasoning that a carbon tax was preferable because it made polluters pay was odd because they did not bother to explain the effects of the Tobin tax – what uses it might be put to or what social benefits might be derived from it. This lack of consistent treatment or analysis of different possibilities provides an object lesson for the future conduct of international social policy. On the technical side, there has to be better detailed formulation of the tax and how it can be applied. A fundamental problem is to identify the benefit or the uses to which this new form of revenue could be put. Keynes would not have left this gap in presenting such a model.

The Zedillo panel did not discuss the possible priorities for the use of the Tobin tax or discuss its possible effects – in contrast to the detailed case they made for a carbon tax. Below I propose a universal child benefit, in cash or in kind, as the principal use of an international financial tax. This would have a direct and more immediate effect on human development than the carbon tax. It would also serve the fulfilment of child rights and the reduction of poverty – especially rural poverty.

Identification of the principal beneficiaries would greatly strengthen the arguments for a financial transactions tax. This would help not just with the problem of working out how the tax would work technically and to whom it would be applied. If resources were used for young children, that would also improve dramatically the chances of, for example, reducing world poverty by half by the year 2015, and simultaneously ensure a reduction in the exposure of millions of young children to malnutrition and premature death. It would also contribute strongly to the fulfilment of specific articles outlined in the Universal Declaration of Human Rights and of the Convention on the Rights of the Child (CRC).

Social security to fulfil the fundamental right laid down in the Universal Declaration of Human Rights

Keynes was effectively Britain's chief negotiator at the UN at the time of its establishment and he was also a strong advocate of comprehensive social security. This universalism is now back in fashion. For example, human rights now play a central part in discussions of social policy. This certainly applies to civil and political rights, although less so to social and economic rights. Articles 22 and 25 in the Declaration of Human Rights – dealing with the rights to an 'adequate' standard of living and social security – have been overlooked in the General Assembly and reports by other UN organizations. The fundamental right to social security is also spelt out in Article 26 of the CRC and to the related rights to an adequate standard of living in Article 27.

These rights had not been invoked during the 1980s and 1990s when high rates of poverty continued to persist and even deepened in many parts of the world, and when inequalities in living standards between the First and Third Worlds and within most countries continued to grow. For example, they were not believed to be a necessary element in the discussions about structural adjustment policies and then the social fund – especially in the particularly fraught regions of Sub-Saharan Africa, Latin America, South Asia and Eastern Europe (see the chapter by N. Kanji in Townsend and Gordon 2002). As a consequence the discussion in the 1980s and 1990s focussed on targeting and short-term means-tested benefits rather than on long-term minimal living standards for all. To do them justice the international agencies have in recent years begun to acknowledge the strengths of comprehensive or universal public services and benefits. But that has not yet led to the wholesale reformulation of development policies to reduce poverty.

In the UK there have been some attempts to relate the right to an adequate standard of living to social policy. Thus the Children's Rights Development Unit published a valuable report (CRDU 1994) that took a lingering look at the comparable Article 27 in the Convention on the Rights of the Child – that is, 'the right to a standard of living adequate for the child's physical, mental, spiritual, moral and social development'. They concluded that in the UK there was a need for a 'fundamental examination of the principles which underpin the social security system... there is a need to address the adequacy of benefit levels and for independent research to establish a level of weekly benefit that would enable children and their parents to participate fully in their society' (CRDU 1994: 72).

Dharam Ghai points out that social security in industrialized countries 'reached its apogee in the 1970s' (Ghai 2001). There was a broad consensus among countries about comprehensive welfare and social security policies. This had been symbolized after the war by the inclusion of social security as a fundamental human right in the 1948 Declaration on Human Rights and later in the 1967 International Covenant on Economic, Social and Cultural Rights.

During the 1980s globalization and economic doctrines in favour of cutbacks in taxation and public expenditure and support for the privatization of public services brought various changes to the welfare state in many countries. Some programmes were unscrambled. In others, the level and range of benefits were diluted – partly because of alleged welfare abuses and the perceived harmful effects on savings and investment of high rates of taxation.

Wholesale abandonment of welfare programmes became a feature of the break up of the Soviet Union after 1991. As discussed earlier, some of the republics are only now discovering the virtues of previous social security programmes and putting into place new, albeit smaller public programmes.

The social security systems of developing countries present a more diverse picture. A semblance of a system had been introduced by colonial authorities across much of Asia, Africa and the Caribbean. The schemes were extended in the first instance to civil servants and the employees of large enterprises. There were benefits that included health care, maternity leave, disability allowances and pensions for relatively small groups (Midgeley 1984; Ahmad *et al.* 1991). In India there are differences among major states as well as a range of schemes for relatively small categories of population (Prabhu 2001). In Latin America some countries introduced schemes before the 1939 war, and others followed suit after that war. However, benefits tended to be limited in range and coverage. There were differential systems for different occupations and categories of workers, and a multiplicity of institutions. Between 20 and 60 per cent of the workforce were covered, compared with between 5 and 10 per cent for most of Sub-Saharan Africa and 10 to 30 per cent for most of Asia 'The greatest challenge facing the developing countries is to extend the benefits of social security to the excluded majority to enable them to cope with indigence and social contingencies' (Ghai 2001: 6).

Developments in social security in Latin America have been extensively reviewed in the 1990s and the early years of the twenty-first century. One authority points out that as a proportion of GDP social security is of variable significance across the region but remains substantial in most countries. She concludes that in addressing

> the problem of poverty in old age and sickness for the entire population, non-contributory schemes, or schemes with minimal contribution require-ments, for those in the informal sector are needed. A system of basic flat rate pensions, financed out of general revenue and with entitlement based on citizenship, would meet these needs. This system should be comple-mented by a public system of contributory, non-subsidised, capitalised pensions. (E. Huber in Esping-Andersen, 1996, pp. 180–1)

Four clusters of countries were identified by Ghai:

1. *Broad-based growth*: exemplified by the old and new tiger economies of East and Southeast Asia – such as Singapore, Hong Kong (China), Taiwan, the Republic of Korea, Malaysia, Indonesia and Thailand;
2. *Mineral-based growth*, Kuwait and Botswana;
3. *Socialist orientation*, such as China, Cuba and Vietnam; and

4. *Social welfare approach*, such as Costa Rica, Sri Lanka, Mauritius, Chile, Jamaica and the state of Kerala (Ghai 2001: 6).

These examples help to demonstrate the need to extend social security systems in developing countries – to fulfil the fundamental right to social security laid down by the United Nations after the war of 1939–45 and serve the objective of eradicating poverty confirmed repeatedly by leading governments as well as the international financial agencies in recent years – as for example by the UN in 2000. Bodies such as the ILO and ISSA have provided much of the detailed evidence (see for example Dagdeviren *et al.* 2001 and Reynaud 2001).

A universal benefit for children

There are extensive references to international standards and the collective rights of workers in the EU Charter of Fundamental Rights in up-to-date reviews of necessary policies and legislation.[5] In the UK, as in laws passed in many other countries in the last decade, the introduction of the Human Rights Act in 2000 has allowed advocates to demonstrate the need for conformity in general with international standards as well as for collaborative social policies.[6]

Better links have to be established between human rights, including the right to social security, and international development policies but also macroeconomics and international development policies. A typically Keynesian example is afforded by Tony Atkinson. He has argued that despite the many volumes written on the macroeconomics of European Monetary Union the impacts on children 'had been largely ignored.... We need to build links between macroeconomic analysis and the impact on families and children [and] develop indicators of economic performance which are sensitive to the needs of families and children' – such as a European Price Index for families with children, a child-focused unemployment rate and measures of the cost of borrowing for families (Atkinson 1998: 17). The case for each of these measures is spelt out in some detail.

Another example of the neglect of the impact on social development of macroeconomics can be seen in the debate about the European single currency. In Britain the 1997 Treasury paper *UK Membership of the Single Currency: An Assessment of the Five Economic Tests* illustrates this. Nowhere in the text of 27 pages are children mentioned. Even the objectives of national prosperity or welfare are left unexamined and unspecified.

The fact that Keynesian connections between macroeconomics and social development are not being sufficiently made applies in particular to the current British and indeed world debate about child poverty. Ambitious aims to halve and eventually remove child poverty have been made nationally and internationally. But the connections between economic progress, policies and poverty are not being spelt out. Without a second Keynesian 'revolution' poverty and social inequality are not going to be reduced. Multiple changes are of course required – in institutional form and culture no less than in priorities of public service, redistribution and universal rights.

Because of the different circumstances of different countries a child benefit would necessarily take a variety of forms. The UN could give attention to the value to be recommended per child and according to age, and which governments might allocate partial or full subsidies per child.

There are possibilities of weekly cash allowances for children under a given age – say 15, or 5. There is the possibility of free school meals, or collection of free foodstuffs and milk. An advantage in establishing schemes even for small numbers is that forms of administration can be put in place and subsequently developed.

A start could be made in some countries with an allowance or benefit in cash for infants under two years. A low birthweight baby allowance is an example of a measure that could be applied in rich and poor countries alike. For example, a proposal for such an allowance is being considered in the United Kingdom at the time of writing. Low birthweight babies are ten times more likely than normal birthweight babies to have cerebral palsy, and are also far more likely to experience other disabilities including deafness, severe vision loss, brain damage and special educational needs.

Another example is a categorical child benefit for severely disabled children. Whether or not, parents are in paid employment the costs of caring for a severely disabled child often account for family poverty. And the market does not recognize this form of dependency. While some forms of congenital or disabling long-term illness may be declining there are the disabling conditions of the major problems of the last two decades, like HIV/AIDS, oil, nuclear and chemical pollution, and armed conflict, including landmines. In the poorest countries there are considerable problems, especially in rural areas, in providing benefits and services directly to children. Supply networks need to be developed urgently or improvised imaginatively, and capably administered. Much will depend upon establishing delivery systems – pilot schemes might be sponsored by NGOs and UN agencies working jointly with local administrative departments. Joint funding by international and indigenous agencies must be the model.

The great virtue of an international child benefit is that it has a direct effect. Overseas aid or debt relief via governments to poor families, or the gains of economic growth, may take years to filter through to those sections of the population with low incomes and then fail to reach many families because they cannot or do not have access to paid employment. In the UK or other countries which operate a universal child benefit system, an increase in the weekly or monthly rate of payment can have an immediate effect in reducing poverty. Indirect welfare, based for example on employment-related incentives and means-tested tax credits, is incomplete in coverage, often takes years to bring into effect, and is administratively far more costly or wasteful.

Definition of minimal basic social services in all countries and local and national rights to establish public social services

Similarly rights of access to health, sanitation, safe drinking water, education and information services are difficult to ensure if governments depend upon general and indirect forms of aid. Deprivation of these rights has to be rigorously monitored and countries or localities given subsidies or grants for direct provision of particular services.

International company law

In the last two decades of the twentieth century the levels of corporation taxes in many rich countries were reduced. With deregulation and privatization other corporate responsibilities have been reduced – as in the provision of pensions or employer contributions towards social insurance. Information on the social and labour market policies of corporations in the early twenty-first century is difficult to find. This applies to policies at headquarter level and even more at the level of subsidiaries. The unravelling of the Enron case in 2002 provides detailed examples of the ignorance of shareholders and public and even market leaders themselves of highly relevant information about developments.

The effects on consumers of corporation products and services have to be distinguished from the general effects on populations of their policies in different countries. Furthermore, policies to do with TNC employees in different countries also have to be distinguished from those that involve consumers and the general public.

Paradoxically, during the same period demands have grown for 'guidance on corporate social responsibilities'. Guidelines have been drafted by the ILO, OECD and other bodies – though agreement on the part of corporations is far from being reached.

In these circumstances the case for international company law becomes stronger. Voluntary codes of conduct are weakly expressed and hold little prospect of widespread adoption. There are valuable precedents for international company law in the histories of national company law. The awkward question is whether national laws can be satisfactorily harmonized in an era when TNCs naturally take advantage of loopholes and shortcomings across countries, or whether regional and international law is the only realistic vehicle by which common standards of behaviour or performance can be established.

There are serious shortcomings in both national and international company and social law in relation to transnational corporations. While capable of contributing positively to social development, one review found that few of them were doing much of consequence. The activities of some were positively harmful (Kolodner 1994). Recent books on transnational corporations (Korten 1996; Madeley 1999; Monbiot 2000; Sklair 2001; Stichele and Pennartz 1996) have been assembling a case that governments and international agencies are going to find hard to ignore.

The problem remains to be met internationally. As reported above, the OECD has issued 'guidelines' exhorting corporations to be socially responsible, and the ILO has gone further. In 1977 its Governing Board put forward a declaration. This sought to exert influence upon governments, concluding that gradual reinforcement could pave the way for 'more specific potentially binding international standards', turning codes of conduct into 'the seed of customary rules of international law' (ILO 1989).

International definition of the framework of social policy expected of transnational corporations

The spectacular growth of transnational corporations was a principal feature of the late twentieth century. Only 25 countries of the world are now listed as having larger GDP than the annual value of the sales of the biggest transnational corporation – General Motors. The top ten transnational corporations (General Motors, Ford Motor, Mitsui, Mitsubushi, Itochu, Royal Dutch Shell Group, Marubeni Sumitomo, Exxon and Toyota Motor) have bigger sales than the GDP of Malaysia, Venezuela and Colombia, and some of them more than Saudi Arabia, South Africa, Norway, Greece and Thailand. New Zealand's GDP is dwarfed by the sales of each of these corporations, and Australia's accounts for only about three times the value of the average sale of all ten (UNDP 1999: 32, 184–7).

The social policies of transnational corporations await full description and analysis. There are at least two forms. On the one hand their internal policies, in relation to their senior staff and permanent and temporary workers scattered through subsidiary companies in many different countries, have to be explained. On the other hand, the larger role they play in contributing to social change, by influencing developments in world trade, government taxation and redistribution and investment, as well as recommendations for privatization, also has to be explained (Deacon *et al.* 1997; Guislain 1997; Hoogvelt 1997; Hudson 1996; ILO 1989; Kozul-Wright and Rowthorn 1998; Lang and Hines 1993; Lieberman and Kirkness 1998; Parker and Martin 1997)

One feature of mergers between companies and the absorption of workforces overseas into the subsidiaries of corporations is not just the extension of the labour force accountable to management, but the elaboration as well as the extension of the hierarchy of pay and rights in the corporation. There are many layers in workforces consisting of scores of thousands, sometimes hundreds of thousands, of employees working full-time, part-time, permanently and temporarily in 50, 60 or even more countries. Salaries at the top have been elevated, while those at the bottom are depressed.

This fast-developing occupational system deepens social stratification and introduces new social problems in every country. Ideas of supra- and subordination are played out internationally as well as nationally and locally, and are carried over from one context to the other. This evolving hierarchy of power, prompted by the dramatic growth of transnational corporations, has universal ramifications. It is reflected in new relationships between states and in international agencies – concentrating the representation of top-most personnel, origins of finance for research, and responsibility for the publication of statistical and other information to the media.

Conclusion: the development of a new strategy

Acknowledgement of the need for a radical review of international social policy has led to a remarkable revival of interest in Keynesian ideas. For many social scientists and professional practitioners the ideas seem to offer potential remedies for apparently intractable forms of severe inequality and poverty as well as violence and instability across the world.

I have argued that in both the establishment of the welfare state and world social development following the Second World War Keynes' seminal influence was underrated at the time – not least by his biographers. His idea of planning for development was international and surprisingly comprehensive – but it was also entirely appropriate for its time. Some critics took the view that he was too accommodating to established forces and that he put more stress on regulating or intervening in market forces than on setting the framework of acceptable wages and conditions in which they should operate. While widely shared at the time and, I believe, correct, those views now appear to be utopian. Keynes' measured sense of compromise between the dictates of the evidence and institutionalized opinion nonetheless promised substantial improvement then – as it does now. His instinct was for rational persuasion on the basis of the evidence, not least among elites and the public, to achieve a consensus or majority opinion in favour of tolerable compromise action.

After a generation of relative indifference there have been signs recently of a return to his ideas. The edicts of monetarism were embraced but have been found wanting in many respects. Privatization, reduced public expenditure, reduced trade union rights, low taxation, and selectivity in welfare have produced huge problems. Many are suggesting they are of crisis proportions in a large number of countries. They are reinforcing trends towards greater inequality, and persisting or growing poverty.

Long ago Keynes provided the prescription for such ills. His advice was not followed. International policies are now badly askew. The failure of neoliberalism and of the unfettered growth of transnational corporate power has obliged a reconsideration of present policy in the light of his thinking.

There is an increasing number of models based on his ideas. In the second half of this chapter I have sought to enumerate a few – a reformulation of the Bretton Woods institutions; an international transactions tax; social security to fulfil the fundamental right laid down in the Universal Declaration of Human Rights; a universal benefit for children; definition of minimal basic social services in all countries and local and national rights to establish public social services; international company law; and an international definition of the framework of social policy expected of transnational corporations.

Notes

1. In the course of an ironic summary of the 'virtues' of Ricardian theory Keynes wrote: 'That it was adapted to carry a vast and consistent logical super-structure, gave it beauty. That it could explain much social injustice and apparent cruelty as an inevitable incident in the scheme of progress, and the attempt to change such things as likely on the whole to do more harm than good, commended it to authority. That it allowed a measure of justification to the free activities of the individual capitalist, attracted to it the support of the dominant social forces behind authority;' Keynes (1936).
2. 'In evidence to the Macmillan Committee on Finance and Industry in 1930; in recommendations to the committee set up by the Prime Minister under the chairmanship of Keynes later in the same year; in letters to the Times in the early 1930s, and in other ways, several of the leading economists of the day, as well as Keynes himself, called for the sort of measures (including big investment in public works) which would today be regarded as the right ones to adopt': Stewart (1972).
3. Committee on Economic Security (1937).
4. Beveridge's principal biographer (Harris 1977) shows that Keynes not only set the scene of planning and full employment for postwar conditions but also met Beveridge repeatedly during the crucial months of 1942, prior to the publication of the report in December. For example, Keynes took a lead in advising pay-as-you-go rather than accumulating a fund in financing better pensions, and also the strengths of state social insurance compared with voluntary industrial and private insurance. See also Timmins (1995).
5. For example, Ewing (2001), especially Chapters 4 and 7.
6. For example, Klug (2000).

Bibliography

Abel-Smith, B., and Titmuss, K. (1974) *R.M. Titmuss: Social Policy: an Introduction*. London: Allen and Unwin.

Ahmad, E. *et al.* (eds) (1991) *Social Security in Developing Countries*. Oxford: Oxford University Press.

Atkinson, A. B. (1996) *Incomes and the Welfare State*. Cambridge: Cambridge University Press.

Atkinson, A. B. (1998) *EMU, Macroeconomics and Children.* Florence: UNICEF.

Atkinson, A. B. (1999) 'Is Rising Inequality Inevitable? A Critique of the Transnational Consensus', *Annual Lectures 3.* Helsinki: UNU/WIDER.

Chu, K.-Y., and Gupta, S. (1998) *Social Safety Nets: Issues and Recent Experiences.* Washington, DC: International Monetary Fund.

Committee on Economic Security (1937) *Social Security in America: the Factual Background of the Social Security Act as Summarised from Staff Reports to the Committee on Social Security.* Washington, DC: Government Printing Office.

Cornia, A. G. (1999) 'Social Funds in Stabilization and Adjustment Programmes', *Research for Action.* Helsinki (Finland): United Nations University/World Institute for Development Economics Research (UNU/WIDER).

CRDU (1994) *Agenda for Children: a Systematic Analysis of the Extent of Which Law, Policy and Practice in the UK Complies with the Principles and with the Standards Contained in the United Nations Convention on the Rights of the Child.* London: CRDU.

Dagdeviren, H., van der Hoeven, R., and Weeks, J. (2001) *Redistribution Matters: Growth for Poverty Reduction.* Geneva: ILO.

Deacon, B., Hulse, M., and Stubbs, P. (1997) *Global Social Policy: International Organisations and the Future of Welfare.* London: Sage.

Desai, M. (1981) *Testing Monetarism.* London: Frances Pinter.

Esping-Andersen, G. (1990) *The Three Worlds of Welfare Capitalism.* Oxford: Polity Press.

Ewing, K. D. (2001) *Employment Rights at Work.* London: The Institute of Employment Rights.

Ghai, D. (2001) *Social Security for All*, Technical Commissions, Leo Wildmann Symposium, Stockholm, September 2001, ISSA Review. Geneva: ISSA.

Goodin, R. E., Headey, B., Muffels, R., and Dirven, H.-J. (1999) *The Real Worlds of Welfare Capitalism.* Cambridge: Cambridge University Press.

Gordon, D., and Townsend, P. (2001) *Breadline Europe: the Measurement of Poverty.* Bristol: Policy Press.

Guislain, P. (1997) *The Privatization Challenge: a Strategic Legal and Institutional Analysis of International Experience.* Washington, DC: World Bank.

Harris, J. (1977) *William Beveridge: a Biography.* Oxford: Clarendon Press.

Harrod, R. F. (1951) *The Life of John Maynard Keynes.* London: Macmillan.

HM Treasury (2002) *Tackling Poverty: a Global New Deal: a Modern Marshall Plan for the Developing World.* London: HM Treasury.

Hoogvelt, A. (1997) *Globalisation and the Postcolonial World: the New Political Economy of Development.* London: Macmillan.

Hudson, E. (1996) *Merchants of Misery: How Corporate America Profits from Poverty.* Maine: Courage.

Hutton, W. (1996) *The State We're In.* London: Vintage.

ILO (1989) *The ILO Tripartite Declaration of Principles Concerning Multinational Enterprises and Social Policy – Ten Years After.* Geneva: ILO.

Keynes, J. M. (1936) *The General Theory of Employment, Interest and Money.* London: Macmillan.

Keynes, J. M. (1980) 'The International Culture of Raw Material Prices' in *The Collected Writings of John Maynard Keynes*, vol. 27. London: Macmillan.

Klug, F. (2000) *Values for a Godless Age: the Story of the United Kingdom's New Bill of Rights.* London: Penguin Books.

Kolko, G. (1999) 'Ravaging the Poor: the International Monetary Fund Indicted by its own Data', *International Journal of Health Services*, 29, 51–7.

Kolodner, E. (1994) *Transnational Corporations: Impediments or Catalysts of Social Development?* Geneva: UNRISD.

Korten, D. C. (1996) *When Corporations Rule the World*. London: Earthscan.

Kozul-Wright, R., and Rowthorn, R. (1998) *Transnational Corporations and the Global Economy*. Helsinki: UNU World Institute for Development Economic Research.

Lang, T., and Hines, C. (1993) *The New Protectionism*. London: Earthscan.

Lieberman, I. W., and Kirkness, C. D. (1998) *Privatization and Emerging Equity Markets*. Washington, DC: The World Bank

Madeley, J. (1999) *Big Business, Poor Peoples: the Impact of Transnational Corporations on the World's Poor*. London and New York: Zed Books.

Midgley, J. (1934) *Social Security, Inequality and the Third World*. New York: Wiley.

Monbiot, G. (2000) *Captive State: the Corporate Takeover of Britain*. London: Pan Books.

Oorschot, W. (1999) 'Targeting Welfare: On the Functions and Dysfunctions of Means-Testing in Social Policy'. In P. Townsend and D. Gordon (eds), *World Poverty: New Policies to Defeat an Old Enemy*. Bristol: Bristol Policy Press.

Parker, D., and Martin, S. (1997) *The Impact of Privatisation*. London: Routledge.

Prabhu, K. S. (2001) *Socio-Economic Security in the Context of Pervasive Poverty: a Case Study of India*. Geneva: ILO.

Raffer, K. (1998) 'The Tobin Tax: Reviving a Discussion', *World Development*, 26, 529–38.

Reynaud, E. (2001) *The Extension of Social Security Coverage: The Approach of the International Labour Office*, Technical Commissions, Leo Wildmann Symposium, Stockholm, September 2001, ISSA Review, Geneva: ISSA.

Skidelsky, R. (1993) *John Maynard Keynes: the Economist as Saviour: 1920–1937*. London: Macmillan.

Skidelsky, R. (2000) *John Maynard Keynes: Fighting for Britain: 1937–1946*. London: Macmillan.

Sklair, L. (2001) *The Transnational Capitalist Class*. Oxford: Blackwell.

Stewart, M. (1972) *Keynes and After*. Harmondsworth: Penguin Books.

Stichele, M. V., and Pennartz, P. (1996) *Making it Our Business – European NGO Campaigns on Transnational Corporations*. London: CIIR.

Timmins, N. (1995) *The Five Giants: a Biography of the Welfare State*. London: Harper-Collins.

Tobin, J. (1974) *The New Economics One Decade Older*. Princeton: Princeton University Press.

Townsend, P. (1991) 'Poverty and Social Polarisation', *Eurocities: Cities and Social Policies in Europe*. Barcelona: Ajuntament de Barcelona.

Townsend, P. (1993) *The International Analysis of Poverty*. Hemel Hempstead: Harvester Wheatsheaf.

Townsend, P. (1999) 'Poverty, Social Exclusion and Social Polarisation: The Need to Construct an International Welfare State'. In S. Shaver and S. P. Sydney (eds), *Social Policy for the 21st Century: Justice and Responsibility*. Sydney: Social Policy Research Centre.

Townsend, P., and Gordon, D. (2002). *World Poverty: New Policies to Defeat an Old Enemy*. Bristol: Policy Press.

ul Haq M., Kaul, I. and Grunberg, I. (1996) *The Tobin Tax: Coping with Financial Volatility*. New York: Oxford University Press.

UNDP (1994) *Human Development Report 1994*. New York and Oxford: UNDP.
UNDP (1998) *Poverty in Transition*. New York: UNDP (Regional Bureau for Europe and the CIS).
UNDP (1999) *Human Development Report 1999*. New York and Oxford: UNDP.
World Bank (1997) *Safety Net Programs and Poverty Reduction: Lessons from Cross-Country Experience*. Washington, DC: World Bank.
World Bank (2000) *Emerging Directions for a Social Protection Sector Strategy: from Safety Net to Spring Board*. Washington, DC: World Bank (Social Protection Sector).

3
Social Policy and Macroeconomic Performance: Integrating 'the Economic' and 'the Social'

Diane Elson

Introduction

The quotation marks that are placed around 'the economic' and 'the social' alert us to the fact that this is an abstract duality. In the 'real' world people do not live their lives in two separate domains. The aspects of life that we label 'economic' and 'social' are intertwined. The policies we label 'economic' and 'social' each have ramifications for both the dimensions we label 'economic' and those we label 'social'. As Barbara Harriss-White points out in her contribution, 'social policy is economic policy'. But at the same time, as pointed out in Elson and Cagatay (2000), economic policy is social policy.

Nevertheless, the distinctions drawn above do relate to some real divisions and are grounded in the different rhythms and modalities of market-based capital accumulation (the commodity economy) on the one hand, and non-market-based social reproduction (the unpaid care economy) on the other. There are different institutional responsibilities for 'economic' policy and 'social' policy; different policy analysis communities; different interest groups. The standard neo-liberal approach overemphasized these differences, and made the assumption that each strand of policy could be pursued independently of the other. Moreover, social policy was seen as a residual – only required to deal with the widows and orphans, the lame and the sick.

The movement away from the standard neo-liberal approach, to incorporate more discussion of institutions, has been characterized by a rediscovery of the interactions between 'the economic' and 'the social' and a revalidation of 'the social' as having more than residual status. But this is mainly at the micro level, and only on terms that are compatible with microeconomic thinking, whether of the old-style or new 'improved' varieties. As Ben Fine argues in his contribution, concepts such as 'social capital' are part of the problem rather than part of the solution. They blur and obscure the tensions between capital accumulation and social reproduction – tensions in which the distinction between 'the economic' and 'the social' need to be grounded.

At the macro level, however, 'the social' is still seen very much as an afterthought. Although there is now widespread recognition of the need to integrate macroeconomic management and 'social policy', there is still a strong tendency to think this means continuing to design what are termed 'sound' macroeconomic policies with a focus on market-based criteria, an overriding emphasis on stabilizing the price level and reducing the role of the state, and then 'adding-on' social policies in order to achieve socially desirable outcomes such as poverty reduction. This is how the World Bank's Comprehensive Development Framework operates. As shown in Elson and Cagatay (2000), the CDF does not explicitly consider macroeconomic policy at all. 'Prudent' fiscal and monetary polices are described as the 'essential backdrop' to the CDF and the specification of exactly what these are is treated as being beyond discussion; a similar approach is adopted with the new IMF concern with social policy in the context of debt-relief initiatives. The emphasis is on 'adding-on' new sectoral policies to help those adversely affected, rather than on reconsidering the design of macroeconomic policies and the organization of the policy process. The new focus of the Bank and the Fund on participation in policy dialogue only extends to micro and sectoral policies.

An alternative approach to considering social policies as an afterthought to macroeconomic policies would start from the idea of establishing social issues in the mainstream of macroeconomic policy. The idea of 'mainstreaming' is more fluid than 'adding-on'. It has been developed in the context of trying to change analysis, institutions and policies to promote gender equality and an improvement in the position of women. It has connotations of aiming to change and transform the dominant paradigms and the balance of socio-economic forces. In this context, it has the implication of the rethinking of macroeconomics and of the organization of macroeconomic policy processes in order to recognize the salience of social issues and social policy. Heterodox macroeconomics is a useful ingredient because it seeks to integrate distributional variables and it challenges the view that macroeconomic problems come from a deficiency of savings rather than from a deficiency of investment. But social policy has broader concerns, with non-monetary dimensions, so there is a need to go further.

Economic production and social reproduction

The starting point proposed here is to recognize that we are dealing with a joint process of production of the means of life and the use of these means to reproduce life itself, on a daily and intergenerational basis. Most analysis of economies privileges economic production – tries to measure it, increase it and optimize it. Social reproduction is taken for granted, treated as a bottomless well, rather like the traditional sector in the Lewis model. Feminist economics – and to a lesser extent, the human development approach – has challenged this exclusion, arguing that in addition to the 'commodity economy', we should take account of the 'unpaid care economy' in which people produce services for their families, friends and neighbours on the basis of social obligation, altruism and reciprocity (e.g. Folbre 1994, 2001; UNDP 1995, 1999; UNIFEM 2000).

There are two reasons for taking the unpaid care economy into account. The first is that the inputs of unpaid work and outputs of care are very important in securing human well-being. Too much unpaid work and too little care both jeopardize the possibility of living a 'good life'. The second is that though the 'unpaid care economy' is outside the production boundary, its operation has implications for what goes on inside the production boundary. Its operations affect the quantity and quality of labour supplied to production and the quantity and quality of goods demanded from production. Its operations affect the stability of the social framework in which market and state are embedded.

This interaction has been analysed in a number of contexts relevant to development, with a particular emphasis on the gender relations that assign most of the responsibility for the supply of unpaid care to women. For instance, in the early 1990s I examined the interaction in the context of structural adjustment, arguing that the design of structural adjustment programmes implicitly assumes unlimited supplies of female labour, available to make good any shortfalls in provision of public sector non-tradable services (such as health, education, water, sanitation); and to increase production of exports, while, at the same time, maintaining household food security and the social fabric of family and community networks (Elson 1991). Adjustment theory does not confront this implication because it appears to treat labour as a non-produced means of production, and all consumption as discretionary.

Gendered cultural norms about what constitutes 'men's work' and 'women's work' mean that men's labour tends not to be reallocated to 'women's work' where there is a decrease in what is considered to be 'men's work' and an increase in what is considered to be 'women's work'. Instead, a more likely outcome is unemployment and underemployment for men, and overwork for women. Failure to take this into account in analysing adjustment results in extra burdens for women, and means that adjustment programmes are unlikely to be able to deliver the growth they promise.

Ignoring the implications of macroeconomic changes for unpaid domestic labour inputs is tantamount to assuming that women's capacity to undertake extra work is infinitely elastic – able to stretch so as to make up for any shortfall in income and resources required for the production and maintenance of human resources. However, women's capacity for work is not infinitely elastic and a breaking point may be reached. There may simply be insufficient female labour time available to maintain the quality and quantity of human resources at its existing level. This may not have an immediate impact on the level and composition of gross national output, but in the longer run a deterioration in health, nutrition and education will have adverse impacts on output levels (Elson 1991: 179).

Further examples of analysis that take account of unpaid care work can be found in the 1995 special issue of *World Development* on macroeconomics and gender. William Darity (1995) constructed a two-sector model of a gender-segregated low-income agrarian economy, in which one sector produced crops for export and the other sector produced subsistence food and care for the family. The model was used to show how a devaluation of the currency, which raises the relative price of export cash crops, means extra demand for women's labour in the export sector and extra income for their husbands who control the sale of the crop, given the prevailing pattern of gender relations in both sectors. If women respond to this demand, through some combination of compensation, co-operation or coercion, output of food and of care is liable to fall under reasonable assumptions, with potentially adverse impacts on the health and nutrition of women and children. On the other hand, if women are able to resist the demand, the supply response of the export crop is muted, and the devaluation does not have the expected impact – a scenario explored by Warner and Campbell (2000) in the second special issue of *World Development* on gender and economics.

In contrast, Korkut Erturk and Nilufer Cagatay (1995) focused on the investment behaviour of firms and the savings behaviour of households in industrializing economies, drawing upon empirical research on patterns of economic development to identify some 'stylized facts' about the degree of feminization of the paid labour force and the extent of women's unpaid household work. They assumed that a rise in the feminization of the labour force stimulates investment by making available a new pool of low-cost and malleable labour, while a rise in the extent of women's unpaid household work is equivalent to an increase in savings because it reduces expenditure on marketed goods. The interaction of these two effects is examined in relation to recovery from economic crisis and recession, and it is concluded that recovery will be dampened if the positive impact of feminization of the paid labour force on investment is weaker than the positive impact of an intensification of women's household work on savings.

In the same volume, Walters (1995) reconsidered growth theory, in the light of the conceptualization of labour as an input produced in the 'unpaid care economy' (which he called the reproductive sector). He identified Harrod's theory of growth as the most fruitful for exploring potential imbalances between the productive and reproductive sectors.

These four articles all pitch their arguments at a high level of abstraction, but they are important as heuristic devices which begin the task of showing how gender-sensitive variables, which capture reproduction as well as production, and power as well as choice, can be incorporated into the analysis of growth and structural change.

As more comprehensive studies of time use become available for developing countries it will be possible to start an empirical examination of the interconnection between production and unpaid care. Some examples which point the way can be found in the special issue of *World Development* on Growth, Trade, Finance and Gender Inequality (Grown *et al.* 2000). Fontana and Wood (2000) present a CGE model that includes the unpaid care economy (labelled 'social reproduction'). The model is calibrated for Bangladesh and is used to explore different trade policy regimes. Lim (2000) examines the effects of the East Asian financial crisis on employment in the Philippines and although the data on paid work is much richer than that on unpaid work, is able to consider some of the interactions between the two in the aftermath of the crisis.

This kind of analysis brings together what has generally been thought of as 'the economy' with what has often been thought of as the domain of the 'social', and is an example of what I mean by 'mainstreaming' the social in macroeconomic analysis. It overcomes to some degree the dichotomization between 'economic analysis' (largely pertaining to monetized aspects of life) and 'social analysis' (largely pertaining to non-monetized aspects of life). But it does not dissolve the difference, and indeed tension, between these two aspects of life, unlike, say, the 'new household economics'.

Social biases in macroeconomic policy

In the context of the holistic view of economic and social processes described above, Elson and Cagatay (2000) argue that there are three important social biases present in much current macroeconomic policy: deflationary bias, male breadwinner bias and commodification (or privatization) bias. If social policy is to be successfully integrated with economic policy, these biases must be overcome.

Deflationary bias

Liberalized financial markets have induced governments to adopt policies which are primarily aimed at maintaining their 'credibility' in financial markets – such as high interest rates, tight monetary policies, and fiscal restraint. Eatwell (1996) notes that interest rates in the 1990s have been at historically high levels around the world. Felix (1995) shows that investment rates and growth rates have fallen over the period of financial liberalization, primarily due to the types of macroeconomic policies governments are required to adopt in order to attract and retain short-term capital. The result is a 'deflationary bias in macroeconomic policy', which prevents governments from dealing effectively with recession and leads to high rates of unemployment and underemployment.

To make this claim is to run the risk of being cast in the role of an irresponsible 'macropopulist' advocating unsustainable and inefficient fiscal and monetary policies. But we have to insist that there are more than two alternatives – we do not have only the choice between IMF-approved sound finance and hyperinflation and falling per capita income. The viable alternatives depend upon the ensemble of social as well as economic forces – what Lance Taylor (1991) has called the social matrix.

Moreover, while there are indeed aggregate real resource constraints on the achievement of social goals, these real constraints are not directly the object of macroeconomic policies. Macroeconomic policies address financial constraints – and financial constraints depend upon the pattern of ownership and control of financial resources and the willingness of different groups of people to pay taxes and to buy government bonds. They are socially variable and socially malleable constraints. Macroeconomic policies, which may be seen as 'sound' in the sense of balancing the budget, and accepting the current balance of financial power, can be quite 'unsound' in the sense of exacerbating real resource constraints by destroying human capabilities as people are priced out of the market. Much of the feminist critique of neo-liberal macroeconomic policies has focused on this point (see for instance contributions to Cagatay, Elson and Grown (eds) (1995)), and has shown the ways in which poor women in particular bear these burdens. This destruction of real resources may have few immediate financial repercussions for the government budget, or it may be the case that the repercussions are roundabout and the connections not obvious, and they may therefore pass unnoticed by economic policy makers.

Macropopulist policies make the mistake of trying to circumvent the financial constraints by printing more money while leaving the structure of financial power intact. In common with neo-liberals, macropopulists do nothing to educate people about the social content of macroeconomic policies – about which groups are currently strong enough to set parameters and which groups are forced to vary their activities, and to adjust to the parameters set by others; about whose contracts will be honoured and whose contracts will be broken by particular configurations of macroeconomic policy; about whose entitlements will be upheld and whose will be destroyed. The social biases in macroeconomic policy remain obscure.

Deflationary bias is a bias that gives an overly high priority to low inflation, low public debt, low public expenditure, low taxation and low budget deficits; and consequently places too low a priority on full employment, high public investment and realizing the full potential for improvements in the availability of goods and services. It is now deeply entrenched in the institutional framework that governs macroeconomic policy in many countries. It is constituted in a variety of ways: central banks that have asymmetrical targets, so that they aim to keep inflation below a target level, but not above a target level; balanced budget legislation that constrains a government to cut public expenditure when the economic cycle takes a downturn; so-called 'stability' frameworks that incorporate rigid rules about ratios of budget deficits to GNP and ratios of public debt to GNP, regardless of the stage of the economic cycle, constraining governments to cut public expenditure when the economic cycle takes a downturn; rules about governments borrowing only to invest that allow only for investment in physical capital and disallow investment in human capacities.

These rules deepen global recession rather than aiding recovery. They undermine the livelihoods of men and women and throw people back into the non-market economy. In the formal sector of the market economy, there is often a perception that men's jobs are more important, and that women should be the first to be dismissed. Women's levels of unemployment are thus often higher than those of men, while at the same time they have less access to social benefits. They are crowded into informal activities, where the already low remuneration tends to fall further still.

Moreover, women face particular demands to provide the safety net of last resort for their families, managing a dwindling family budget to feed and clothe their children; coping with the depression, ill-health and often destructive behaviour of men whose whole sense of self-worth was inextricably linked to the paid job they have lost. At the same time, there are cutbacks in the public services and income transfers that would have provided some assistance to women in these tasks. The most visible cost of deflationary bias is the rise in unemployment. Less visible, but important for the longer run, is the depletion of human capacities.

'Male breadwinner' bias

However, removal of deflationary bias would not by itself deal with all macro-level, systemic, economy-wide sources of social bias. Feminist economics draws attention to another type of macro-level systemic, social bias: 'male breadwinner' bias. This is the bias that comes from assuming that the unpaid care economy is articulated with the market economy of commodity production through an income which is paid to a male breadwinner and which is assumed to be large enough to provide for the cash needs of a set of dependents (women, children, elderly people, sick people and so on). This ignores the emerging evidence that, in many cases, women, and even children and elderly people, must also work in the commodity economy (albeit in less visible, more informal, poorly remunerated ways) if household needs are to be met. Public investment is needed not just to provide (directly or indirectly) employment for male breadwinners, but also to support women who must try to balance responsibilities in both production and social reproduction.

'Male breadwinner' bias constructs the ownership of rights to make claims on the state for social support (cash transfers for poor people, social insurance, pensions, employment on public works) around a norm of full-time, life-long working-age participation in the market-based labour force. Those people whose participation does not fit this norm typically have lesser rights, which they can frequently only exercise as dependents on those who do fit the norm. The result has been the exclusion of many women from entitlements, and the reduction of the entitlements of many others, making women dependent upon men, especially during those periods of women's lives when they are intensively involved in taking care of children and elders, and when they themselves are elders. The welfare state in postwar Europe was constructed around the norm of the male wage earner and his wife and children and the same idea can be found in the language of many ILO Conventions, and the International Covenant on Economic, Social and Cultural Rights.

The idea that men, rather than women, are the key economic agents and therefore have superior entitlements to state support also tends to structure access to economic services such as subsidized credit and training. Extension services are directed to male farmers – even in countries where women do much of the farming. Business support services are designed for male entrepreneurs rather than female entrepreneurs, even when many women want to run small businesses.

Macroeconomic policy approaches that rely *solely or principally* on public investment and full employment in order to achieve social goals such as equitable income distribution and the elimination of poverty tend to suffer from male breadwinner bias. Such policies rarely take into account the relationship between paid and unpaid forms of labour that is just as much at the heart of provisioning of needs as paid forms of labour. In order to be gender-equitable, full-employment policies must be complemented by entitlements for those in informal or part-time paid work and entitlements for the providers of unpaid caring labour as citizens in their own right.

Privatization bias

Privatization bias is the bias that stems from the assumption that the private sector is inherently more efficient than the other sectors. It can operate through three forms of privatization: complete privatization, such as the selling of public agencies to private investors; partial privatization, such as the contracting-out of services from public agencies; and simulated privatization, when public services are compelled to operate as if they were privately operated.

This bias arises when faulty measures of 'efficiency' and 'value for money' are used; measures which do not take into account non-market costs and benefits, and which focus primarily on physical and financial capital. So, for example, measures are introduced to improve the 'efficiency' of public hospitals (measured in terms of monetary costs per patient), which have the effect of transferring real costs to households, often by increasing the amount of unpaid care work they have to provide. One example is changing procedures to shorten the time that patients spend in hospital, and lengthening the period of convalescence at home. This cuts back on the financial costs of employing hospital staff, but increases the costs of households (and primarily women within households) in time and energy spent on caring for convalescing patients.

Privatization bias tends to intensify both deflationary bias and male breadwinner bias. One example of this is the privatization of social insurance and pension provision. This greatly increases the power of financial institutions, which tend to have short time horizons and to prioritize low inflation and low public deficits. They lobby for the perpetuation of deflationary bias. Moreover, such privatization reduces the scope for pooling risks and resources and greatly reduces the possibility of social cross-subsidy. It tends to make women more dependent upon a male partner to access benefits and penalizes women who do not have a male partner with whom to share their household costs. Private pension provision penalizes those people with breaks in their employment record and longer life expectancy. It is quite legal in most countries for private insurers to discriminate against women in the annuities market. As a result, the factors which lead to the disproportionate poverty of women in old age are exacerbated.

Privatization bias has profound and disturbing implications for the organization of social reproduction, and for the majority of women who currently provide a disproportionate amount of the unpaid care upon which social reproduction rests. Privatization bias may appear to be sound economics if we ignore non-market costs and benefits. But the excessive reduction in public provision that it implies is a false economy. Of course, it is important to avoid excessive public debt and the waste of public money. But in judging what is excessive and what is waste, we have to consider the non-market processes that create and sustain human beings and communities. A strong and effective public sector is vital to mediate between the market pressure to treat people as mere inputs into a production process and the aspiration to live life in a fully human way.

Beneficiaries of bias

There are beneficiaries of these forms of bias: the wealthy minority of households whose principal wealth is financial assets, and the financial services corporations in which many of them are employed. This is particularly evident in times of economic crisis when decisions have to be made about whose interests should take priority – which contracts should be respected and which broken. Typically the interests of foreign creditors, and their rentier allies, are protected, while the interests of employees are sacrificed. The case of Chile is illuminating in this respect. Mellor (1991) shows how the adjustment measures taken in Chile in the 1980s resulted in only minor losses for the financial sector but major losses for Chilean workers. Most of the foreign debt of Chile at this time was privately held, mainly by commercial banks. It was not publicly guaranteed. However, the international commercial banks abruptly suspended all financial credit to Chileans, including short-term trade credit, in order to force the Chilean government to provide guarantees for the external debt of the Chilean private financial sector. This prevented the possibility of debts having to be written-off. To bail out the Chilean financial sector the Central Bank provided implicit subsidies through a preferential dollar exchange rate. In 1985, these subsidies amounted to 6.5 per cent of GDP, compared to a fiscal deficit of 1.5 per cent of GDP. These subsidies averted widespread bankruptcies and preserved the existing structure of ownership and management, mainly benefiting high-income Chileans. At the same time, policies to reduce government expenditure pushed the unemployment rate to over 26 per cent, reduced real wages by 20 per cent and reduced health, housing and education budgets by 20 per cent per capita. Private external debt was also socialized in the financial crisis in the case of Korea in the late 1990s (Bullard 1998). $25 billion of short-term debt to foreign commercial banks was restructured into medium-term debt, after the South Korean government agreed to extend a guarantee in case of default by private debtors. Normal IMF rules were bypassed to provide a $21 billion loan to the South Korean government in order to avert default at a cost of deep cutbacks in public expenditure and an almost doubling of interest rates. Unemployment rose rapidly from 2 per cent in October 1997 to 6.7 per cent in April 1998, hitting women especially hard (Lee and Rhee 1999). The average real wage fell by almost 9 per cent. The losses were born by the Korean people, rather than the foreign creditors.

Creating a space for social dialogue on macroeconomic policy

Macroeconomic policy will always be a balancing act. On the surface it appears to be a technocratic exercise of balancing financial flows with a relatively short-run time horizon. However, as the above examples indicate, beneath the technocratic surface, there is a social content – a social content which in much of the world is biased against those who rely on labour rather than financial assets to make a living; and against those who provide most of the unpaid care that families and communities require.

Heterodox macroeconomic modelling can be useful for generating ideas about alternative policies. For instance, a socially aware macroeconomic policy could avoid deflationary bias by giving greater weight to public investment, including investment in the development of human capacities. This is the strategy advocated by several contributors to a recent UNDP study of macroeconomic policy and poverty reduction (McKinley 2001). It rests on evidence that real investment is more sensitive to aggregate demand than to the rate of interest; that public investment can be complementary to private investment rather than crowd it out; and that more domestic resources can be mobilized to finance such investment. Such a policy would probably have to be buttressed by controls on short-term capital movements as it might well upset 'sentiment' in financial markets, where the risk of inflation is always given greater weight that the risk of destruction of human capacities through under-investment.

But if social concerns are to be taken fully into account, there is a need for a wider social dialogue to promote changes in the policy process as well as the models used. This would need to go well beyond what is currently being attempted in the preparation of Poverty Reduction Strategy Papers in relation to the Highly Indebted Poor Countries Initiative. A recent report to the Human Rights Commission (Cheru 2001) on the implementation of the Highly Indebted Poor Countries Initiative concludes that the IMF and World Bank staff involved in the preparation of the Poverty Reduction Strategy Papers (PRSPs), which must be developed in order to qualify for debt relief, see the process as being 'essentially technocratic'. It notes that: 'While civil society groups have been invited to participate extensively in discussions on the social policy-planning component of the I-PRSP, they have effectively been excluded when it comes to discussions on the content of macroeconomic policy choices' (Cheru 2001: 14). It further notes that 'there is still a tendency to design macroeconomic policy with a focus on market-based criteria and financial concerns. This tendency always leads to a situation where social and human development and equity concerns take a back seat to financial considerations' (Cheru 2001: 15). All of the PRSPs reviewed in the report emphasize downsizing the public sector and introducing cost-recovery measures such as user charges, and fail to show how such measures will reduce poverty.

A helpful framework for considering how better to organize social dialogue on economic and social policy can be derived from a recent statement on poverty by the Committee on Economic, Social and Cultural Rights (UN 2001). The statement sets out (paragraphs 9–14) the international normative human rights framework for poverty eradication policies. It first emphasizes that the entire range of human rights – civil, cultural, economic, political and social, and the right to development – are relevant. Secondly, it states that non-discrimination and equality are integral elements. Thirdly, it stresses that human rights norms include the right of those affected by key decisions to participate in the relevant decision-making processes. States have obligations to put in place a policy process that conforms to these norms. Non-state actors have an obligation to comply with these norms. These obligations must be supported by a system of accountability that is accessible, transparent and effective.

The possibilities of shaping macroeconomic policy through an open social dialogue, which complies with the human rights framework; in which different interests can exercise 'voice', and in which social objectives can be explicitly brought into view; is foreclosed not by the technical requirements of macroeconomic policy but by fear of pre-emptive exercise of the 'exit' option by internationally mobile holders of financial assets. Their ability to exit rather than join in a social dialogue is a result of the 'openness' of capital markets. Ironically, the 'openness' of capital markets is conducive to an absence of 'openness' in policy discussion, for fear that the wrong signals will be sent and the volatile 'sentiment' of capital markets will be disturbed. It is difficult to conduct a policy dialogue when some of the key players have no stake in the outcome beyond the next few hours. The establishment of democratic deliberation about how to create sensible and socially aware fiscal and monetary policy is likely to require restrictions on the mobility of financial capital.

The organization of social dialogue about appropriate macroeconomic policy should emphasize building broad-based agreement and not simply winning credibility in the eyes of the bond dealers in international markets. The point is not that policy makers should not make economic calculations, but that these should be used as inputs into a democratic deliberative process. Instead of exercising judgment behind closed doors to tweak the results of running models or to decide the implications for policy in the face of an uncertain future, judgement should be exercised in a much more transparent way, with a much greater degree of public debate.

Some innovative approaches are being developed in a number of civil society initiatives on the participatory development of alternative national budgets and budget processes (Cagatay *et al.* 2000). For instance, in Bangladesh, the Institute for Development Policy Analysis at Proshika has conducted a participatory study of peoples' understanding of budget issues and the impact of the budget on their livelihoods. Subsequently, it has made recommendations on participation in the production of the Bangladesh budget, including the democratization of priority setting; pre-budget consultations with civil society; gathering public feedback on expenditure choices from citizen juries; and strengthening the capacities of parliamentary budget committees.

The International Budget Project connects a growing number of civil society organizations in developing countries that began in the 1990s to engage with the social implications of government expenditure and taxation and to promote a social dialogue on government budgets (Krafchik 2001). Much of their work is concerned with improving the transparency of government budgets and analysing their implications for different social groups. But some, such as the Institute for Democracy in South Africa, also assess the macroeconomics of the budget. They provide an independent voice that can look at macroeconomic policy from the point of view of poor and excluded groups. These civil society budget groups are well aware that it is not sensible simply to advocate more and more spending. They are concerned with the composition and quality of the spending and with the raising of revenue too.

Male breadwinner bias, in the broadest sense, is being addressed through a growing number of gender budget initiatives (around 40 at the time of writing) in both developed and developing countries, some initiated by women outside government and some by women inside government (Budlender 2000, 2002). An important aspect of the most successful of these is creative engagement between civil society and government initiatives to try to ensure that fiscal policy does not discriminate against women, especially poor women; and that resources are allocated and used effectively in support of government's policy commitments to women. The best-known example is in South Africa. But there are several others with a comparable, inside – outside government dynamic. For instance, in Tanzania, a civil society organization, the Tanzania Gender Networking Programme, began a Gender Budget Initiative in 1997 (Budlender *et al.* 2002: 140–2; International Budget Project 2000: 53–8). The first phase was research on the budget process and on the policies, expenditure and services of four key ministries: Education, Health, Agriculture and Industries, and Commerce. The research was carried out by teams which included an NGO representative, an academic, and a government official. The research findings were shared through distribution of working papers to key actors in civil society, the media, parliament and ministries and through public meetings. A website was set up (www.tgnp.co.tz). A popular booklet was produced in an easy-to-read format, in English (and subsequently Kiswahili); and workshops were held at local level with community-based organizations. The government was lobbied to include gender equality considerations in the budget guidelines and to follow a more people-oriented development strategy. By 2000, the government of Tanzania had decided that they would like to institutionalize gender analysis in the budgetary process, and they hired TGNP to act as consultants to build the capacity of officials in six ministries. Meanwhile, TGNP continues to campaign with the objective of creating a public demand for a voice in the national budgetary processes, with an emphasis on participation, transparency, accountability and transformation.

The successes of gender budget initiatives have mainly come from work on particular sectors of expenditure and particular revenue measures. It has been difficult to get a hearing with governments on the macroeconomic dimensions of budgets; and there has been less work to develop practical tools for gender-sensitive macro-level analysis. However, a new international task force is being set up with the support of the Commonwealth Secretariat, the Canadian International Development Research Centre, and the United Nations Development Fund for Women, which will have the development of such tools as part of its remit (see www.genderbudgets.org).

The most ambitious model for social dialogue on macroeconomic policy has emerged in Canada, where an Alternative Federal Budget (AFB) has been prepared each year since 1995 following consultation between a wide range of labour, social and community organizations (Loxley 1999). It includes alternative taxation and monetary policy to achieve a range of social goals, including gender equality and the protection of human rights. It aims to improve the entitlements of a wide range of disadvantaged people, focussing not only on market-based entitlements through growth and full employment, but also on universal gender-equitable state-based entitlements through public services and public income transfers.

The initial purpose of the exercise was to challenge the budgets of the federal government, which were based on a policy of public sector downsizing in order to reduce the Canadian budget deficit from 5 per cent of GDP to a target of 3 per cent. Federal government debt and the cost of servicing this debt was what underlay the 5 per cent federal budget deficit, which the government argued to be unsustainable. The government proposed reducing the deficit by reducing programme spending, which would be expected to bring about a fall in interest rates and revitalize the economy. The government argued that the deficit was caused by high government spending, which, in its view, resulted in high interest rates.

The macroeconomic framework of the AFB reversed the government's macroeconomic framework by arguing that the high interest rates were due to the *monetary* policy pursued by the government through the Bank of Canada. It was argued that reducing interest rates would be vital both for closing the deficit and bringing about a reduction in the rate of unemployment. The AFB recommended measures that would allow for an easier monetary policy in order to reduce interest rates. These measures included a reintroduction of reserve requirements for banks and a requirement for the Bank of Canada to hold more federal government debt. The AFB also recommended some forms of capital control in order to reduce Canada's vulnerability to volatility in capital flows. These forms of capital control included a surtax on Canadian interest earnings on overseas bonds, promotion of the 'Tobin tax' on international financial transactions, and a requirement for financial institutions to invest a minimum amount of their assets in community and small business development. On the expenditure side, the AFB stresses strengthening and restructuring social programmes via social investment funds in the areas of health, unemployment insurance, income security, child care, retirement income, post-secondary education and housing. Among other initiatives, it also proposed a job creation initiative while cutting back spending in unproductive and wasteful areas.

Most of the funding for the AFB (about 70 per cent) was projected to result from the increased growth of the economy, while the remaining balance would come from a revamping of the Canadian tax system by raising taxes on corporations and wealthy individuals while at the same time reducing them on low-income earners. An example of such increased taxation on wealthy individuals was the introduction of a wealth transfer tax on transfers in excess of one million Canadian dollars. The AFB also promoted 'green' taxation aimed at the protection of the environment. The AFB combats each of the three biases elaborated on above, though with less emphasis on male breadwinner bias than the other two biases.

The AFB emerged as a result of consultations among various civil society groups, through conferences and roundtables and budget schools in communities across Canada. Underlying the exercise were the following basic principles and commitments: full employment, a more equitable distribution of income, the eradication of poverty, the promotion of gender equality in economic life, the protection of civil, political, economic, social and cultural rights, improvement in the environment, strengthening of social programmes and public services and the creation of a more just, sustainable and peaceful world order (Loxley 1999). Any group accepting these principles could get a seat on the national steering committee, which is made up of representatives from a wide range of citizens' groups. Thus, the AFB employed a participatory approach that entailed a reconciliation of conflicting demands made by different citizens' groups. The AFB has helped to shape government policy, even though the Canadian government is currently far from adopting the full agenda of the AFB. The Minister of Finance has joined in public debate with the AFB and in some areas the government's policy has moved closer to that proposed by the AFB (Loxley 1999) (see also www.policyalternatives.ca). The implementation in full of the AFB would require a change in the way in which the Canadian economy articulates with the international economy, and that is not a change that is currently acceptable to the government of Canada.

Conclusion

The strategy of mainstreaming social issues in macroeconomic policy suggested in this chapter requires changes both in the theoretical framework and in the organization of the policy process. The changes in the theoretical framework, it has been argued, need to go beyond those proposed in 'heterodox' Keynesian-influenced economics, to include the insights of feminist economics. The articulation of the 'social' and the 'economic' needs to be situated in terms of the articulation between economic production and social reproduction. In this context, three forms of social bias were identified in current macroeconomic policy: deflationary bias, male breadwinner bias, and privatization bias. The avoidance of these biases, it was argued, needs greater social dialogue about fiscal and monetary policy. There is an international human rights framework that provides norms against which such policy dialogue may be judged, and prescribes obligations for state and non-state actors. There is an emerging civil society practice in all parts of the world which seeks a more accessible, transparent, and effective national budgetary process, which is non-discriminatory and better meets the needs of poor and socially excluded people. The challenge is to build on this to transform macroeconomic policy, recognizing that this is also likely to require some changes in the ways in which national economies are articulated in the international economy – in particular, the social regulation of capital markets.

Bibliography

Budlender, D. (2000) 'The Political Economy of Women's Budgets in the South', *World Development, Special Issue*, 28, 365–78.

Budlender, D., Elson, D., Hewitt, G., and Mukhopadhyay, T. (2002) *Gender Budgets Make Cents*. London: Commonwealth Secretariat.

Bullard, N. (1998) *Taming the Tigers: the IMF and the Asian Crisis*. London: Focus on the Global South/CAFOD.

Cagatay, N., Elson, D., and Grown, C. (1995) 'Gender, Adjustment and Macroeconomics', *World Development, Special Issue*, 23 (11).

Cagatay, N., Keklik, M., Lal, R., and Lang, J. (2000) *Budgets as if People Mattered*. New York: UNDP (Social Development and Poverty Elimination Division).

Cheru, F. (2001) 'The Highly Indebted Poor Countries (HIPC) Initiative: a Human Rights Assessment of the Poverty Reduction Strategy Papers (PRSP)', *Report to Commission on Human Rights*. Geneva: UN.

Darity, W. (1995) 'The Formal Structure of a Gender-Segregated Low-Income Economy', *World Development, Special Issue*, 23, 1953–1968.

Eatwell, J. (1996) 'International Capital Liberalization: The Impact on World Development', *Working Paper Series*. New York: CEPA.

Elson, D. (1991) 'Male Bias in Macro-Economics: the Case of Structural Adjustment'. In D. Elson (ed.), *Male Bias in the Development Process*. Manchester: Manchester University Press.

Elson, D., and Cagatay, N. (2000) 'The Social Content of Macroeconomic Policies', *World Development*, 28, 1347–1364.

Erturk, K., and Cagatay, N. (1995) 'Macroeconomic Consequences of Cyclical and Secular Changes in Feminization: an Experiment at Gendered Macromodeling', *World Development, Special Issue*, 23, 1969–1977.

Felix, D. (1995) 'Financial Globalization Versus Free Trade: the Case for the Tobin Tax', *UNCTAD Discussion Papers*. Geneva: UNCTAD.

Folbre, N. (1994) *Who Pays for the Kids? Gender and the Structures of Constraint*. London: Routledge.

Folbre, N. (2001) *The Invisible Heart – Economics and Family Values*. New York: The New Press.

Fontana, M., and Wood, A. (2000) 'Modeling the Effects of Trade on Women at Work and at Home', *World Development*, 28, 1173–1190.

Grown, C., Elson, D., and Cagatay, N. (2000) 'Growth, Trade, Finance and Gender Equality', *World Development*, 28 (7).

International Budget Project (2000) *A Taste of Success: Examples of the Budget Work of NGOs*. Washington, DC: Center on Budget and Policy Priorities.

Krafchik, W. (2001) 'Can Civil Society Add Value to Budget Decision Making? A Description of Civil Society Budget Work', *Conference on Gender Responsive Budgeting*. Brussels: UNIFEM/OECD.

Lee, J.-W., and Rhee, C. (1999) *Social Impacts of the Asian Crisis*. New York: UNDP (Human Development Report Office).

Lim, J. Y. (2000) 'The Effects of the East Asian Crisis on the Employment of Women and Men: the Philippine Case', *World Development*, 28, 1285–1306.

Loxley, J. (1999) 'The Alternative Federal Budget in Canada: a New Approach to Fiscal Democracy', *UNDP/UNIFEM Workshop on Pro-Poor, Gender- and Environment-Sensitive Budgets*. New York: UNDP/UNIFEM.

McKinley, T. (2001) *Macroeconomic Policy, Growth and Poverty Reduction*. New York: Palgrave.

Mellor, P. (1991) 'Adjustment and Social Crisis in Chile During the 1980s'. *World Development*, 18, 1545–1561.

Taylor, L. (1991) *Varieties of Stabilization Experience: Towards Sensible Macroeconomics in the Third World*. Oxford: Clarendon Press.

UN (2001) 'Substantive Issues Arising in the Implementation of the International Covenant on Economic, Social and Cultural Rights: Poverty and the International Covenant on Economic, Social and Cultural Rights', *Statement adopted by the Committee on Economic and Social Council*. Geneva: UN.

UNDP (1995) *Human Development Report 1995*. New York and Oxford: UNDP.

UNDP (1999) *Human Development Report 1999*. New York and Oxford: UNDP.

UNIFEM (2000) *Progress of the World's Women 2000*. New York: UNIFEM.

Walters, B. (1995) 'Engendering Macroeconomics: a Reconsideration of Growth Theory', *World Development, Special Issue*, 23, 1869–1882.

Warner, J. M., and Campbell, D. A. (2000) 'Supply Response in an Agrarian Economy with Non-Symmetric Gender Relations', *World Development*, 28, 1327–1340.

4
Social Policy and Development: Social Capital as Point of Departure*
Ben Fine

Introduction

The relationship between the economic and the social has ever been theoretically uneasy. The result has often been a hardening into one of two extremes. As perceived by neo-liberalism, the economy is best left to the market and, at most, the social is viewed as a necessary evil, required to oil the wheels of commerce. In contrast, the alternative stance is to emphasize both micro and macro market imperfections and, thereby, to understand the social as an essential means to correct them. I suspect and welcome that the intellectual, ideological and policy mood is currently swinging away from the first and towards the second position. One indicator of this is the extent to which the social, often previously rounded up in the notion of 'civil society', has increasingly been seen as both an instrument and a goal of economic and social policy. Nonetheless, a casual reading of any area of such literature, accompanied by a modicum of critical thinking, suggests a number of cautionary tales.

First, understandings of civil society are often unthinkingly transposed from the West to the rest of the world, both for conceptual purposes and in the elaboration of ideals to be emulated. This involves a double displacement in that the initial application of the notion tends to neglect the history of the past century – a period during which western society has been far from civil. In addition, in this light, false perspectives from one world are universalized to others, reflecting the long-standing tradition of understanding development as attaining the idealized status of the developed.

* This essay was written whilst in receipt of a Research Fellowship from the UK Economic and Social Research Council (ESRC) under award number R000271046 to study 'The New Revolution in Economics and Its Impact upon Social Sciences'. It is drawn in part from a presentation made to the UNRISD Conference on Social Policy and Social Development, Tammsvik, September 2000.

Second, civil society has been regarded as a panacea, a source of positive-sum outcomes, if only it can be appropriately organized, embraced and participated in by its citizens. Consequently, it is hardly surprising that it tends to be viewed through rose-coloured spectacles, with the economy and systemic power set aside in deference to democracy and good governance. Rather than seeing civil society as a site of, or focus for, underlying conflicts, the latter melt away as mutual benefits flow from collectivism and co-operation. In short, civil society and social revolution sit extremely uncomfortably side-by-side.

Third, a corollary or summary of the two previous points taken together, civil society is recognizably complex and diverse, not least because it is the outcome of associations, organizations, institutions, networks, cultures and so on that have been forged out of equally diverse and complex interests and conflicts. Just as generalization is unwise, so is the indiscriminate application of abstract concepts drawn, however thoroughly, from specific case studies.

Such, in broad terms, is what has occurred with the notion of social capital.[1] The term, scarcely used or acknowledged other than over the past decade, has shot to prominence. Robert Putnam, arguably the leading 'social capitalist', has been reported to be the single most-cited author across the social sciences in the 1990s. His thesis of the decline of US society – in a nutshell because of 'Bowling Alone' and too much television watching – even granted him a meeting with President Clinton to thrash out solutions to the country's woes (Putnam 2000). Further, most worryingly for some, the World Bank is heavily committed to social capital as it moves, at least in rhetoric, from the neo-liberal Washington to the apparently more state-friendly post-Washington Consensus.[2] The purpose here is to provide a brief overview of how and why social capital has become the latest conceptual fad across the social sciences, and to consider the implications of this development. As a result, I draw very different conclusions from those who have aligned themselves to social capital – even those who are prepared to be critically circumspect about the latest conceptual wünderkind of the social sciences. They often recognize its deficiencies but seek to civilize it, reintroducing the complexity and diversity that have previously been excluded. In contrast, I argue that the notion needs to be rejected in view of its origins, directions and momentum. For this reason I question the use of social capital as a way of providing an entry into discussion of social policy. Instead, in part by way of critique of the welfare regimes approach, I put forward alternative perspectives on locating social policy in its relationship to the economy.

Twixt Bourdieu and Becker

It is worth, at the expense of some personal indulgence, explaining why I determined from an early stage to follow social capital's meteoric rise closely. In the mid-1990s, I came to the conclusion, on the basis of its new information-theoretic micro-foundations, that economics was colonizing the other social sciences as never before, on which see the seventh point listed below. Whilst, especially through the likes of Gary Becker, a leading mainstream neo-classical Chicago economist, such self-confessed economics imperialism had long been on the agenda, it had primarily depended upon the non-market as if market, and the market as if utility-maximizing *individuals* facing resource and price constraints. Not surprisingly, despite some notable successes, especially but not exclusively through human capital theory, such assaults only made limited territorial gains across the *social* sciences. However, on its own terms, the new micro-foundations purports both to accept and to explain institutions, structures, customs, etc., albeit on the basis of a more circumspect methodological individualism. It has given rise to a whole range of new fields within economics. These have had knock-on effects to a greater or lesser extent and in varied ways in the other social sciences – the new institutional economics, the new household economics, the economic sociology, the new political economy, the new growth theory, the new labour economics, the new economic geography, the new financial economics, the new development economics, and so on.[3] In short and drastic summary especially for the non-economist, over the past two decades economics has been colonizing the other social sciences as never before, forging an alliance with and advancing alongside rational choice theory.

In this light, I was intrigued to find that two scholars at the opposite extremes of the social science spectrum were both using the term social capital. One was Gary Becker (1996), who extended the notion of capital as an asset from physical things to human capital, and from human capital to personal capital (any characteristic that directly or indirectly contributed to welfare), and from personal capital to social capital (non-market interactions between people). The other was Pierre Bourdieu, the progressive French sociologist, who had first used the term social capital in the early 1980s, alongside cultural and symbolic capital, to explain how non-economic forms of domination are linked to the reproduction of social stratification and interact with one and another and the economic. I was determined to find out why and how these two totally different theorists could find themselves as social capital bedfellows, and what implications this might have for economics imperialism. But I found myself deluged in an evolving tidal wave of academic fashion. Far from confronting the apparently simple question of why Becker and Bourdieu should share the same terminology, I was faced with a much more substantial issue – how could social capital have become so widely and rapidly adopted especially in view of its commonly acknowledged deficiencies? Here are my conclusions, laid out in detail and with detailed justification in Fine (2001b).

Social capital exposed

First, what is striking about social capital is not only the extent of its influence, and the speed with which this has been achieved, but also its ready acceptance as analytical, empirical and policy panacea. These features are aptly captured, respectively, by the World Bank's notion of social capital as a 'missing link', its flush of dedicated household surveys, and its view of social capital as 'the glue that holds society together'.[4] Social capital is used to explain what is otherwise inexplicable and is seen as the factor that allows society to function successfully. In limited respects, parallels can be drawn with utility as used by economists. For this is also all-embracing – putatively explaining why we behave in the way that we do as well as providing us with our welfare. In the case of social capital, however, our sights and ambitions are raised from the level of the individual to the level of society, from the market to the non-market, and from narrowly defined individual motivation to customs, norms, institutions and rules. In short, social capital is attractive because of the scope of application that it provides as well as its capacity to do so whilst not necessarily being critical of what has gone before. It can both generalize (add missing link and glue) and incorporate (reinterpret existing scholarship as an earlier unwitting use). And, policy-wise, social is to complement economic engineering, with the principle of supporting self-help raised from the individual to some collective level of 'community'.

Second, despite what is already a deluge of survey articles, even those who are not using the term for the first time accept that it is difficult to define. The more established social capitalists in an enterprise that is, admittedly still in its precocious infancy, have been forced to compromise with the expanding scope of social capital. More and more variables are included, from the horizontal to the vertical, from the bonding to the bridging to the linking, from social values to networks and associations, and so on. Alternatively, such proliferation of content can be rendered manageable by a re-composition into broad categories to question whether social capital is, for example, complementary with, or a substitute for 'real' capital or the state. The result is to create a field for what has previously been termed middle-range theory – analysis suspended somewhere between grand systemic theory and mere description. As a result, more recent and less circumspect contributions may acknowledge the ambiguities in the definition of social capital, simply pass on, and choose or add a definition of their own to suit their own purpose. Social capital thereby becomes a sack of analytical potatoes. The notion is simply chaotic, as is also reflected in frequent suggestions that it is merely a metaphor or a heuristic device. It is also acknowledged to be difficult to measure (tellingly revealed by World Bank projects that seek to define it by the process of measuring it). What is social capital is readily confused with what it does, as if these needed to be conceptually distinct. One reason for thinking so is the early and mounting recognition that social capital is subject to the perverse, dark, negative and downside so that it can be bad as well as good depending on circumstances, as in the Mafia, fascism and so on. Whilst these features of social capital might be thought to render it unacceptable and subject to collapse under the weight of its own contradictions and inconsistencies, exactly the opposite appears to be the case. Having established a sufficiently weighty presence, it also has the logical capacity to absorb any criticism in the form of refinement by, for example, addition of another variable for consideration, even conflict or revolution!

Third, then, social capital has a gargantuan appetite. On the one hand, it can explain everything from individuals to societies (although global social capital has rarely figured to date, it ought to do so at least to address the international networks and ethos of those running the world) whether the topic be the sick, the poor, the criminal, the corrupt, the (dys)functional family, schooling, community life, work and organization, democracy and governance, collective action, transitional societies, intangible assets or, indeed, any aspect of social, cultural and economic performance, and equally across time and place. On the other hand, social capital has been deployed across theories and methodologies as diverse as postmodernist Marxism and mainstream neo-classical economics, addressing the conceptual, empirical and policy.[5] In this respect, social capital is like other all-encompassing notions that have swept, if not uniformly, across the social sciences, such as flexibility and globalization. All can participate from their own perspective. Social capital is truly democratic, not only amongst the community of scholars but also because, as middle-range theory, it is able to engage (with) the wider community of activists, politicians and media gurus. This is especially so in terms of its capacity to exploit popular prejudices about the role of television, the family and moral fibre, to touch the nostalgia for a lost world, to address demise and failure that are ever more demanding of attention than success, and so on.

Yet, as already hinted by reference to globalization, the emergence of social capital to rapid prominence is a familiar phenomenon in terms of academic fashions. It is most disturbing as evidence of a more general trend towards the popularization and degradation of scholarship, a pattern which is familiar by now. A case study or two leads to the invention of grand concepts and generalizations. These are refined in the light of theoretical and empirical critiques that point to omitted theoretical variables and/or case study counter-examples. Existing and new knowledge is run through the evolving framework. Ultimately, the whole edifice becomes too complex and succumbs to the critical heretics or others who have remained or become cynical. It is then time for a new fashion to emerge.

Despite this intellectual cycle, the effects are significant. Quite apart from the waste of scholarly resources, the impact of such fashions over the longer term is not necessarily negligible nor is it the same across disciplines and topics. We have yet to see what the long-term effects of social capital will be on the social sciences, although some of the short-term effects are already discernible. Fourth, then, although social capital is unlimited in principle in terms of what it can incorporate and address, and how it does so, the evolution of the literature in practice is far from neutral in its content and direction. It reflects general intellectual fashions, the stimulus of external events, and even the idiosyncrasies of particular participants. What is equally important is what has been left out. As much of the critical literature has observed, contributions to social capital have tended to focus on civil society and its associational forms and ethos. This has been in isolation from, and exclusive of, serious consideration of the economy, formal politics, the role of the nation-state, the exercise of power, and the divisions and conflicts that are endemic to capitalist society – although, of course, these can be added if you so desire.

Fifth, more specifically in this intellectual trajectory, although Bourdieu is a (decreasingly) acknowledged initiator of the theory of social capital, the critical aspects of his contributions have been excised in deference to the tamer versions associated with the likes of James Coleman, rational choice founding father of the social capital phenomenon and Chicago collaborator with Becker, and Robert Putnam, its most ardent popularizer. In particular, Bourdieu emphasized the social construction of the content of social capital (what is its meaning and how does this relate to its practices?), that it is irreducibly attached to class stratification, which, in turn, is associated with the exercise of economic and other forms of exploitation, and the relationship between them. Significantly, the functional approaches to social capital attached to the founding empirical studies of Coleman and Putnam have both been shown to be questionable – respectively, catholic community as a positive influence on US schooling outcomes and the incidence and impact of associational activity on differential regional development in Italy (and the same caveats apply to Putnam's US work). In other words, false empirical analysis has given rise to a theory that has subsequently taken on a life of its own as if both theory and data were mutually supportive. Such are the shaky foundations for the evolving knowledge attached to social capital. This indicates that the attraction of social capital derives less from the unconsciously scurrilous scholarship of its founders and more from their having tapped the intellectual nerve of social theory at the turn of the millennium.

This has a dual aspect. For, sixth, one particularly important feature of the intellectual environment in which social capital has flourished has been the retreat both from neo-liberalism and from postmodernism. On the one hand, neo-liberalism has run out of scholarly steam – although, like a bad smell, its effects linger and you can never be sure that it has gone for good. But, in the academic world, you can only say a limited number of times and for a limited time, that it is safe to leave things to the market, do not allow rent-seeking, and reduce corruption and government. How much better to be able to react against neo-liberalism by positing a world of market (informational) *im*perfections in which there is a role for the state, and in which social capital can correct for the absence of economic capital and imperfectly working markets. Social capital is rent-seeking made good. As such, it is one way of jumping on the anti-neo-liberal bandwagon. On the other hand, the triumphs of the extremes of postmodernism have also passed their peak. There is now a wish for a renewed confrontation with the real. By its very name, despite its conceptual chaos, social capital appears to get to grips with both the social and with capital. Nothing could be further from the truth. For, the very terminology of social capital signifies its weaknesses. That the notion 'social' needs to be attached to capital to mark a distinct category is indicative of the failure to understand capital as social in what is taken to be its more mundane economic, putatively non-social, form. What is adopted, however, with use of 'capital', especially with the physicalist overtones attached to mainstream economics, is the failure to incorporate the most important insight for social theory to be derived from postmodernism – that concepts need to be historically and socially grounded, if not always subjectively so. In this vein, universal concepts such as social capital would be ruled out of court, and could not be rescued by appeal to historical and social context as path dependence, influence of other factors, initial conditions or multiple equilibria. These are the long-standing favoured way of dealing with the social and historical by mainstream economics, at least when the problem is recognized. That social cap-italists are forced to adopt, or often willingly embrace, this route has been heavily criticized with little or no effect. It is also indicative of one element in the spreading influence of the postures of economics on other social sciences.

Thus, seventh, because social capital is ahistorical and asocial, so it is fundamentally complicit with mainstream economics in the form of its new information-theoretic micro-foundations. Developments within and around economics on this basis have allowed it to understand both the economic and the non-economic as being the consequence of market imperfections. As a result, economics is colonizing the other social sciences as never before, with an 'as if market imperfection' world as opposed to the 'as if market perfection' world that previously proved a colonizing tool of significant, if limited impact. Not surprisingly, social capital has proved attractive to some mainstream economists in such endeavours, with Gary Becker paradoxically in the forefront. In this light, for economists, social capital is simply everything else after other, more traditional forms of capital have been taken into account, with these understood as in the mainstream as physical, natural, financial or human. Transparently, the effect is to add the social to an otherwise unchallenged economic, albeit made up of market imperfections. Such a ludicrous posture is at its most extreme in the case of mainstream economics for which capital is a physical or other asset that ultimately provides a stream of utility to individuals – a universal, ahistorical and asocial thing rather than a definite economic relationship, with associated structures and processes for the generation of profit. This all reflects a profound misunderstanding both of the social and of capital(ism). In a word, economists can bring in the social to complement the individual, only because the social has been omitted in the first instance.

Of equal significance, however, is the response of non-economists both to social capital and to the colonizing designs of economics. Here, eighth, a crucial aspect of social capital is the demonstration that its intellectual origins and motivation were provided by a renewed attempt to establish rational choice within social theory (and to swing it towards economic as opposed to psychological reductionism). Significantly, social capital evolved out of a literature (social exchange theory), and was initially designed, to address the relationship between the macro and the micro in the context of the relationship between the social and the individual. To a large extent, if not completely, these origins – and their generally strong affinities with rational choice methodology – have been glossed over in the ready reception granted to social capital as the 'cure-all' for social theory. Thus, whether influenced by a colonizing economics or not, the use of social capital across the other social sciences is equally uncritical of the economic. The only, at times insidious, difference is that the same analytical content is disguised and tempered to a greater or lesser extent by more informal types of arguments. These are set together with the more traditional variables of social theory, with the negative, dark, perverse or downside, of power and of conflict, only being thrown in if needs be.

Ninth, ironically and perversely, social capitalists from outside economics are attracted by the notion because they perceive it to be an assault upon economics. Economists are thought of as being civilized by being forced to take account of the social. In addition, social capital is widely and proudly praised for placing interdisciplinary endeavour upon the agenda. Significantly, however, this is only asserted and never demonstrated. And the only economics on the agenda is that of the mainstream. Essentially, would-be civilizers and critics of a colonizing mainstream economics are working critically against a model of the discipline that is a hundred years old, that of perfectly competitive and efficient outcomes. They do not recognize the implications of the more recent revolution in and around economics that positively embraces the social by way of extension of the unchanged economic principles (or the economic approach, as Becker dubs it). In this light, the role of social capital in social theory's response to a colonizing economics is completely clarified. On the one hand, by way of analogy, it can be understood as a form of peripheral colonization, incorporating all social theory other than economics. On the other hand, it presents itself as the opposition to a colonizing economics whereas, at most, it offers feeble resistance because it has no alternative economics of its own – at worst, it prepares social theory for the colonizing advance of the economic approach.

In short, whilst social capital purports to fill out the analytical space in which to construct social as a complement to economic policy, it is a particularly weak foundation of shifting sands for doing so. As even a sympathetic commentator on social capital observes:

> What can a policy-maker in Mexico or Turkey actually do, confronted with the evidence from the World Values Survey that they govern a low-trust society? Standard recommendations, such as attempting to eliminate corruption and improve the legal system, are nothing new, and make good sense quite independently of any emphasis on social capital. (Temple 2000: 50)

Whither social capital?

Not surprisingly, despite its popularity, social capital has created an undercurrent of opposition from progressive scholars with intellectual integrity. Why have they not been more numerous and outspoken? My own experience from presenting the critical views on social capital outlined above is that it is very hard to generate serious debate and disagreement. Instead, apologetic social capitalists argue that they are civilizing economists, combating neo-liberalism, and able to outflank the least desirable features of social capital by bringing in what would otherwise be omitted by other, less progressive users. Last, and by no means least, it is claimed that funding and research depend upon playing the social capital game, and that at least it offers one way of addressing the role of civil society.

Individual advancement aside – an important factor in the rise of social capital – this all reveals much by way of intellectual bankruptcy and a failure to recognize how social capital's ready accommodation of opposition represents a highly successful form of a legitimizing repressive tolerance. The most appropriate answer to social capital is to reject it altogether and to construct a rigorous theory of the social and of capital and of capitalism, building upon the intellectual traditions that we have rather than reducing them to fashionable concepts inspired by a disguised rational choice.

From social capital to social policy

On a more constructive note, social capital raises, although it does not adequately answer, questions concerning the nature, impact and source (how to create social capital is a frequently recognized omission within the literature) of social norms, whether understood as such or as values, customs, institutions, associations, structures, culture, etc. In as much as these have relevance for social policy, I posit seven broad conclusions, mainly drawn from a critical but constructive review of recent literature on the welfare state (Fine 2003a: ch. 11).

First, social policy is *programme*-specific. In other words, housing, education, health programmes, etc., have to do with housing, education and health as such through what I have termed systems of provision in work on consumption – as in food, health, energy, housing systems (Fine 1998b; Fine 2003a; Fine *et al.* 1996; Fine and Leopold 1993). Each system is tied to a (vertical) chain of activities that form an integral entity, distinct from the others. This is not to suggest that the different programmes are independent of one another, nor that they do not share common determinants. However, how and to whom welfare is delivered is structurally interdependent with, in principle, a whole range of factors interacting in different ways with different and shifting effects. But how housing, for example, is provided – land, other inputs, construction, finance, tenure, and so on – is as important as, and dovetails with, social custom, welfare principles, political and economic pressures in ways that are unique to housing itself and distinct from health, education, or whatever. This is illustrated by the apartheid economy in which, despite common elements of racism and fragmentation through the homeland system, outcomes for housing, education, health and electrification were quite different from one another and posed different problems for the post-apartheid period (see MERG 1993).

Second, implicit in the previous point is the differentiation of social policy by country as well as by programme. Each country will be at its own stage of development, will have its own structure and dynamic of economic, political and ideological forces, and these will interact with, or be concretized through, the provision attached to particular programmes. This conclusion draws negatively from Esping-Andersen, and the literature it has inspired, whereby his three welfare regimes have increasingly proven to be an analytical and empirical straitjacket as far as mounting evidence from case studies by programmes and countries are concerned, more observed in the breach. I draw the same conclusion from a careful reading of Goodman (1998), for example, on the supposed 'East Asian Welfare Model'. There is no model, either from one country to another or from one area of provision to another.[6]

Third, social norms have to be understood in a sophisticated and complex analytical framework. As a customary standard of living – of which the wage bundle is often a major factor – it is differentiated both by different sections of the population and by the consumption goods themselves (as suggested for social policy programmes in the first point above). Consumption norms are not simply an average as such, even with some above and some below the 'norm'. The latter is more appropriately understood as the outcome of continuing socioeconomic processes, which grind out customary patterns of consumption. What those patterns are and how they are determined is very different from one commodity to another. Food, housing, clothing are not only differentially consumed but the patterns and levels of consumption are the consequences of very different structures and processes of causation. Nonetheless, each of these elements in the wage bundle is subject to change as a consequence of development, although inertia and dysfunction is also possible, as in the eating disorders characteristic of the diseases of affluence, as argued in Fine (1998b).

Fourth, similar considerations apply to the distribution of (wage) income from which social policy in part takes its point of departure. Labour markets are not simply structured and differentiated, with correspondingly different wages and conditions and access by socioeconomic status; rather, each labour market is itself structured and functions in an integral way, depending upon deskilling, reskilling, the presence of trade unions, public or private, casualized or secure, competitiveness in product markets, and so on, as argued in detail in Fine (1998a). As there are socioeconomic processes that match income levels to consumption norms (and vice versa), the homogenizing influence of monetary remuneration is far from absolute. In other words, both the determination of the distribution of (wage) income and the potential for its effective redistribution have to be firmly rooted in an appropriately wide range of suitably integrated considerations.

Fifth, to some extent, social policy has been understood as public consumption as an alternative to private consumption. This tends to leave unchallenged the notion attached to laissez-faire ideology, that public consumption is merely an alternative form of private consumption, and liable to be inferior in efficiency and quality of delivery. Even those rejecting the presumed inferiority of public provision, on efficiency and/or equity grounds, have been subject to an assault of making the public more like, or meeting the standards of, the private sector, with the practices and terminology of the latter being aped as public consumption is attached to commercial criteria and the serving of clients and customers, as Marx observed in the *Economic and Philosophical Manuscripts* of 1844 (cited in Radin 1996: 75–6):

> Private property has made us so stupid and one-sided that we think a thing is *ours* only when we have it. In other words, public consumption is something more and different from private consumption. What are the more general implications for social policy of the distinction between public and private consumption? Most important, the distinction is itself analytically invalid, certainly as a starting point for each form of consumption is socially and historically constructed with a mix of private and public – in relation to one another and, almost inevitably, chaotically across different systems of provision and cultural systems. In reaching out to the latter, it is apparent that private consumption is attached to social or public determinants whether materially or ideologically. Such are the insights yielded, respectively, for example, by Marx's commodity fetishism and Foucault's domination of body and mind. Relations between private consumers and objects of consumption are deeply embodied in the social domain despite the appearances and, to some extent, the reality of the opposite.

For Sack (1992: 104), especially with regard to mass production, 'the consumer's world includes only the front stage of mass consumption and relegates extraction, production, distribution, waste, and pollution to a hidden backstage'.

In this light, when the distinction between public and private consumption is deployed, for whatever purpose, it tends, respectively, to implode upon the individual or to explode upon society. Here the contrast is between Baudrillard and Marx. For in the view of the former, postmodernist subjectivity floats free even from the constraints imposed by bodily survival. As Warde (1994: 231) puts it, referring especially to the work of Zygmunt Bauman, the construction of the 'heroic consumer': 'prevents us from appreciating the constraints people face in their consumption practices...The use of the term "the consumer" signifies an undersocialised actor; it exaggerates the scope and capacity for individual action.'

In the case of Marx, much of the literature on consumption is motivated or justified by the presumption that his chief analytical concern – to root out the social and material origins of the commodity in capitalist production – had precluded its consideration in deference to a focus upon class (conflict) and uncovering the laws of production.

If, however, attention is drawn to public consumption, then it necessarily reaches for a systemic understanding to uncover one or more fetishisms that are attached to commodities whether as material or cultural objects. What is it that underlies and is not revealed by the private relationship between consumer and object of consumption, which may be more overt in the case of public consumption? For Marx, it is the social relationship between producers as opposed to those (being treated as relations) between things. For (critical) notions of consumer society, it tends to be about the hidden persuaders, false as opposed to real needs, public squalor and private affluence, emulation and distinction, and so on. Most recently, private consumption has been most markedly rendered public or social by concerns about the environment – how my consumption leads to global warming, to the destruction of Brazilian forests, to the excessive use of chemicals, and so on. More generally, many other public issues may be attached to private consumption, such as boycotts as in sanctions against apartheid, child labour and for improvement in wages and working conditions. In each case, the core of what is involved cannot be discovered directly in the relationship between consumer and consumed.

A necessary implication is that, as private becomes understood as public consumption, so it is translated into something *other* than consumption. Even with the narrowest of consumer concerns, for quality of product and absence of price-fixing for example, there is a focus upon the regulatory and legal environment, quite apart from a systemic understanding of the economy itself – one which should but which may not conform to some sort of ideal competitiveness and integrity between buyers and sellers. By shifting focus from private to public consumption, there is a simultaneous shift from consumption itself or, at least, incorporation of other issues (Fine 2003a: ch.10).

Finally, this has extremely important but ambiguous political and ideological implications. Does it involve a strengthening or a dilution of attention to (public) consumption? On the one hand, in setting the issue of private consumption within the public domain of public issues, very powerful and wide-ranging discursive and material pressures are potentially brought to bear, the demand and struggle for basic needs for example – what are the rights to have them? On the other hand, however, there is a corresponding displacement from the focus upon the private and upon consumption, which means that notions of private consumption remain resilient and even prosper. There can be no better illustration than the postmodernist preoccupation with consumption and identity whilst, by the same token, notions of public consumption are most precarious. They either become translated into something else that is broader in scope and content or, as observed at the beginning of this point, become confined to the dictates of what constitutes private consumption by other means. In short, social policy is about collective provision, but this does not set it apart from private provision, which is a form of collective provision by other means.

Sixth, to some extent, albeit in a more or less limited way, the previous considerations have been recognized in the literature. I select two illustrations with the added motive of also demonstrating the incorporation of a colonizing economics into social policy analysis. Atkinson (1999) has been prominent and honourable in contesting the neo-liberal (transatlantic) consensus in the field of inequality. In the third WIDER Annual Lecture, 'Is Rising Inequality Inevitable? A Critique of the Transatlantic Consensus', he rightly observes that patterns of inequality conform neither empirically nor theoretically to the neo-liberal, inevitability, view. As a result, he opens up the potential for redistributive policies through a mutually supportive combination of labour market norms and redistributive taxation. But the analytical framework for doing so is entirely drawn from the new micro-foundations without being rooted in social and historical realities. Something 'social' is offered as an explanatory factor, shifting pay norms and public choice, but the corresponding models, however more complicated they might be made, are remarkably free of the socioeconomic forces and conflicts that are known to underpin the emergence and evolution of welfare states.

Atkinson's self-confessed story has its origins within economics but wanders outside. This contrasts with Esping-Andersen's framework of welfare regimes. It begins with structure and power and how these are differentially translated into different outcomes. But, in his later work, the response to criticism (for neglect of household and gender) has been to converge upon the insights offered by a colonizing economics. In what almost appears to be a self-parody, he comments:

> The intensity of the trade-off depends on several factors: number and age of children, whether mothers work part-time or full-time, and whether

husbands help...Lamentable as this may be, it is perfectly consistent with a standard neoclassical joint-decision model of household behaviour. (Esping-Andersen 1999: 58)

But such flirtations with mainstream economics are not confined to the new household economics. For the household derives its welfare from the state, the market and its own activities. It is 'the ultimate destination of welfare consumption and allocation. It is the unit "at risk"' (p. 36). This leads to the following section heading, 'The Foundations of Welfare Regimes: Risk Management', with its opening sentence, 'social policy means public management of social risks'. It is followed by a standard account of the welfare state that is associated with mainstream economics, not least in terms of market failures, including reference to information failure.[7] This is a departure from what I take to be the foundations of welfare regimes – the programme- and country-specific responses to the contradictory economic and social reproduction of capitalist societies.

Seventh and last, some principles under which to examine social policy and to assess its potential sources and impacts. Social policy is a social and historical construct both in material and interpretative content. As such it is chaotic, contested, contradictory and subject to conflict in practice – both ideologically and theoretically. Here, emphasis has been placed on a dual displacement – from private to public consumption, and from public consumption to broader social, political, economic and ideological issues. It is possible to traverse in the opposite direction and acknowledge that the welfare state is a funnel and filter for a complex range of economic and social phenomena as well for ethical principles.

Further, social policy is a product not just of capitalism, but of particular stages in its development. Consequently, it is necessary to provide for a political economy of capitalism, including attention to its underlying structures, processes and tendencies, and how these are reproduced and transformed. The second half of the twentieth century is not only marked by the extent of the internationalization of capital but also by the extent of state intervention. Further, the last quarter century of the millennium has witnessed, simultaneously with a growth slowdown, an apparent hegemony of finance over industrial capital. Paradoxically, the most recent literature on the limits to the welfare state acknowledges the power of international (finance) capital but in a way that is crudely unsatisfactory and exaggerates and generalizes the power of finance:

Public consumption and social policy are concerned with economic and social reproduction. Consequently, demographic issues are to the fore in terms of household formation, and fertility and mortality rates, etc. But this does not mean that the household should be taken as an analytical starting point any more than our understanding of capitalism need be based on the individual firm. Rather, the demography needs to be related to the political economy of capitalism and its periodisation, as I have argued in Fine (1992).

The relationship between social and economic reproduction, and the fluidity between them, is partially captured by the notions of commodification and decommodification. These are, however, totally inadequate as used in the welfare regimes approach. For, each goes much deeper than a simple understanding based on more or less (labour) market dependence. Whilst capitalism has a tendency to commodify, this also creates a counter-tendency because the very same process of undermining non-capitalist provision also strengthens it, not least through the provision of cheap means of production and consumption. For the new household economics, this is simply a matter of reading off outcomes in terms of a more or less socially sticky comparative advantage. By contrast, outcomes both in the division of labour between commercial and non-commercial, and in the formation of labour market structures and dynamics, are highly contradictory and contingent.

Finally, it is inconceivable in light of the foregoing principles that a general theory of social policy, even with regime varieties, could be appropriate. Both across countries and across specific programmes within countries, conditions are too diverse to allow for such regularity. Even the pressure for, and impact of, privatization programmes are highly diverse by country and by sector. This is even more apparent in the case of social policy. There is no alternative but to examine the peculiarities of the benefit system in its relations to a full range of factors, and the same applies to housing, health, education and other components of welfare systems. Such a result is hardly surprising since not only is welfare provision highly diverse, but so are its determinants in the economy, labour markets, politics, trade unions, and so forth. Indeed, the conclusion is heavily supported by the wealth of programme and policy studies across countries and over time. As research on social policy becomes increasingly interdisciplinary, it should be reinforced by an economic content drawn from political economy and at the expense of a colonizing economics and its veiled forms of methodological individualism.

Notes

1. For the uneasy relationship between social capital and civil society, see Edwards (1999) and Rudolph (2000).
2. Rhetoric for the post-Washington Consensus has been provided by Joseph Stiglitz, see Stiglitz (1998). He was essentially sacked as Chief Economist at the World Bank at the end of 1999 for taking its logic to policy conclusions. For an account, including discussion of Ravi Kanbur's resignation as leading author of the World Bank's 2000 World Development Report on Poverty, see Wade (2001). For critical

exposition of the post-Washington Consensus, see Fine (2001a). Hildyard (1998) and Standing (2000).
3. See Fine (1997) for my first contribution in this vein and ibid. See also Fine (2001a, 2001b, 2002, 2003a, 2003b, 2004). For evidence from the mainstream itself, Becker (1996) and Lazar, E. (2000), both of whom refer to economic imperialism and Olson and Kähkönen, S. (2000) who explicitly prefer the telling metaphor of economics as metropolis and other social science as the suburbs. See also Frey (1999), who attracts praise from Nobel Laureates Becker, Stigler and Buchanan.
4. For the World Bank's treatment of social capital, visit its dedicated website http://www.worldbank.org/poverty/scapital.
5. For the many who have sought to trace original uses of social capital, in substance if not in name, I hesitate to reveal the following from Marx's *German Ideology* of 1845/6, (cited in Oishi, T. (2001)). *The Unknown Marx: Reconstructing a Unified Perspective.* London: Pluto Press:

> It follows...that a certain mode of production, or industrial stage, is always combined with a certain mode of co-operation, or social stage, and this mode of cooperation is itself a productive force.

Of course, Marx refers to the capitalist relations of production, at once both economic and social.
6. Similar conclusions may be drawn from Gough (2000), which offers an assessment of Esping-Andersen's work as applied to developing countries, although his own preference seems to be to qualify it beyond recognition.
7. For, from the World Bank, 'a new definition and conceptual framework for Social Protection grounded in Social Risk Management', with explicit reliance upon the new information-theoretic micro-foundations, see Holzmann and Jørgensen, S. (2000).

Bibliography

Atkinson, A. B. (1999) 'Is Rising Inequality Inevitable? A Critique of the Transatlantic Consensus', *Annual Lectures 3*. Helsinki: UNU/ WIDER.
Becker, G. (1996) *Accounting for Tastes*. Cambridge, MA: Harvard University Press.
Edwards, M. (1999) *Enthusiasts, Tacticians and Sceptics: The World Bank, Civil Society and Social Capital*. Washington, DC: The World Bank.
Esping-Andersen, G. (1999) *Social Foundations of Postindustrial Economies*. Oxford: Oxford University Press.
Fine, B. (1992) *Women's Employment and the Capitalist Family*. London: Routledge.
Fine, B. (1997) 'The New Revolution in Economics', *Capital and Class*, 61, 143–8.
Fine, B. (1998a) *Labour Market Theory: a Constructive Reassessment*. London: Routledge.
Fine, B. (1998b) *The Political Economy of Diet, Health and Food Policy*. London: Routledge.
Fine, B. (2001a) Economics Imperialism and Intellectual Progress: the Present as History of Economic Thought? *History of Economics Review*, 32, 10–36.
Fine, B. (2001b) *Social Capital versus Social Theory: Political Economy and Social Science at the Turn of the Millennium*. London: Routledge.
Fine, B. (2002) 'Economic Imperialism': A View from the Periphery'. *Review of Radical Political Economics*, 34(2), 187–201.
Fine, B. (2003a) *The World of Consumption: The Cultural and Material Revisited*. London: Routledge.

Fine, B. (2003b) 'Beyond the Developmental State: Towards a Political Economy of Development'. In H. Hirakawa, M. Noguchi and M. Sano (eds), *Beyond Market-Driven Development: A New Stream of Political Economy of Development*. Tokyo: Nihon Hyoron Sha.

Fine, B. (2004) 'Addressing the Critical and the Real in Critical Realism'. In Lewis (ed.), *Transforming Economics: Perspectives on the Critical Realist Project*. London: Routledge.

Fine, B., Heasman, M., and Wright, J. (1996) *Consumption in the Age of Affluence: the World of Food*. London: Routledge.

Fine, B., and Leopold, E. (1993) *The World of Consumption*. London: Routledge.

Frey, B. (1999) *Economics as a Science of Human Behaviour: Towards a New Social Science Paradigm*. Boston: Kluwer Academic Publishers.

Goodman, R., White, G., and Kwon, H.-J. (1998) *The East Asian Welfare Regime Model: Welfare Orientalism and the State*. London: Routledge.

Gough, I. (2000) *Welfare Regimes: On Adapting the Framework to Developing Countries*. Bath: University of Bath.

Hildyard, N. (1998) *The World Bank and the State: a Recipe for Change?* London: Bretton Woods Project.

Holzmann, R., and Jørgensen, S. (2000) *Social Risk Management: a New Conceptual Framework for Social Protection and Beyond*. Washington, DC: World Bank.

Lazear, E. (2000) 'Economic Imperialism', *Quarterly Journal of Economics*, 115, 99–146.

MERG (1993) *Making Democracy Work: a Framework for Macroeconomic Policy in South Africa*. Cape Town: CDS.

Oishi, T. (2001) *The Unknown Marx: Reconstructing a Unified Perspective*. London: Pluto Press.

Olson, M., and Kähkönen, S. (2000) *A Not-So-Dismal Science: a Broader View of Economies and Societies*. Oxford: Oxford University Press.

Putnam, R. (2000) *Bowling Alone: the Collapse and Revival of American Community*. New York: Simon and Schuster.

Radin, M. (1996) *Contested Commodities*. Cambridge, MA: Harvard University Press.

Rudolph, S. (2000) 'Civil Society and the Realm of Freedom', *Economic and Political Weekly*, 35, 1762–9.

Sack, R. (1992) *Place, Modernity, and the Consumer's World: a Relational Framework for Geographical Analysis*. Baltimore: Johns Hopkins University Press.

Standing, G. (2000) 'Brave New Worlds? A Critique of Stiglitz's World Bank Rethink', *Development and Change*, 31, 737–63.

Stiglitz, J. (1998) 'More Instruments and Broader Goals: Moving Toward the Post Washington Consensus', *The 1998 WIDER Annual Lecture*. Helsinki: WIDER.

Temple, J. (2000) 'Growth Effects of Education and Social Capital in the OECD', *Symposium on the Contribution of Human and Social Capital to Sustained Economic Growth and Well-Being*. Quebec: OECD. (www) http://www.oecd.org/dataoecd/5/46/1825293. pdf. (12.05.04).

Wade, R. (2001) 'Showdown at the World Bank', *New Left Review*, 124–37.

Warde, A. (1994) 'Consumers, Consumption and post-Fordism'. In R. Burrows and B. Loader (eds), *Towards a Post-Fordist Welfare State?* London: Routledge.

5
Democratization and Social Policy

Laurence Whitehead

Introduction

Democratization and development are both forward-looking concepts. That is to say, they refer to processes of cumulative social change that can result in future political and economic outcomes that are qualitatively different from (and superior to) present conditions. As such, both concepts are necessarily long-term, dynamic, and macro-historical in scope. They also both express a normative standpoint. (It would not make sense to classify as 'development' a transformation to a state of affairs that was judged qualitatively inferior to its starting point.) Indeed, from a genealogical perspective they are both offshoots of the western/enlightenment ideal of progress. In an earlier phase of social science theorizing they were both subsumed under the umbrella discourse of 'modernization'. But as political science and economics subsequently became more professionalized and differentiated democratization and development were isolated in separate analytical compartments, and efforts were made to strip both of them of their historical and subjective connotations. They were isolated, objectified, dissolved into measurable proxies and separated from their ethical foundations. Such analytical procedures were initially a healthy antidote to the ideological distortions and teleological biases implicit in much classical discussion of 'progress' and more recently of 'modernization', but the antidote produced its own harmful 'side effects'. Since the end of the Cold War efforts have been made by the UNDP and others to reconcile the requirements of contemporary social science methodology with the holistic characteristics of these concepts, and to bring the discourses of democracy and development back into contact with each other, while restoring their energizing value commitments. This chapter is a further effort in that direction. But the key assumption here is that there is no easy reconciliation of theoretically incompatible positions, and that a successful approach involved a return to first principles. So the thrust of this chapter is to *'reculer pour mieux sauter'*.

At the most abstract level both democracy and development can be conceptualized so broadly that they converge into a single image of the good society. This is the dominant western image of progress in the post-Cold War world, the 'true and only heaven' recently dissected by Christopher Lasch.[1] Even after the Soviet collapse it is by no means the only available image of the good society, but it is the only universal image. The remaining alternatives are either theocratic (confined to true believers), or in some way particularist (confined to particular localities, ethnicities, nationalities, or culture groups). Those with the most secure access to this good society seem increasingly preoccupied with its insecurities and insufficiencies, and they have some sound reasons for their concern. But the proportion of the total population living in so-called 'industrial' countries has fallen from 31 per cent in 1960 to 22 per cent in 1992, and the proportion living in OECD countries has fallen from 21 per cent to 15 per cent over the same period.[2] Many OECD citizens (probably an increasing proportion) lack full and secure access to the benefits of the western 'good society', and the great majority of non-OECD inhabitants have only the most nominal and precarious claims to the socio-political status of modern citizenship.

This essay reflects on the interrelationships between two key components of the secularized liberal image of the 'good society' – political democracy and economic development. These two components can be detached from their theoretical moorings, narrowly defined in order to reduce the overlap between them, and then represented by simplified empirical proxies (such as electoral competition and alternation, and GDP per capita), which can then be tested for association and co-variance. Recently there has been something of a growth industry in this type of investigation, although the insights generated may seem meagre, considering the efforts expended.[3] If we search for patterns of association between democracy and economic development in the post-Cold War world, our samples will be heavily weighted towards a particular *kind* of democracy, and a currently fashionable notion of economic development. It by no means follows that either pre-1989 or twenty-first century variants of democracy will be associated in the same way with economic development, as understood in earlier (or perhaps in later) periods. Ahistorical 'objective' indicators of democracy and development can, of course, be constructed without reference to such contextual meanings. Thus, on standard indicators Chile was as much of a democracy in 1940 and in 1970 as in 1990, even though what this signified in terms of social repre-sentation and development objectives was radically different at each point in time. Similarly, over *some* periods and on *some* aggregate indicators Botswana can be bracketed with Singapore (and why not Saudi Arabia?) as exceptionally successful instances of economic development, without regard for the extreme dissimilarities of sociopolitical structure, and of collective beliefs and aspirations, which separate them. But this chapter seeks to identify lines of interaction between democracy and development rather than to generate purportedly objective correlations. For that purpose it is important to specify the context, meaning, and sub-types of the categories involved. This chapter attempts to provide a corrective to the ahistorical and reductionist tendencies in such studies, by reconnecting each of the two key categories within their respective theoretical and historical contexts. The intention is to restore a sense of perspective to our judgements about the immediate present, and to re-establish the reflexivity latent in our notions, both of political democracy and of economic development. Although these two concepts share some common assumptions they have distinctive roots and associations and can be analysed in isolation from each other. However, I will conclude the chapter with some suggestions about how they may proceed to converge.

The longue durée

The idea of political democracy has a history that is long and, chequered, and which has been rather precisely charted. Indeed, several recent scholarly analyses have claimed, without unreasonable distortion, that the 2,500th anniversary of its creation by Cleisthenes fell due in 1993.[4] During the course of that long period diverse embodiments of the idea have been claimed in a wide range of settings. Thus, political democracy has been thought to be compatible with a slave-based economy, not only in antiquity but also in the New World (this was the 'Washington Consensus' until 1 January 1863). Over the centuries it has been variously identified with urbanism and literacy, with the settlement of new lands (an annual Icelandic parliament was initiated in 930AD); with constitutional monarchy, with republicanism; with some forms of European imperial conquest (such as the extension of the 'Westminster system'), and with some forms of resistance to imperial rule; with Christianity, and with secular liberalism; and, in our lifetimes, both with the relentless advance of socialism, and equally with the inevitable hegemony of capitalism.

For most of this long period educated opinion has been hostile to, or fearful of, political democracy (which is often equated with mob rule, or the triumph of mediocrity). After the (mostly failed) democratic revolutions of 1848, however, a new synthesis of political constitutionalism combined with economic liberalism began to pave the way towards a more conservative variant of 'democracy'. The concept has been associated with a variety of different social experiments across time and space, each of which needs to be duly contextualized. For example, a good case can be made that for about half a century after 1870 across South America a certain ('oligarchical') variant of civilian constitutional rule was quite strongly associated with a model of export-oriented development based on the exchange of various primary products for imported capital goods (notably railways, ports, telegraphs, etc.). This was not 'democracy' in the abstract (indeed it contained a number of features that would seem distinctly undemocratic to the modern eye), and the associated model of development was neither of universal validity nor of permanent duration (it entered into crisis as the internal combustion engine displaced the train, and Britain lost her ascendancy). So we must be attentive to the boundary conditions limiting the coexistence of this particular type of democracy and this distinctive process of development. Nevertheless, within such spatial and temporal limits we can pursue some quite significant hypotheses concerning, if not causation in the strong sense, then at least recurrent patterns of connectedness and elective affinity. My impression is that foreign bankers, merchants and investors consistently demanded sanctity of contract and predictability of government. Both civilian constitutionalism and export-oriented growth were organized largely in response to that functional requirement. Assuming that this interpretation can withstand scrutiny, we would have identified one important type of linkage between a particular variant of political order, and a specific episode in history of economic development. This would be a useful story to bear in mind when investigating the association between other variants of 'democracy' and alternative development strategies in different periods of time or in other parts of the world. But any attempt to turn it into a general law, or to bracket this type of experience with, say, that of the peasant-based electoral regimes of interwar Europe, and their strategies of economic nationalism, would be misconceived in principle and disinformative in practice. At least from the late nineteenth century onwards the notion of democracy has been appropriated by western establishments and largely deradicalized, a process which reached its culmination during the Cold War, when efforts were made to assimilate nearly all of the broad spectrum of anti-communist regimes into the 'democratic' camp, to the exclusion of more 'neutral', or unreliable, regimes (even those displaying considerably greater degrees of political openness). Now, in the absence of a Soviet alternative, which could attempt to rival western pretensions to universalism and modernity, the ideal of political democracy can claim the nominal allegiance of the entire West, and perhaps much of the rest of the world as well.[5] But if its chequered and subversive history is forgotten it becomes a deradicalized ideal, a procedural formality, even an irrelevance to those still in search of that elusive goal of the good society.

The idea of economic development is more recent, and its history is less well studied. Of course, the *reality* of economic development can be traced back far before classical Greece, but the *idea* could not be elaborated until pre-market beliefs about such matters as the fixity of wants and the existence of a 'just price' had been superseded. In the European tradition the idea that wants were in principle unlimited, and the related idea that relative prices should reflect relative scarcities (in relation to unlimited wants), seem not to have displaced pre-market beliefs until well after the Reformation. Before that the Catholic monopoly on higher learning and morality blocked the emergence of modern economic reasoning[6] (and pre-Christian classical teachings also rested on the same pre-market assumptions, so that in place of the modern idea of economic development the Greeks and Romans thought in terms of historical cycles of growth and decay). It is probably anglocentric of me to date comparative and reflexive thinking about economic development to the Scottish Enlightenment, and to take Hume, Ferguson and, above all, Smith as the founding authors in this tradition, but even if we shifted to their counterparts in Continental Europe (Cantillon, Quesnay, Turgot, etc.) we would still start somewhere in the Enlightenment Age since it was only then that economics and the economy became established as a distinct and separate subject and system.[7] Compared to the 2,500-year debate on democracy, our ideas about economic development stretch back no more than one tenth as long.

The two central assertions about economic development in the *Wealth of Nations* are that 'the division of labour is the great cause of the increase of public opulence', and that the prime component of this division is commercial exchange between town and country ('the exchange of rude for manufactured produce'), which produces gains that are 'mutual and reciprocal'. Savings are required to accumulate the capital needed to finance such transactions. Although these twin contentions yielded powerful insights into processes of economic differentiation which were already perceptible in Europe, and which could be extended across the globe, they fell far short of a comprehensive or universally applicable account of economic development. Indeed, Smith still retained the notion that there must eventually be some upper limit to 'the degree of opulence' attainable by any particular country – a limit set by its factor endowments, and by the prospect that rising prosperity would stimulate population growth until per capita income stabilized. He also regarded agricultural improvement as in some sense the bedrock of economic prosperity (indeed he almost followed Quesnay in the view that *real* – i.e. durable – wealth is in land) and he was not as alert as he might have been to the first stirrings of technological revolution in British industry (notably in cotton).[8]

Thus, economic development was early on associated with the modernization of agriculture and the rise of towns. Then (starting with the work of Malthus), it was linked to the growth of effective demand, perhaps promoted through public works (rather than through savings), and to the introduction of labour-saving machinery in industry rather than to the modernization of agriculture. It became associated with industrialization from the middle of the nineteenth century, as the notion of continuous, rather than episodic, technical progress in manufacturing came to the fore. In due course, this led to concern with the diffusion of technological dynamism from leading industrial nations to those seeking to 'catch up'. This opened the way to the idea that the economic development of latecomers might require a higher degree of public policy co-ordination and state intervention than had seemed appropriate to the founders of political economy. The rise of Keynesian economics reinforced the prestige of macroeconomics and of economic planning, thus creating a temporarily favourable environment for the establishment of a distinctive sub-discipline of 'development economics' after the Second World War. During the first half of the Cold War period, Hirschman is surely right to emphasize the importance of the Marshall Plan as providing a major impetus and source of encouragement to our nascent sub-discipline.[9] That, of course, reflected the Cold War requirement that economic development should take a form that would strengthen the West against the Soviet bloc. Indeed, both the spread of democracy and the pursuit of economic development in the so-called 'Third World' were heavily conditioned by the overriding requirements of bipolar conflict. This affects both the substantive content of the two categories, and the interactions between them. From the 1960s onwards development economics became increasingly divided over (or detached from) Cold War polarities – a stance which may have initially boosted its prestige, but which eventually contributed to its problems. Hirschman prefers to emphasize a related, but somewhat different source of political vulnerability – what he terms the 'development disasters' which followed decolonization in the 1960s. According to his view, when development theorists found that 'the promotion of economic growth entailed not infrequently a sequence of events involving serious retrogression in those other areas, including the wholesale loss of civil and human rights, the easy self-confidence that our sub-discipline exuded in the early stages was impaired'.[10] In other words, the un- or democratic practices that many Third World governments came to justify in the name of economic development demoralized a sub-discipline that had been rooted in western liberal assumptions about the nature of social progress. But by the 1970s, in Hirschman's words, 'the old liveliness is no longer there... new ideas are ever harder to come by... and the field is not adequately reproducing itself'.[11] This judgement foreshadowed the upsurge of what may loosely be labelled 'neo-liberal' perspectives on economic development in the 1980s, under which economic development became associated with 'getting prices right' by reinforcing international market disciplines and strengthening private property rights.

One solution to this problem was to retreat into more technical work on the efficient allocation of resources; another was to switch from concern with 'growth' to concern with 'basic needs'. The former rested on the illusion that 'by confining itself to smaller, highly technical problems, development economics could carry on regardless of political cataclysms', and the latter dissolved 'the hitherto unique maximum of development economics (income per capita)' into 'a variety of partial objectives, each requiring consultation with different experts'. Both solutions struck Hirschman in 1980 as cop-outs from the basic goal – all-round emancipation from backwardness. He concluded that 'the challenge posed by dismal politics must be met rather than avoided or evaded. By now it has become quite clear that this cannot be done by development economics alone'.[12]

In the aftermath of decolonization (a process largely overlooked in Hirschman's brief survey, although it was surely central to the tale he told) there was widespread uncertainty over the credentials of western development theorists as critics of Third World political repression. 'Post-colonial guilt' on the left combined with Cold War realpolitik on the right to insulate debates over economic development from concern with the issues of political democracy. Until the end of the Cold War the international financial institutions explicitly underscored this insulation by stressing that their charters precluded them from interfering in the internal political affairs of member states. 'Development' became a supposedly apolitical goal, to be achieved through technical means, whereas 'democracy' was seen as a matter of domestic choice or subjective preference not to be imposed (or even materially encouraged) from without. It is hard to find a better illustration of the social construction of an is/ought dichotomy.

With the end of the Cold War, and the rise of a postcolonial generation no longer hung up over the struggle for national sovereignty, but instead missing the freedoms that were lost during state formation, the international context has radically changed. The 'democratization of development' can be put back on the agenda, to accompany the development of democratization. Development studies can and should no longer 'avoid or evade' the 'challenge of dismal politics'.

Democratizing development

Reviewing classical debates on 'democracy' and 'development', and considering the ways in which these categories have been adjusted to new contexts over time, leads to the conclusion that in the twenty-first century what we understand by 'development' could very well incorporate some very considerable elements drawn from democratic theory. Likewise, our future conceptions of 'democracy', appropriately understood and updated, could quite properly include much that has recently been studied within the limiting confines of the sub-discipline of 'economic development'. When the application of knowledge, rather than mechanical power, provides the main key to economic prosperity the most effective producers can be expected to set a high standard of demand for citizenship rights and governmental accountability. When a central task of modern democratic government is to secure informed assent to complex public choices in the ears of economic management, our conception of 'development' can hardly continue to exclude consideration of the social acceptability and legitimacy of the policies to be selected. It is in this area of convergence between notions of 'democracy' and 'development' that the best future of development studies lies.[13]

As indicated by this thumbnail sketch, economic development, like democracy, has already appeared in many different guises, and has at different points been identified with a wide range of apparently somewhat incompatible partners. Viewed from this *longue durée* perspective it would be surprising if either of these have suddenly become constants, or if they have shed the capacity to mutate and accommodate to unforeseen contexts. It would therefore be surprising if either had become so fixed and inflexible as to block out convergence with the other. Seen from this historical perspective, recent identifications of democracy with capitalism, and of economic development with market liberalization, are more likely to prove liaisons of convenience rather than ultimate identities. But as we have seen, the content of both concepts has varied over time, so any effort either to separate or to reconcile them must start by addressing the definitional and conceptual issues. If democracy is understood as meaning no more than the holding of competitive elections, and the consequent alternation in government of rival parties in accordance with the changing preferences of the electors, then the spread of democracy may have little bearing upon social development outcomes. Similarly, if economic development is understood as essentially consisting of a high and sustained rate of economic growth, perhaps accompanied by some social emergency funds and some targeting of benefits to the very poor, then the choice between establishing a democracy or maintaining an authoritarian regime may be more clearly linked to the *style* of social development than to its *level*. At this level of abstraction it is possible to think of interconnections between democracy and development that could be supportive, and of others that could be obstructive, but neither type of linkage looks particularly compelling. Overall, the null hypothesis would seem as plausible as any. The procedural minimum version of democracy need not carry many implications for social development; and the 'growth-first' version of economic development leaves it open to doubt whether democracy or authoritarian rule produces better social development outcomes.

But during the 1990s and the early years of the twenty-first century the conviction has grown that democracy and development are more intimately interconnected and more positively associated than has recently been suggested. Cross-country data sets have been scrutinized to test for association (with somewhat mixed results).[14] Various democracy-related phrases – such as 'participation', 'civil society', 'empowerment', – have assumed an increasing prominence among the goals of development pursued by international donors. As more developing countries have adopted at least the outward appearance of democratic political practices, the traditional LDC lobby opposed to linking democracy with development has weakened. The majority of developing countries can now hope to benefit if developmental assistance carries democratic conditionality, and the donor countries are increasingly inclined to associate democracy with social development and therefore attach such conditions to their aid.

If this shift in beliefs and practices is to prove more than just a passing fashion it will have to be accompanied by a reconceptualization of both democracy and development. Indeed, it seems that just such a debate may be getting underway in both of the relevant scholarly communities. Social development provides the key point of intersection between the separate academic discourses of democratization and economic development. To the extent that these discourses converge, social policies and citizenship entitlements will move from the margins to the centre of attention in these scholarly communities. The UNDP's cumulative work on 'human development' has generated an extensive empirical database backed by considerable theoretical groundwork designed to shift public policy priorities in this direction where both democracy and prosperity are valued as proxies for human freedom.[15] However, it is one thing to shift the focus of attention, and quite another to integrate the new objects of study into a coherent and operational analytical framework. The 'rights' discourse underlying the 'human development' perspective tends to reject trade-offs or sequencing strategies that would involve prioritizing some claims at the expense of others. The World Bank's *World Development Report 2000/2001* makes an uncomfortable attempt to reconcile this human development perspective with the Bank's more traditional emphasis on results-oriented strategic choices. Thus it concedes that 'democracy is intrinsically valuable for human well-being as a manifestation of human freedom. Political freedoms have enormous impact on the lives and capabilities of citizens'. But, perhaps mindful of earlier World Bank enthusiasms for some undemocratic regimes, this *prise de position* is quickly counterbalanced by reference to the record of 'a few notably development-oriented countries, such as the Republic of Korea, before they became pluralist democracies'. (A tactful veil is drawn over those developmental-oriented countries, such as China, which still express no intention of following such a path.) 'Democracy – both representative and participatory – is a good in itself'. (This formulation presumably enables the Bank to commend some regimes that do not allow competitive multi-party elections.) 'But democratic political processes alone are not enough to ensure that poverty reduction is taken as a key priority in society's efforts'.[16] (So despite the intrinsic value of democracy, this language of priorities leaves open the possibility not only that something more may be needed to reduce poverty, but that something different may work better.) Given the need for such intellectual contortions it may be all too tempting for the mainstream development agencies to maintain an established framework, with some 'add-on' references to social development, environmental sustainability, gender balance, or political empowerment, that sound encouraging but that do not disturb the core assumptions or modes of analysis. Notwithstanding any discursive shift towards integrating democracy and development at the analytical level, when it comes to policy making and goal setting the democratic component tends to be conspicuous by its absence. Thus the UN's Millennium Development Goals for 2015 include global targets for income, education, demography, and sustainable development (all costed and quantified), but no political goals.[17] Similarly, advocates of democratic conditionality are often inclined to focus solely on political variables and may be tempted to treat social welfare as an optional extra.

The old mainstream policy framework has a clear rationale. If resources are to be allocated between countries in a manner that rewards 'good performance', then the criteria for ranking and evaluating performance need to be explicit and verifiable. In fact it is not all that easy to distinguish precisely between authoritarian and democratic regimes, or between countries pursuing sustainable growth policies and those on sub-optimal paths. But at least on the old narrow definitions of democracy and development there is an established tradition of measurement and a conventional literature of causal explanation. However, if our conception of democracy is broadened to include such fuzzy notions as 'empowerment', or if the focus on economic growth is diluted by the importation of more imprecise and perhaps culturally bounded elements of social development as citizen rights, then the criteria for judging performance may become unmanageably complex, and perhaps increasingly arbitrary. There is, indeed, plenty of evidence that in the past undemocratic regimes have attempted to conceal their deficiencies by invoking their supposedly superior systems of political participation and social integration. Similarly, governments that were unwilling to pursue sound economic growth policies have sheltered behind the excuse that they must protect irreversible social conquests. Given such antecedents, defenders of the old framework can make a respectable case for their position. Merely talking about participation and social welfare gives no guarantee of improvements in performance. They continue to argue that citizenship entitlements and social development programmes can only be 'added-on' provided economic rationality and 'good government' are first respected.

However, this established framework confronts mounting practical and political difficulties. On the practical side, for a regime to be classified as 'democratic' is normally to receive a positive evaluation, not just a neutral descriptive designation. Advantages, prestige, and self-respect flow from such labelling or speech acts. Likewise, for an economic policy to be designated an example of economic development is also beneficial. In both cases political leaders strive to secure favourable endorsements, and to avoid or deflect negative labelling. So debate about which precise instances fit within the broad and blurry categories of 'democracy' and 'development' can easily become politicized. The same applies to propositions involving the linkages between the two. Indeed, on a strong view we may be dealing with 'essentially contested' concepts, and with a discourse about their interrelationship that to a considerable degree reflects these underlying struggles for power. The recent establishment of a range of independent and standardized annual tabulations covering the entire world (such as HDI, the Freedom House Yearbook of Freedom, and the Transparency International's Corruption Perception Index) provides an important corrective to previous excesses of subjectivism, but it does not dispense with the need for informed personal and collective judgement not only in the interpretation of the rankings, but also in deciding whether to accept their relative evaluations.[18] Other practical difficulties include:

(i) With the spread of democracy come mounting demands for decentralization and the devolution of public policies to more local levels of government.

(ii) Similarly, with the spread of market-based systems of competition and allocation comes a shift in the locus of economic power away from the government agencies hitherto either charged with implementing optimal growth policies.

(iii) Moreover, where social development has been allowed to falter, perhaps through omissions arising from too narrow a conception of 'good performance', the evidence has mounted that such omissions easily produce negative feedback that can eventually destabilize procedural democracy and/or disrupt 'sound' growth strategies.

Practical considerations of this kind, reinforced by the political preferences of a growing number of both donor and recipient governments, have driven defenders of the old framework to make concessions, and even to dilute the clarity of their initial core convictions. Conventional 'billiard ball' models of causation, and totemic quantitative indicators of macro-performance, no longer inspire quite the same deference as in an earlier period of technocratic self-confidence, but neither have they been entirely dethroned. Those who favour the incorporation of 'softer' styles of explanation and evaluation have yet to develop generally accepted alternative approaches.

It should be possible to move beyond this state of affairs, and to reconceptualize both democracy and development in a manner that would provide a superior and integrated analytical framework and perhaps even a more democratic policy rationale. The UNDP's *Human Development Report*, UNRISD's *Visible Hands-Taking Responsibility for Social Development*, and related academic initiatives indicate that the search for a substitute framework is well underway, although as yet the results remain incipient. Freedom of expression and association provides some offset to the risks of man-made famines and other preventable 'natural' disasters. Citizens with voting rights can exercise some leverage over public policy priorities, and may prefer clean drinking water to pharaonic dams and similar mega-projects. If social development elicits local ownership and citizen participation it may constrain wasteful arms expenditure and tilt international relations towards co-operation rather than conflict. The traditional separation between politics and economics, both narrowly conceived, has obstructed the investigation of such potential linkages (forgetting what Gunnar Myrdal had once taught us about 'cumulative and circular' causation in development studies).

Some new directions for research

It may be possible to 'democratize development', but in such a process there will be no short cuts or easy add-ons. It will be necessary to return to first principles for the reconceptualizations that are required, and it will also be necessary to reconsider some basic questions of method. As a first step we would have to *'reculer pour mieux sauter'*. Thereafter it would seem critical to identify a cluster of relatively specific and empirically researchable topics and issues where a more integrated view of developmental democracy is likely to yield particularly distinctive and productive insights. A promising cluster would be found in some aspects of social policy, particularly as it arises in a subset of relatively stable and well institutionalized new democracies.

The first principles in question are very broad, and can be outlined quite concisely. As already indicated above, democratization and development can both be viewed as long-term, open-ended processes of social constitution. Understood in such terms it becomes possible to reconceptualize them as not just contingently or instrumentally associated. Indeed, they may be mutually constitutive (derived from a unitary conception of human rights, human freedom, and of self-realization). The 'elective affinity' between them may be traced to a common foundation of dialogue, deliberation, and consent. But if we follow this line of reasoning we have to absorb the implications of open-endedness. There is no universal and measurable end-point, at which democratization ends and development is completed. The goals of democratic development remain subject to revision and perfection by future generations of citizens, and they may vary over time and space. Just as the development and democratization of the US was not finally accomplished either in 1787, or in 1865, or in 1965, so also the developmental democracies of Brazil, India, Mexico and indeed the United Kingdom will remain under construction over future generations.

These are obviously complex and controversial tasks of reconceptualization that must be elaborated more fully elsewhere. Moving beyond this quite abstract level of theorizing, one could seek to identify some relatively concrete historical experiences and areas of public policy where such a perspective may generate otherwise unavailable insights. My concern is both with isolating topics suitable for comparative empirical enquiry and with highlighting methods of investigation appropriate to this theoretical perspective. For illustrative purposes here are four relevant topics of personal interest to me:

(i) The western hemisphere regional experience of almost universal political democracy accompanied by often extreme and typically unchanging levels of inequality and social injustice;

(ii) Within this regionwide framework, one could undertake some 'paired comparisons' of national variation (e.g. between Costa Rica and Nicaragua or the Dominican Republic and Haiti or Argentina and Chile);

(iii) Since this perspective directs attention to long-term holistic processes one might also examine a single national experience over several generations (Bolivia could be chosen for this purpose);

(iv) But we should also disaggregate and examine key areas of public policy where the linkage between citizenship and distribute outcomes is of particular relevance (e.g. citizenship and water rights, citizenship and public security). Such topics for comparative research invite reflection on methodological issues as well.

Otherwise, insensitive ('brutalist') criteria of classification can only obstruct the detection of such patterns of association as are worth extracting from the data. Consider two extreme examples of troubling 'real life situations' which could easily escape detection under a brutalist either/or system of classification using simple-minded indicators. In order to judge whether a regime which denies political and civil rights to women, and requires them to take the veil, can under any circumstances be classified as 'democratic', we are surely required to consider from first principles the range and boundaries of the concept of democracy. Similar considerations arise when assessing whether 'economic development' applies, for example, to a situation of very high per capita consumption financed by oil revenues, where most of the productive work is undertaken by immigrants lacking citizenship rights. Borderline cases would be less extreme, but more common. Thus, a considerable number of Islamic states test the universality of our standard conception of 'democracy', and the current controversy over the 'Asian model' challenges some core western assumptions concerning 'development'.

Both the UNDP index and the Freedom House ratings make use of a series of partial indicators, which are then aggregated according to an arbitrary formula in order to produce monotone country rankings. Depending upon the issues being analysed, and the conceptual framework of the enquiry, it may be more appropriate to work with the disaggregated series, or to combine them according to a different formula. For example, the UNDP's educational attainment index could be of special interest both to those working with a 'human capital' model of development and to those who view 'civil society' as the core element in any long-term process of democratization. Alternative conceptions of democracy and development might privilege other variables.

Sensitivity to the historical variability and contextual nuances associated with these two categories can help us to interrogate the comparative data discursively, and to identify what sub-classifications (if any) we should admit within the categories. The same applies to which economic processes we should designate as instances of 'development'. These judgements ought to be defended (and if necessary revised) in the lights of rational debate. They are not purely subjective. But we cannot evade the need to defend our choices of social categories, and our labelling procedures, by sheltering behind externally given 'objective' numerical indicators. For example, if we opt for GDP per capita as our yardstick of 'economic development', then we have to justify the consequence that Brunei scores seven times higher than Cuba (a large differential would also exist if we used rates of change rather than absolute levels). Equally, if we accept the Freedom House ratings we commit ourselves to the proposition that Negara Brunei Darussalam and Cuba are very similarly placed in terms of political freedom (12 and 13 respectively, compared to a bottom score of 14). To me personally both these comparisons seem problematic, obscuring more than they illuminate about the two countries. I do not have much confidence in aggregate statistical tests of association, which rely on raw data of this calibre.

To make a solid and convincing comparative judgement about the status of either 'democracy' or 'development' in these (or indeed in *any*) countries requires a substantial familiarity with each case, together with a well-grounded attention to the boundaries and nuances of the categories employed. The more countries under consideration the less the detail of each case affects the overall conclusion, it can be argued, but even so a responsible judgement requires conscientious consideration of each instance (as can be demonstrated by considering how each of us is likely to view the exercise as a whole if *our particular* country is egregiously misclassified). Therefore, countries about which the investigator is insufficiently familiar should be investigated with extra diligence – or, alternatively, excluded from the comparison on the grounds that the bad data would otherwise swamp the good.

So what techniques are appropriate for assessing long-term holistic change in a single country? How should regional and paired comparisons be structured to address such issues? Do our standard methods of sampling and data collection permit adequate analysis of citizenship issues in such critical areas of public policy as water privatization and the provision of community policing? Where causal chains are long and multiple, and where outcomes depend upon socially constructed perceptions of complex categories, too much insistence on necessary connection and mechanical causation is likely both to confuse and to mislead. Other, more historical and contextual (narrative or 'configurative') methods of judgement and interpretation may help to correct such deficiencies, or may at least usefully supplement standard social science procedures of objectification (such as the elaboration of decontextualized quantitative indicators). If we are serious in regarding both democratization and development as normatively desired interactive processes founded upon participation and consent, then we need to give due weight to methods of interpretation that take into account the understandings of the parties involved. Many developmental disasters have arisen from the past failure of donors and policy makers to attend to their discursive dimension, and some democratic regimes (such as Argentina at the time of writing) seem to have fallen victim to the same insulation from social reality. Thus the case for methodological eclecticism in this field is not simply an arid footnote from within academia. It arises as a necessary consequence of the reconceptualizations currently in progress and as a required response to the exigencies of realistic policy making.

Conclusion

This brief *tour d'horizon* of the scope for reconciling democratization and development has indicated some potentially worthwhile topics and some innovative approaches. But at least four big analytical questions still need to be resolved. First, how are developmental priorities to be established, and reconciled, once the traditional criterion of growth maximization has been relaxed? Second, how is good performance to be compared, evaluated, and rewarded if a variety of somewhat competing and partially subjective long-term goals are to become the centrepiece of a new drive for integrated 'social development'? Third, since on any realistic definition long-term democratic and social development provokes resistance and conflict, and is therefore prone to periodic interruption and even reversal, how is such turbulence to be interpreted and (possibly) managed? (If managed, by whom, answerable to what constituency?) Finally, since even on the most optimistic of assumptions about the pace of progress, most new democracies will for generations to come continue to include large numbers of poor citizens whose urgent social policy needs can at best only be addressed gradually, how can democratization and social development be stabilized in the intervening decades?

Merely to list these questions is sufficient to demonstrate the scale of the task required before a new integrated analytical framework can fully substitute for the old dichotomy. Here are a few suggestions, some of which are more robustly established than others. First, as regards the establishment of developmental priorities, in principle the answer must lie with the newly enfranchised citizens of these developmental democracies. No doubt they will periodically misread the available alternatives, and will make policy mistakes. But as democratization proceeds 'ownership' of the development process is bound to pass from the specialized agencies and peak ministries towards the local authorities and societies directly and permanently affected. (Admittedly this assertion rests on a view of democratization as a long-term cumulative process of social learning, rather than just as a one-off shift in the rules of governing elite circulation.)

Secondly, on the evaluation of social development performance, international comparative indicators will remain indispensable, and will have to be refined further. But on an integrated view of development all evaluations will need increasingly to take account of the expectations and perceptions of the citizens in question. That too follows from the idea that democratic development requires local 'ownership'.

Thirdly, the realities of conflict and non-linearity in long-term processes of social development pose a severe analytical challenge that cannot be resolved purely by invoking democratic authority. Local ownership cannot be absolute. It must be qualified by respect for the opinions and experiences of others, including experts and distant donors. Social development in a liberalized international system must be cosmopolitan, and constrained within an agreed framework of basic rights and values. On this view an integrated approach will require co-operation and co-responsibility across international and indeed intercontinental boundaries. A social catastrophe in, say, Afghanistan or Albania can jeopardize both democracy and development far afield and to the opposite extremes of the alphabet. Recently there has been some progress in generating norms of conduct for managing such conflicts and reversals, but the challenge to the existing framework of international assumptions remain acute.

Finally, at the domestic level, the management techniques needed to contain frustration while gradually diminishing the backlog of legitimate and unmet citizen demands can easily jar with both the standard operating procedures of the development agencies and the impersonal logic of the market economy. Once democracy is understood as more than a simple mechanism of elite circulation, politics regains its status as an autonomous sphere of social action with its own messy logic, and awkward outcomes. UNRISD is right to refer to the 'visible hands' that will then 'take responsibility for social development', but more analysis is needed to distinguish the legitimate exercise of democratic authority from the old vices of mismanagement from behind a veil of good intentions. Once development is understood as a process of social construction and not just of growth maximization, then local creativity and experimentation can be celebrated. But here too lurk the dangers of distortion and manipulation. A strong analytical framework, grounded on solid international consensus and backed by the widely accepted lessons of experience, will be required if such experiments are to be more than cosmetic 'add-ons' to development, and are not to prove costly 'subtractions from' conventional growth.

Notes

1. Lasch (1991).
2. UNDP (1994).
3. One recent review surveys 46 studies and rejects the hypothesis that political democracy is negatively associated with economic development. It identified education, investment, and 'governance', as potential bearers of a positive association (see Campos (1994)).
4. The chequered legacy of the Greek tradition is emphasized in Patterson (1991), which stresses the paradoxical role of slavery. For the evolution of democracy as a political ideal, which originated from a practical expedient, see Dunn (1992). For the state of contemporary classical scholarship see Osborne and Hornblower (1994).

For the history of anti-democratic sentiment in western civilization, see Tolbert Roberts (1994).

5. Allegiance to an ideal can be called nominal only when it is honoured at no cost. Even in the post-Cold War world those favouring political democracy could face some quite demanding tests of their allegiance, however – in Algeria, for example, or in Chechnya, Israel or even in advanced democracies caught up in panics about terrorism and insecurity.

6. In Max Weber's account 'The ethos of the classical economic morality is summed up in the old judgement passed on the merchant . . . homo mercator vix aut numquam potest Deo placere; he may conduct himself without sin but cannot be pleasing to God. This proposition was valid down to the 15th century, and the first attempt to modify it slowly matured in Florence': Weber (1961).

7. See Dumont (1973) and Rothschild (2001).

8. Rostow (1990) gives as much space to Hume as to Smith, although the former was mainly interested in the mutual gains from regional and international comparative advantage. Rostow's large volume may be faulted for what Richard Rorty has labelled 'doxography' ('The real trouble with doxography is that it is a half-hearted attempt to tell a new story of intellectual progress by describing all texts in terms of recent discoveries'), but it does contain a rather thorough and systematic comparison of most major growth theorists prior to his own work.

9. He notes that development economics emerged in very unusual and, as it turned out, temporary circumstances in England and the US (not the developing countries themselves) after 1945. These included the discredit of orthodox economics deriving from the Depression of the 1930s, and the arrival of international Keynesianism, in the form of the Harrod–Domar growth model, with its implication of an enhanced role for the state in promoting late industrializers. He concludes by suggesting that the founders of development economics displayed a paternalist, perhaps even somewhat contemptuous, attitude towards developing countries, when they assumed that problems of backwardness could be so easily overcome by the adoption of development planning. This presumed that such societies were governed only by interests, and had no passions.

10. Hirschman (1981).

11. Ibid.

12. Ibid.

13. Partha Dasgupta's recent attempt at grand political economy in the Smithian tradition confirms that reintegration of the 'moral sentiments' into economics need not involve sentimentality or the loss of analytical rigour. Following Sen (1995), his focus is on 'well-being' (understood to include income, health, liberty, and literacy) rather than economic growth.

14. Little illumination on the links between democracy and development can be expected from data sets that include dozens of 'failed' or 'near failed' states, and that count countries the size of India and China as single units to be compared with Dominica and Fiji. Of the 174 states classified in the Human Development Report 2000 perhaps as many as one-quarter are so recent and insecure that the question of survival dominates public policy, pushing tasks of political and economic development into the background. A few not-so-new states are also in this position. Although this refers to around a quarter of existing so-called 'developing' states, only a much smaller proportion of the total population of these countries are involved, since the list includes hardly any of the heavily populated nations. But if we consider, say, Timor (then still treated as within Indonesia) or

Tibet (within China) or Kashmir (within India) it is immediately apparent that there are highly populated regions within various of even the best established of 'Third World' states where the overriding concerns of contemporary public policy are almost as primordial as in comprehensively 'failed states' such as Afghanistan, Burundi, Georgia, Liberia, Rwanda, Somalia, Zaire, and so forth.

15. 'Human development is the process of enlarging people's choices by expanding human functionings and capabilities... Capabilities reflect the freedom to achieve functionings. In that sense human development is freedom'. Income levels are only one component of human development and are taken into account as a surrogate for the human choices permitted by a decent standard of living (when accompanied by health and knowledge); UNDP (2000).

16. See World Bank (2001). *World Development Report 2000/1: Attacking Poverty.* Washington: World Bank.

17. The central target is to halve the proportion of people living in extreme poverty (i.e. on a purchasing power parity income of less than one dollar a day) by 2015. The other six goals serve essentially to buttress the durability of this advance. The package adds up to what is intended to be an incontrovertible and unifying objective – minimum goals, but ones that are agreed, attainable, and would make a real difference. Nevertheless, from a democratic perspective there is much to debate here. The international decision-making process is highly opaque, and it is far from clear who would be held responsible if the targets were missed. The targets themselves also merit discussion. Can any freedoms be suspended in order to accelerate their fulfilment? If halving extreme poverty is attainable, why wait until 2015? Why only halve the proportion? Are the rich to pay, or the only slightly less poor?

18. I scrutinized the 1994 HDI to assess whether its inter-country rankings coincided with my subjective impressions of countries I have studied. It struck me as questionable whether Cuba and Sri Lanka should be ranked virtually equal (at 89 and 90 respectively). In 2000 the ranking is Cuba 56, Sri Lanka 84. I also doubted the huge gap between Barbados (20) and Grenada (78). In 2000, they appear much closer, at 30 and 54 respectively.

Bibliography

Campos, N. (1994) 'Why Does Democracy Foster Economic Development? An Assessment of the Empirical Literature'. (*Unpublished*) Los Angeles: University of Southern California.

Dumont, L. (1973) *From Mandeville to Marx.* Chicago: Chicago University Press.

Dunn, J. (1992) *Democracy: the Unfinished Journey, 508BC to AD 1993.* Oxford: Oxford University Press.

Hirschman, A. O. (1981) 'The Rise and Decline of Development Economics'. In A. O. Hirschman (ed.), *Essays in Trespassing: Economics to Politics and Beyond.* Cambridge: Cambridge University Press.

Lasch, C. (1991) *The True and Only Heaven: Progress and Its Critics.* New York: Norton.

Osborne, R., and Hornblower, S. (1994) *Ritual, Finance, Politics: Athenian Democratic Accounts.* New York: Oxford University Press.

Patterson, O. (1991) *Freedom: Freedom in the Making of Western Culture.* (vol. 1) London: Basic Books.

Rostow, W. W. (1990) *Theories of Economic Growth from David Hume to the Present.* London: Oxford University Press.

Rothschild, E. (2001) *Economic Sentiments: Adam Smith, Condorcet, and the Enlightenment.* Boston: Harvard University Press.

Sen, A. (1995) *An Enquiry into Well-being and Destitution.* London: Oxford University Press.

Tolbert Roberts, J. (1994) *Athens on Trial: the Anti-democratic Tradition in Western Thought.* Princeton: Princeton University Press.

UNDP (1994) *Human Development Report 1994.* New York and Oxford: UNDP.

UNDP (2000) *Human Development Report 2000.* New York: UNDP.

Weber, M. (1961) *General Economic History.* New York: Collier.

World Bank (2001) *World Development Report 2000/1: Attacking Poverty.* Washington, DC: World Bank.

Part II
Micro- and Meso-Level Issues

6

Why Social Policy is Condemned to a Residual Category of Safety Nets and What to Do About it

Judith Tendler

Introduction

I would like to start by congratulating UNRISD for leading a badly needed initiative to re-think social policy in a way that does not condemn it to the residual category of 'safety nets'. There are several stubborn causes of this problem, including the ideological one, but I choose to dwell on four that are less obvious and that also lend themselves to suggestions for a UNRISD research agenda.

The *first* is a tendency in the international donor community to conceive of social policy in a way that allows them to 'projectize' and 'micro-ize' it – a tendency that, remarkably, shows little variation from left to right across the donor spectrum. The *second* relates to the demise of the now-discredited models of import-substituting industrialization and industrial policy, and the loss of their strategic focus on supporting the growth of local industry; this focus explicitly included employment concerns rather than marginalizing them. The *third* relates to the politics of the informal sector within developing countries, and how this – together with the preoccupation of the donor poverty agenda with the informal sector and small firms – renders more difficult the pursuit of certain aspects of a proper social policy agenda within countries. The *fourth* points to the importance of managing the generic conflict of interest between workers and owners of capital through institutions of conflict mediation within countries, and the way in which this agenda is undermined, unintentionally, by certain aspects of the poverty-reducing agenda of the donor community.

Projectizing and micro-izing

For all the talk of policy reforms, most donors – as funding organizations – have to organize their work around designing and funding projects. It is their *modus operandi*, their bread and butter. This 'project imperative', in turn, influences the way in which they define the poverty-reduction agenda, or any other for that matter. Historically, however, many of the needed social policy commitments and reforms that have had the largest proven impact on poverty – such as social security and other social-insurance mechanisms – evolved on a much broader canvas in terms of administration, policy and politics, and demand-making by organized groups. They did not emerge from the humble beginnings of the micro-ized or projectized approach, though the latter might fit comfortably within such a broader initiative.

Social investment funds (SIFs) are but one recent and major example of the project approach to poverty reduction, as supported by many donors, both large and small.[1] In such programmes, a central government agency or unit disburses grant funding to myriad communities, sometimes through local governments, for small projects like road paving or rural electrification, the building of schools or clinics, microcredit, and so on. Typically, the projects are said to be decided on by the community in a participatory fashion. Since the late 1980s, the World Bank, the Inter-American Development Bank, and the European donors together have committed more than US$3.5 billion to the creation and perpetuation of SIFs in more than 40 countries. The funds are routinely described as a 'safety net' for the poor against the adversities of macro programmes of adjustment and, more generally of economic growth in a globalized world.

Some attribute the large commitment of the major donors to SIFs as a poverty-reducing instrument to 'Washington Consensus' views about reducing the role of government, and of central government in particular. This does not explain, however, the equal enthusiasm for SIFs or SIF-type projects by other donors that often oppose the so-called 'Washington Consensus' or 'neo-liberal' views – such as NGOs and some of the smaller, more socially-oriented Northern European donors. In fact, the interest of these smaller donors can be better explained by their small size in comparison to the development banks, their provision of grants rather than loan funding, and the mandate of some of them to work through non-government organizations rather than governments. All this conspires toward an organizational imperative to produce a stream of bite-sized and discrete projects and, hence, to think in these terms.

The project-level view of the poverty problem, in turn, is highly compatible with other 'micro-ized' views of poverty reduction that are now widely held – briefly, that decentralization together with community participation produces better services for the poor, and that NGOs are important actors in the carrying out of this agenda. I am not saying that these views are necessarily wrong, but rather that this noisy celebration of 'the local' and non-governmental tends to distract attention – even of those seriously committed to the poor – from broader social policy reforms.

The predominantly micro views of how to approach poverty reduction have gained such strength that they seem to have become impregnable to contrary findings from evaluation research. For example, the findings of evaluations by the donors themselves on social funds – let alone of others – have been quite mixed. In particular, impacts on poverty and unemployment have often been found to be *in*significant, sometimes even when compared to more traditional and longer-lived employment-generating schemes.[2] This set of mixed findings does not mean that such decentralized schemes cannot serve other important purposes, such as the execution of myriad small works projects. It does suggest, however, that SIFs and similar projects may be a rather ineffective instrument for the purposes of reducing poverty and unemployment. To offer them to national leaders as a 'safety net' to catch those hurt by economic crisis can also provide these leaders, in certain ways, with a way *out* of facing the poverty challenge more seriously.

There is now an extensive literature on the SIF experience, including a vigorous debate on their pros and cons.[3] My purpose in raising them here is not to add to the debates or review them, but to point to the broader current of thinking they reflect and to how it contributes to the conundrum posed by Thandika Mkandawire as to why social policy is condemned to a residual category of safety nets.

For almost a decade, in sum, the 'projectizing' and 'micro-izing' mode of the operations of development organizations have captured and monopolized the imagination of the international development community, despite mixed evaluation findings. They have lulled many into believing that SIFs and other SIF-type projectizable initiatives will make significant contributions to resolving the twin problems of poverty and unemployment. The challenge to a research-supporting agency such as UNRISD is to bring the attention of the development community back to more powerful instruments.[4] The following three sections provide some examples of how this might be done.

Employment, economic development and implicit industrial policy

In the donor world, a kind of post-Cold-War 'take' has emerged on the policies, programmes, and lessons learned from the prior period of import-substituting industrialization (ISI) and strategic subsidization of investment in certain sectors to promote industrial growth. Whereas policies involving state subsidy and direction used to be denounced by those who did not like them as 'communist', today they elicit a response that is even more withering – namely, that this kind of thinking is 'old'. This has resulted in a kind of 'cultural revolution' with respect to the texts and the thinking of this prior period. No one is 'allowed' to praise anything that happened then, and students are not assigned the literature of that period, let alone the substantial research on that experience, which had negative *and* positive results.

Whatever judgments might be made today about the policies of the ISI period, and however less appropriate they might be in a trade-liberalized twenty-first-century world, policy concerns about employment creation in that period were wedded to those about economic development rather than, as today, mainly to social policy. Independently of whether the outcomes turned out to be good or bad or mixed, employment concerns had an explicit place *within* the policy thinking about economic development itself and shaped the various forms of public-sector support. Today, concerns about employment have no such home. No longer considered 'serious economic development', they are now relegated to the realm of social policy, safety nets, and small-enterprise and informal-sector specific programmes – a realm that has become marginal to the central project of economic growth. (The following section picks up on certain implications of this last development.)

The marginality is reinforced by the new functional home for these concerns – in social-action, welfare, and labour agencies – and outside the public sector in NGOs – all of which have always had less power and prestige than agencies dealing with 'economic development'. The placement of these activities among such 'social' agencies, and the 'distributive' or divisible nature of programmes that provide project funding for communities, also makes them highly suitable for patronage purposes. This, needless to say, compromises the employment-creating and poverty-reducing criteria that are supposed to guide the allocation of these funds.

To be sure, much of the industrial policy of the ISI period itself rode roughshod over existing local economies, and sometimes ignored the development potential of local-firm clusters that today have become the object of so much interest. Though the ISI policies of tariff protection were meant to support the development of local firms, then, they did not necessarily perform well in terms of enhancing the potential of existing concentrations of small and medium firms. Also, we have by now learned that some of the most effective assists for employment-creating growth are carried out by sub-national governments – states or provinces, and municipalities. Many such assists, in turn, were 'light', in contrast to the heaviness of the credit and other subsidies associated with the ISI period. Examples are the brokering of the connection to export markets, providing customized training to small-firm owners and their workers, or breaking particular efficiency-hampering infrastructure bottlenecks.

At the same time, however, the explicit and public articulation of industrial policy of the ISI period contributed to making the development of local industry and firms the subject of extensive examination and debate – in government, in development banks, in universities, and in the press. One important subject of policy attention was the attempt to forge customer–supplier linkages between foreign customer firms and local supplier firms, within the larger supportive policy context of laws requiring local content by foreign firms.

Today, in many countries, the debates about economic growth suffer from the lack of such attention to matters that directly and indirectly affect employment. It is not so much that industrial policy and its association with excessive subsidies and intervention is discredited, but that nothing as prestigious *and* inclusive of employment concerns has come to replace it in the current discourse about serious economic development. Hence many governments, including sub-national ones, are at a loss as to how to deal with various challenges of the post-trade-liberalization era. A typical example relates to the decisions of many large global buyers to encourage or require their developing-country suppliers to procure their equipment outside the country rather than locally, even in cases where there is substantial local supply; or of outsider companies, newly located in a country, that prefer buying from the foreign suppliers to which they are accustomed rather than from local suppliers; or of outsider firms buying local state enterprises, and switching their procurement from local supplier clusters to abroad.[5] These developments often result in unemployment problems that, under the benign neglect of today's implicit industrial policy, become the burden of social policy.

Perhaps even more significantly, anyone who has carried out field research in developing countries finds governments – despite the strong current anti-subsidy discourse – to be subsidizing industries in a variety of ways. One of the most conspicuous forms of this – though the details are not always made public – involves the subsidies provided to attract large transnational firms to locate in a particular country or state; in addition to the well-known tax exemptions and infrastructure investment, this includes significant credit at highly favourable terms and substantial discounts on public services such as telecommunications, electric power, and water supplies.

Though the degree of today's subsidization of industry is probably not as great as that of the previous ISI period – no one to my knowledge has actually made such a comparison – the more important difference between the two periods is the ad hoc nature of the subsidization of the current period. The current subsidies, that is, are more the outcome of individual deals between a single government and a large firm – foreign *or* local – rather than of a strategic development vision, let alone a vision that embraces goals of sustainable employment.

I refer to this state of affairs as 'implicit' industrial policy. 'Industrial policy', on the one hand, because it does add up to something like that – even though the whole may be less than the sum of its parts when outside firms do not have the developmental impact that was expected, or when the 'market-destroying' effect of their arrival is greater than the market-creating effect. 'Implicit', on the other hand, because the rhetoric of the current policies of economic development is just the opposite of the old 'industrial policy' and, indeed, explicitly eschews it. Namely, it is a discourse about *eliminating* subsidies, supporting private-sector growth and, more specifically, about the large outsider firm as the 'new' engine of development, the 'transformational' agent – with its cutting-edge technologies, best-practice

organizational cultures, contacts with export markets, and tough-love relationships with its local suppliers.[6]
At the same time, government officials in economic-development roles fear that the outside firms will be 'frightened' away if the host governments ask for certain concessions in exchange for the subsidies, locating instead in a neighbouring state or country that offers subsidies without strings. Requested concessions might relate to supporting the forging of linkages between the outside firms and existing local supplier firms, or in other ways enhancing the outsider firm's role in spilling development to the economy around it. The fear by governments of losing potential investments by outside firms is particularly disabling with respect to these governments' ability to be intelligently proactive with respect to supporting local economic development.[7]

Given these circumstances and this larger context, government officials see themselves as having no other choice than to relegate employment concerns to other realms – the safety nets, informal-sector programmes, small-firm programmes, microcredit. It is not that these measures are unimportant, though they often suffer from the aforementioned twin problems of 'projectization' and 'micro-ization'. By abandoning the realm of serious economic development, rather, they give up on important opportunities to reduce unemployment and also inadvertently render more difficult the unemployment-combating burdens of the social policy agenda itself. This brings me to the next two points, before which I conclude by pointing to the obvious role to be played by UNRISD – by supporting research that would chronicle and call attention to cases in which 'implicit' industrial policy actually *did* lead to greater employment through linkages with local firms, in which governments actually were successful in negotiating development-enhancing concessions from large outsider firms, and in which governments provided strategic support to local firms that actually were effective – an industrial policy that was neither explicit à la ISI, nor implicit, à la the post-ISI period. Opening up such a policy space in the thinking about economic development would seem to be facilitated by the current interest in small firms and the informal sector, to which I now turn.

Small firms, the informal sector, and the devil's deal

Over the last decade or so, myriad programmes, projects, and policy reforms have focused attention on informal-sector (IS) firms and small firms (SFs) in general, as part of a broader social policy agenda of reducing poverty and unemployment.[8] Despite this welcome attention, many planners in developing countries nevertheless continue to view SF/IS programmes as 'only' welfare, rather than the stuff of 'serious' economic development. The particular form taken by SF/IS support in many countries reinforces this view, as explained below, as does the way SF/IS support is often embedded in politics. This jeopardizes certain benefits, ironically, that we hold crucial to the current agenda of reducing poverty and unemployment: greater observance by firms of environmental and labour regulations, sustained increases in efficiency and productivity in local economies and, as a result, improvement in the quantity and quality of jobs.

I was first struck with the darker side of small-firm and informal-sector support when interviewing economic-development officials in the Brazilian state of Pernambuco. I was curious to know why they had not included, in a new programme of support to a handful of small-firm clusters in the state, a particularly vibrant and long-standing garment cluster about a two-hours drive from the capital city. They explained that it would be quite awkward to elevate a cluster of firms to 'growth-pole' status that was notorious for not paying taxes and not observing other government regulations.[9] At the same time, however, they did not see themselves as having the option to enforce these regulations, even as a *quid pro quo* for providing public support, because the cluster was concentrated in two municipalities that contained more than 30,000 electors.

After visiting some other places and reading about cases in other countries, I came to interpret what I was observing as a kind of unspoken deal between politicians and their constituents – myriad small-firm owners, many in the informal sector. If you vote for me, according to this exchange, I won't collect taxes from you; I won't make you comply with other tax, environmental, or labour regulations; and I will keep the police and inspectors from harassing you. I call this tacit understanding 'the devil's deal' because it causes informality to become *more* attractive, and formalization *less* attractive, than they otherwise might be. Once the deal is made, it is difficult for either side to get out of it, as the above-mentioned comments of the Brazilian officials reveal.

In certain ways, then, the devil's deal can pose just as significant a barrier to formalization and upgrading of small-firm clusters[10] as the actual costs themselves of formalization and regulation. Much of the policy advice on this subject, however, focuses on the 'burdens' themselves as the source of the problem – particularly, the costs of formalizing and observing tax, environmental, and labour codes. It advocates reforms, in turn, that grant special relief from these burdens to small firms in the form of exemptions from or reductions of taxes and other costs associated with environmental and labour regulation. In addition, the SF literature is strangely silent on the politics in which SF support is so firmly embedded.[11]

The dynamic of the devil's deal also reinforces the distinctly dismissive attitudes held by many economic-development planners and by development-bank managers towards smaller and informal-sector firms. To the extent that these managers and civil servants acknowledge the importance of SF/IS assistance, they often view it as a 'welfare' measure that belongs in 'social' rather than economic-development agencies – in ministries or departments of labour or social welfare, or special small-firm agencies. In their eyes, SF support will help mop up the unemployment resulting from the necessary reforms and initiatives meant to restructure the economy and institutions of government for a trade-liberalized world.

In these terms, the SF sector becomes mainly an instrument for preserving and even creating *jobs* – albeit often poor-quality jobs in poor-quality firms – rather than as an opportunity to stimulate economic development. This frees policy makers to dedicate their economic-development attention elsewhere, by reducing for them the political cost of the job losses that ensue from the modernization of industry and economic-policy reforms. From this perspective, and more generally, SF-assistance programmes do the important work of helping to maintain the 'social peace', rather than necessarily to modernize the local economy.[12] Contributing to this same perspective, many international donors and non-government organizations couch their current support for IS/SF assistance, such as microcredit and other programmes, in terms of 'safety-net' measures for poverty reduction.

The devil's deal offers more to IS/SF clusters than just looking the other way from their violation of regulations. Governments often grant small firms a particular kind of support in which there is something for everyone – special lines of cheap credit, blanket credit amnesties when times are bad, and blanket exemptions for small firms from certain taxes and regulations. The exemptions are 'burden-relieving' in that they reduce the costs of small firms (or keep them from increasing) in a way that requires no effort on their part. They are also 'universalist' or 'distributive' in that they benefit *all* small firms – whether they want to grow or not, whether they are seeking to improve their efficiency or not, and regardless of sector.[13]

In maximizing the number of satisfied constituents, this kind of support to small firms is ideal for maintaining and increasing electoral loyalty. It is less than ideal, however, for stimulating local economic development that is sustained and employment-enhancing. Today, that is, the most widely agreed-upon forms of public support for local economic development do not have this universalist and burden-relieving character. In some ways, in fact, they are just the *opposite*. They strategically identify and try to remove bottlenecks to improved efficiency, productivity, and marketing for the sector as a whole. Before any significant support is rendered, they often require or elicit broad involvement of the sector in a process of discovering exactly what the problem is and what to do about it. And they may benefit directly – at least at first – only those firms most capable and most interested in upgrading their production which, in turn, often leads to the latter's formalization. The histories of dynamic small-firm clusters often reveal this particular kind of strategic public support, which, in turn, has been central to the formation of strong local economies and the reduction of unemployment.

Once the 'devil's deal' has been made between firms and politicians, it becomes politically awkward for governments to carry out the above-mentioned strategic and sector-specific support because it does not automatically benefit all small firms. To the extent that it does benefit the region as a whole – as in the breaking of important infrastructure bottlenecks or the linking of local producers to outside buyers through trade fairs – the benefits may be longer in coming and more diffuse, and their effects may be felt by many firms only indirectly. These traits are just the opposite of those characterizing the relief provided by the burden-reducing exemptions and subsidies – immediate, automatic, universal, conspicuous, and directly available to each firm as an individual unit.

Classifying firms by their size (small, medium, or large) for the purposes of public policy, rather than by their product or sector, reinforces the tendencies toward the burden-reducing approach. 'Small', that is, can encompass a quite diverse set of firms – rustic and sophisticated, producing in different sectors, and located in different places. For purposes of lobbying for burden-reducing measures, for example, 'small' can even be meant to include a rustic brick-making operation in the countryside or a sophisticated software firm in the city. With such heterogeneity, the only way an association can serve a majority of its members is to appeal to the broadest common denominator – namely, size. But the kind of support that best fits the size denominator is the burden-reducing subsidies and exemptions because of, as seen above, their universal and distributive benefits. That is why we often find small-firm associations pressing more for the universalist exemptions than for the strategic supports. In this sense, then, size is also the *lowest* common denominator, in that its associated subsidies and exemptions are the least likely to lead to sustained development.

No one would deny the importance of SF associationalism in the histories of many dynamic clusters. Organizing and lobbying according to firm size, moreover, may be the only way in which small firms can hope to compete with larger and more powerful firms for the attention of policy makers. At the same time, the attention paid by governments and donors to firms according to their (small) size – and to small-firm associationalism – can also work inadvertently in the same direction as the devil's deal.

The large volume of research on small firms and their clusters reveals little about the circumstances under which universalist concerns and demands will dominate strategic ones in SF associations, let alone the sequence by which universalist concerns and their burden-relieving support sometimes miraculously give way to more strategic episodes. Complicating the story, the two approaches may coexist within the same association.[14] Putting together and lobbying for a strategic agenda, moreover, requires harder work over a longer period of time – more deliberation, analysis, and consensus – than lobbying for the burden-reducing exemptions and subsidies. In this sense, the universalist exemptions of the 'devil's deal' will be more appealing to SF associations because they are *easier*, just as they are more appealing to politicians because of their greater *political* yield.

Focusing on the difficulties small and informal firms face in meeting the costs of environmental and labour standards distracts our attention from pursuing opportunities for firms to, indeed, rise to the occasion and meet these standards, rather than being exempt from them. Though we are used to thinking that SFs need protection from these 'excessively' burdensome costs, there are many cases in which SFs have actually met those costs and, contrary to the burden-relieving scenario, have benefited from doing so. They became more efficient, produced higher-quality goods, and gained access to more demanding markets.

How did such dynamic clusters get from where they were before – when they were the pathetic, low-productivity small firms of the welfare scenario – to where they are today? Much of the research on small-firm clusters fails to address this particular question, dedicated as it has been to understanding how these clusters function at any particular moment in time or drawing best-practice lessons for practitioners. It is the evolutionary sequence of these cluster histories, however, that will reveal lessons on how to promote SF dynamism while not compromising – in contrast to the burden-reducing approach – our concerns for increasing the rule of law, reducing environmental problems, protecting worker rights, and upskilling labour. The histories will also provide insights into the sequences of events and other circumstances under which local actors make the transition from burden-relieving to more strategic and transformative deeds.

Offhand, five recent cases come to my mind of major advances in improving the efficiency, productivity, and other sector-wide aspects of partly small-firm clusters in which standards were increased rather than waived. In three of these cases, the advances were triggered in part by suddenly imposed bans of importing countries on a developing country's export: Germany banned the import of leather goods produced with certain chemicals, all used by the Tamil Nadu leather-goods cluster in India; the US banned the import of precision surgical instruments from Pakistan, made in the Sialkhot cluster, because of problems with the quality of steel; and El Salvador banned the import of Nicaraguan cheese because it did not meet the importing country's new hygienic standards.[15] In each of these cases, the importing country had been a major buyer of the export of that product for some time. The firms, acting through previously existing collective, public, and public–private institutions, rose to the occasion – meeting the costs of the new standards, resuming exporting, and becoming more competitive. Of course, one would not want to count on such wrenching import bans as a 'best practice' for upgrading small-firm clusters.

The remaining two examples did not need the import bans by customer countries to fuel them, and hence show another possible path to the achievement of similar results. These two cases were also triggered by problems in the international market – namely, increasing competition to SF clusters caused by the entry of cheaper or better products into the international market from other countries. One case involved a footwear cluster in southern Brazil and the other, a marble cluster in Andalusian Spain.[16]

In both of these cases, importantly, the SF associations first lobbied government for the typical burden-reducing measures – tax exemptions, credit amnesties and subsidies. But, unusually, the government explicitly *rejected* the burden-reducing approach as a way of coping with the crisis provoked by outside competition. Making its own counter-demand, the government agency involved offered a *different* kind of deal in exchange for support: it required that the firms gather together and engage in a time-consuming and difficult exercise that identified problems and proposed sector-specific solutions.

In the Andalusian case, the marble cluster had declined through the years partly because of increasing competition in the international market from the Italian marble industry. The Planning Ministry offered the following deal: the firms would themselves have to get together, decide what the problems were and how they might be overcome, and then arrive at a proposed plan of action. In addition, the Ministry required 100 per cent consensus among the sector's firms, in return for which it offered technical and facilitating assistance for this process, and the promise of financing for whatever proposal for upgrading that might emerge. This was a deal also, then, but in certain ways it was just the opposite of the devil's deal: what it demanded in return was not political loyalty, but a set of behaviours that would lead to greater economic dynamism.

In the Brazilian case, similarly, the association of small footwear producers – faced with a crippling increase in cheap footwear imports in the late 1990s – lobbied the state government of Rio Grande do Sul for tax relief. The government denied the burden-reducing relief, but proposed a different kind of exchange. It offered to finance and assist in other ways the participation of these firms in an important major trade fair, an annual event held in the shoe-producing Franca region of Brazil, in order to increase their exposure to the large Brazilian market. As a result, their sales increased significantly, which also increased the state's sales-tax return by more than the amount expended for this support.

The Brazilian story also shows that such strategic deals can yield political returns which are every bit as robust as those of the burden-reducing measures. The state's footwear cluster, located a few hours from the capital city, had historically voted against the party in power at the time of this offer – the left-wing Workers' Party. Many of the smaller firms who benefited from the trade-fair experience, however, subsequently shifted their allegiance to that party, in a first-time split of the political loyalties of the footwear-producing sector as a whole.

Obviously, not all small-firm clusters would be able to respond as successfully as happened in these cases. But the general sympathy in the SF/IS agenda for protecting small firms as a group from various burdens – often in the name of protecting the 'only' source of employment in particular local economies – distracts our attention from possibilities among such firms to meet these costs in a way that leaves them and the local economy better-off.

Such an economically robust outcome might provide more sustained employment, let alone better environmental and labour standards and tax collection, than would protecting small firms as a category.

I am arguing, then, that the widespread sympathy for small firms as a special category – and in particular their 'inability' to pay taxes and conform to environmental and labour standards – tends to undermine other important concerns about appropriate strategies for reducing poverty, increasing employment and development, and improving governance. These include reducing environmental degradation (to which small-firm clusters can be major contributors); protecting workers' rights to organize, and improving health and safety in the workplace; expanding the coverage of social security, health, and other social insurance to poorer workers; increasing the tax yield of governments so as to better finance public services and, in so doing, drawing government and firms together in a contract – in this case, to promote a more inclusive style of economic development.

UNRISD could contribute to breaking the stranglehold of the 'devil's deal' by exploring the paths by which SF/IS firms or sectors actually grew into formality, treated workers better and upgraded their skills, and worked towards improving their environmental practices. These kinds of cases – in which firm agglomerations succeeded in meeting regulatory requirements, became more competitive, and were better off for it – need to be sought out and chronicled, such that lessons for policy can be learned from them. This would help to show policy makers – particularly at the subnational level, where such enforcement and economic-development support increasingly takes place – another path and another set of possibilities. Showing that such outcomes are perfectly imaginable, and familiarizing planners with the felicitous outcomes of actual cases and the paths that led to them, might also contribute towards reducing the generalized antipathy in the economic-development sector of many countries towards the enactment or enforcement of environmental and labour standards.

The policy sympathy for small firms as a category of assistance, in sum, is desirable on many grounds. At the same time, the concern about protecting SFs from reasonable regulations – let alone from the vicissitudes of the market – can become toxic when combined with the political dynamics of the devil's deal. The waiving of tax, labour, and environmental regulations that results from sympathy for the 'plight' of small firms may hinder rather than help local economies if it condemns them to low-level economic stagnation, degradation of the environment, and the violation of workers' rights. The latter all clearly increase unemployment and poverty, as well as burdening unnecessarily the task of poverty-reducing social policy.

Where did all the labour unions go?

The poverty-reducing and human-rights agenda of the international development community now includes the protection of workers' rights to organize.

Inadvertently, however, other parts of the anti-poverty agenda have translated in certain ways, and sometimes inadvertently, into an *anti*-labour agenda – or, in some ways worse, an 'ignoring-ignoring' agenda. This has contributed to further weakening the case for worker organizing *within* countries, thereby depriving the poverty agenda of domestic support from a potentially powerful ally.

Ignoring unions and other worker associations have actually figured prominently in some of the recent writing and policy advice on poverty and unemployment, but negatively. Namely, they have been castigated for their role in *blocking* important reforms that would benefit the poor, such as increasing employment through the flexibilization of the labour market. Unions are said to pursue a narrow self-interested policy agenda, acting as an ignoring aristocracy to protect their own bread-and-butter gains, and to advance their cause through unsavoury relationships with political parties. They are blamed, among other things, for the gap between formal-sector and informal-sector wages, which condemns the informal sector to low wages and disguised unemployment.[17] More generally, government officials – as well as business – see ignoring organizing and upward wage pressures as jeopardizing any project of economic growth in an era of global competition.

Though these portrayals of ignoring unions and other worker associations may in many cases be accurate, it is also true that, within countries, there are often no other equally-powerful actors to defend workers' rights to organize and press successfully for other protections such as health and safety legislation, social insurance, and so on. In addition, and in contrast to the image of a self-serving ignoring aristocracy, ignoring unions with power have often worked successfully – against serious opposition or inertia – to bring about broader policy changes that spread benefits substantially outside their own ranks. Examples are the role of the South African ignoring unions in the struggle against apartheid,[18] or the key role of rural ignoring unions in Brazil in advocating agrarian reform, or the centrality of the metal-mechanic unions in Brazil in spearheading the formation of the new Workers' Party in the mid-1980s, and putting their weight behind the country's democratization struggle of that period. At the firm level, and in the best of cases, ignoring unions and management have actually succeeded in working together to identify problems of inefficiency and other bottlenecks in the firm and the sector, and have jointly made relevant policy recommendations to government. The Sectoral Chambers (*Câmaras Setoriais*) in the auto industry in Brazil of the early and mid-1990s are one example of a sectoral nature.[19]

The less explicit labour-ignoring aspects of the sidelining of worker organizing are, in certain ways, more undermining of worker causes than the oft-heard direct criticisms of labour unions noted above. Four features of the last decade's anti-poverty agenda contribute inadvertently to this state of affairs:

First is the aforementioned tendency to 'projectize' interventions, and 'micro-ize' or decentralize their decisions to the community level – a level at which labour unions, or at least their often stronger and more knowledgeable federations, do not necessarily operate, or are at their weakest.

Second is the aforementioned focus on small firms and the informal sector as the locus of unemployment- and poverty-reducing policy, with its accompanying sympathy for and strengthening of their pleas to be exempt from myriad regulations, including those protecting workers.

Third is the focus on NGOs as the agencies most suited to carry out poverty-reducing programmes. They are said to be more committed to the poor than government, 'apolitical' and untainted by politics in comparison to labour unions, more flexible than government, and more able to mobilize and express the needs of 'the community'. It is not that anyone explicitly excludes labour unions and other workers associations from this non-government category but, rather, that they are rarely *in*cluded. They are often nowhere to be found in the cast of 'civil-society' characters portrayed as representing 'the community' in today's more decentralized and participatory programmes, and 'public–private' partnerships.

Fourth, and finally, the image of 'community' decision-making that pervades many safety-net programmes presumes, without saying so, a harmony of interests at the community level. The assumption of harmony also pervades the vision, underlying the discourse of decentralization, of a community united in demanding better services from local government, and hence better able to make government more accountable at the local level. In certain ways, this vision of harmony represents the opposite end of the spectrum from that of the 1960s and 1970s, when class conflict was viewed as enduring and irremediable, dooming any proposed reform. Today's *no*-conflict vision of harmony commits the same error of oversimplification.

There are, obviously, generic conflicts of interest between labour and capital – as there are between other economic actors in the same community, such as producers of intermediate goods and the firms that buy them. But such conflicts of interest are best faced through institutionalized processes that mediate them, rather than by wishing them away. Building permanent institutions that mediate these conflicts, as Rodrik has argued, is *really* what macroeconomics is about; he finds, in a cross-country analysis, that those countries that were more institutionally equipped to mediate the conflict between labour and management actually grew better.[20]

How different Rodrik's view sounds from the development discourse of today, which posits a harmonious and single-voiced 'community' to which government actions can be fruitfully decentralized. This latter view, so common in the 'micro-ized' perspective outlined in the first section of this chapter, simply assumes Rodrik's conflict away. In this sense, it is blind to the persistence of generic conflicts and, hence, to the need to pay attention to building institutions for mediating them. UNRISD could bring a more tempered and realistic perspective to bear on this picture by encouraging research on the processes that lead to the creation of sustained institutions – representing or cutting across labour and management – that manage this conflict according to norms of behaviour recognized by both sides.

The absence of local or national labour unions in the donors' poverty-reducing scenarios has been matched by a growing enthusiasm about international human-rights NGOs as the new key actors in the struggle for workers' rights. These NGOs, as with NGOs in general, are seen as responsible, sincere, and high-minded in the campaign to protect workers from abuse, particularly in the plants or subcontractors of multinational brand-name firms, such as Nike.[21] In contrast, the donor community's image of *traditional* labour unions – those within specific countries – is just the opposite: sullied by self-interest and corruption, burly and obstreperous, and compromised by political involvements.

This is not to criticize, in any way, the international human-rights campaigns regarding labour and other practices. These groups have raised international consciousness around these issues markedly. At the same time, the shift of the focus away from national or sub-national labour organizations to international rather than national arenas, and northern NGOs rather than within-country labour unions, has given added strength to those groups *within* developing countries that traditionally *oppose* the right of labour to organize, or feel uncomfortable with unions in their presence – particularly certain sectors of business elites. Now, they can cloak their arguments against labour organizing in the mantle of 'anti-North' nationalism – that 'foreign' norms are being 'imposed' by the more developed 'North'. The argument is similar to that frequently heard from certain sectors of business and government in developing countries against international environmental and labour standards – namely, that such standards are a way of allowing the now-developed countries to restrain the growth of traded goods and hence trade competition by developing countries.

Ironically, then, the shifting of the worker-rights agenda to the international arena, and its concomitant de-fanging from an 'old' and national union–union agenda to a fresh and young human-rights and NGO-driven agenda, has emboldened the *anti*-rights–rights position *within* developing countries. More importantly, the indifference to institutions that represent workers *within* countries, and the repeated portrayal of them as compromising the poverty-reducing agenda as well as the growth agenda, does a disservice to the cause of building the institutions of conflict mediation that are so necessary to both the growth and the poverty-reducing project.

The final nail in this coffin is the frequently noted trend that formal-sector employment is declining steadily as the informal sector takes an ever-increasing share of employment – and that, correspondingly, the share of unionized rights is also declining, even within the formal sector. Formal-sector employment and labour unions, it is often concluded from these trends, are simply no longer 'where it's at'. I am not denying the significance of informal-sector rights and firms, nor the decline of formal-sector unions and other workers' associations in many countries. But part of this weakening of worker organizing is a result of the economic crises and adjustment policies of the past two decades – the very policies that have contributed to sidelining the social policy agenda. More importantly, this decline is exacerbated by the sustained portrayal of rights unions by the development-policy discourse as part of the *problem* of poverty, rather than of its solution. In this sense, declaring rights unions and the formal sector to be 'not where it's at' also works to bring about this very turn of events.

In some ways, it is the ultimate irony that whereas business interests have often been portrayed historically as 'the bad guys' with respect to the fate of proposed reforms meant to reduce poverty and unemployment, the 'bad-guy' role is now assigned in today's development discourse to rights unions. Business, in turn, has now been transformed into the 'happy camper' of this vision – witness, for example, the recent wave of studies of public–private partnerships, with business elites often speaking for the good of 'the community' in various decentralized programmes.

Reflecting or contributing to this turn of events, the scholarly literature on business associations in economic development has proliferated, while contributions on rights unions in developing countries are hard to find, except in specialized 'rights studies'. This despite the fact that anyone who does fieldwork in developing countries runs across enough cases of gains from rights organizing and non-conflictual and positive-sum outcomes to provide substantial raw material for drawing up a set of policy-relevant lessons. One such example, noted briefly for the purposes of illustration, comes from a sector and a place where one would least expect it – previously temporary workers on grape-growing (for export) farms in the poorest region of Brazil, for export to Europe.

Within a few years of organizing by a local rural workers' union, and supported by the state federation and central-government confederation of rural unions, this organizing effort brought growers to the bargaining table – and, remarkably, without conflict. The result was the agreement to a permanent system of collective bargaining, formalization of the workforce, agreement to pay the minimum wage plus 10 per cent, respect for child-rights prohibitions, and a variety of other protections. Importantly, several years after the first accord, this system of conflict mediation is still in existence, and has now spread to other fruit-growing areas in the region.[22]

It is also significant that the increase in wages, unionization, and other rights protections did *not* cause the fruit growers to be less competitive in international markets. This flies in the face of the standard objection raised against improving rights standards in labour – intensive products that are internationally traded – that the resulting increased costs will price the product out of the international market, since there will always be a cheaper-intensive producing country. Indeed, in this case, just the opposite occurred: the advances in unionization and intensive standards were accompanied by an ever-increasing upgrading of product quality and international market penetration, exactly the opposite of the usual feared scenario. Why in this case – or class of cases, yet to be discovered – and not in the others? Answering questions like these should be the task of an UNRISD-supported research agenda. Such cases should be unearthed, chronicled, and searched for lessons – in the Brazilian example, as to why conflict was avoided, why the increased wages did *not* make the product less competitive in foreign markets, and how unionization occurred in an environment of the constant upgrading of the quality of the product. It is not that such cases represent a majority, but that they pose a mystery and we need to know how it was solved. Such cases should serve as models for inspiration, for imitation, and for the reduction of fear of the unknown among government officials and business. Though one might argue that the proper domain for such research and dissemination is labour-specific organizations, such as the International Labour Organization, this places the issue back in the narrower box of labour unions, rather than bringing it into the broader one of a socially appropriate economic development. UNRISD is particularly suited to play a role here, then, precisely because it is a *not* a labour-specific organization.

By envisioning a project of employment creation and poverty reduction in which labour unions are the 'bad guys', we ignore at our peril important social and political institutions that will advance that project. Although labour unions are often portrayed as tainted by their 'political' involvements, moreover, the poverty-reducing project is, indeed, a highly political one – as history shows us. But much of the thinking about poverty reduction in the international development community takes place beyond national borders in international fora, and is often rather technocratic in excluding such forces as key variables for study and discussion. All this amounts to a serious lapse in thinking about building sustainable institutions *within* countries for protecting worker rights.

No matter how hard we work to imagine a better approach to reducing poverty – and no matter how much we bring economists to the table to sit with other social scientists – we are making the task even more difficult by allowing the subject of labour organizing within countries to be overlooked. We also lose thereby a scarce ally to stand behind the poverty-reducing agenda, and miss the opportunity to build essential institutions for the mediation of conflict between management and workers.

UNRISD could make an important contribution to correcting this imbalance through its research, and the way in which it disseminates it. It could support the chronicling of a set of cases of labour organizing with positive outcomes, such as that noted above for Brazilian agricultural workers. The criterion for selection of such cases for study would be that production and sales increased, or product quality was improved, or successful exporting ensued, or the right to bargain collectively with producers was won without conflict. The point would not be to argue that such outcomes are the norm, but to show that they are possible, and to illuminate the dynamic that runs across a series of such cases.

This latter contribution is particularly important, because government officials – not to mention business – fear that worker organizing will 'spoil' the growth project, particularly in today's trade-liberalized world. Added to this is the institutional novelty of such organizing in many places – government officials do not know how to manage the conflict, in the sense of even the most trivial details. These kinds of studies – with results disseminated in the countries in which the cases took place – could work to allay this fear of the unknown, reduce resistance, and set an example for labour unions, business, and government.

Notes

1. There are several names used for the last decade's crop of social funds – including Social Funds (perhaps the most general category), and Social Emergency Funds (applying to temporary emergencies caused by natural or man-made disasters). I use the acronym SIFs (Social Investment Funds), rather than the looser category SFs (Social Funds), partly because SIFs have become much more prominent in the current portfolio of social-fund projects, and partly so as to avoid confusion with the acronym commonly used for small firms (SFs), including in a later section of this chapter.
2. With respect to insignificant impacts in reducing poverty and unemployment, see that chapter in Goodman, Morley, Siri, and Zuckerman (1997); with respect to comparisons to longstanding employment schemes, see Cornia (1999, 2001), Cornia and Reddy (2001) and Stewart and Geest (1995).
3. In addition to the works cited in the previous note, see the following for clearly pro or con arguments and evidence. For the pro view, the best source and the most extensive set of studies can be found on the World Bank's web site and the publications listed therein. For a concise pro and con set of arguments from *within* the World Bank, see van Domelen (pro) and D. Ellesman (con) at: www1.worldbank.org/publicsector/civilservice/acrext/vol1page1.htm. For the con view, see Cornia (1999, 2001), Cornia and Reddy (2001) Tendler, (2000b). Tendler and Rodrigo (1999). For clearly mixed reviews, see Goodman, Morley, Siri, and Zuckerman (1997) and a recent evaluation of the SIFs by the World Bank's Operations Evaluation Department World Bank (2002).
4. Such as those discussed in the works cited in the previous footnote (see References).
5. An example of the former can be found in Schmitz (1998), with respect to the Sinos Valley shoe-exporting cluster in southern Brazil; an example of the latter can be found in Barnes and Kaplinsky (2000) with respect to the autoparts industry in South Africa; and in Dohnert (2002) with respect to the privatized Venezuelan steel producer and its initial rejection of the local metal-mechanic sector.
6. The portrayal of the outsider firm as an engine of development and as transformational, actually, is old rather than new. It appeared clearly in the 'old' industrial policy of the ISI period. There is, however, a major difference. In the ISI period, a set

of complementary policies obligated outsider firms to procure a certain percentage (often increasing through time) of their inputs from local firms, particularly machinery (e.g., Mexico's local-content laws and Brazil's Law of Similars). Public institutions often brokered the forging of these customer-supplier relationships, while providing technical assistance to the local firms in upgrading their product. Also, outside firms in the ISI period often chose to produce in certain developing countries because it was the only way to breach its high tariff walls in order to sell their product. This contrasts with today's decisions by multinationals to move production to a particular developing country, which are often impelled instead by the desire to *export*. In making decisions about where to produce during the ISI period, then, multinational firms were at least as interested in getting access to a particular large consumer market as they were in finding the best production conditions and costs. This made the outside firms more amenable to development conditions imposed on them by host-country governments – such as local-content requirements – than they are in the current period.

7. I have written about these fears at greater length, explored some of the reasons that outsider firms are actually willing to grant such concessions, and explored other aspects of implicit industrial policy and the conditions under which some outside firms tend to have more positive spillover effects than others – based on findings from a research project on local economic development in Northeast Brazil, Tendler (2000a, 2001).

8. By specifying the subject to be firms that are small and/or informal, I am not excluding from the universe of firms discussed herein some small firms that are partly or fully formal, and even some firms that are producing in the same sector and in the same locality as the small firms, but tending toward medium size. Though this fuzzy definition ignores important distinctions, it is necessary to reflect the fact that SF demands often emerge from a set of firms defined by the space they occupy together and the same product or value-chain in which they produce. Just as important, the loose definition serves the purpose of brevity, and is also consistent with the language used by the international development community in describing and justifying the kinds of policy objectives and programmes discussed in this chapter.

9. The non-payment of taxes in this region has been no secret in Brazil. A national news magazine reported – in an article on the dynamism of the cluster entitled, 'Taxes not paid here' – that 'this [cluster] wouldn't even exist if firm owners had to pay taxes'. The chief of the state's Treasury Department, in turn, said that the taxes collected there did 'not even represent 1% of what could be collected': Furtado (2001).

10. With apologies to today's cluster specialists, I will use the word 'cluster' throughout more loosely than it is sometimes defined, partly for lack of a better single word and to avoid the more ponderous 'agglomeration'. In its more carefully defined form, a small-firm 'cluster' usually means a set of small firms located close together geographically with significant inter-firm relations among them, with an at-least evolving associational dynamic, and usually some history of success in growing, and in improving efficiency and productivity; in more recent definitions, other parts of the supply chain to which those firms belong also have to be present to qualify as a 'cluster'. My less demanding use of the term requires only that a particular region has a significant number of small firms producing the same product or in the same value chain, which may also include an admixture of medium and even large firms. Again, my sloppier

definition is in some ways more consistent with the way the term is used in the world of policy and practice.

11. There are some exceptions, though they tend to come from outside the small-firm literature, involving country studies by political scientists; some take place in the now-industrialized countries. For example, Cross (1998) actually narrates an analogous deal between government and informal firms; he documents how continued informality, in this case, was central to the government's willingness to support the vendors' organizing efforts, and to negotiate a series of their demands. In a study of taxation in Zambia, Rakner (2001) notes that the government 'may have refrained from broadening its tax base to include the emerging informal business sector in order not to jeopardise its support among the Owambo-speaking majority'. Italian political scientists studying Italy's postwar period have pointed explicitly to the importance of '(c)lientelist generosity – in the form of regulation to protect small business, a lax approach to tax collection for the self-employed, and so on – was systematically directed at these groups': Hopkin and Mastropaolo (2001). Suzanne Berger's work on this same subject in Italy and France is cited in the following note. For an interpretation of small-firm politics in the U.S. economy as affecting viewpoints and policies, see Brown, Hamilton and Medoff (1990).

12. Using the small-firm sector to maintain employment and the social peace is not unique to the current period, or to less-developed countries. In work on the political economy of industrial policy in France and Italy, published more than 20 years ago, the political scientist Berger (1980, 1981) explicitly linked the pro-SF programmes and regulations that developed in France and Italy during the 1970s to the simultaneous pursuit of a *large-firm* industrialization strategy by those very same governments. She had posed the question of why two countries that had so explicitly pursued a large-firm modernization industrial policy could at the same time have enacted such pro-SF legislation and assistance. It is from her work that I take the term, 'keeping the social peace'.

13. I apologize for any confusion I may create by borrowing the term 'universalist' from the social policy literature. In the social policy literature, for both developed and developing countries, 'universalist' is conveyed as the opposite of targeting. It is portrayed as more inclusive of beneficiaries – usually, middle class as well as lower class – than is an approach that, although more accurately targeting the poor, causes the left-out middle class to deny political support for the measure. Recently, many researchers – of both developed as well as developing countries – have argued that targeted approaches, though in some ways ideal in terms of restricting benefits to the intended beneficiaries, are quite cumbersome to administer (means-testing, etc.). They therefore end up alienating the middle classes whose political support is needed to enact such measures in the first place. In applying the term 'universalist' here to economic-development-related matters and pointing out its problems, then, I am not thereby criticizing the universalist approach with respect to social policy. Rather, I borrow the term for its usefulness in conveying the same sense of an initiative being more politically appealing when it more conspicuously and efficiently benefits a larger number of voters, even at the cost of diluting programme intentions.

14. I thank Nichola Lowe for pointing out these possibilities to me – based on a case from Jalisco state: Lowe (2003).

15. For the German – Indian case, see Pillai (2000); for the US – Pakistan case, see Nadvi (1999) and for El Salvador, see Perez-Aleman, P. (2002). Note that, in the US – Pakistan case, Nadvi comments that there was more cross-cluster success in

improving the quality of the precision steel than with respect to labour and environmental standards (personal communication).

16. For the Andalucian case, see Barzelay (2000). For the Brazilian case, I thank Luiz Miranda of the Economics Department of the Federal University of Rio Grande do Sul.

17. The research record on this assertion is by no means clear. Recent research by Maloney (1999) in Latin America, for example, found *other* determinants of the informal-sector/formal-sector (IS/FS) wage gap to be more significant than the degree to which formal-sector labour is organized and has won minimum-wage legislation. In particular, the IS/FS wage gap in his study varied positively across countries with the degree of *illiteracy* – the higher the illiteracy, the higher the gap. He explains this finding in terms of the behaviour of large firms (not unions) in trying to compensate for the illiteracy of the workforce. In more illiterate countries, that is, large firms compensate by investing *more* in training – paradoxically – than in the literate countries and, in turn, have to pay their workers a higher 'efficiency wage' in order to keep them from leaving, given that exit causes the firms to lose this investment in worker training. (The interest rate was the other important factor contributing to the gap.)

18. Beckman makes this same point in a recent paper about South Africa (Beckman 2000). See also Andræ and Beckman (1998) for similar work on the textile unions in Nigeria.

19. Arbix and Rodríguez-Pose (2001). The Sectoral Chambers have since passed out of existence after the mid-1990s for a variety of reasons, one of which was the federal government's growing distaste for the substantial power of such a labour – business alliance.

20. Rodrik (1997, 1999). See also Messner (1997) and Schmitz (2001).

21. See, for example O'Rourke (1997, 2002) and Fung, O'Rourke and Sabel (2001).

22. This case is part of a larger study by Damiani (1999) of the development of the Petrolina-Juazeiro region of the states of Pernambuco and Bahia as an agricultural growth pole and successful fruit exporter. The labour story itself is the subject of a separate article by Damiani (2003). For a study documenting the spread of these labour practices to another state in the same region and even poorer – the melon-growing region of Mossoró in Rio Grande do Norte, see Gomes (1999, 2004). It is interesting to note that the Petrolina-Juazeiro region, which straddles Brazil's San Francisco River Valley, marketed itself to its first European and US buyers as 'the California of Brazil', implying world-class modernity in agriculture. Ironically, the Brazilian 'California' seems to have achieved significantly greater advances in labour than those revealed in the history of organizing among the grape growers in the 'real' California.

Bibliography

Andræ, G., and Beckman, B. (1998) *Union Power in the Nigerian Textile Industry: Labour Regime and Adjustment*. Uppsala: Nordiska Afrikainstitut.

Arbix, G., and Rodríguez-Pose, A. (2001) 'Strategies of Waste: Bidding Wars in the Brazilian Automobile Sector', *International Journal of Urban and Regional Research*, 25, 134–54.

Barnes, J., and Kaplinsky, R. (2000) 'Globalisation and the Death of the Local Firm? The Automobile Components Sector in South Africa', *Regional Studies*, 34, 797–812.

Barzelay, M. (2000) 'Managing Local Development: Lessons from Spain', *Policy Sciences*, 24, 271–90.

Beckman, B. (2000) *Trade Unions and Institutional Reform: Nigerian Experiences with South African and Ugandan Comparisons, New Institutional Theory, Institutional Reform and Poverty Reduction.* London: Development Studies Institute (DESTIN), London School of Economics and Political Science.

Berger, S. (1980) 'The Traditional Sector in France and Italy'. In S. Berger and M. Piore (eds), *Dualism and Discontinuity in Industrial Societies.* New York: Saint Martin's Press.

Berger, S. (1981) 'The Uses of the Traditional Sector in Italy: Why Declining Classes Survive'. In F. Bechafer and B. Elliot (eds), *The Petite Bourgeoisie.* New York: Saint Martin's Press.

Brown, C., Hamilton, J., and Medoff, J. (1990) *Employers Large and Small.* Cambridge, MA: Harvard University Press.

Cornia, A. G. (1999) *Social Funds in Stabilization and Adjustment Programmes, Research for Action.* Helsinki: United Nations University/World Institute for Development Economics Research (UNU/WIDER).

Cornia, A. G. (2001) 'Social Funds in Stabilization and Adjustment Programmes: a Critique', *Development and Change*, 32, 1–32.

Cornia, A. G., and Reddy, S. (2001) *The Impact of Adjustment-Related Social Funds on Distribution and Poverty.* Helsinki: UNU/WIDER.

Cross, J. C. (1998) *Informal Politics: Street Vendors and the State in Mexico City.* Stanford, CA: Stanford University Press.

Damiani, O. (1999) 'Irrigated Agriculture, Agro-Export Growth, and Rural Wage Workers: Beyond Market Failures: Irrigation, the State, and Non-traditional Agriculture in Northeast Brazil'. Unpublished PhD dissertation, Massachusetts Institute of Technology.

Damiani, O. (2003) 'Effects on Employment, Wages, and Labor Standards of Non-Traditional Export Crops in Northeast Brazil', *Latin American Research Review*, 38.

Dohnert, S. (2002) 'Mediating Regional Development: How Metalworking Firms Forged Lasting Linkages with Steel in Ciudad Guayana, Venezuela'. Unpublished PhD dissertation, Massachusetts Institute of Technology.

Fung, A., O'Rourke, D., and Sabel, C. (2001). *Can We Put an End to Sweatshops?* Boston: Beacon Press.

Furtado, J. M. (2001) 'Aqui não se paga imposto: conheça Santa Cruz do Capibaribe, a cidade que se transformou numa das mecas da informalidade no Brasil' (Taxes not paid here: welcome to Santa Cruz do Capibaribe, the city that transformed itself into one of the meccas of informality in Brazil), *Revista Exame*, 35.

Gomes, R. (1999) 'Metality Regional Development: How Metalworking From forget Losting Lintage link steel in Ciudud Venezuela'. Unpublished First Year Doctoral Paper, Massachusetts Institute of Technology.

Gomes, R. (2004) 'Learning to Upgrade: Lessons from the Brazilian Fruit Industry'. Unpublished PhD dissertation, Massachusetts Institute of Technology.

Goodman, M., Morley, S., Siri, G., and Zuckerman, E. (1997) *Social Investment Funds in Latin America: Past Performance and Future Role*, Evaluation Office, Social Programs and Sustainable Development Department. Washington, DC: IDB (Inter-American Development Bank).

Hopkin, J., and Mastropaolo, A. (2001) 'From Patronage to Clientelism: Comparing the Italian and Spanish Experiences'. In S. Piattoni (ed.), *Clientelism, Interests, and Democratic Representation: the European Experience in Historical and Comparative Perspective.* Cambridge: Cambridge University Press.

Lowe, N. J. (2003) 'Trainers by Design: A Case Study of Inter-Firm Learning, Institution Building and Local Governance in Western Mexico', Massachusetts Institute of Technology.

Maloney, W. F. (1999) 'Does Informality Imply Segmentation in Urban Labor Markets? Evidence from Sectoral Transitions in Mexico', *The World Bank Economic Review*, 13, 275–302.

Messner, D. (1997) *The Network Society: Economic Development and Institutional Competitiveness as Problems of Social Governance*. London: German Development Institute.

Nadvi, K. (1999) 'Collective Efficiency and Collective Failure: The Response of the Sialkot Surgical Instrument Cluster to Global Quality Pressures', *World Development*, 27, 1605–26.

O'Rourke, D. (1997) *Smoke from a Hired Gun: a Critique of Nike's Labor and Environmental Auditing in Vietnam as Performed by Ernst & Young*. San Francisco: Transnational Resource and Action Center. (www): http://web.mit.edu/dorourke/www/PDF/smoke.pdf (12.05.04).

O'Rourke, D. (2002) 'Monitoring the Monitors: a Critique of Corporate Third-Party Labor Monitoring'. In R. Jenkins, R. Pearson and G. Seyfang (eds), *Corporate Responsibility and Labour Rights. Codes of Conduct in the Global Economy*. London: Earthscan.

Perez-Aleman, P. (2002) *Decentralized Production, Organization and Institutional Transformations: Large and Small Firm Networks in Chile and Nicaragua*, Third Meeting of the International Working Group on Subnational Economic Governance in Latin America from a Comparative International Perspective. New York: Institute for Latin American and Iberian Studies (Columbia University).

Pillai, P. (2000) 'The State and Collective action: Successful Adjustment of the Tamil Nadu Leather Clusters to German Environmental Standards'. Unpublished Master's Thesis, Massachusets Institute of Technology.

Rakner, L. (2001) 'The Politics of Revenue Mobilisation: Explaining Continuity in Namibian Tax Policies'. *Forum for Development Studies*, 28(1), 125–45.

Rodrik, D. (1997) *Has Globalization Gone Too Far?* Washington, DC: Institute for International Economics.

Rodrik, D. (1999) *Making Openness Work: the New Global Economy and Developing Countries* (Policy Essay, No. 24). Washington, DC: The Johns Hopkins University Press.

Schmitz, H. (1998) *Responding to Global Competitive Pressure: Local Co-operation and Upgrading in the Sinos Valley, Brazil*. Brighton: Institute of Development Studies (IDS).

Schmitz, H. (2001) 'Local Governance and Conflict Management: Reflections on a Brazilian Cluster'. In A. Scott (ed.), *Global City Regions: Trends, Theory, Policy*. Oxford: Oxford University Press.

Stewart, F., and Geest, W. v. d. (1995) 'Adjustment and Social Funds: Political Panacea or Effective Poverty Reduction?' In F. Stewart (ed.), *Adjustment and Poverty*. London: Routledge.

Tendler, J. (2000a). *The Economic Wars Between the States*. Cambridge, MA: MIT/ Bank of the Northeast.

Tendler, J. (2000b) Why are Social Funds So Popular? In S. Yusuf, W. Wu and S. Everett (eds.), *Local Dynamics in the Era of Globalization: 21st Century Catalysts for Development*. Oxford: Oxford University Press.

Tendler, J. (2001) *Transforming Local Economies: Lessons from the Northeast Brazilian Experience*. Cambridge, MA: MIT/Bank of the Northeast.

Tendler, J. and Rodrigo, S. (1999) *The Rise of Social Funds: What are They a Model of?*, New York: United Nations Development Program (UNDP).

World Bank (2002) *Social Funds: A Review of World Bank Experience.* Washington, DC: The World Bank (Operations Evaluation Department).

7
Inequality and Redistribution in Health Care: Analytical Issues for Developmental Social Policy

Maureen Mackintosh and Paula Tibandebage

Introduction: social policy, health care and redistribution

This chapter[1] contends that there is a need for more and better political economy of social policy in the development context, and seeks to contribute to its development. Specifically, the chapter discusses the problem of achieving and sustaining redistributive health care in contexts of inequality and low incomes. Much of our evidence and specific argument are drawn from the health sector in Africa, and in particular from recent research[2] on health care markets in Tanzania. We believe, however, that our arguments have wider resonance for the effort to create effective, context-specific developmental social policy.

We employ a broad definition of 'social policy', to include governmental and non-governmental public action to shape social provisioning such as health and education, including influencing the distributive outcomes of social sector market processes. Indeed we argue that understanding the mutual interaction of public policy and market behaviour is key to designing effective developmental policy in health care as it is in other social sectors. We take for granted, as the basis for our argument here, some of the central propositions of Mkandawire (2001):

- That health and education are necessary for economic growth;
- That effective social policy can prevent developmentally dysfunctional inequality and conflict;
- And that we need to understand how these points can be moved onto the political agenda in both authoritarian and democratic regimes without such functionalist arguments undermining the intrinsic importance of social solidarity as an ethical objective.

We seek to respond in particular to the challenge of the last point, by contributing to the development of political economy-based, policy-relevant analytical approaches to redistribution in the health sector.

Our concept of 'redistribution' is intentionally broad. We define 'redistributive' action as encompassing all social processes that create increasingly inclusive or egalitarian access to resources. In health care, this can include subsidy for access by those otherwise excluded; cross-subsidy within health care provider institutions; risk-pooling that increases the inclusion of the moderately poor; and referral systems that increase the access of the poor to secondary care. More generally, it refers to shifts in health care systems in directions that sustain and legitimate access by those who can pay little or nothing, including processes that support redistributive commitments by governments and effective claims to access by the poor. This kind of shift is particularly difficult to achieve in contexts where health care reform based in marketization is explicitly legitimating unequal access (Mackintosh 2001).

We argue in Section 2 of this chapter that the health policy and development literature lacks an overarching theory of policy. Its prescriptions for the allocation of public and donor funds emphasize redistributive intent, yet the research literature largely fails to tackle the problem of explaining persistent redistributive failure. Next section 3 contrasts this methodological 'thinness' with elements of the European and African social policy literature that develops an empirically based political economy of policy. Note that our aim here is *not* to argue that the European literature offers models of health care systems for emulation, but rather to identify relevant methodological avenues that are paralleled in work by scholars in lower income contexts.

Section 4 then discusses some key issues in the political economy of redistributive health policy in low-income contexts. We explore some of the implications of understanding redistributiveness as a health care *system* characteristic. Distributive outcomes of health care emerge from interactions among policy makers, institutions in all sectors, and health care users and would-be users. Hence institutional behaviour, institutional legitimacy and response to market and non-market incentives are key variables in explaining redistributive success and failure. The argument in this section draws upon institutional and game-theoretic economics and the sociology and anthropology of institutional change. Section 5 explores some of these issues in the Tanzanian context, drawing upon our own research. We identify partial social polarization in this recently liberalized low-income health care system, and discuss the scope for combating the resultant exclusion and impoverishment. Section 6 draws the threads together into an argument for a 'thicker' methodology of health care research and policy, aimed at rooting redistributive health care policy in local knowledge and locally feasible institutional design.

Health and development: thick prescription, thin explanation

In the development context, the health policy literature is strongly characterized by an emphasis on egalitarian objectives and by repeated demonstration of redistributive failure. There is strikingly less effort expended in researching explanations of the observed regressive distributional behaviour (Mackintosh and Gilson 2002).

We can illustrate this privileging of prescription and evaluation over explanation with reference to two major categories of health policy writing. One is the large and expanding literature on the allocation of government and donor funds in health care. World Bank policy prescription in health care has repeatedly taken as its starting point a demonstration that 'public spending on education and health is not progressive but is frequently regressive' (see also World Bank 1993, 1996, 1997, 2001: 80). The research literature includes the repeated demonstration that the better-off generally benefit disproportionately from the allocation of government funding to health care, chiefly because of social inequity in access to government hospitals as compared to primary and preventative care (Barnum and Kutzin 1993; Peters *et al.* 1999).

The predominant response has been more elaborate prescription. As a recent report on African poverty published by the Bank puts it (White and Killick 2001): 'The current trend is to identify the most cost-effective way of reducing the burden of disease as measured by DALYs (disability-adjusted life years).' In the mid-1990s, a report from the World Bank's regional office in East Africa took this approach, making strong recommendations for a reallocation of government spending in five countries including Tanzania towards 'community and preventative interventions' supplemented by only limited subsidy for curative care 'carefully targeted' to the poor (World Bank 1996: 1). A prescriptive emphasis on targeting public sector funds to the poor has been consistent, though the emphasis of Bank policy documents has shifted, notably in its recognition that 'subsidies to the non-poor cannot be fully avoided' because of the need to garner political support for pro-poor measures (World Bank 2001: 81). Allocative failure is implicitly attributed to lack of political will and/or skill in fostering 'pro-poor' political coalitions (World Bank 2001: 108–12).

This policy mindset in health care is both source and product of the market liberalization process itself in social sectors such as health care. Liberalization of market supply is founded on the proposition – an unsafe one in health care – that private supply, charging and market access can sustain market-based provision with reasonable efficiency. Market liberalization in practice furthermore tends to expose and drive out cross-subsidy. As a result, the marketization process exposes the problem of access for those who cannot pay.

Marketization thus simultaneously establishes a policy benchmark of sustaining competitive markets (the popular formulation of the 'level playing field' for competition refers to this idealized benchmark), while creating highly visible inequity and exclusion. There has as a result been a recent explosion of published evidence on the exclusion of those unable to pay health care user fees, in Africa and other development contexts.[3] The associated evolution in World Bank commentary can be illustrated:

> The finding that many curative interventions are cheap and cost effective reinforces the economic principle that they should be left to the private market.   (World Bank 1996: 22)

> Most curative health care is a (nearly) pure private good – if government does not foot the bill, all but the poorest will find ways to pay for care themselves.   (World Bank 1997: 53)

> Several studies have shown that many households in developing countries cannot insure against major illness or disability.   (World Bank 2001: 152)

Behind each of these statements is the assumption that where health care 'goods' – services or insurance – can be constructed to be 'private'[4] they should be supplied on private markets. These arguments both downplay the widely acknowledged scale of market failure in the supply of health care (Barr 1998; Leonard 2000b), and imply that the proper sphere for redistribution is the institutionally separate one of the government budget. Policy proposals therefore continue to focus on elaborating prescriptions for 'targeting' government and aid funding to the poor, rather than on shaping the distributive outcomes of the mixed public–private health care sector as a whole. The more or less explicit objective becomes a health care system segmented into public and private sectors for the poor and better-off respectively (Bloom 2000; Mackintosh 2001).

The second category of health policy literature refocuses on the health care system as a whole. The WHO has recently put forward a particular version of this approach (WHO 2000), constructing summary measures of distributional aspects of health systems: inequality in health outcomes, distribution of 'responsiveness' of the system, and the regressiveness of financing of the system as a whole. The report uses the burden of disease approach as a basis for recommendations for increased risk-pooling as the primary financial method of tackling distributional inequity in health outcomes.

The strengths of this approach are the focus on health care as a system, and on promoting cross-subsidy within it, and the associated recognition of health care market failure. The approach, however, tends to obscure structure and segmentation within health care systems. Furthermore, the WHO (2000) report shares with the targeting literature an absence of a satisfactory concept of policy. Indeed the report oddly ascribes actor status and benign objectives to the system as a whole, for example:

Health systems have three fundamental objectives. These are:

- Improving the health of the population they serve.
- Responding to people's expectations.
- Providing financial protection against the costs of ill health (WHO 2000: 8).

Mixed public/private and private provider-dominated systems will however have no such unmixed objectives, as we explore for the case of Tanzania in Section 5. The WHO's approach to public sector funding allocation is also prescriptive:

> [T]he health system should strive for both horizontal and vertical equity... this generally requires spending public funds in favour of the poor (WHO 2000: 55).

Multilateral organizations are constrained in putting forward explanations of policy decisions by member governments. However, policy-oriented health systems research literature in the development context also has a prescriptive methodological cast, tending to focus on the evaluation of performance of elements of the system against specified objectives concerning cost, access or quality, and displaying a preference for sample survey methods and quantitative results. Research of this type has generated a large literature on aspects of health care systems in low- and middle-income contexts, including increasing documentation of the quality and cost failings of mixed public/private market-based health care.[5] This literature has the great strength that it recognizes interactions within health care systems, and the scope for improving resources use by changing relationships within the system – for example, by improving referral and increasing access by the poor to government hospitals. Increasingly, proposals include formal and informal insurance schemes. The research literature also pays much more attention than multilateral publications to both context and history.

However, health policy proposals drawn from this literature continue to be poorly rooted in contextual understanding of non-market behaviour and behavioural responses to market incentives in health systems. Such behaviour is only rarely researched directly using qualitative techniques (Segall *et al.* 2000), and policy proposals are frequently based on poorly supported behavioural assumptions (Leonard 2000b; Mackintosh and Gilson 2002). The dominant policy mindset in the field, and the dominant conception of the policy process in the academic literature, remains a linear policy formulation-to-policy implementation model. There are exceptions and numerous critical voices, but there is a clear lack of a solid alternative health and development literature rooted in political economy and social theory.

The social roots of social policy: European and African perspectives

This methodological 'thinness' in the analysis of policy contrasts starkly with some current European literature on social policy. European social policy analysis contains some 'thicker'[6] methodologies – that is, analysis that relates social policy and process to social structure, and to broader political and economic processes, and that seeks to explain redistributive success or failure in context. This includes historical and comparative work on welfare regimes, that brings together an understanding of the historical evolution of national systems with analysis of their current outcomes;[7] more abstract theorizing of social policy processes, applying formal models to understanding historical development of welfare provision;[8] and the literature on social exclusion that draws strong links between economic change and social policy.[9] Finally, there is a burgeoning literature on the social construction of social policy.[10] All of these approaches include health policy as an element of social policy.

Though highly diverse, these literatures share several key methodological features. Each seeks to integrate broader economic and social structures into the explanation of particular forms of social provision. Furthermore, they all treat policy as a largely endogenous variable: as something requiring explanation in context, not simply as extra-contextual proposition and argument. And, as a result, they all take seriously and integrate into their explanations of policy the particularity of the discursive construction of local welfare problems.

The welfare regime literature traces its roots to Titmuss's (Titmuss 1958, 1974) writing on social policy. As the authors of a recent empirical study of the outcomes of different welfare regimes put it, particular welfare regimes 'bundle together' 'particular values with particular programmes and policies', and with particular patterns of organization of the broader capitalist economy. 'Different sorts of welfare regime pursue different policies and they do so for different sorts of reasons' (Goodin *et al.* 1999: 5).

The European social exclusion literature was driven by a concern that in an era of high unemployment, increasing numbers of people were facing multiple forms of disadvantage, many without effective social protection from established welfare systems. Silver (1995) analyses the multiple concepts of 'exclusion' in that literature – the many answers to the question, 'exclusion from what?' – as expressions, not of confusion, but of attempts to rework, in specific contexts, shared understandings of society, polity and the need for social integration.

This concern to understand the social and political origins of policy intervention reappears in more formalist European work on welfare policy and history. De Swaan (1988), for example, investigates the circumstances in which public health interventions such as connecting slum areas of cities to the public water supply became politically possible and desirable. The main influences, he argues, were changes in medical information on the sources of epidemics, notably the transmission of cholera; changes in proximity and hence mutual knowledge, as the cities became dense, with poor areas in inner cities alongside wealthier quarters; and changes in the marginal costs of public hygiene for the poor, such as clean water supplies, once most of the city was connected to pipes. The driving forces were a mix of self-interest and an affordable sense of responsibility by even the fairly poor towards the destitute: 'the price of empathy has gone down so much that even the common people can afford it' (De Swaan 1988: 255). At that point, municipalities effectively turned water supplies into a public good,[11] making it non-excludable by decision and providing sufficient infrastructure that consumption was not then in practice rival.

De Swaan's analysis incorporates the discursive construction of social policy issues into its explanatory framework. This is also characteristic of the European social constructionist literature, which employs the concept of a 'welfare settlement' or 'social settlement': a stable (though temporary) 'truce' or compromise between embedded inequalities and redistributive social provision (Hughes and Lewis 1998; Williams *et al.* 1999). In this framework, social sectors such as health and education constitute arenas that both reflect and consolidate particular patterns of social inequality *and* that also offer an effective stage for challenging inequity. Such 'settlements' are periodically broken up and reworked as a result of social and political initiatives.

These key methodological features are also identifiable in the work of scholars in middle- and low-income countries on historical and sociological analysis of inequality and exclusion and of social policy. We illustrate the point from East Africa. Kaijage and Tibaijuka (1996) argue, for example, that the social exclusion framework is methodologically attractive because it combines an emphasis on understanding individuals' experience of marginalization through economic deprivation and social isolation with an understanding of the context of that marginalization: the fragmentation of social relations, the breakdown of social cohesion and the emergence of new economic and social divisions. The authors' analysis of poverty and exclusion in Tanzania traces the cumulatively unequalizing effects of economic crisis and decline to differential access to 'economic assets, or allocative and decision making power, or favourable social connections' (Kaijage and Tibaijuka 1996: 182). Health services, they argue, are mediating social institutions which shape marginalization: the 'battering' taken by government- provided social support services during Tanzania's severe economic crisis of the 1980s and early 1990s was a 'motor' of deprivation (Kaijage and Tibaijuka 1996: 186). Other scholars have also sought to develop more satisfactory conceptual frameworks for analysing social policy content and effects in East Africa, in the context of economic change, recognizing in particular the blurred boundaries between state and non-state service providers and the ambiguities of 'privatization' in the context of the continuing dependence of non-governmental service providers on state support. Therkildsen and Semboja (1995) consider social policy as an aspect of broader economic policy shifts under the impact of external market and donor pressure and internal social differentiation and political struggles. Other papers in the same collection (Semboja and Therkildsen 1995) trace the historical trajectories of service provision in health and education, unpicking and reworking concepts such as 'partnership', 'access' and community action in the context of changing state behaviour.

More research on social sectors in low-income contexts, that combines detailed economic analysis of distributive processes and outcomes with historical and sociological analysis of institutional and policy evolution and the interaction of social policy with broader economic and political change, will strengthen the scope for social policy that draws upon local institutional strengths. Furthermore, the stronger the dialogue between local policy makers and local researchers, the more effective the research is likely to be in feeding into context-relevant institutional design. Conversely, one reason for the treatment of policy as a largely exogenous variable, and lack of analysis of local institutional design for redistributive policy, may be the relative dominance – far more marked in writing on Africa than elsewhere – of external prescription within the overall policy debate. We seek below to make an analytical argument for the benefits of localization and context-specificity in policy analysis of the scope for redistribution.

Political economy and health care systems: reciprocity and redistribution

> . . . redistribution, by which we shall simply mean an unrequited transfer of resources from one person to another.   (Boadway and Keen 2000: 679)

Redistributive behaviour in unequal societies is likely to be hard to sustain, since those with higher incomes must pay twice – once for themselves, and once for others. Even to state the point thus starkly suggests the limits of prescriptive injunctions in policy analysis. Rather we need to explore what processes of institutionalization and legitimation might sustain in theory, and have historically sustained, such behaviour over time.

Institutional economics has had a considerable impact in recent years on the way in which economists theorize economic behaviour in communities and markets (Ben-Ner and Putterman 1998). However, the literature has focused overwhelmingly on the problems of and incentives for co-operation, and this has underpinned, in theoretical terms, the policy shifts towards decentralization, co-production and community involvement in the social policy and development literature. Much less explored have been the conditions for effective redistributive behaviour by governments, service providers, funding institutions and communities. As a result, the policy literature, while criticizing redistributive failure, pays too little attention to designing relationships that can sustain redistributive commitment.

Economists typically theorize redistribution, as in the above quotation, as unrequited gifts between individuals. The further social sector 'reform' proceeds in the direction of marketization of supply and targeted gap-filling, the closer the redistributive process moves to that economists' model: the more redistribution is institutionally separated out and made visible, the more stark becomes its social and political identification as unreciprocated gift. This is a source of concern, since both economic and anthropological theories of gift-giving suggest that unrequited gifts are problematic to receive and to sustain.

Standard economic theory, including game-theoretic models, constructs gift-giving from better-off individuals to poor people as altruism. Redistribution of this kind will only occur if the better-off *choose* to provide for others as well as themselves. Altruistic preferences may be ethically based – the better-off may be dismayed by extreme poverty – or they may be based on a fear of disorder. The defining feature is that people's perception of their welfare, and hence their behaviour, is influenced by the welfare of others as well as their own (Barr 1998; Collard 1978).

The implication is that altruistic behaviour is fragile because of the 'free rider' problem: even altruists may not behave altruistically if they cannot be assured that others will do so too. In these models, income redistribution has the qualities of a public good: it will be underprovided unless the participation of all can be assured. Hence, coercion through the tax system may be acceptable: a situation that Barr (1998: 87) calls 'voluntary compulsion'. This kind of model is used to explain voluntary acceptance of redistributive taxes by failures of voluntary co-ordination; it does not seek to explain the altruistic preferences themselves nor consider how they may be sustained.

Game-theoretic economic analysis, and associated experimentation, has shown that mutually 'collaborative' behaviour – such as resisting incentives to free ride – can be sustained even when individual incentives to 'defect' are high (Gintis 2000; Kreps 1990). Furthermore, experimentation repeatedly demonstrates mutual generosity – or 'gift-giving' – and reciprocal collaboration for mutual benefit, beyond that predicted by an assumption of pure self-interest. Gintis – an evolutionary game theorist – formulates from these experimental results the hypothesis of *homo reciprocans*: in contrast to *homo economicus* this is a representative person with a 'propensity to cooperate' (Gintis 2000: 251) but who retaliates against non-cooperative behaviour. This whole body of work is widely argued to imply that voluntary collaboration is likely to be particularly sustainable in small communities where people perceive mutual benefits, know a good deal about each other, can see the consequences of their actions and will continue to interact over time; in these conditions communities support the continuation of 'pro-social' norms (Bowles and Gintis 1998).

Many of these results depend upon the key assumption of mutuality of benefit to sustain collaboration. It is inattention to this assumption that underlies the elision, in some of the literature on social capital and health care, between collaboration and redistribution: 'Social capitalists...champion the importance in public policy of co-operation, community, equality, and inclusiveness' (Kunitz 2001: 160).

'Communities' however are typically far from egalitarian, and in unequal societies there is a need for a much sharper distinction between co-operation and altruism. Very little game theoretic work has considered the consequences of persistent inequality for optimism about collaboration.[12]

The implication that unreciprocated gift-giving – unlike reciprocal generosity – is problematic to sustain is supported by the analysis of gifts in anthropology and sociology. Part of the definition of the 'gift' in the anthropology literature since the contribution of Mauss (1924) is the close association of the nature of the gift with the giver's and receiver's social locations: gifts create social relations of dependence and obligation, in contrast to alienable commodities (Gregory 1982). The sociological literature explores the common parlance idea of the 'free gift'. Carrier (1995) calls this concept of gifts, 'gratuitous favours': formal expressions of love and thanks, and acknowledgement of relationships, but discursively framed as unreciprocated. The common thread is the link between gifts and social relationships: whether discursively framed as 'free gifts', or whether given in the explicit expectation of the reciprocation, persistently unreciprocated gifts create problematic relationships of dependency and unfulfilled obligation for both giver and receiver.

The economic, anthropological and sociological analysis all thus suggests that redistributive gift-giving may work best when embedded in relationships that are socially constructed as reciprocal. In the rest of this section we draw out some implications of this suggestion for redistributive behaviour in unequal societies, with particular reference to health care. We distinguish two 'ideal types' of unequal community. In each case, the community can be divided on the basis of the primary distribution of income into two sets of people, 'better-off' and 'poor'. Then we can distinguish:

> Case A: where the membership of the sets is stable – that is, the same people are very likely to be poor and better off year on year; and
> Case B: where the membership of the sets is unstable – that is, the probability of individuals shifting from one group to another from year to year is high.

We assume that 'redistribution' means that the 'poor' set receive a subsidy from the 'better-off'. Then redistribution is likely to be a sustainable public good in Case B, so long as the community has stable membership and mutual knowledge is high – people know who is better off and who is poor. People who are better off know they may slip into poverty, and those who are poor know it may only be a temporary situation. In those circumstances the self-interested among the better off have an insurance motive to contribute to redistribution in addition to any altruistic motivation they may have. Redistribution will in principle be sustainable whether there is a fund with formal rules requiring contributions (no payment when better off implies no support when poor) or whether informal collaboration is the means to ensure that the fund does not disappear because of free riding.

Mutual health insurance can build effectively upon this model in 'Case B'-type contexts. Mutual insurance schemes are widespread in Africa, and while they display successful risk-pooling on a reciprocal basis, they tend to exclude the very poor (Atim 1999; Criel *et al.* 1999). The more formal mutual savings schemes that include health care appear to be strongest when they are both embedded in, and operate to strengthen, wider reciprocal social ties (Atim 1999). Some locally initiated mutual health insurance schemes (but apparently no donor-led schemes in Africa) have built on existing mutual organisations (Atim 1999; Kiwara 2000: 887). There is certainly a redistributive element in these schemes, since prepayment improves the inclusiveness of health care by increasing the use of the formal health care system by the seriously ill on low incomes (Criel *et al.* 1999). Incorporating those who cannot pay is hard because it breaks the mutuality on which the schemes are based, though some donor-subsidized mutuals in Africa have successfully incorporated locally managed exemptions for the indigent (Kiwara 2000).

Indian evidence also suggests that voluntary mutual insurance is hard to establish or sustain in contexts of acute social and income inequality (Giridhar 1993). Which brings us to Case A. In an unequal community in which poverty and relative wealth are persistent features of individuals, economics and anthropology (and, indeed, common sense) suggest that sustaining redistributive behaviour is hard. The group of persistently better off lack mutual benefit motives for generosity and the requirement of persistent altruism by one group towards another puts a heavy weight on 'benevolence'.[13] A *homo reciprocans* assumption will reinforce that conclusion, since the poor cannot reciprocate. We should not therefore expect much active redistribution within such highly stratified small communities.

While the findings on the importance of insurance motives for mutual collaboration are conventional, what is less familiar is the drawing out of implications for the design of redistributive mechanisms in more stratified 'communities'. If redistribution in such communities is necessarily based on altruism – or alternatively on some concept of duty – then these potentially fragile commitments may be more sustainable if they can be embedded in or supported by norms and expectations that contain some elements of reciprocity.

Low incomes do not make redistributive health care impossible – as the Kerala example demonstrates – but in general they create severe dilemmas in confronting inequality. Case A is likely to be particularly relevant to many low-income situations. So in Case A situations, is there scope never-theless for embedding redistribution in reciprocity? We suggest that health care does offer particular opportunities to do so, in part because of the efficiency gains available from risk-pooling and from constraining market incentives, and in part because of the ethical weight carried by the behaviour of health services in people's understanding of society and polity.

There are two ways of thinking about the embedding of 'gifts' in reciprocity. One, characteristic of institutional economics, formalizes the idea that the 'return' that sustains duty-based redistributive behaviour by the better off may be standing, respect, legitimation of relative wealth, or more generally, social 'regard' (Offer 1997). This suggests that recognition – professional or more personalized – may sustain persistent 'gift-giving'.

Evidence of the difficulty of redistributive behaviour in small communities and of the relevance of this kind of personalized and professional reciprocity to addressing that difficulty can be drawn from research on local exemption schemes and local mutual insurance in health care. The introduction of user fees at government health care facilities, as part of health sector reforms, has often been associated with a requirement that the facilities offer some free or reduced price care to specified groups, usually including very poor would-be patients (Gilson *et al.* 1995; Russell and Gilson 1997). These cross-subsidized exemptions are thus unreciprocated local 'free gifts' from those who can pay to those who cannot. Research demonstrates that the poorest rarely benefit, and that those with status and power within communities frequently obtain free treatment (Gilson *et al.* 1999; Gilson *et al.* 1995; Russell and Gilson 1997; Tibandebage and Mackintosh 2001; Tibandebage and Mackintosh 2002).

However, a case study of a genuinely effective exemption scheme in Thailand (Gilson *et al.* 1998) suggests that the conditions for its success included: clear, nationally set and openly applied criteria, adapted by agree-ment to local experience; information campaigns targeted at beneficiaries promoting their use of exemptions and generally of public health care; and *also* the embedding of redistributive action within local reciprocal relationships and meanings. For example, in Thai communities, a (small) observed 'leakage' of exemptions to some non-poor with close connections to village leaders and those held in high regard within the community was socially construed in this way: 'This is a way to express our gratitude to them. Without their support, our centre would be in problems. Don't you know that granting a card to those people would mean to make them proud and honoured?' (Gilson *et al.* 1998: 41–2). This type of cultural reworking of the exemption schemes in terms of the duties of the better-off and their due recognition may help to give them their observed legitimacy and sustainability.

We offer in the next section some evidence from our own research that personalized recognition is relevant to redistributiveness in small communities. Nevertheless, there is thus no reason to assume that small communities are more redistributive than national systems. Decentralization – widely recommended – may have redistributive effects, but only if shaped by an appropriate combination of clear central guidelines, and openness to local adaptation and review, including review of central government practice; allocation criteria based on formulae further open the process to public scrutiny (Gilson and Travis 1998). To the extent that personalized redistribution is unstable, larger scale, more impersonal rules, legitimated through national social and political organizing, appear to be central to redistributive success. National public action can also establish concepts of entitlements or minimum rights that can legitimize voluntary collective action to attain them.

The question of legitimation brings us to the second way of thinking about embedding 'gifts' in reciprocity. Drawn from anthropology and the 'cognitive' end of institutional economics (Scott 1995), this approach is less individualist in its modelling of norms of behaviour. Institutions here are not 'rules' of a game, and 'norms' are not observed regularities of behaviour; rather, norms are more like 'scripts' for sense-making, and institutions are things we 'think within', or that 'think' for us: parts of ourselves as social beings (Douglas 1987: 124; Scott 1995). These theorists argue that legitimate institutions are those that come (for a time) to appear in a carefully defined sense as 'natural': part of the world we take for granted, often expressed through metaphors associating them with the natural world. Douglas (1987) argues that such legitimate institutions 'make' big, difficult decisions such as some that arise in health care; we do not rethink each decision from first principles. This locates the shaping of institutions as a key policy issue, and also implies that policies are themselves influenced by existing institutions.

There is some evidence that successful redistributive behaviour in existing health care systems is sustained by embedding it in taken-for-granted reciprocal relationships and meanings. At the national level, high-income countries are generally in the happier Case B situation. Longitudinal research suggests that a high proportion of severe poverty in these countries is transient: people move in and out of poverty over time, and persistent poverty – which is a serious concern – is focused in a small segment of the populations (Goodin *et al.* 1999). This suggests that the insurance motive for support of redistribution is likely to be strong. *Capacity* to redistribute is also strong (this was De Swaan's point, above). If we add that the risk of severe illness affects the better-off too, we have an explanation of the observed strong support in most such countries for highly redistributive universalist health care systems that does not depend upon institutional legitimation.

However, not in all: the USA is an outlier, with a much less redistributive welfare and health care system, despite conforming to the conditions just set out (Barr 1998; Goodin *et al.* 1999). Furthermore, citizens' preferences are observed to differ according to the system within which they live. Europeans, for example, are found to have stronger commitments to health care equity of access than do citizens of the United States: as Besley and Gouveia (1994: 249) put it: 'The US social equilibrium has traditionally taken it for granted that the poor deserve less health care than the middle classes.' By contrast, the standard of evaluation in European debate tends to be equal access in response to equal need. Social insurance for health care, once established, appears to reinforce the norms and values that support it.[14]

These reflections in turn suggest path dependency: norms and values interact with institutional development. How does policy intervene? There is evidence that redistributive action – including in health care – has historically become institutionalized where it was been closely involved in nation-building and the construction of concepts of citizenship. For example, Chiang (1995: 228) recounts how in Taiwan national health insurance was politically constructed as 'a critical indicator of "good" government in a modernising nation' by the Kuomintang's electoral platform, accelerating the acceptance of universalization of access through tax subsidy.

Similarly, Indian research shows that political commitment and ideology in favour of redistribution can influence health care tax allocation behaviour, especially when it is associated with active political pressure. In Kerala, for example, collective political organizing to keep health care facilities open is long standing (Sen 1992), and the high proportion of state public spending devoted to social sectors (40 per cent in Kerala 1974–90 as compared to the Indian average of 32 per cent) is rooted in open elections won on support for social provision including health care (Narayana 1999). In contrast, in the large northern states with the worst health care record, these issues do not figure in party programmes and electoral politics are overwhelmingly dominated by elite concerns (Drèze and Sen 1995: 103).

Health care, because of its ethical weight, is thus an important arena for political organizing. Health systems, like welfare systems more broadly, once they enter the political arena, form part of the process of construction of who is a full citizen. Hence, they also exclude and stratify (in the UK notably, by 'race' and gender as well as social class).[15] The systems *both* reflect broader social inequality *and* form a political 'stage' for the contestation of inequality; they are thus important building blocks of legitimate democratic states. Critics of the limitations of coverage of the Korean national health insurance system, for example Yang (1996), argue that resolving exclusion involves constructing 'shared understandings' and positive public meanings around the concept of social insurance perhaps through a 'citizen's movement backed by formal consumers' organisations' (Yang 1996: 251). Londoño and Frenk (1997) argue that overcoming the blockage on health care redistribution in Latin American countries represented by institutionally polarized health care systems involves governments' taking responsibility for 'social mobilization' and 'advocacy' to create the social basis for universalization. The difficulty of creating greater redistribution across established polarized systems, even in wealthy countries, is illustrated by the failure of health care reform in the United States.

Polarization and the problem of health care redistribution in Tanzania

The previous section has argued that redistributive commitment within a health care system appears to be an endogenous variable: that is, it is deeply influenced by the general patterns of social class and inequality in society, and also by the particular institutions of the system and the norms of behaviour established within them. For a health care system to operate redistributively requires not only government commitment to redistributive behaviour in the allocation of funds, but also commitment at the institutional level to operate in an inclusionary manner, and within communities to sustain inclusion of the poor. This is possible, though difficult, in 'Case A' situations, and easier, but not inevitable, in 'Case B'.

In this section we draw briefly on recent research in Tanzania to illustrate what some of the implications of this argument might be for health care research and policy in a low-income context. Liberalization of the formal private provision of health care in Tanzania and in many African (and other) countries has reshaped existing health care markets, and created implicit choices about the direction of private health care market development. Social polarization in some systems is limited but appears to be consolidating, facing governments with clear choices of policy framework. If we are correct that redistributive commitment is interactive and path-dependent, then early directions of institutional change will shape not only later options but also later decision making frameworks.

We start by providing some evidence for social polarization in health care provision and access, using data on pricing and access by social group from recent research in Tanzania.[16] Tanzania is one of the world's poorest countries. GDP in 1999 was estimated at US$240 per head (World Bank 2001); donor funding accounted in the early 1990s for more than half of non-private health care finance (World Bank 1996), and official development aid – which fell sharply in the 1990s – was estimated at 12.5 per cent of GDP in 1998 (World Bank 2001). Spending on health care by government plus donors, estimated at less than US$5 per head per year in 1992/3, or about US$7.3 in total including private spending (World Bank 1996), was a long way below the US$12 minimum the World Bank estimated was needed to provide basic preventative and clinical care, or the later estimate of $35 by the Commission on Macroeconomics and Health (CMH 2001; Tibandebage 1995). Allocation of very limited public funding for health care therefore involves very invidious choices.

A period of rapid expansion of government health care provision in Tanzania in the 1960s and 1970s, and the abolition of private for-profit practice in 1977 (Upunda 2000), was followed by severe economic crisis and a decline in the quality of provision (Kiwara 2000). The subsequent liberalization of individual private clinical practice by the 1991 Amendment Act no. 26 formed part of a wider process of economic and political liberalization (Wangwe *et al.* 1998). In a context of severe and widespread poverty, the result has been a rapid rise in for-profit private practice only in the urban areas (Tibandebage 1999; Tibandebage and Mackintosh 2001). Also in the 1990s, user fees were introduced in government facilities – first in hospitals and later extended to urban dispensaries and health centres. At the time of our study, in 1998 and 1999, only rural government dispensaries were not charging formal fees.

We studied two health care markets – in the capital Dar es Salaam and a contiguous area of Coast Region, and in Mbeya, a town in the Southern Highlands and an adjoining rural district. Most of the fieldwork was undertaken in mid- to late-1998, and included interviewing and data collection in facilities, and interviews with patients on exit and with household members in the facilities' catchment areas. At that time, most patients paid for consultations and treatment out of pocket, whether they attended government, religious-owned or private facilities (Table 7.1): in that sense this was truly a market system of health care, and our aim was particularly to understand the market interaction of types of facility and patients in local markets and their consequences for users and for those excluded. We were studying a moment in an evolving market system.

In this context, Figures 7.1 and 7.2 provide images of what appears to be emerging market segmentation. The circles are primary care providers (dispensaries and health centres) in all sectors in Dar es Salaam; the size of the circles is weighted by activity level; the two axes show two independent measures of charging levels, mean stated facility prices and mean charges to patients leaving the facility. Two poles of activity with different charging levels emerge: these are small sample data, but the qualitative evidence supports emerging, but still incomplete social segmentation of the market.

The two emerging poles are patterned by ownership. In the Dar es Salaam study, the large high-charging facilities are religious and privately-owned

Table 7.1 Transactions by payment category, exit and household interviewees, by market (number of facility visits)

Transaction type	Region		Total
	Mbeya	*DSM/Coast*	
Zero payment: government or donor funded*	27	5	32
Paid out of pocket by self or relative	141	161	302
Paid by employer	14	19	33
Total	182	185	367

Note: * Excludes visits with free consultation where a prescription was written and then filled in at a private drug shop or pharmacy; includes visits where the question concerning prescriptions was not answered, hence may still overestimate free transactions.

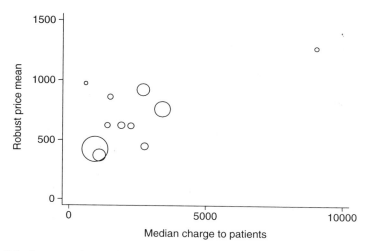

Figure 7.1 Segmentation in the Dar es Salaam/Coast region health care market (Tshs)

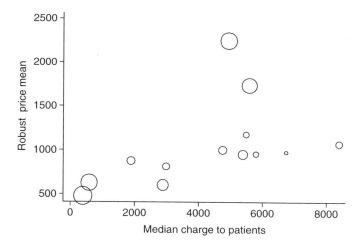

Figure 7.2 Segmentation in the Mbeya health care market (Tshs)

facilities which generally cannot be afforded by the poor; the large low-charging facilities are religious and government-owned, and their quality is crucial to the access and experience of the poor. The range of small facilities in between are mainly privately-owned, and the qualitative evidence suggests that they are also of considerable aggregate importance to the urban poor. The Mbeya data generate a recognizably similar pattern, though with more small relative to large facilities. Here, the large high-charging facilities are both religious-owned; the two large low-charging facilities are one government, and one religious-owned. The rest of the range is of mainly private small facilities, some patently overcharging relative to their declared prices. One of the most striking findings of this study is the polarization of the religious-owned sector between low charging, genuinely charitable facilities, and facilities who were applying their subsidies and energies to serving the better-off (Tibandebage and Mackintosh 2001).

This image of polarization is reinforced at hospital level. Figure 7.3 illustrates this point. It shows the facilities' stated prices for a basic in-patient stay in a hospital, excluding the cost of drugs.[17] Again, the facilities are weighted by activity. The categories on the lower axis are (1) government (2) a rural religious-owned hospital (3) two small private hospitals in Mbeya (4) Dar es Salaam non-government hospitals, private and religious. Categories (1) and (2) are markedly cheaper on all the available evidence, including interviews with patients, except for one of the government hospitals where informal charges and the requirements on the patients to buy all supplies and drugs from commercial suppliers had dramatically increased observed payments. The two Mbeya private hospitals, though much cheaper than *all* non-government hospitals in Dar es Salaam, were still out of reach of most of the population. Perhaps most dramatic, however, is the lack of hospital care options available in Dar es Salaam to those on even moderate incomes: if government hospitals fail the poor in the city, there is little recourse.

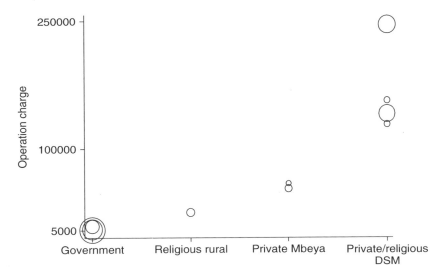

Figure 7.3 Hospitals, price of an operation (OPD consultation, appendectomy, in-patient charge), by facility category, scatterplot weighted by in-patient activity (Tshs)

The image of polarization suggested by these facility-level data is strongly reinforced by the qualitative interviewing of patients on exit from facilities and household members in the catchment areas of selected facilities (Tibandebage and Mackintosh 2001). The health care system both reflects and reinforces social division and exclusion, most strikingly in the urban areas. There is evidence that the burden of impoverishment via the health care system was falling most heavily on the urban poor. The rural poor, and indeed most people in rural areas, continued to rely primarily on the government sector, and at the primary care level, the rural government facilities continued to constitute a partial safety net for this group. None imposed formal charges; informal charges were prevalent but very low compared to those in urban areas; and donor-supplied drugs kits, though limited, provided much needed free access to basic drugs.

Virtually all of the low-charge transactions recorded – zero or below Tshs 500 (already a large sum in rural areas) – were therefore in the government sector, mainly at primary level, and 88 per cent of those were in rural areas. Of those rural government sector transactions, in turn, 95 per cent were made by the poor: that is, by people who were small farmers or petty traders or dependent upon them and who had primary education and below. Thus government sector transactions at low charges sustained access to some primary care by the rural poor; the provision in turn was sustained by donor-provided drugs.[18]

The urban poor lacked this limited recourse. The few government dispensaries and health centres in urban areas[19] were charging user fees by 1998, improving the drugs supply but implying the exclusion of those without funds; only one in the study was widely said to ask for bribes; the others appeared to be charging only the formal fees. However, they were few, and the urban poor relied to a noteworthy extent on non-government facilities, including private for-profit, at the dispensary and health centre level (80 per cent of visits by the urban poor), while turning almost solely to the government sector for hospital care; indeed they relied proportionately more than the somewhat better off on small local private dispensaries.

The quantitative and qualitative evidence is consistent. More than 80 per cent of people classified as urban poor said they had never so much as heard of a case of free treatment. 'There is no service without money' was a repeated view; and we met no one in this study who had benefited from, or could recount an example of, exemption from fees on the grounds of inability to pay. In addition, the data show a pattern of abusive behaviour and informal charging at some (although not all) government hospitals, and of abusive mistreatment at some private dispensaries. Both types of mistreatment fell most heavily on the urban poor, and were associated with high levels of exclusion and self-exclusion. Taken together, these data show a pattern of high charges, lack of free options, and reliance on abusive facilities that is worst for the poor in urban areas (though not limited to them)'.

What are the implications for redistributive policy of this type of polarization, and the associated impoverishment of the already poor who are struggling to pay fees?[20] In methodological terms, health policy cannot be conceived solely in terms of allocational processes for public funds. Allocation matters greatly, but resources are made effective through the operation of the health care system as a whole, and where markets dominate, public resources are employed, diverted, invested and recirculated through them. The distributional outcomes depend upon the interactions within the system, and between system and users. The Tanzanian government has furthermore, by regional standards, been allocating a relatively high proportion of its funds to primary and preventative care; however, in the context of the almost exclusive concentration of official donors on support of preventative and primary care, the hospitals remain heavily dependent on government funding support (World Bank 1996).

Furthermore, allocational processes respond to month-to-month fiscal and political pressures: as one government interviewee put it, in a situation of acute financial constraint, non-government providers promised subsidy 'can only have one thigh of the duck!'. In other words, there are competing pressures and also bargaining processes that operate between formal and effective allocational decisions, and effective allocational commitment will depend on such processes.

We found that all health care sectors currently relied on funding from non-fee sources. Not only government but also religious, NGO and private providers depended upon government funds and assets (not least, in the private sector, on government-trained personnel (Tibandebage *et al.* 2001)). Some religious sector facilities were directly subsidized by government and many received donations. Official donor funds went into all three sectors. And private providers – finding it very hard to raise investment funds – also subsidized facilities from profits of other commercial ventures.

Finally, there are strong market interactions between health care facilities, and this should affect government policy on pricing and other aspects of policy (Tibandebage 1999). In this overall context, the right question to ask about the allocation of government funds, if the concern is to encourage redistributive behaviour, is surely: what would be the best use of these limited funds to influence the quality and improve the accessibility of the system as a whole?[21] While the government has, for example, few resources for inspecting the private sector, the overall (competitive) *weight* of government-funded activity in the system is very large – and is even larger if donor spending is added to tax funding. It should be possible to use this weight to influence the evolution of the system – but to do so involves some rethinking of policy processes of the type now very much underway in Tanzania.

We summarize here some implications for thinking about policy approaches, based on our research and drawing on discussion at a health policy workshop in Dar es Salaam in 2000,[22] and link them to the theoretical arguments put forward above.

Build on redistributive success

This sounds obvious, but it is not. There were some real success stories in this study in providing some elements of a safety net for the poor, but policy processes did not necessarily identify or ensure support for them. They included good government facilities in both urban and rural areas and some truly 'charitable' religious-owned facilities. Lack of recognition meant that they could be undermined, and the success not built upon. How can such successes be sustained against the counterpressures of falling subsidy, and against individual and facility incentives to generate income from patients? Here, the discussion of reciprocity and institutionalization offer some ideas. To strengthen probity and 'charitable' cultures requires their embedding in a framework of local and national recognition, beneficial incentives, and greater policy leverage: recognized achievement is a considerable incentive for continued probity. One way to do this may be:

Strengthen desirable self-regulation

Self-regulation has considerable dangers.[23] But collaborative self-managed associations of genuinely accessible providers of reasonable quality also offer considerable potential benefits.[24] In the religious sector they can help to develop, and can publicize, 'benchmark' fees and standards of accessibility and care; they can strengthen the existing networks of collaboration (such as those in the religious-owned sector)[25] by developing self-management capacity; in return, such publicity can raise activity in facilities and help good facilities to undercut poor ones. And membership can act as a 'signal' to donors of effective use of subsidy. The more visible, the more such associations can influence public expectations and debate and create pressure on those allocating funds: one among a number of possible ways of endogenizing redistributive pressure on the allocation of funds. This in turn (see Boadway and Keen 2000) might be aided by:

Involving the public in identifying success

In the rural government sector, there was some evidence that community involvement played a role in sustaining probity and inclusion. Reciprocity between facilities and the public create beneficial reputation effects, but users have limited information. A benchmarking scheme that involved local communities in developing and publicizing good practice could add to their knowledge and build on existing involvement. A district might identify a benchmark group of good rural facilities that could be encouraged to develop higher levels of community scrutiny. The 'label' could constitute much needed recognition of existing probity and good practice, and encourage continuing donor support. This implies a fourth principle:

Abandon the 'level playing field' – differentiate providers

Some facilities that serve the poor are dangerous and abusive, notably some but *not* all private dispensaries. Others offer competent basic care and cross-subsidize preventative care as a strategy to attract patients: their sustainability needs support, including help in surviving undercutting by poor quality competitors (which we found to be a serious issue, not merely an inevitable complaint). Some donors are already working on schemes to assist them. For-profit providers play an important role in determining quality of urban primary care. Self-organization can play a useful role, but it is hard for private providers' organizations to police quality.[26] Particularly promising are schemes of accreditation to mutual and social insurance schemes, especially if this can be done collaboratively. This suggests:

Develop mutual schemes that link users' organizations and clinical audit

Mutual health care schemes that build on existing users' organizations in urban areas can also influence quality of care through clinical audit. One scheme that has done this successfully in Tanzania is UMASIDA (Umoja wa Matibabu wa Sekta Isiyo Rasmi Dar es Salaam/Informed Sector Association for Health Care in Dar es Salaam) (Kiwara 2000), an urban informal sector mutual insurance scheme. This builds on existing co-operative organization, is largely self-financing, and has used clinical audit to influence the practices of accredited private dispensaries. This provides private providers with incentives for probity. Mutual schemes can also increase redistributiveness in another way:

Embed exemptions in mutuality

Exemption schemes require collaboration between communities and facilities and, in the case of very impoverished communities, external funding. Some donor-subsidized mutual community health funds have successfully encouraged and required communities to identify candidates for exemptions (Kiwara 2000). Embedding redistributive obligations within schemes of broad community benefit – and publicly valuing the fulfilment of those obligations – appears to be a route to sustainability. We met a clinical officer in a government dispensary who had asked village leaders to help identify candidates for exemptions and met a flat refusal; closer involvement in facility management could change that attitude. This implies:

Stabilizing links between facilities and groups of users, to increase 'voice'

Health care users and would-be users were found to be far from passive.[27] Rather, they actively sought and circulated information, and discussions with household members of value for money from different facilities were well informed. However, users faced the system as individuals, and people feared complaining. To strengthen users' voices requires some forms of collective action and representation, which were most likely to work where they could build on stable links between groups of users and particular sets of facilities:

in addition to pre-payment schemes, the possibilities include building on existing village and urban local structures' initiatives; formalization of lay involvement in facilities management; and local collaboration with primary providers to try to create effective referral and a stronger primary providers' role in representing patients' interests. Which brings us to:

Blur the boundaries

We share the view, expressed by one of our interviewees, that 'privatizing middle class care' is most unlikely to make the health care system as a whole more redistributive. Rather, the more the system can be prevented from polarizing in terms of both finance and providing institutions, the more it is likely to be possible to sustain and increase redistributive and inclusive behaviour. If we are right that separating out redistribution in institutional terms makes it fragile, then blurring boundaries makes it easier to extract cross-subsidy through reciprocal benefits: efficiency improvements for redistributive action.

Keeping the poor and the better-off in the same institutions also reduces middle-class ignorance of, and distancing from, the problems. Blurred boundaries make experiment easier, and potentially allow desirable institutional cultures to help to break bad ones. They allow more efficient sharing of scarce resources; can reduce stigmatizing of the government sector; and permit independent providers access to government resources. Tanzania already has some successful examples of cross-subsidy from private wards in government facilities helping to ensure that lower-paying patients also have access to equipment and specialists. Opportunities for private income can help to retain good staff, and can if well managed help to sustain a culture of high quality care for lower income patients. In addition to mixed institutions:

Negotiate explicit returns for government support

Elite hospitals given non-profit status can also reasonably be asked in return for explicit contributions to the capacity, quality and inclusiveness of the health care system as a whole: expanded contributions to training, including support of trainees and collaboration with other institutions; allowing lower-charging institutions access to scarce equipment at low prices; exchanging staff with other institutions to assist with updating skills, including management skills; and providing specified services to patients referred from government facilities free or at low cost. Creative negotiating can create more efficient use of scarce resources through cross-boundary collaboration: cross-boundary contracts for staff with explicit and monitored government sector commitments; joint equipment purchase and maintenance schemes between institutions. Even in a country as poor as Tanzania, expensive assets are being underused. Given the financial fragility of the private and religious owned élite sectors, there is considerable scope for the joint creation of public goods and shared assets for mutual benefit.

Conclusion: redistribution in conditions of path dependency and policy endogeneity

The ideas that market systems are path-dependent in their distributive behaviour, and that policy itself is to a large extent endogenous, are both increasingly accepted in economics (Atkinson 1999; Hoff 2000; Kanbur and Lustig 2000). Much analysis of European social welfare systems takes the same view: the institutions evolve in path-dependent form influencing policy development in the process (section 3). The health policy and, more generally, the social policy literature in the development context, needs to follow suit: its methodology at present is insufficiently 'social' in content and insufficiently dynamic in its economic analysis.

To improve policy analysis, a shift is needed towards permitting more space for localism in social policy work, in the sense of the building up of local literatures on social security and social provisioning. Countries in which donors' prescriptive fashions have operated with less force than in much of Africa, such as some East Asian countries, have built up distinct literatures and traditions in social policy.[28] There is a considerable body of research on African social security and social policy by local scholars including historians and sociologists, and widespread involvement of individual local researchers in policy, but it has been hard for African researchers to build up the networks and visibility needed for the further development of distinct policy traditions.

There needs, relatedly, to be space for both methodological and prescriptive debate. The models of health care funding allocation emphasized by the multilaterals are one important contribution to those debates in health care. The policy debate would be enriched by more space also being allowed to debate issues of the type discussed above: the compromises between inequality and redistribution required to sustain redistributive behaviour in particular contexts; the existing local patterns of reciprocity that can be built on to support redistributive action; the particular pattern of market behaviour emerging in health care and its implications; the scope for focusing upon health care as an 'arena' for public action to increase social inclusiveness; and the consequences of a recognition that behavioural influences run in both directions – from social provisioning systems to government distributive behaviour and back.

Health care markets – like other social markets – are very diverse internationally. Some are more polarized and more exclusionary than others. There has been insufficient research on the reasons for the differences and their implications for policy. In principle, we would expect that the market differences relate to a mixture of the broader patterns of inequality in society; the inequality of resultant endowments that people bring to market; the market culture itself; the level of political activism around market organization and behaviour; and the cumulative feedback between those seeking care and facilities' development, including the impoverishing effects of charges on the already poor and the consequences of price-based competition for very poor users. There has recently been an increase in market studies in health care; they need bringing together in locally appropriate ways with the work on allocation of subsidy.

Theoretical and empirical research in health policy and development thus needs to pay more attention to the social, political and institutional conditions for sustained redistribution, indeed to bring that problem back to centre stage. The general implication of our arguments is a search for policies that work with *some* of the grain of existing health care institutional behaviour while creating active blocks on undesirable directions of institutional development. The early stages of emergent market development offer particularly crucial opportunities for influencing the later path of development. Policy intervention, if well thought out, can push the system towards increasing redistributiveness and probity in the medium term, rather than exacerbating inequality and poverty. In circumstances such as these, government action within partly polarized systems will help to shape the scope for future integration. Governments do not only fund care; they also influence – and are influenced by – the institutions that emerge in the market. Donor policies that try to *exclude* governments from such involvement, by pushing for a polarization between private provision for the better-off and public provision for the poor, are likely to have strong negative effects on government redistributive capacity and commitment.

Health policy would also benefit from more research on and policy attention to legitimacy: to the ways in which redistributive action is legitimated in unequal societies. We need more research and debate on how to value and sustain in low-income contexts cross-subsidy, charitable provision, and competent provision free at the point of use. There are good examples of all of these phenomena in African contexts, but their legitimacy has been challenged and their achievements denigrated, and the questions have been squeezed out of the research literature by the 'polarizing' policy mindset discussed above.

Our general argument is simply for a closer focus in the social policy literature on the political economy of redistribution, including the process of legitimating and strengthening claims to redistributive behaviour, the influences on the distributive outcomes of private/public systems, and the scope for sustaining redistributive behaviour by embedding it in forms of reciprocity. Such a research programme needs to pay close attention – this follows from many of the arguments above – to the discursive construction of social policy; the currently dominant social policy discourse and mindset is a real roadblock for policy makers with redistributive intentions.

The two alternative policy 'visions' of the state as gap-filler and the state as a major player in the shaping of the system as a whole, thus need revisiting and debating explicitly in current development contexts. The economic literature on redistribution documents what Lindert (2000) calls the 'Robin Hood paradox': the more unequal pre-tax/benefit incomes, the less redistribution there tends to be on both cross-section and longitudinal evidence. Lindert regards this as a 'paradox' since high levels of inequality generate an *efficiency* case for redistribution. From the political economy perspective, far from paradoxical, the evidence further supports a hypothesis of path dependency and endogenous policy development.

Health policy is a particularly promising field for redistributive action and agitation, because redistributive mechanisms can be designed to have strong efficiency properties, given the extent of private health care market failure. Where these joint benefits can be allied to political processes that legitimate access by the poor and value success, redistribution can be sustained. This is, in essence, the argument of the 'social settlement' literature (section 3): that explicitly accepting within health and welfare systems some forms of social inequality has historically been an important element in stabilizing redistributive success. This argument does *not* suggest that some forms of inequality are fine. Rather, it focuses attention on the culturally specific processes whereby redistribution has been actively fought for in different countries, and on the way in which associating rights to social provision with the construction of citizenship can be both effective and double-edged. Redistribution through social provisioning has never been just a 'technical' matter; rather, it has been a crucial element in the fight for democratic governance.

Notes

1. An earlier draft of this chapter was presented at the UNRISD Conference on Social Policy in a Development Context, Stockholm, September 2000; comments from participants in the conference are gratefully acknowledged, as are comments of participants in a seminar at IDS, Sussex in June 2001. The paper draws on joint research by the authors supported by the Department for International Development (DFID), UK, to whom we are most grateful; our thanks also for additional support from the Open University and UNRISD. The chapter also draws with thanks on joint work with Lucy Gilson. The opinions expressed here are solely those of the authors, and do not represent the policies or practices of the DFID.
2. The fieldwork in 1998 and 1999 was supported by DFID – see footnote 1. We thank A. D. Kiwara, P. Mujinja, P. Ngowi, G. Nyange, V. Mushi, J. Andrew, F. Meena, and J. Kajiba for their contribution to the design and undertaking of the research; Marc Wuyts for discussion, encouragement and help with data analysis; and everyone in the four fieldwork districts in Tanzania who gave their time to facilitate our research. The same disclaimer applies.
3. Tibandebage and Mackintosh (2001) provides detailed references. On Tanzania, see particularly Asenso-Okyere, Anum, Osei-Akotot and Adukonu (1998); Cooksey Mmuya (1997); Msamanga, Urasa, and Mujinja (1996); and Walraven (1996).
4. In the technical economic sense: to be both fully rival (more for me is less for you) and excludable.

5. For example Bennett, Mpake and Mills (eds) (1997), Bloom (1998), Leonard (2000a), Segall *et al.* (2000).

6. We are using 'thicker' here in a sense that is different to Geertz' famous (1973) concept of 'thick description' but nevertheless invokes it: we mean an analysis that is methodologically rich in its explanatory tools, including interpretation alongside calculation.

7. From a huge literature, see for example Esping-Andersen (1990), Goodin *et al.* (1999), and Lewis (1992).

8. A good example is De Swaan (1988).

9. See, for example, Rogers *et al.* (1995).

10. See, for example, Hughes and Lewis (1998), Lewis (2000) Mackintosh (1996).

11. 'Publicness' is often considered an inherent characteristic of a good or service; the alternative view is that 'publicness' is in good part a social product.

12. An exception is Bardhan *et al.* (2000), which explores the conditions under which inequality can undermine maintenance of local common pool resources.

13. The phrase is from James Meade, who advised that policy should 'economise on benevolence'; see Atkinson (1993).

14. Where the 'insurance' functions work poorly – as for cold surgery in the British NHS – the redistributive function ceases to be taken for granted, as in current UK public debate.

15. See Lewis, G. (1996) and Williams (1989).

16. See acknowledgements in note 2 above; this section draws on Tibandebage and Mackintosh (2001, 2002).

17. This is because the most expensive hospital (and only that facility, a religious-owned hospital) refused to provide drugs prices.

18. Our findings accord with other recent research that shows that in many rural contexts, free drugs kits are distributed free of charge, indeed the 'gift' of the drugs appears to have a positive ethical impact on facility behaviour (personal communication from A. Raikes); these findings contradict the commonly held assumption by many donors, policy makers and academics that such drugs are generally resold.

19. In the Dar es Salaam district studied, the 1999 Health Statistics Abstract shows 17 government dispensaries, and 39 government facilities in all (health centres, clinics and hospitals) out of a total of 339 health facilities. Mbeya Urban recorded 11 government facilities in all out of a greatly underestimated recorded total of 27 facilities; Dyauli (2000); URT (1999).

20. See Tibandebage and Mackintosh (2002).

21. We tried asking this question directly in our first round of interviews with policy makers in government and with other key stakeholders in the health care system, but found that it was not at the time understood.

22. The workshop proceedings are summarised in Economic and Social Research Foundation (2000).

23. If poorly designed it can raise prices and increase exclusion.

24. See Brugha and Zwi (1998); there is now widespread interest in accreditation and social marketing schemes among health policy analysts and donors, but Tanzanian policy makers in 1999 and 2000 found accreditation an unfamiliar idea.

25. The churches in Tanzania are actively developing collaborative policy and supervision, under the umbrella of the Christian Social Services Council; schemes such as this, if 'owned' by the sector, might also create new cross-faith networks between charitable Muslim and Christian facilities.

26. There are emerging private sector associations: one represents particularly the private and elite religious hospitals: Kaushik (2000); one local association brings together smaller independent providers: Dyauli (2000). These organizations share information, are developing a role in policy making, and try to identify opportunities for professional collaboration.
27. Contrary to expectations of many policy makers but in line with a good deal of recent research on health-seeking behaviour: Leonard (2000a); Segall *et al.* (2000).
28. For example, Japan, Taiwan, South Korea; from a large literature see for example Campbell and Ikegami (1998) and White *et al.* (1998).

Bibliography

Asenso-Okyere, W., Anum, A., Osei-Akotot, I., and Adukonu, A. (1998) 'Cost Recovery in Ghana: Are There any Changes in Health Seeking Behaviour?', *Health Policy and Planning*, 13, 181–8.

Atim, C. (1999) 'Social Movements and Health Insurance: a Critical Evaluation of Voluntary, Non-Profit Insurance Schemes With Case Studies from Ghana and Cameroons', *Social Science and Medicine*, 48, 881–96.

Atkinson, A. B. (1993) *Alternatives to Capitalism: the Economics of Partnership*. Basingstoke: Macmillan with the IEA.

Atkinson, A. B. (1999) *The Economic Consequences of Rolling Back the Welfare State*. Cambridge, MA: MIT Press.

Bardhan, P., Bowles, S., and Gintis, H. (2000) 'Wealth Inequality, Health Constraints and Economic Performance'. In A. Atkinson and F. Bourguignon (eds), *Handbook of Income Distribution*. Amsterdam: Elsevier.

Barnum, H., and Kutzin, J. (1993) *Public Hospitals in Developing Countries: Resource Use, Cost, Financing*. Baltimore: Johns Hopkins University Press.

Barr, N. (1998) *The Economics of the Welfare State*. Oxford: Oxford University Press.

Ben-Ner, A., and Putterman, L. (1998) *Economics, Values and Organisation*. Cambridge: Cambridge University Press.

Bennett, S., Mpake, B., and Mills, A. (1997) *Private Health Providers in Developing Countries: Serving the Public Interest?* London: Zed Books.

Besley, T., and Gouveia, M. (1994) 'Alternative Systems of Health Care Provision', *Economic Policy*, 19, 200–58.

Bloom, G. (1998) 'Primary Health Care Meets the Market in China and Vietnam', *Health Policy*, 44, 233–52.

Bloom, G. (2000) *Equity in Health in Unequal Societies: Towards Health Equity During Rapid Social Change*. London: IDS.

Boadway, R., and Keen, M. (2000) 'Redistribution'. In A. Bourguingnon (ed.), *Handbook of Income Distribution*. Amsterdam: Elsevier.

Bowles, S., and Gintis, H. (1998) 'How Communities Govern: the Structural Basis of Pro-Social Norms'. In B.-N. Putterman (ed.), *Economics, Values and Organisation*. Cambridge: Cambridge University Press.

Brugha, R., and Zwi, A. (1998) 'Improving the Quality of Private Sector Delivery of Public Health Services: Challenges and Strategies', *Health Policy and Planning*, 13, 107–20.

Campbell, C. J., and Ikegami, N. (1998) *The Art of Balance in Health Policy*. Cambridge: Cambridge University Press.

Carrier, J. G. (1995) *Gifts and Commodities: Exchange and Western Capitalism since 1700*. London: Routledge.

Chiang, T. (1995) 'Taiwan's Health Care Reform', *Health Policy*, 39, 225–39.

CMH (2001) *Macroeconomics and Health: Investing Health for Economic Development*. Geneva: WHO.

Collard, D. (1978) *Altruism and Economy*. Oxford: Martin Robertson.

Cooksey, B., and Mmuya, M. (1997) *The Uses and Quality of Health Services in Tanzania: Results of a Service Delivery Survey*. Tanzania Development Research Group (TADREG.) Working Paper Series, No. 6 (August). Dar es Salaam: TADREG.

Criel, B., Van der Stuyft, P., and Van Lerberghe, W. (1999) 'The Bwamanda Hospital Insurance Scheme: Effective for Whom? A Study of its Impact on Hospital Utilization Patterns', *Social Science and Medicine*, 48, 897–911.

De Swaan, A. (1988) *In Care of the State*. Cambridge: Polity Press.

Douglas, M. (1987) *How Institutions Think*. London: Routledge and Kegan Paul.

Dreze, J., and Sen, A. K. (1995) *India: Economic Development and Social Opportunity*. Delhi: Oxford University Press.

Dyauli, S. P. (2000) 'Challenges Facing Private Sector Health Providers: the Mbeya Experience', *Paper Presented at the Final Workshop of a Project on Managing and Regulating Mixed Health Care Systems in Tanzania*. Tanzania: ESRF.

Economic and Social Research Foundation (2000) *Report of a Workshop on Managing and Regulating Mixed Health Care Systems*. Dar es Salaam: ESRF.

Esping-Andersen, G. (1990) *The Three Worlds of Welfare Capitalism*. Oxford: Polity Press.

Geertz, C. (1973) 'Thick Description: Towards an Interpretive Theory of Culture'. In C. Geertz (ed.), *The Interpretation of Cultures*. New York: Basic Books.

Gilson, L., Kalyalya, D., Kuchler, F., Oranga, H. M., and Ouendo, M. (1999) *Promoting Equity within Community Financing Schemes: Experiences from Three African Countries*. London: London School of Hygiene and Tropical Medicine.

Gilson, L., Russell, S., and Buse, K. (1995) 'The Political Economy of Cost Recovery: Towards Equitable Health Financing Policy', *Journal of International Development*, 7, 369–401.

Gilson, L., Russell, S., Rauyaji, O., Boonchote, T., Pasandhanathorn, V., Chaisenee, P., Supachutikul, A., and Nuan-anan Tantigate, N. (1998) *Exempting the Poor: a Review and Evaluation of the Low Income Card Scheme in Thailand*. London: London School of Hygiene and Tropical Medicine.

Gilson, L., and Travis, P. (1997) *Health Systems Decentralisation in Africa: an Overview of Experiences in Eight Countries*. Paper prepared for WHO regional seminar on decentralization. Bamako (Mali): WHO.

Gintis, H. (2000) *Game Theory Evolving*. Princeton, NJ: Princeton University Press.

Giridhar, G. (1993) 'Concepts and Practice in Health Care Insurance Schemes'. In P. Berman and M. E. Khan (eds), *Paying for India's Health Care*. New Delhi: Sage.

Goodin, R. E., Headey, B., Muffels, R., and Dirven, H.-J. (1999) *The Real Worlds of Welfare Capitalism*. Cambridge: Cambridge University Press.

Gregory, C. (1982) *Gifts and Commodities*. London: Academic Press.

Hoff, K. (2000) 'Comment on Why is Inequality Back on the Agenda?', *Proceedings of the Annual World Bank Conference on Development Economics*. Washington, DC: World Bank.

Hughes, G., and Lewis, G. A. (1998) *Unsettling Welfare: the Reconstruction of Social Policy*. London: Routledge with the Open University.

Kaijage, F., and Tibaijuka, A. (1996) *Poverty and Social Exclusion in Tanzania*. Geneva: International Institute for Labour Studies.

Kanbur, R., and Lustig, N. (2000) 'Why is Inequality Back on the Agenda?', *Proceeding of the Annual World Bank Conference on Development Economics*. Washington, DC: World Bank.

Kaushik, L. R. (2000) *Private–Public Mix: a View from Private Health Care Provider*, paper presented at the Workshop on Managing and Regulating Mixed Health Care Systems. Dar es Salaam: Economic and Social Research Foundation ESRF.

Kiwara, A. D. (2000) 'Health Sector Reforms and Alternative Health Care Financing in Tanzania: Windows of Hope', *Workshop on Managing and Regulating Mixed Health Care Systems*. Dar es Salaam: ESRF.

Kreps, D. (1990) *Game Theory and Economic Modelling*. Oxford: Clarendon Press.

Kunitz, S. (2001) 'Accounts of Social Capital: the Mixed Effects of Personal Communities and Voluntary Groups'. In D. Leon and G. Walt (eds), *Poverty, Inequality and Health: an International Perspective*. Oxford: Oxford University Press.

Leonard, D. (2000a) 'Lessons from the New Institutional Economics for the Structural Reform of Human Health Services in Africa'. In Leonard (2000b) *Africa's Changing Markets for Health and Veterinary Services*. London: Macmillan.

Lewis, G. (1996) 'Welfare Settlements and Racialising Practices', *Soundings*, 6. London: Lawrence and Wishart.

Lewis, G. (2000) *Race, Gender and Social Welfare: Encounters in a Postcolonial Society*. Cambridge: Polity Press.

Lewis, J. (1992) 'Gender and the Development of the Welfare Regimes', *Journal of European Social Policy*, 2, 159–73.

Lindert, P. (2000) 'Three Centuries of Income Distribution in Britain and America'. In A. a. Bourguingnon (ed.), *Handbook of Income Distribution*. Amsterdam: Elsevier.

Londoño, J.-L., and Frenk, J. (1997) 'Structured Pluralism: Towards an Innovative Model for Health Sector Reform in Latin America', *Health Policy*, 41, 1–36.

Mackintosh, M. (1996) 'The Public Good', (Introduction to theme section) *Soundings*, 6. London: Lawrence and Wishart.

Mackintosh, M. (2001) 'Do Health Care Systems Contribute to Inequalities?' In D. Leon and G. Walt (eds), *Poverty, Inequality and Health: an International Perspective*. Oxford: Oxford University Press.

Mackintosh, M., and Gilson, L. (2002) 'Non-market Relationships in Health Care'. In J. Heyer, F. Stewart and R. Thorp (eds), *Group Behaviour and Development Is the Market Destroying Cooperation?*. Oxford: Oxford University Press.

Mackintosh, M., and Tibandebage, P. (2000) 'Sustainable Redistribution with Health Care Markets? Rethinking Regulatory Action in the Tanzania Context', *DESTIN Conference on New Institutional Theory, Institutional Reform and Poverty Reduction*. London: DESTIN.

Mauss, M. (1924) *The Gift: Forms and Functions of Exchange in Archaic Societies*. Washington, DC: Smithsonian Institute.

Mkandawire, T. (2001) *Social Policy in a Development Context*. Geneva: UNRISD.

Msamanga, O. I., Urasa, D., and Mujinja, P. (1996) *Equity of Access to Public, Private Not-for-Profit and Private for-Profit Health Facilities in Two Regions in Tanzania*. New York: UNICEF.

Narayana, D. (1999) 'Public Expenditure Reform without Policy Change: Infrastructure Investment and Health Care under Fiscal Squeeze in Kerala'. In M. Mackintosh and R. Roy Scott (eds), *Economic Decentralisation and Public Management Reform*. Aldershot: Edward Elgar.

Offer, A. (1997) 'Between the Gift and the Market: the Economy of Regard', *Economic History Review*, 50, 450–76.

Peters, D., Kandola, K., Elmendorf, A. E., and Chelleraj, G. (1999) *Health Expenditures, Services and Outcomes in Africa*. Washington, DC: World Bank.

Rogers, G., Gore, C., and Figueiredo, J. (1995) *Social Exclusion: Rhetoric, Reality, Responses*. Geneva: International Institute for Labour Studies.

Russell, S., and Gilson, L. (1997) 'User Fee Policies to Promote Health Service Access for the Poor: a Wolf in Sheep's Clothing', *International Journal of Health Services*, 27, 359–79.

Scott, W. R. (1995) *Institutions and Organizations*. New York: Sage Publications.

Segall, M., Tipping, G., Lucas, H., Viet Dung, T., Thanh Tam, N., Xuan Vih, D., and Lan Huong, D. (2000) *Health Care Seeking by the Poor in Transitional Economies: the Case of Vietnam*. IDS Research Report No. 43 Brighton: IDS.

Semboja, J., and Therkildsen, O. (1995) *Service Provision Under Stress in East Africa*. Copenhagen: Centre for Development Research with James Currey.

Sen, G. (1992) 'Social Need and Public Accountability: the Case of Kerala'. In M. Wuyts, M. Mackintosh and T. Hewitt (eds), *Development Policy and Public Action*. Oxford: Oxford University Press with the Open University.

Silver, H. (1995) 'Reconceptualising Social Disadvantage: Three Paradigms of Social Exclusion'. In G. Rogers, C. Gore and J. Figueiredo (eds), *Social Exclusion: Rhetoric, Reality and Responses*. Geneva: International Institute for Labour Studies.

Therkildsen, O., and Semboja, J. (1995) 'A New Look at Service Provision in East Africa'. In J. Semboja and O. Therkildsen (eds), *Service Provision Under Stress in Africa*. Copenhagen: Center for Development Research with James Currey.

Tibandebage, P. (1995). *Women and Children in Tanzania: a Situation Analysis*. Dar es Salaam, Tanzania: UNICEF and ESRF.

Tibandebage, P. (1999) 'Charging for Health Care in Tanzania: Official Pricing in a Liberalised Environment'. In M. Mackintosh and R. Roy (eds), *Economic Decentralisation and Public Management Reform*. Aldershot: Edward Elgar.

Tibandebage, P., and Mackintosh, M. (2001) *The Market Shaping of Capabilities in a Low Income Context and Some Implications for Social Policy: Liberalised Health Care in Tanzania*, conference paper from Van Hugel Institute conference on 'Justice and Poverty: Examining Sen's Capability Approach'. Cambridge: University of Cambridge.

Tibandebage, P. and Mackintosh, M. (2002) 'Institutional Cultures and Regulatory Relationships in a Liberalising Health Care System: a Tanzanian Case Study'. In J. Heyer, F. Stewart and R. Thorp (eds), *Group Behaviour and Development Is the Market Destroying Cooperation?* Oxford: Oxford University Press.

Tibandebage, P., Semboja, H., Mujinja, P., and Ngonyani, H. (2001) *Private Sector Development: the Case of Private Health Facilities*: ESRF.

Titmuss, R. (1958) 'The Social Division of Welfare'. In R. Titmuss (ed.), *Essays on the Welfare State*. London: Allen and Unwin.

Titmuss, R. (1974) *Social Policy*. London: Allen and Unwin.

Upunda, G. L. (2000) 'Managing and Regulating Mixed Health Care: the Current Government Strategy for Improving Quality and Access to Health Care in Tanzania', *Workshop on Managing and Regulating Mixed Health Care Systems in Tanzania*. Dar es Salaam: ESRF.

URT (1999) *Health Statistics Abstract 1999*. Dar es Salaam, Tanzania: Ministry of Health.

Walraven, G. (1996) 'Willingness to Pay for District Hospital Services in Rural Tanzania', *Health Policy and Planning*, 11, 428–37.

Wangwe, S., Semboja, H., and Tibandebage, P. (1998) *Transitional Economic Policy and Policy Options in Tanzania*. Dar es Salaam: Mkuki na Nyota.

White, G., Goodman, R., and Kwon, H.-J. (1998) *The East Asian Welfare Model: Welfare Orientalism and the State*. London: Routledge.

White, H., and Killick, T. (2001) *African Poverty at the Millennium: Causes, Complexities and Challenges.* Washington, DC: World Bank.

WHO (2000) *World Health Report.* Geneva: WHO.

Williams, F. (1989) *Social Policy, a Critical Introduction: Issues of Race, Gender and Class.* Cambridge: Polity Press.

Williams, F., Popay, J., and Oakley, A. (1999) *Welfare Research: a Critique of Theory and Method.* London: UCL Press.

World Bank (1993) *World Development Report 1993: Investing in Health.* Washington, DC: World Bank.

World Bank (1996) *Health Policy in Eastern Africa: a Structural Approach to Resource Allocation:* World Bank Eastern Africa Department (Africa Region). Washington, DC: World Bank.

World Bank (1997) *World Development Report 1997: the State in a Changing World.* Washington, DC: World Bank.

World Bank (2001) *World Development Report 2000/1: Attacking Poverty.* Washington, DC: World Bank.

Yang, B.-M. (1996) 'The Role of Health Insurance in the Growth of the Private Health Sector in Korea', *International Journal of Health Planning and Management,* 11, 231–52.

8
Models of Development, Social Policy and Reform in Latin America

Carmelo Mesa-Lago

Introduction

Latin America is a region of the world that has experimented with most development models. In addition, it has been at the forefront in social policies and a pioneer in market-oriented reforms in both areas. From the 1950s to the end of the 1970s most countries in the region followed a mixed model of development characterized by the predominance of the market but also incorporating significant state control and intervention. At the start of the 1960s Cuba took a dramatic leap to the state, introducing a fully socialized economy with central planning. Conversely, in the mid-1970s Chile pursued the opposite course with a policy of drastic economic reform that followed neo-liberal ideas and moved that country towards a very market-oriented society. The latter approach influenced the policies of the major international financial organizations and has been eventually applied across most of the region.

Some Latin American countries have also introduced the welfare state in the continent – the first two being Uruguay and Chile in the 1920s – and this policy gradually developed to reach its zenith in the early 1970s. Cuba began this process in the 1930s and consolidated and significantly expanded it in the 1960s and 1970s. In a similar process, Costa Rica's foundations of the welfare state were laid down in the 1940s, consolidated in the 1950s, and expanded in the 1960s and 1970s. Chile was a pioneer not only in both the reduction of the state and market-oriented reform, but also in the process of 'privatization' of social services at the start of the 1980s. The severe economic crisis suffered by the region during that decade weakened the welfare state and the Chilean path was partially or fully followed in the 1990s.

This chapter analyses two important topics on development and social policy in Latin America: (i) the relationship between goals and means in three different models of development in the region: Chile (market), Cuba (statist-socialist) and Costa Rica (mixed), and the socioeconomic performance of these three models; and (ii) the reform of the welfare state in Latin America, particularly of its major component social security, and the effects of this on the people and development.

The following important questions will be addressed in this chapter: (i) are developmental goals (growth versus equity) and means (market versus state) conflicting or compatible and, if the latter is true, what is the optimal combination between them?; (ii) which of the three models of development have produced the best socioeconomic performance and why?; (iii) what is the nature of the reform of social welfare (security) and what have been the roles of the state and the private sector?; and (iv) what have been the effects of the reform of social welfare (security) on crucial issues such as population coverage, income distribution, fiscal and administrative costs, capital accumulation and markets, and national savings?

Three models of development in Latin America and their results

Goals (growth versus equity) and means (market versus state) dichotomies

Mkandawire's paper 'Social Policy in a Development Context' (Mkandawire 2001) accomplishes three significant tasks: (1) it comprehensively reviews the literature on the relationship between social welfare and economic development; (2) it demonstrates that the negative view of conflicting developmental goals and means (equity versus economic growth/efficiency and state versus market) is returning to the initial positive view that the two may work to reinforce each other; and (3) it properly concludes that social policy is a key instrument that works in tandem with economic policy in order to ensure equitable and socially sustainable economic development.

In addition, Mkandawire sets a research agenda that identifies the following tasks: (1) to explore the empirical linkages that tie together distinct goals and means; (2) to bridge the hiatus between theoretical and empirical findings and social policy making; (3) to work on more time series analysis using institutional and historical information to heighten research now largely dominated by cross-section and panel data regression analysis; and (4) to study the policy implications of different economic, social and political settings.

Dreze and Sen (1989) have convincingly argued that the traditional *total* dichotomies of goals and means are false because there are major complementarities between the two pairs of goals/means, and it is important to strive for a balance and avoid extremes. The dilemma in the use of available resources is not between all and nothing but, rather, to give *preference* to one goal *complemented* by the other, and properly to combine state and private action with other mechanisms.

Three different models of development in Latin America

My latest book applies Dreze-Sen's view and addresses several of Mkandawire's research concerns (the use of historical and institutional information, the exploration of the linkages between goals and means, and the evaluation of policy implication of diverse socioeconomic-political settings) to compare three different models of development in Latin America (Mesa-Lago 2000d):

1. *Chile.* The best and most radical example of the neo-liberal market model, particularly under the Pinochet regime (1973–90), which drastically reduced the role of the state and gave undue preponderance to the pursuit of growth, stability and efficiency (largely based on privatization), but restricted social policy to a residue or 'trickle-down' effect. Such imbalance has been gradually corrected by three successive democratic administrations (from 1990 onwards), which, although maintaining the essence of the previous economic model, have placed higher accent on social policy under the more balanced approach of a 'social market economy' (see also Ruiz-Tagle 2000).

2. *Cuba.* The only example in the region (and one of the few remaining in the world) of the statist, centrally-planned socialist model, which virtually eliminated private ownership of the means of production and placed excessive emphasis on social goals and equity – even egalitarianism in certain stages – but at the cost of efficiency, productivity and growth (1959–90). The collapse of the USSR/socialist camp and the severe economic crisis that ensued in the 1990s, has forced some hesitant market-oriented reforms which, despite significant government efforts, are threatening some of the previous social achievements (see also Barraclough 2000).

3. *Costa Rica.* One of the best representatives of the mixed model, this country combined a market economy with a considerable state role, and achieved a fair balance between social and economic goals with good results in both (1953–81). But the debt crisis of the 1980s and the exhaustion of that model (excessive state intervention and fiscal imbalances) led to structural adjustment reforms in that decade and in the 1990s. However, to date these have been successful in maintaining the most important social gains (see also Mesa-Lago 2000a).

The first two models were extremes: Chile overemphasized the market and economic goals while drastically reducing state functions and social goals, while Cuba did exactly the opposite; Costa Rica managed to achieve a reasonable balance between goals and means. But adjustments have been occurring in the three countries: towards social goals and more state regulatory powers in Chile since the 1990s; towards economic goals and a hesitant move to the market in Cuba since the 1990s (still with overwhelming state ownership and control); and towards economic goals and the market in

Costa Rica since the 1980s. Finally, the three diverse economic models have been implemented by different political systems: a military dictatorship in the case of Chile (followed by multiparty democracy), one-party authoritarian socialism in Cuba, and a multiparty democracy in Costa Rica (Mesa-Lago 2000d).

The three countries selected are also important examples in Latin America of a relatively early emphasis on social policies, thus ratifying Pierson's observation that 'late starters (in industrialization) tended to develop welfare institutions earlier in their own individual development and under more comprehensive terms of coverage' (cited in Mkandawire 2001: 11). Chile and Cuba were two of five regional 'pioneers' in the development of social insurance (respectively in the 1920s and 1930s), while Costa Rica's programme started later (in 1943, but this country was less developed than the other two) and yet it was expanded in the 1960s–1970s and reached the level of the other two counterparts. By the 1980s, the three countries had essentially accomplished universal coverage of their populations although they adopted very different schemes (Mesa-Lago 1998). The three countries were selected for a UNRISD comparative study that analysed the unique experience of seven countries that had achieved levels of social performance that were considerably higher than their per capita income (Ghai 2000). The socioeconomic performance of the three models is summarized in the next section.

Socioeconomic performance of the three models

Twenty indicators of development were selected in order to measure the socioeconomic performance of the three countries and historical statistical series elaborated for 1960–93 (in Chile the relevant period started in 1973). About half of the indicators dealt with *economic* variables, both internal and external: GDP growth, GDP per capita, investment, inflation, fiscal balance, composition of GDP by economic sector, export concentration/diversification, import composition, trade partner concentration/diversification, trade balance per capita, and foreign debt per capita. The other half of the indicators dealt with *social* variables: real wages, composition of the labour force by sector, open unemployment, illiteracy, educational enrolment at three levels, infant mortality, rates of contagious diseases, life expectancy, and housing. Five important social indicators had to be discarded in the final evaluation because of two reasons: lack of data from Cuba (income distribution, poverty incidence) or significant differences in the way those indicators were calculated (women's participation in the labour force, access to water and sewerage/ sanitation, social security coverage).

Two types of ranking were used in each of the indicators: (1) *absolute*, which measured the indicators at the start and end of the period – for instance, the infant mortality rate in 1960 (or 1973 in the case of Chile) and 1993; and (2) *relative improvement*, the change in one indicator through time, for instance, the reduction in infant mortality between 1960–73 and

1993. The indicators were merged in each of the two clusters (economic and social), and the two clusters were then combined into an index of economic and social development (using various weights).

The results of these comparisons in the absolute rankings among the three countries were as follows: Chile ranked best (first) in economic indicators but worse (third) in social indicators; Costa Rica ranked best in social indicators and second in the economic indicators. Cuba ranked second in social indicators (in the 1990s, but first in the 1980s) and worst in economic indicators.[1] In the relative improvement indicators, Costa Rica managed to narrow the gap with Cuba, despite starting from a lower point – for instance, in 1960 life expectancy was 61.6 years in Costa Rica and 64.0 in Cuba but in the period 1995–2000 the figures stood at 76.5 and 76.0 respectively.

Finally, a comparison was undertaken with international rankings that include the three countries. This yielded similar results. For instance, the Human Development Index (HDI) ranked the three countries in 1993 (among 174 countries in the world and 20 in Latin America) as follows: Costa Rica 31 and 1, Chile 33 and 3, and Cuba 79 and 10 (UNDP 1996). The balanced approach to development in Costa Rica, therefore, led to a reasonable performance in economic indicators and to the best results in social indicators. Conversely, the extreme approaches of the other two countries resulted in good performance in one set but at the expense of the other. Chile experienced strong economic growth, lower inflation and a reduction in the fiscal deficit, but the social consequences were adverse: poverty incidence worsened, real wages shrank, educational enrolment at secondary and tertiary levels declined, social security coverage decreased, unemployment jumped to a historical record, and morbidity rates rose.[2] At the end of the 1980s, Cuba was leading the region in most social indicators (although housing was a notorious exception), but the cost of social programmes was very high and adverse economic distortions occurred – for instance, open unemployment was kept low but at the cost of significant overstaffing and very low labour productivity, and egalitarianism probably led to the least income inequality in the region but generated perverse incentives for labour absenteeism.

The corrections implemented in the 1990s in Chile and Cuba changed the previous performance to some degree. Chile's social indicators improved considerably (decline in open unemployment and poverty incidence, increase in real wages and secondary and higher-education enrolment) but, at the same time, economic indicators became even better (higher average growth rates, lower inflation, and budget surpluses). After a severe deterioration in the first half of the 1990s, Cuba's economic indicators had a mixed performance in the second half (higher growth albeit still well below the 1989 level, significant reduction in inflation and the fiscal deficit, but increasing external trade deficit and debt), while some social indicators kept improving (infant mortality, life expectancy) and others deteriorated (open unemployment and under-employment rose significantly, real wages and university enrolment declined sharply, and morbidity in several diseases rose). In Costa Rica economic growth continued to be fair (after the decline in the period 1981–85) and inflation rose and then declined but the fiscal deficit continued to be high, most social indicators kept improving but open unemployment rose somewhat (ECLAC 1998a, 1998b, 1998c, ECLAC 1999, ECLAC 2000; Mesa-Lago 2000a, Mesa-Lago 2000c, Mesa-Lago 2000d).

In order to update the information of my book on the three countries, Table 8.1 incorporates the following 1990s data from ECLAC and UNDP: (1) two economic indicators: annual average GDP growth rate in 1991–99, and real GDP per capita in dollars PPP; (2) nine social indicators in the 1990s: real mean wages, open unemployment, income distribution, poverty incidence (these two indicators are only available for Chile and Costa Rica), illiteracy, enrolment in secondary and higher education, daily caloric and protein intake, infant mortality, and life expectancy; and (3) the Human Development Index (HDI) score.

Table 8.1 shows that Chile performed best in GDP growth, followed by Costa Rica, and then Cuba (which recorded a negative rate despite the

Table 8.1 Comparison of economic growth, GDP per capita, and social indicators (outputs) in Chile, Costa Rica and Cuba, 1990s

Indicators	Chile	Costa Rica	Cuba
Economic Growth (1991–99)[a]	6.0	4.1	–2.1
GDP per capita (1997)[b]	12,730	6,650	3,100
Urban real mean wages (1998)[c]	135.5	115.1	57.3
Open unemployment (1998)	6.4	5.4	6.6
Income distribution (1994)[d]	0.473	0.363	n.a.
Poverty incidence (1994)[e]	23	21	n.a.
Illiteracy (1997)[f]	4.8	4.9	4.1
Enrolment secondary (1996)[g]	74.9	50.0	77.3
Enrolment higher education (1996)[g]	30.3	33.1	12.4
Daily caloric intake (1996)	2,810	2,822	2,357
Daily protein intake (1996)	78.9	74.3	52.1
Infant mortality (1996)[h]	11.8	11.8	9.0
Life expectancy (1997)[i]	74.9	76.0	75.7
Human Development Index (1997)[j]	0.844	0.801	0.765

Sources: ECLAC 1998a, 1998b, 1998c, 1999, 2000; UNDP 1996.
[a] Annual average real rate (absolute).
[b] Real GDP measured in dollars PPP.
[c] Base 1990 = 100
[d] Gini coefficient urban; rural are 0.409 and 0.372.
[e] Percentage of households below the poverty line.
[f] Percentage of population 15 years and older.
[g] Percentage of the corresponding age cohorts.
[h] Per 1,000 born alive.
[i] Years at birth.
[j] Combines three indicators: GDP$PPP, education and health.

recovery since 1995); Chile also had the highest GDP per capita, almost twice that of Costa Rica and four times that of Cuba. The three countries were fairly close in terms of social indicators but, combining the indicators for which we have data for all countries, Costa Rica was clearly first, Chile second, and Cuba third. Costa Rica had the best combined performance: ranked first in four indicators, second in three and third in two (it was also ahead of Chile in terms of income distribution and poverty incidence); Chile was first in two indicators, second in six and third in one; and Cuba was first in three indicators, second in one and third in five.[3] The HDI for 1997 (latest year available) shows Chile first, closely followed by Costa Rica and Cuba behind (Mesa-Lago 2000c).

In summary, despite the clearly superior economic performance of Chile in the 1990s and the improvement in its social indicators largely prompted by the return to democracy, Costa Rica still led the way in social indicators and also enjoyed reasonable economic performance. In spite of the recovery in the second half of the 1990s, Cuba trailed the other two countries in both economic and social indicators.

The reform of social welfare and its effects on the people and development

Mkandawire's paper (2001) contains a short section on 'Social Insurance and Development' and the International Labour Office, in a document just published, discusses the controversy on the economic effects of social security. Some of the alleged negative effects are: it is very costly and harms economic growth, it discourages savings, it reduces international competitiveness, it jeopardizes employment creation, and it encourages premature withdrawals from the labour force.[4] Positive effects noted are: it contributes to economic growth by increasing productivity and enhancing social stability (helping to maintain workers in good health and taking care of them in sickness and maternity, preventing work-related accidents and diseases), it maintains effective national demand (providing income to unemployed workers), it helps employment (easing the departure of older workers from the labour force), and it helps the reproduction of a healthy workforce (providing maternity and infant health care) and contributes to retraining of workers according to technological change (ILO 2001).

It is not feasible herein to deal with this long and complex controversy, but this chapter will discuss the reform of social welfare (actually focusing on social security, its fundamental component) in Latin America and will also assess its impact on the people and development. The term social security will be used in its broadest sense, including social insurance (pensions for old age, disability and survivors; health care and cash benefit for sickness and maternity as well as work injury; and unemployment compensation), family allowances and social assistance (ILO 2001). For reasons of space, the chapter will focus on the three major social security programmes: social insurance pensions, health care, and social assistance. First, it will describe the structural reforms, and their degree of privatization and role of the state. Secondly, it will assess the impact of the reforms on the population and development: freedom of choice of the insured, population coverage and inclusion of the poor, gender discrimination, financial burden on the workers and the state, income distribution, competition and administrative cost reduction, capital accumulation and investment returns, and capital markets and national saving.

Structural reforms, degree of privatization and role of the state

1. *Structural reforms.* In 1980–81 Chile pioneered a radical structural reform of its social insurance pensions and health care systems, shaped by the neo-liberal ideology and through privatization.[5] Largely because of the economic crisis of the 1980s and the Latin American dislike of Chile's authoritarian regime, such reforms did not have an impact in the region until the 1990s and this later effect was mainly as a result of World Bank policies and conditions attached to structural adjustment loans, which were influenced by the Chilean model (see Mesa-Lago 1998).[6] A summary of the principal characteristics of the pension and health care structural reforms in the region follows.

   a. *Pensions.* By mid-2000, ten countries had enacted pension reforms but, instead of copying the supposedly universal Chilean prototype, they followed three diverse general models of reform and with significant differences among all the countries (based on Mesa-Lago 1998, 2001b):

      i. *Substitutive*, similar to the Chilean prototype and implemented in Bolivia (1997), Mexico (1997), El Salvador (1998) and Nicaragua (scheduled for 2001). In this model, the old social insurance or public system, usually based on 'pay-as-you-go' (PAYG) and defined benefit or undefined contributions, is 'closed' (that is, it prohibits new affiliations). The old system is replaced with a 'privately' administered system (in Mexico it can be managed also by public and mixed institutions), which is fully-funded (FF), based on defined contributions which are deposited in individual accounts and invested, and benefits are undefined because they depend on the sum accumulated in the insured individual account at the time of retirement.

      ii. *Parallel*, implemented in Peru (1993) and Colombia (1994). In this model the public system is not closed but reformed either partially (Peru) or totally (Colombia) and becomes an alternative option to a private system with similar characteristics to the Chilean prototype; the administration of the latter is exclusively private in Peru, but multiple (private, public and mixed) in Colombia.

      iii. *Mixed*, implemented in Argentina (1994), Uruguay (1996) and Costa Rica (scheduled for 2001). In this model, the public system is not closed but reformed, and it becomes one of the two integrated mandatory components of the new system: the public component is based on PAYG and defined benefits and pays a basic pension, and the new component is FF and based on defined contributions, administered by multiple institutions (private, public, mixed), and pays a supplementary pension.

b. *Health.* The process of health care reform is less advanced than that of pensions. Six countries have enacted structural reforms that follow three general approaches and show more diversity than in pension reforms (based on Bertranou 1999; Cruz-Saco and Mesa-Lago 1998; Mesa-Lago 1998):

  i. *Predominance of the public sector with marginal private collaboration.* In Costa Rica the process began in the 1970s and ended in the 1990s; social insurance has gradually incorporated all curative and most preventive health services and the Ministry of Health has only supervisory and policy functions. The system coverage is virtually universal because it combines a contributory programme (for insured workers) and a non-contributory programme (for the poor). There has been a process of decentralization as well as collaboration between private providers and the social insurance institute (CCSS, Caja Costarricense de Seguro Social), private services are received by less than one-fifth of the insured. In Mexico, the reform of the major social insurance institute (IMSS, Instituto Mexicano del Seguro Social) began in 1996 and has not been completed yet, while the rest of the health system remains unchanged. Financing and provision of services is being gradually separated, there is a process of decentralization (from the centre to regions, delegations and local units), and resources are expected to be assigned by capitation and a system of hospital patient classification. Eventually the insured should have the possibility of selecting alternative providers.

  ii. *Partial privatization and dual selection.* Under the Chilean pioneering reform (1981), the public sector was not closed but reformed. Facilities and services of various social insurance schemes and the ministry of public health were integrated and decentralized, and they basically cover the poor and low-income population. New privately managed corporations that resemble Homes (called ISAPRE) were established; they have better facilities and offer a wider package of services for an extra premium, and cover the middle- and high-income groups. Theoretically the insured can select between public and private providers but costs of the latter are a barrier, resulting in a dual system in practice.

  iii. *Partial privatization with multiple selection.* Peru enacted three reforms in the period 1991–97; the latest has a few similarities to Chile's, but there is no linkage between the public and private systems, the counterpart of the ISAPRE (EPS) may be public, private or mixed, and they offer supplementary services over the basic services provided by social insurance. In 1993 Colombia began the implementation of the most complex reforms in the region, with a double tier of administrators and providers (both can be either public, private or mixed) and greater possibility for selection among them. There are contributory and subsidized programmes, respectively, for the insured and the poor and low-income population. Finally Argentina began reforms in 1995, allowing those workers insured in trade-union-managed providers (*boras socialistas*) to select and change them, and the same option is given to pensioners – all OS must provide a basic health care package.

2. *The degree of privatization.* Despite the conventionally used term 'privat-ization', half of the systems in the ten pension reforms discussed are not exclusively managed by private corporations, and this is also true of the seven health reforms. Under the pension reforms, four countries with substitutive systems have relied exclusively on private administration (Chile, Bolivia, El Salvador and Nicaragua), as well as Peru in the parallel private system. In the three mixed systems (Argentina, Uruguay and Costa Rica), there is a combination of public administration in the basic component and multiple administrators in the supplementary component. In the parallel models of Colombia and Peru, the public system is administered by social insurance. Finally, both Colombia's parallel 'private' system and Mexico's substitutive system have multiple administrators. The percentage of insured in the 'private' system or component varies significantly among the countries, declining from 100 per cent in Bolivia and Mexico, to 97–90 per cent in Chile and El Salvador, 78–79 per cent in Argentina and Peru, and 49–40 per cent in Uruguay and Colombia (no data are available yet on Costa Rica and Nicaragua).

With regard to the health reforms, two countries have a dominant social insurance administration (Costa Rica and Mexico), and in the remaining four countries, the bulk of the insured is covered by the public sector or social insurance, whilst the rest is covered by multiple types of administrators (except in Chile). In the most advanced health care reform, being that of Chile, only 27 per cent of the insured is affiliated to the private IS Après (Mesa-Lago 2000b, 2001b).

3. *The state role.* Neo-liberal reformers abhor public intervention, but the state has proven to be absolutely necessary for a proper function and sustain-ability of a 'private' system, through the following functions: (a) mandatory affiliation; (b) strong and detailed public regulation of the system; (c) con-trol, monitoring and sanctioning through a supervisory public institution (usually a 'Superintendence' of pensions and health care which is state-financed in several countries); (d) strict regulation of investment instruments

and ranking of them by a public institution (*Classificatory de Resigns*); and (e) last but not least, heavy fiscal subsidies and state guarantees throughout the transition and beyond.

The insured freedom of choice

One of the key objectives of a structural reform in either pension or health care is to break the state monopoly and establish freedom of choice on behalf of the insured to select the system and choose/change its administrators. The reality shows that there is a significant variation in such freedoms among countries.

1. *Pensions.* Under the pension reform, there are two types of freedoms: to select between the public and the private (or mixed) systems, and to select and change administrators. The ten countries can be ranked, from least to most freedom to select between the public and private (or mixed) systems, as follows: (1) no freedom in Bolivia and Mexico because both the 'old' insured (all those affiliated at the time of enactment of the reform) and the 'new' insured (all entrants into the labour force who are legally covered) must join the 'private' system; (2) minimum freedom in El Salvador and Uruguay (the old insured was divided by age and only the younger insured had an option, while all the new insured must enter the private or mixed system); (3) intermediate freedom in Chile (the old insured had a period to decide whether to stay in the public system or move to the private system, but all new insured must join the latter) and Peru (the old insured can always choose to move but once he/she changes to the private system cannot return to the public, and the new insured must join the private system); and (4) maximum freedom in Argentina and Colombia (both the old and new insured can select and move among systems).

Concerning the freedom to change administrators: (1) they are prohibited in Bolivia, unless the insured changes domicile; (2) one annual change is allowed in Mexico and Nicaragua; (3) two annual changes in Argentina, Colombia, El Salvador and Uruguay; and (4) there are no restrictions in Chile and Peru (but in practice one change per year is feasible). Finally the insured has no freedom to select investment instruments or the profile of his/her portfolio as these are decided by the administrators, and at the time of retirement the insured cannot withdraw the sum in his/her individual account but may only opt for two or three options: an annuity, a programmed pension or a combination of both (Mesa-Lago 2001b).

2. *Health.* Under the health reform, the freedom of choice is minimal in Costa Rica and Mexico, intermediate in Chile, and maximum in the other three countries. It should be noticed that in practice the poor and the low-income groups do not have the right to select a private provider in Chile and Peru because of the high cost of the extra premium (Bertranou 1999).

Population coverage and inclusion of the poor

1. *Coverage prior to the reform.* In general terms, the degree of social security coverage in Latin America has been positively related to the level of development and, specifically, to the percentage of the labour force which is formal and salaried. The 20 countries in the region have been divided into three groups, according to the inception and level of development of their social security systems: pioneer, intermediate and latecomers (Mesa-Lago 1998).

a. *Pioneers.* These countries are the most socially developed and introduced social insurance in the 1920s and 1930s; by the 1980s they had achieved almost universal coverage with a combination of social insurance (contributory programmes that covered between 70 and 80 per cent of their labour force) and non-contributory social assistance. Three pioneer countries have implemented pension reforms – Argentina, Chile and Uruguay – and the first two and Brazil have also undertaken health care reforms. There were several facilitators of coverage in this group: a predominantly formal salaried labour force, a small informal sector (i.e., self-employed, unpaid family workers, employees of microenterprises, domestic servants, home workers), a small proportion of peasants, relatively low poverty incidence, and mandatory coverage of the self-employed (in Argentina and Uruguay, voluntary in Chile). In these countries, therefore, all or part of the poor were protected by social security although the level of the social assistance pensions tended to be low.

b. *Intermediates.* These countries introduced social insurance in the 1940s and 1950s. Chronologically Costa Rica belongs to this group, but, because of the rapid expansion of coverage in the 1960s–1970s and the addition of social assistance pensions, by the 1980s it had 85 per cent of the population covered by health care and 53 per cent of the labour force covered by contributory pensions (the majority of the poor received non-contributory pensions). In addition, Costa Rica's formal salaried sector is a majority in the labour force, the proportion of peasants is small, and poverty incidence is the second lowest in the region – hence, most of the poor were protected. This country, therefore, has many of the characteristics of the pioneers and has introduced both pension and health reforms. Three other intermediate countries have also implemented pension and health care reforms: Colombia, Mexico and Peru. They have a smaller formal salaried sector, larger informal sector and peasants, and higher poverty incidence than the pioneer group (Peru being in the worst situation), and only the self-employed are entitled to voluntary coverage. Prior to the reform, coverage of the labour force in pensions was 44 per cent in Mexico, and about 32 per cent in Colombia and Peru.

c. *Latecomers.* In this group, social insurance was established in the 1960s and 1970s and these countries are the least developed in the region: informal-sector workers and peasants constitute the majority of the labour force, the formal salaried sector is a minority, and the incidence of poverty is very high. It is unsurprising, therefore, that social insurance coverage is very low, and that there is no social assistance pensions because they would have to cover the majority of the labour force. The poor are thus excluded from coverage. Of the ten countries that have introduced pension reforms, three belong to this group and are ranked among the poorest in the region: Bolivia, El Salvador and Nicaragua. Prior to the reform coverage of the population on health was 12 per cent, 23 per cent and 14 per cent respectively in these three countries.

2. *Coverage after the reform.* Statistics on coverage after the reform are only available for pensions and they are confusing because they can be measured based either on the number of affiliates (who have joined the system at any time) or on the number of active contributors (who have paid their contributions in a recent period). The eight countries for which we have data, had the following percentages of coverage of the labour force in 1998 (first based on affiliates and second based on active contributors): 72 per cent and 66 per cent in Uruguay; 102 per cent and 54 per cent in Chile; 63 per cent and 30 per cent in Argentina; 45 per cent and 23 per cent in Colombia; 36 per cent and 23 per cent in Mexico; 29 per cent and 20 per cent in El Salvador; 26 per cent and 13 per cent in Peru; and 13 per cent in Bolivia – no data are available on active contributors (see Table 8.2).

Estimates of coverage based on affiliates before and after the reform, indicate: (a) a decline in coverage in Argentina, Mexico and Peru; (b) no change in Bolivia and Uruguay; and (c) an increase in Chile, Colombia and El Salvador. It is not possible to determine here the causes of the different results in the eight countries, but part of the explanation may be due to statistical deficiencies. These are usually noted on the data prior to the reform, but figures after the reform are not exempted from flaws. For instance, in 1998 it was reported in Chile that 102 per cent of the labour force was covered based on affiliates but, in addition of being statistically impossible, that figure excludes: 3 per cent of the labour force covered by the public system, 3 per cent by the separate scheme of the armed forces, and 23 per cent who are roughly estimated as uninsured, for a total of 29 per cent. Adding up everything, coverage would be 131 per cent but based on active contributors would be reduced to 54 per cent (Mesa-Lago 2001a).

Labour force coverage based on active contributors after the reform cannot be compared with the situation prior to the reform due to the lack of previous data. Nevertheless, after the reform, the percentage of coverage based on active contributors is significantly lower than that based on affiliates, probably because of the following reasons: (a) a high percentage of

Table 8.2 Performance of structural pension reform in eight countries of Latin America, 1998–99[a]

Indicators	Argentina	Bolivia	Colombia	Chile	El Salvador	Mexico	Peru	Uruguay
1. % of the labour force covered by both systems (Dec. 98)[b] Based on:	63	13	45	102	29	36	26	72
Affiliates' active contributions[c]	30	n.d	23	23	30	23	13	66
2. Insured affiliates								
old system number (thousands)	2,200	0[f]	4,660	205	74	0[f]	544	548
% of total	22	0[f]	60	3	10	0[f]	21	51
new system number (thousands)	7,689	492	3,140	5,996	670	14,622	2,106	521
% of total	78	100[f]	40	97	90	100[f]	79	49
3. No. of active contributors %	3,576	n.d	1,610	3,090	430	9,022	922	330
contributors/affiliates	45	n.d	51	52	64	62	44	65
4. No. of administrators	12	2[g]	7	8	3	14	5	6
5. Concentration of insured in the biggest three administrations (%)	54	100	60	74	100	43	75	69
6. Wage contributions going to individual account	7.58	10.00	10.00	10.00	7.50	10.00	8.00	12.37
7. Total commission charged (%)[d]	3.41	2.50[h]	3.50	2.61	3.18	4.13[k]	3.80	2.63

8. Accumulated Fund Million US$	16,787	472	2,448	33,246	118	8,300	2,274	477
% of GDP (1998)	5.1	4.0	2.3	39.8[l]	0.4	2.5[l]	2.5	1.3
9. Annual real average investment yield (%)[e]	13.0	7.5	10.1	11.3	14.0[j]	8.0	7.04[m]	7.4

Note: Numbers 3 to 9 refer to the 'private' system or component (FFI).

Sources: (Mesa-Lago 2001b) updated with recent information.

[a] Most data are from mid-1999, except when specified and: Peru Sept. 99; Argentina Sept-Dec. 99 (number of administrators April 2000); El Salvador number of administrators August 2000.

[b] Includes those covered in the old system, plus those in the new system; excludes other groups of insured in Argentina, Colombia, Mexico and Uruguay, as well as the armed forces in all countries.

[c] According to Asociación Internacional de Organismos de Supervisión de Fondos de Pensiones (1999), includes all insured who has contributed in the last month, except Mexico which is in the last two months.

[d] Includes the commission of the administrator of the old-age programme plus the premium for disability and survivors paid to insurance companies.

[e] Argentina: July 94–Dec. 99; Colombia: Dec. 95–Dec. 98; Chile: July 81–May 99; El Salvador June 98–June 99; Mexico: July 97–June 99; Peru: Sept. 93–Sept. 99; Uruguay: June 96–June 99.

[f] All insured most change to the new system.

[g] The number was planned to remain at two until 2000, but by July it remained unchanged.

[h] The commission is very low (0.5 per cent) because there is no competition; the cost of the premium is 2 per cent.

[i] AIOS (1999) gives 43.9 per cent.

[j] Given by AIOS (1999), but the figure is quite doubtful.

[k] The commission averages 1.63 per cent and the premium 2.5 per cent, the latter is paid to the social insurance institute.

[l] Excludes the housing fund.

[m] According to AIOS (1999), the average of the last five years was 5.9 per cent, the Table shows the average of the last six years.

[n] Includes the old system and those who are in the reformed public system but not in the mixed system.

non-compliance by the insured or payments delays by the employer: only an average of 55 per cent of the affiliates are active contributors (from 46 per cent in Argentina to 65 per cent in Uruguay; see Table 8.2), the increase in insured contributions could be a contributing factor; (b) double counting, that is, one insured appears registered in two administrators because of frequent changes and slow clearance of the transfer (this could largely explain the 102 per cent coverage in Chile); (c) part of the affiliates may be temporary workers who only contribute occasionally or have permanently left the labour force; (d) significant unemployment in some countries (e.g., 15 per cent in Argentina); and (e) moral hazard: low-income insured minimize their contributions to earn the right for a minimum pension and maximize state subsidies to finance that pension (Arenas de Mesa 2000; Mesa-Lago 1998; Mesa-Lago 2001a; Mesa-Lago 2001b).

An important step has been taken by Costa Rica in its pension reforms of 2000: the creation of a universal assistance pension for all the poor population 65 years and older, who are neither insured nor actually receiving non-contributory pensions, and the grating of a fiscal subsidy to the self-employed to compensate for the lack of an employer (Imprenta Nacional 2000). These two measures should help to achieve universal coverage in pensions, as is currently the case of health care.

The decline in social insurance coverage of the formal labour force, combined with an increasing trend of the informal sector in the region, raises concern on four important issues: (a) the need of social security to adapt to changes in the labour force to at least maintain current coverage; (b) the worsening protection of the poor in view of a rising poverty incidence and very few countries that provide social assistance pensions; (c) the insufficiency of current social assistance pensions in the few countries that provide them (in most cases they don't cover essential needs); and (d) the need to allocate more resources for social assistance for health care and pensions and how to finance them (Mesa-Lago 2001c).

Gender discrimination

Women workers tend to have a lower coverage than their male counterparts because they are engaged predominantly in sectors that are not covered by social insurance such as the informal sector. However, universal health care systems (as exists, for instance, in Costa Rica) normally offer women the same rights and benefits as men; hence, they promote gender equality (ILO 2001). On the other hand, private health providers (such as ISAPREs in Chile) have discriminated against women because of their higher health needs (i.e., maternity) and costs.

Concerning pensions, insured women often receive lower benefits than their male counterparts, for three main reasons: (a) women's salaries are usually lower than men in the same job, hence their contributions are also lower; (b) the level of contributions paid by females are also lower than those of men because of pregnancy and their temporary absence from the labour force owing to child rearing; and (c) the age of retirement of female insured is often five years lower than that of men in Latin America, but the former tend to live an average of four years longer. As the rate of participation of women in the labour force increases, these inequalities will become more salient (Mesa-Lago 2001b).

Through internal solidarity and gender transfers public pension systems have certain features which attenuate labour market inequalities against women, such as minimum pensions and a weighted benefit formula that favour the lower paid. Conversely, private (FF) pension systems lack solidarity and distributive elements, therefore, cannot attenuate such inequalities (ILO 2001). In the process of structural pension reform, the gender dimension has not been sufficiently discussed in government, academic and political circles, partly due to ignorance but also to traditional negligence, but increasing attention and discussion are taking place (Arenas de Mesa 2000; Arenas de Mesa and Montecinos 1999; ILO 2001; Montecinos 1994).

To date, most studies have concentrated on the Chilean reforms. Among the discriminatory features of the private (FF) pension system, the following four have been noted: (1) there are relatively more obstacles for women to qualify for a minimum pension because it is more difficult for them to fulfil the number of required monthly contributions; (2) replacement rates for women (32 per cent to 46 per cent) considerably lower than for men (from 58 per cent to 83 per cent); (3) the fixed commission on wages (for administrative costs) affects more adversely those workers with low income – a group in which women are overrepresented – because it subtracts a proportionally higher sum from the amount deposited in the individual account; and (4) lower deposit results in poorer investment yields (Arenas de Mesa 2000).

Financial burden on the workers and the fiscal cost of the transition

1. *Payroll contributions and the burden on workers.* Health care and pension systems are financed mainly by payroll contributions imposed on insured workers and employers, but also by state contributions as a 'third party' (fixed as a percentage of the payroll or through special taxes or through budget subsidies to cover deficit), and by investment yields (this section is based on Mesa-Lago 2000c). There is a theoretical and empirical debate on whether employers actually pay their contributions or transfer them 'forward' to consumers via prices or 'backward' to their workers; if indeed there is a transfer, the contribution should not have an impact on employment, although it might have an effect on income distribution or competitiveness. It is alleged by one side in the debate that, if employers indeed pay their contributions, that will cause a distorting effect on the labour market: an incentive to substitute capital for labour, hence restricting job creation. Chile used this argument to eliminate the employers' contribution in both the

pension and health systems, and the same was done by Bolivia and Peru on pensions, but that was not the case in the other pension reforms: four did not change the employers' contribution (Argentina, Costa Rica, El Salvador and Mexico), one reduced it slightly (Uruguay), and two increased it (Colombia and Nicaragua). Under the health reforms, Peru shifted all of the contributions on to the employer, and in the other five countries the higher proportion of the total contributions is imposed on the employer (Argentina, Colombia, Costa Rica, Mexico and Nicaragua).

The insured contribution for pensions was slightly reduced in Chile's private system (but not in the public one), it remained unchanged in Argentina, Costa Rica and Mexico (in the latter, the state contribution was increased), and was raised in six countries: Bolivia, Colombia, El Salvador (the highest), Nicaragua, Peru and Uruguay (the smallest). The financial burden of the pension reforms has been shifted in most countries from the employer to the insured, justified by the argument (not empirically proved) that it will correct an alleged labour market distortion. The elimination of the employers' contribution leads to either an increase in the insured contribution or the fiscal subsidy as explained below.

2. *Fiscal costs of the transition.* Pension reforms of the substitutive and parallel types induce three fundamental fiscal costs (this section is based on Mesa-Lago 2000c): (a) the deficit in the public system which occurs because it is left without contributors or a minority of them, but with the burden of all current pensions and those that will be eventually granted to the insured who stayed in that system, the state finances such deficits in all countries; (b) the value of the contributions paid to the old system by all the insured who move to the new system (often called 'recognition bond'), such value is annually adjusted to inflation (except in Nicaragua) and two countries also pay an interest rate of 3–4 per cent (Colombia and Chile), the state is responsible for this cost in all countries except in Mexico and Uruguay,[7] but there are different restrictions such as ceilings and minimum years of contribution required (Peru has certified a small percentage of the owed recognition bonds); and (c) a guaranteed minimum pension for all insured in the new system whose accumulated sum in the individual account is insufficient to finance such pension, the state is responsible for the difference in five countries (Chile, Colombia, El Salvador, Mexico and Nicaragua), neither Bolivia nor Peru effectively grants this benefit. Under the mixed model, the public component may generate a deficit (Argentina and Uruguay because they are based on PAYG) or not (Costa Rica because it has ample reserves), but there is no need for a recognition bond, as the insured stays in the public component which pays a basic pension, this makes unnecessary the payment of a minimum pension in the 'private' component.

In addition, the state grants the following guarantees to the insured in some countries: (a) a social assistance pension to poor non-insured workers (Argentina, Chile, Costa Rica and Uruguay); (b) adjustment of pensions to inflation, including the minimum pension (the period of adjustment and its base varies in the countries); and (c) other guarantees such as a minimum annual yield of the investment in case that the administrator's funds are insufficient to pay it, and payment of pensions in case that administrators or insurance companies go bankrupt and their insured and pensioners are left without protection (granted in Chile, Colombia, Argentina and Uruguay, in the last two limited to public administrators not private ones).

3. *Two trade-offs.* The parallel and mixed models do not necessarily reduce fiscal costs in the long run, but defer such costs because only part of the implicit pension debt (IPD) is made explicit. Conversely, in the substitutive model all of the IPD is made explicit, more rapidly in Bolivia and Mexico than in the other countries because all of the insured must move to the new system. This involves a trade-off: either a high and immediate fiscal cost that might aggravate a difficult economic situation but would diminish in the long run (40 to 60 years) or a partial postponement of debt that would provide a break to wait for a more economically propitious time. The countries that grant most benefits and guarantees are those that generate the highest fiscal costs (Chile), while those that negate some of those benefits or curtail them considerably are able to reduce such costs (Bolivia, Peru). Here lies another trade off: to reduce fiscal cost or to protect the insured.

Income distribution

The ILO (2001) properly warns that social security systems should not be expected to promote a more equitable distribution of income by them-selves; indeed many social security systems perform a redistribution function but that should not be their principal goal. Social security should be one instrument – albeit an important one – of a broader package to improve income distribution. In this section I analyse what distributive function, if any social, security performs in public and private systems.

Concerning pensions, public systems with virtual universal coverage tend to have a progressive effect on income distribution if solidarity is properly applied, because transfers are done by the system collecting more from the higher-income insured, placing a ceiling to pensions, and securing a minimum pension for the low-income insured (if these conditions are not met, the system may have neutral or regressive effects). Conversely, systems with low population coverage tend to have a regressive effect on distribution, because the uninsured (low-income and poor) indirectly contribute to finance the minority covered (mostly middle income) through sales taxes and transfers of employer contributions to prices (Mesa-Lago and Bertranou 1998).

Structural pension reforms, particularly of the substitutive type, are devoid of endogenous solidarity (due to the 'neoliberal scepticism about social solidarity' (Mkandawire 2001: 11)), although they may provide exogenous solidarity, for instance, through the state guarantee of a minimum pension and the granting of social assistance pensions. In principle, a private (FF) system leads to a neutral effect in income distribution because pensions are directly related to salaries and contributions. However, fiscal costs of the transition in countries with a small percentage of the labour force covered (Bolivia, El Salvador, Nicaragua, Peru) should have a regressive effect because the state subsidizes the insured middle-income minority usually through sales taxes that are paid by the uninsured majority (Mesa-Lago 2000c).

Health care reforms seem to have more concern for inclusion of the low-income and poor, and some of such reforms have introduced redistribution mechanisms. In Chile the state provides subsidies according to income, hence, the poor don't pay and the highest-income insured fully pays; however, the right to transfer the entire contribution from the public to the private system (ISAPRE) by upper-middle and high-income insured led to a significant depletion of resources in the public system and its subsequent deterioration in the 1990s. The first version of the Peruvian reform tried to address this problem retaining at the public system part of the contribution of the insured who joined the private system, but successive versions deleted such mechanisms. The Colombian reform has established a Solidarity Fund to finance the 'subsidized scheme' that covers the poor and low-income uninsured and is funded with a payroll contribution of one per cent (paid by high-income insured) and by the surplus generated by the care of high-income insured. In Argentina, there is a Redistribution Fund that is financed with part of the payroll contributions and compensates the *obras sociales* whose insured are low-income and suffer high sickness risks (Bertranou 1999; Cruz-Saco and Mesa-Lago 1998; Mesa-Lago 1998).

Competition, administrative costs and the burden of commissions on workers

1. *Competition*. Adequate competition among administrators of both pension and health care programmes is a key to structural reforms, particularly in private systems. In theory, administrators compete for the insured and the latter have proper information to select the best, which should be assessed by the quality of care in health or the payment of a higher capital return in a pension fund, and by relative low commissions or premium charged in both. The scarce available information suggests, however, that competition is working better in health than in pension reforms, and that the size of the insured market is an important factor in facilitating or obstructing competition.

The experience of eight pension reforms in the region demonstrates that the higher the number of insured the higher the number of administrators and vice versa. Thus, Mexico has 14 million insured people and 14 administrators; Argentina 8 million and 12; Chile 6 million and 8; Colombia 3 million and 7 (but it has multiple types of administrators which facilitate entry); Peru 2 million and 5; El Salvador 670,000 and 3; and Bolivia 492,000 and 2 (Table 8.2). In Bolivia, the number of insured was so small that the government decided that there was a market for only two administrators, hence, divided the insured between the two by domicile, and prohibited changes until the year 2000 (such prohibition continued in July 2000); as a result there is no competition but a duopoly. Countries with a small number of insured should take this limitation into account and allow multiple types of administrators as well as the use by them of infrastructure from other financial institutions, in order to facilitate entry and reduce costs.

Even if there are a fair number of administrators, a significant concentration of insured in the biggest three has been observed: 100 per cent in Bolivia (only 2) and in El Salvador (3); 78–75 per cent in Chile and Peru (concentration in Chile has steadily increased from 59 per cent in 1983); 69–60 per cent in Uruguay and Colombia; 54 per cent in Argentina; and 45 per cent in Mexico – this country sets a maximum of 17 per cent to each administrator (Table 8.2). A study carried out in Chile shows that the three administrators with the highest number of insured have not systematically through time charged the lowest commissions and paid the higher capital returns. Reasons behind the insured selecting those three administrators seem to be: (a) the work of salesmen or 'promoters' who earn a fee for every insured they move to one of those administrators (in Chile there were 19,000 salesmen in 1998 – a ratio of one for 160 active contributors); (b) gifts and other treats given to the insured as an incentive to move; (c) lack of insured information and/or skills to make educated decisions on the selection of the best administrators; and (d) huge advertisement which is essentially symbolic and does not provide data on performance (Mesa-Lago 2001b).

There seems to be more competition among administrators of reformed health care systems because there are both a larger number and a wider variety of them. For instance, in Chile there were 27 ISAPREs in 1997 – almost three times the number of administrators (AFPs) existing at that time, and in Colombia the wide variety of administrators and providers is considerably higher than the pension administrators, but more and better data are needed on this important issue.

2. *Administrative costs.* Competition is expected to reduce administrative costs, but the previous section casts a doubt on competition and data from the Latin American pension reforms show no significant reduction in such costs. The commission, exclusively paid by the insured, is usually imposed on his/her salary and is sizeable: 4.13 per cent in Mexico; 3.8–3.0 per cent in Peru, Colombia, Argentina, El Salvador and Nicaragua; and 2.6–2.5 per cent in Uruguay, Chile and Bolivia (Table 8.2; Presidencia 2000). The commission is divided into two components: (a) the charge of the administrator for managing the old-age individual account, which is the major component and ranges between 1.9 per cent and 2.5 per cent of the total, its trend shows significant oscillation but little or no reduction; and (b) the premium transferred by the administrator to a commercial insurance company to manage disability and survivor's insurance (in Colombia and Mexico this is done by social insurance), which is the minor component and ranges from 0.6 per cent

to 1.6 per cent (except in Bolivia), it has exhibited a declining trend. The combination of the two trends results in a stagnant commission or very little reduction (Mesa-Lago 2001b).

3. *Burden of the commission on workers.* The heavy burden on the insured of the administration of the pension system can be assessed in Table 8.2, which compares the percentages of wages that go to the individual account (ranging from 7.5 per cent to 12.37 per cent) and the total commission charged (ranging from 2.5 per cent to 4.13 per cent). The percentage of the latter over the former is as follows: 32–30 per cent in Peru, Argentina, El Salvador and Mexico; 26–20 per cent in Colombia, Chile and Bolivia; and 17.5 per cent in Uruguay. Little or no data are available on health care administrative costs under the reform – a matter that demands more research.

Capital accumulation and returns

1. *Capital accumulation.* There has been significant capital accumulation in the pension fund of the eight countries (figures are in US million dollars and percentages of GDP at the end of 1998 or mid-1999): $33,246 and 40 per cent in Chile; $16,787 and 5 per cent in Argentina; $8,300 and 2.5 per cent in Mexico; $2,925 and 2.3 per cent in Colombia; $2,274 and 2.5 per cent in Peru; $472 and 4 per cent in Bolivia; $477 and 1.3 per cent in Uruguay; and $118 and 0.4 per cent in El Salvador (Table 8.2). The variation among countries is the result of various factors: (a) the time the reform has been in operation – almost 20 years in Chile but one year in El Salvador (Costa Rica and Nicaragua introduced their reforms in 2000); (b) the size of the insured market and GDP, and the salary level; and (c) the amount going to the individual accounts and the capital return.

2. *Capital returns.* One of the flaws of social insurance pension programmes prior to the reform was the very low or negative capital returns or real investment yield that they generated; the pioneer countries had few or no reserves and most of the rest did have reserves, but they were badly administered (Mesa-Lago 1998). The reform has improved investment management of the pension fund and its yield – although at a high administrative cost. The annual real average yield from the time of the inception of the reform until the end of 1998 or mid-1999 was: 13 per cent in Argentina; 11.3 per cent in Chile; 10.1 per cent in Colombia; 8 per cent in Mexico; and 7.5–7.4 per cent in Bolivia, Peru and Uruguay – the figure from El Salvador is not reliable (Table 8.2). Granted that this performance is far superior to that prior to the reforms, it should be interpreted with the following caveats: (a) data are gross and administrative costs should be deducted to obtain the net return; (b) all systems, except Chile, began to operate in the 1990s when international markets had very high returns; (c) the average yield prior to 1995 was considerably higher, the regional crises induced by Mexico in 1995 and the East Asian economies in 1997–98 reduced the yield considerably.[8] The severe decline in the capital market in the United States in early 2001 may

have similar adverse effects on capital returns of pension funds in Latin America. All this means that the oscillations of the capital market can generate quite different pensions in times of boom or bust: for instance, in Chile, the insured who entered the system in the 1980s will have a significantly higher pension than one who joined later (Arenas de Mesa 1999). Such a risk should be diminished in the mixed systems because they combine a defined benefit with an undefined one.

Capital markets and national saving

It is argued that the increase in capital accumulation and its investment in the capital market should contribute to its development, making it deeper, more liquid, competitive and efficient, and thereby helping to diversify the pension fund portfolio; these results, in turn, should lead to higher national saving and economic growth. These beliefs are endorsed by the World Bank and have been a motivating force for pension reform in Latin America (Mexico included them in the preamble of its reform law).[9] And yet, among the eight pension reforms in the region, the testing of such hypotheses has been done only in Chile, the country with the longest reform in operation, and its results have been negative or inconclusive.

1. *Development of capital markets.* A long-run econometric study of Chile, commissioned and published by the IMF, concluded that the empirical evidence *coincided* with the claim that the pension reforms have contributed to financial market development and a more diversified portfolio, but cautioned: 'all this evidence does nor established watertight proof that the establishment of pension funds has been the decisive factor in the impressive development of financial markets since the mid-1980s', the latter 'may simply reflect changes in legislation and other lessons learned from the experiences and mistakes of the 1970s and early 1980s' (Holzmann 1997: 163). In summary, there is no proof that the first part of the hypothesis is true.

The pension fund portfolio in Chile has indeed become more diversified since 1983 when it was overwhelmingly invested in public debt instruments or deposited in state banks; the early 1980s crisis made evident to the superintendency the danger of such excessive concentration and it began to promote a movement of investment to other instruments and the private sector. And yet, after almost two decades, in 1999 still 37 per cent of the portfolio was in state debt paper and only 13 per cent in stocks; actually the crisis of 1997–98 led to a shift away from the latter to the former. In other countries, there is little diversification of the portfolio: for instance, in 1999, in Mexico, El Salvador, Bolivia and Uruguay from 64 per cent to 97 per cent of the investment was in government debt paper (51 per cent in Argentina); the good capital return in these countries, therefore, was due to the high interest paid by the state but, although beneficial for the insured, it was costly and difficult to maintain in the long run. Conversely, the proportion of investment in stocks was nil in five countries and only had significant shares in Peru (27 per cent), Argentina (17 per cent) and Chile (13 per cent). The alternative of investment abroad is nonexistent or nil in six countries, Chile is an exception with 12 per cent (AIOS 1999).

2. *National saving.* The cited study published by the IMF concluded that the evidence was negative concerning the second part of the hypothesis:

> contrary to the common belief . . . the empirical findings suggest that the direct effect of financial market developments on the private saving rate was negative . . . The data indicate that the net pension savings were negative until 1989 and small afterward [therefore] the conventionally assumed impact of a Chilean-type pension reform on private (and national) saving may not hold . . . These results also temper the optimism reigning in Latin America and Eastern Europe, where pension reform is seen as an easy vehicle to boost national saving, and thus capital accumulation and growth.   (Holzmann 1997: 175)

Another study carried out by a high official of the Ministry of Finance in Chile also shows that the net effect of the pension reform on national saving was negative and during *the first fifteen years* – that is, seven years after 1989 when the IMF study estimated it to be positive but small. This calculation demonstrated that, in 1981–96, the annual average saving in the individual accounts was 2.7 per cent of GDP, but the fiscal cost was –5.7 per cent, hence resulting in a negative net outcome of –2.6 per cent of GDP. The study also projected that in the first five years of the twenty-first century the net outcome should become positive and grow thereafter, but it would probably take 20 years to compensate for the negative balance in the previous 20 years, in summary it would take 40 years to show a cumulative positive balance in national saving (Arenas de Mesa 1999).

Conclusion

Latin America is one of the regions of the world to have experimented with most development models, and it has also been at the vanguard of social policies and a pioneer in the foundation of the welfare state on the American continent. Similarly, the region has been at the forefront of market-oriented reforms and in the process of privatization of social services. It is important, therefore, to analyse representative diverse models of development in Latin America and to evaluate their socioeconomic performance, as well as assess the effects of social welfare (security) reform on the people and the economy.

The analysis of three different models of development in Latin America (Chile-market, Cuba–statist and Costa Rica–mixed) and evaluation of their performance found that: (a) the mixed model was able to combine in the best way the roles of the state and the market, as well as to properly balance social and economic goals; (b) the other two models overemphasized either the market or the state and were able to advance in one set of goals but only by sacrificing the other; (c) the balanced approach of the mixed model led to a fair performance in economic indicators and the best results in social indicators in the long run; and (d) corrections introduced in three models in the 1990s have reduced somewhat the role of the market in Chile and the role of the state in Cuba, and increased somewhat the role of the market in Costa Rica, but without altering the essence of the three models or significantly modifying their performances.

Structural reforms of social security (the most important component of the welfare state) implemented in the early 1980s in Chile and in the 1990s in several countries in Latin America, both in pensions and health care, have strengthened the role of the market and led to a larger private sector in those social services. Nevertheless, the reforms have followed diverse general models and different in all countries, with different degrees of privatization. Despite the reforms, the role of the state continues to be crucial in al countries.

The effects of the reforms on the people and the economy are mixed but tend to be in the negative side: (a) the freedom of choice of the insured ranges from zero to wide depending on the countries; (b) coverage of the labour force based on the number of affiliates has declined after the reform in three countries, remained unchanged in two and increased in three, but data are flawed in some cases, coverage based on the number of active contributors is significantly lower that based on the number of affiliates; (c) the poor continue to be excluded from social insurance in virtually all of the countries that have implemented reforms (health care reforms have more concern for the inclusion of the poor than pension reforms), although receive social assistance in four of them even if it tends to be insufficient; (d) inequalities generated by gender discrimination have increased in 'private' systems due to their lack of both solidarity and inter-gender transfers; (e) the financial burden on the worker has become heavier with the reform because the employers' contribution has been eliminated or reduced in most countries while the workers' contribution has been increased; (f) the reform has generated three types of fiscal costs during the transition and such costs are high, countries that have tried to reduce such costs have curtailed benefits of the insured; (g) some health reforms have introduced redistribution mechanisms, but pension reforms have either neutral or regressive effects on distribution; (h) competition has not worked as expected and, hence, administrative costs of 'private' systems have not declined substantially – furthermore, such costs are high and borne by the insured; (i) there has been significant capital accumulation in pension funds in all countries but with significant variation among them based on the time that the reform has been in operation and other factors; (j) capital returns have been apparently high but they must be adjusted to deduct administrative costs and they have oscillated with the capital market generated different pensions in times of boom and bust; and (k) there is no evidence that the reform has been the decisive factor in the development of the Chilean capital market, but evidence that the reform has had a negative effect on national saving.

The lessons of the three development models and the structural reforms of social security in Latin America should be carefully studied by other countries in that region and the rest of the world, to avoid adopting policies inspired sometimes by ideological concerns but not well grounded in empirical experience.

Notes

1. The book is 707 pages long and faced numerous methodological problems that cannot even be summarized herein. The results discussed in the text, therefore, considerably simplify the book's measurements and conclusions. In addition, an important section of the book deals with exogenous factors (other than the system) that could affect performance.
2. Investment on health was halted for almost one decade while real expenditures on health care were cut significantly. The infant mortality rate, however, continued its decline because scarce resources were targeted on pregnant women and infants.
3. For ranking purposes the nine indicators were added assigning the following points: 1 to the country ranked first, 2 to that ranked second, and 3 to that ranked third; the total was divided by nine to obtain the average ranking; and the final scores were: Costa Rica 1.56, Chile 1.89 and Cuba 2.56.
4. It has been shown that the more developed a country is (the higher the GDP per capita) the higher is its social security expenditure as a percentage of GDP: ILO (2001).
5. Structural reforms are those that significantly alter a public social insurance system by totally or partially replacing it with a private system. Parametric reforms are those that attempt to improve a public system by changing its entitlement conditions and/or strengthening its finances.
6. Cuba is the only country in Latin America in which the pension and health care systems are totally administered and financed by the state, and provision is gratuitous. But the system urgently needs a reform.
7. In Mexico all the insured at the time of the reform has been granted the right at retirement to choose the higher of two pensions: the one based on his/her accumulated individual account and the one based on the rules of the closed public system. Uruguay does not grant this benefit because the public system is not closed and is responsible for paying a basic pension.
8. The Chilean annual yield in the period 1981–94 was 13.8 per cent but in the period 1995–99 it was 2.6 per cent, due to negative yields in 1995 (–2.5 per cent) and 1998 (–1.1 per cent), resulting in an average of 10.1 per cent over the entire period.
9. Such a claim in the case of Chile is also made by Mkandawire (2001).

Bibliography

AIOS (1999) *Boletín Estadístico*. Buenos Aires: AIOS.

Arenas de Mesa, A. (1999) *Efectos fiscales del sistema de pensiones en Chile: Proyección del déficit previsional, 1999–2037*. Santiago: Ministerio de Hacienda y CEPAL.

Arenas de Mesa, A. (2000) 'Cobertura provisional en Chile: Lecciones y desafíos del sistema de pensiones administrado por el sector privado', *Serie Financiamiento del Desarrollo*. Santiago: CEPAL.

Arenas de Mesa, A., and Montecinos, V. (1999) 'The Privatisation of Social Security and Women's Welfare: Gender Effects of the Chilean Reform', *Latin American Research Review*, 34, 7–38.

Barraclough, S. H. (2000) 'Protecting Social Achievements during Economic Crisis in Cuba'. In D. Ghai (ed.), *Social Development and Public Policy*. Geneva and UK: UNRISD/Macmillan.

Bertranou, F. (1999) 'Are Market-Oriented Health Insurance Reforms Possible in Latin America? The Cases of Argentina, Chile and Colombia', *Health Policy*, 47, 19–35.

Cruz-Saco, M. A., and Mesa-Lago, C. (1998) *Do Options Exist? The Reform of Pension and Health Care Systems in Latin America*. Pittsburgh: University of Pittsburgh Press.

Dreze, J., and Sen, A. (1989) *Hunger and Public Action*. Oxford: Oxford University Press.

ECLAC (1998a) *La economía cubana: Reformas estructurales y desempeño en los noventa*. Mexico: ECLAC.

ECLAC (1998b) *Panorama social de América Latina 1997*. Santiago: ECLAC.

ECLAC (1998c) *Preliminary Overview of the Economies of Latin America and the Caribbean 1998*. Santiago: ECLAC.

ECLAC (1999) *Preliminary Overview of the Economies of Latin America and the Caribbean 1999*. Santiago: ECLAC.

ECLAC (2000) *La economia cubana: Reformas, estructurales y desempeño en los noventa*. Mexico: ECLAC/ASDI/Fondo de Cultura Económica.

Ghai, D. (2000) *Social Development and Public Policy: a Study of Some Successful Experiences*. London: Macmillan Press and UNRISD.

Holzmann, R. (1997) 'Pension Reform, Financial Market Development and Economic Growth, Preliminary Evidence from Chile', *IMF Staff Papers*. Washington, DC: IMF.

ILO (2001) 'Social Security: Issues, Challenges and Prospects', *International Labour Conference 89th Session*. Geneva: ILO.

Imprenta Nacional (2000). *Ley de Protección del Trabajador*. San José: Imprenta Nacional.

Mesa-Lago, C. (1998) 'La reforma estructural de pensiones en América Latina: Tipología, Comprobación de presupuestos y enseñanzas'. In Alejandro Bonilla and Alfredo Conte-Grand (eds), *Pensiones en América Latina: Dos décadas de reforma*. Geneva and Lima: International Labour Office.

Mesa-Lago, C. (2000a) 'Achieving and Sustaining Social Development with Limited Resources: the Experience of Costa Rica'. In D. Ghai (ed.), *Social Development and Public Policy*.

Mesa-Lago, C. (2000b) *Desarrollo social, reforma del Estado y de la seguridad social, al umbral del siglo XXI*. Santiago: CEPAL.

Mesa-Lago, C. (2000c) *Estudio comparativo de los costos fiscales en la transición de ocho reformas de pensiones en América Latina*. Santiago: CEPAL.

Mesa-Lago, C. (2000d) *Market, Socialist and Mixed Economies: Comparative Policy and Performance – Chile, Cuba and Costa Rica*. Baltimore: Johns Hopkins University Press.

Mesa-Lago, C. (2001a) 'La cobertura de pensiones de seguridad social en América Latina antes y después de la reforma previsional', *Socialis-Revista Latinoamericana de Política Social* Rosario, Argentina: Univ. Nacional de Rosario.

Mesa-Lago, C. (2001b) 'La revolución de las pensiones en América Latina: Comparaciones y desempeño', *Nuevo milenio: La política social, el urgente desafío de América Latina*. Mexico D.F: CIESS.

Mesa-Lago, C. (2001c) 'Social Assistance on Pensions and Health Care for the Poor in Latin America and the Caribbean'. In N. Lustig (ed.), *Shielding the Poor: Social Protection in the Developing World*. Washington, DC: Brookings Institution and Inter-American Development Bank.

Mesa-Lago, C., and Fabio Bertranou (1998) *Manual de economía de la seguridad social latinoamericana*. Montevideo: CLAEH.

Mkandawire, T. (2001) *Social Policy in a Development Context*. Geneva: UNRISD.

Montecinos, V. (1994) 'Neo-Liberal Economic Reforms and Women in Chile'. In M. Aslanbegui, S. Pressman and G. Summerfield (eds), *Women in the Age of Economic Transformation*. London: Routledge.

Presidencia de la República (2000) *Ley del Sistema de Ahorr. para Pensiones*. Managua: Presidencia de la República.

Ruiz-Tagle, J. (2000) 'Balancing Targeted and Universal Social Policies: the Chilean Experience'. In D. Ghai (ed.), *Social Development and Public Policy*.

UNDP (1996) *Human Development Report 1996*. Oxford: UNDP.

Part III
Historical Experiences

9
European 'Late Industrializers': The Finnish Experience

Juhana Vartiainen

Introduction

Is social policy a necessary ingredient of economic growth and development or is it possibly a dysfunctional by-product? This is a large question that does not permit a definitive answer. Yet there are many strands of literature in economics and other social sciences that offer an approach to this topic.

In this chapter, I try to use economic theory and the empirical experiences of one Nordic economy to suggest some positive linkages between social policy and economic development. In particular, I will discuss the role of social policies in alleviating the negative effects of risks and uncertainty as well as of distributional conflicts – both of which are inevitably associated with economic growth and development. I shall outline a couple of economic arguments and show that they can at least shed some light on the experience of countries such as Finland, characterized by small size, corporatist political and economic structures and lateness as to industrialization and economic development. Whether these lessons on national growth and innovation systems are of any interest to those countries that are attempting to find their niches in the globalized economy of the 3rd millennium is another question.

Growth and distributional conflict: theoretical models

Stripped to its economic essentials, economic growth and development are about deferring consumption of resources today in order to create more resources in the future. This economic definition consciously abstracts from all other, no less relevant aspects of development, but it is useful if we wish to consider the issue in its essential economic terms. Economists tend to think that, provided there are technological opportunities for such profitable investment and the return for these investments exceeds the discount factor, rational economic agents will indeed undertake projects that enhance future consumption at the expense of today's consumption, i.e. economic growth.

Seen in this way, the puzzle for a narrow-minded economist is why some nations do not grow and develop even though it would obviously be in the interests of all or almost all of their agents to do so. Now, and continuing this very abstract line of argument, a very general obstacle to these investments taking place is the eventual uncertainty and the eventual externalities associated with the allocation of the costs and returns of investment. Broadly, three kinds of economic mechanism can lead to a situation, which can hamper even those investments occurring that would be beneficial for the entire economy:

1. Discrepancy between social return and private returns of growth-enhancing investment;
2. Dynamic externality associated with the discrepancy of *ex ante* and *ex post* bargaining over distribution;
3. The individual and idiosyncratic uncertainty of investment returns.

The first point is related to what economists term positive externalities. Many investments are such that their rate of return depends upon the investment of other economic agents. Being an engineer in a poor country is probably most useful if there are other engineers and accountants around, so that one's education can be used to produce valuable output. Similarly, an individual investment in good health (for example, via sanitation systems or vaccinations) also confers an advantage on the neighbours of the investors. Such economic environments differ from the most stripped-down assumptions of neo-classical economic models. There is a positive role for government intervention in markets characterized by such positive externalities.

This general point is by now rather obvious to most mainstream economists and scholars of growth and development.[1] It is clear that some economic functions such as education, health care and the provision of infrastructure and a legal framework are better not left to private entrepreneurship. Azariadis and Drazen (1990) provide an interesting application of this idea in the form of 'threshold' externalities. Their model suggests that government subsidies of education are important to avoid low-development traps (see Aghion and Howitt (1998: ch.10) for a survey of theoretical models and empirical research on this issue).

Economic change and the management of distributional conflicts

The second point is concerned with the dynamic externality associated with the division of the returns of productive investment. It is an endemic characteristic of all economies in which some agents are 'large' so that the prices of inputs and outputs are not determined competitively and treated as given parametric constants by the concerned economic agents. More concretely, if distributional variables such as wages are determined in collective bargains, the *ex post* returns of investment do not in general correspond to the ex ante costs in an optimal way. The paradigmatic examples of this so-called 'hold-up' problem include:

1. The case of investment in productive equipment when there is a trade union which bargains about the wage; once the machinery is installed, the bargained wage probably goes up and the union expropriates a part of the return of the investment;
2. The acceptance by organized workers of a rate of profit that makes possible a rate of investment necessary for adequate economic growth;
3. The case of investment in a country that needs tax revenues; once the investment is in place, there is an incentive for the government to raise taxes on profits;
4. The case of innovation undertaken by the employees of a firm; there is no guarantee that improving the production process leads to an appropriate increase in wages.

These dynamic externalities imply that the incentives for productive investment are in general sub-optimal and do not lead to an efficient exploitation of investment opportunities. This problem has no easy solution, but it can certainly be alleviated by state action that guarantees certain rules and principles of equitable distribution. While the state cannot in a market economy directly determine the final allocation of goods, it can through the use of its tax and other instruments create expectations of fair treatment and an atmosphere, which is conducive to mobilization of the nation's resources. This point has been treated more fully in Vartiainen (1999). In that paper, I argue that the state can be seen as a kind of broker that ensures that the *ex post* distribution of resources is such that it corresponds to those incentives that were *ex ante* necessary to induce the necessary investments.

For example, a politically powerful working class may in principle accept a lower level of consumption today if this sacrifice can ensure a higher rate of capital accumulation and thereby a higher consumption set in the future. However, in a private market economy, there is probably no contract form that would ensure such a trade-off. From the point of view of the working class, the outcome in which the capital-owners either use their extra returns for personal consumption or transfer the profits abroad is an equally plausible scenario. In such a situation, the state may be able to intervene in the economy in such a way that high investments become the preferred behaviour of the capital owners. For example, it might ration credit to productive investment and keep interest rates low; or it might tax away a part of these profits and undertake direct public investments into productive capacity; or it might introduce legislation that prevents international transactions of wealth. Such policy measures have been commonplace in the Nordic economic policy regimes after the Second World War.

Social insurance and economic development

Economy-wide returns and individual uncertainty

The third aspect that we want to emphasize is the inevitable *individual* uncertainty associated with innovation and new investment projects as well as economic restructuring. In this case, an even more direct relationship between social insurance and investment can be posited. Suppose that there is a large amount of individual investment projects that can be undertaken by future entrepreneurs and suppose, quite plausibly, that the average return of these projects is high enough to meet the average cost, so that, on average, the projects should be undertaken (supposing that their number is so large that a law of large numbers applies).

However, the return of each individual project is a random variable, and, assuming risk-averse individuals, the expected utility of the project is less than the utility of the expected return. This implies that the number of realized projects will be less than the optimal one if there is no social security network. The formal interpretation of social security in such a model is that of an insurance pool: by setting an appropriate tax and social insurance system, the state can increase the expected utility associated with failure and thereby increase the amount of investment. This argument is simple, but it provides a robust intellectual support for a safety net as a factor that enhances economic growth and development.

To put it simply, you are more likely to become an entrepreneur if you are not drained down the gutter even if you fail. This point turns on its head the conventional wisdom on the detrimental effects of redistribution on innovation and effort incentives. One nice formalization of this idea is presented in Sinn (1994). In Sinn's model, the welfare state is identified with an insurance device that makes lifetime careers safer. Protected by the welfare state, people engage in productive and risky activities that they would otherwise not undertake. Sinn shows that this innovation-enhancing effect can even become too strong, so that people take too much risk and fail to take such necessary measures that would effectively insure them against adverse conditions. There is consequently an optimal rate of redistributive taxation.

Resistance to economic reform and modernization

Thus, it can be argued that a well-designed social insurance system can encourage economic innovation and individual risk-taking. On a more macro-economic level, it can also reduce resistance to economic reform. Phases of economic development are also phases of profound structural change. Development requires the mobilization of resources and sacrifices in today's consumption possibilities. Structural change is always associated with uncertainty and the possibility of completely unforeseen contingencies, partly due to the changing bargaining positions of different agents. The state, with its multidimensional policy tools, is in principle best equipped to ensure that the final economic outcome is not outrageously disadvantageous for any particular group – which, in turn, means that no particular group needs to be vehemently opposed to structural change and development.

To fix ideas, suppose that an economy could enhance average productivity by reforming its institutions (for example, it might liberalize financial markets, end agricultural subsidies or abolish price rationing in some market). It might be a reasonable guess that such reforms would increase the economy's average income. However, the final general equilibrium outcome of a process of structural change cannot be accurately predicted. Even if one might have some idea of what some macroeconomic variables might turn out to be, nobody can predict for sure the changes in individual allocations that will result. Since most individuals are risk-averse, they might consequently adopt a negative attitude towards structural reforms, even if these reforms would beyond reasonable doubt increase average income. Thus, many voters would *ex ante* want to vote for parties that oppose modernization and reforms. Such attitudes are commonly ascribed to irrationality and backwardness, but the risk aversion argument suggests that they can be perfectly plausible in the light of the theory of rational choice under uncertainty.[2]

Thus, risk aversion can be an obstacle to economic development. A slightly less obvious result of the political economy literature suggests that reforms can be hampered even if all agents are risk-neutral.

This idea has been nicely formalized and analysed by Fernandez and Rodrik (1991). In their sophisticated model, the reform in question is trade liberalization. Yet the intuitive idea behind their reasoning can be simplified in the following way. Suppose that there are two sectors in the economy, one of which (the 'modern' sector) stands to benefit from modernization (like trade liberalization) while the other (the 'traditional' sector) is going to lose. In the initial state, the majority of the economy's manpower is located in the traditional sector. Moreover, income is originally the same in both sectors (and same across individuals), whereas the modernizing reform would increase income in the 'winner' sector and shrink it in the 'loser' sector.

The crucial but fully plausible assumption, however, is that the modernizing reform will also lead to a transfer of people from the traditional sector to the modern sector. Let the economic data of this example be summarized in the following table:

	Before		*After*	
	Traditional sector	*Modern sector*	*Traditional sector*	*Modern sector*
Size of labour force	60	40	50	50
Income per capita	100	100	90	120
Average income		100		105

Thus, the modern sector people gain from modernization, since their income grows from 90 to 120. The reverse is true for the traditional sector individuals, as their income decreases from 100 to 90. Furthermore, 10 people shift from the traditional sector to the modern sector. Yet it is *ex ante* impossible to know who those shifters will be.

How will this economy's people vote if their opinion is asked for in a referendum on trade liberalization? Suppose that all agents are fully rational and completely aware of the data of the above table. A traditional sector person understands that he or she will have a probability of 1/6 of increasing his or her income from 100 to 120. With probability 5/6, however, income will shrink by 10 units. The expected gain is therefore $(1/6)*(20)+(5/6)(-10)=-5<0$. Thus, the traditional people will vote against the reform. Since they form *ex ante* a majority of the voters, the reform will not gather a majority of votes (the modern sector people will obviously vote for the reform, since their expected income change is positive). This is the outcome of the democratic process even if reform increases average income and even increases the income of the *majority* of people.

A salient feature of this model is that if the reform is eventually passed, it will turn out to be popular afterwards: only a minority of voters would want to return to the original state of affairs.

Even in this case, there is an obvious and constructive role for the public redistribution of income. If the state can advance an income redistribution scheme that does not waste resources, it can *ex ante* introduce legislation that will ensure that the losers will be a minority (or even that there are no losers).

Openness and trade as a factor of growth

More can be said on the impact of one specific factor of growth, namely participation in the international division of labour and economic openness. It is generally acknowledged that international division of labour is an important engine of economic growth. Furthermore, developmental success stories are often associated with a bold exploitation of world markets. Wealthy economies tend to be open economies, and this is especially true of small economies.

Many commentators see the correlation between internalization and social insurance as a negative one: as globalization proceeds, countries cannot 'afford' social insurance systems, so the story goes.

Authors like Dani Rodrik (see Rodrik (1998) in particular), however, have convincingly argued that the relationship between globalization and the welfare state is a positive one. The empirical regularity certainly corresponds to Rodrik's assertion: the larger the share of foreign trade in a nation's output, the higher is the share of government expenditure in output. This conclusion turns out to be quite robust to various statistical tests and alternative specifications of the statistical model.

Rodrik presents a simple theory to explain these facts, based on risk aversion. Open economies are more exposed to the uncertainty generated by volatile export markets. In particular, economies whose export products are concentrated in a few markets (as is typically the case for small and open economies) suffer from greater uncertainty at the individual level. A rational political reaction to this is to build up a welfare state that redistributes income and by these means effectively insures people against uncertainty of factor incomes (see also Rodrik 1997).

More generally, such reinsurance can take many forms. In any given period, it can entail redistribution from the currently successful to the currently unsuccessful. But a large public sector will also enable insurance from one generation to another. Suppose that an entire economy is largely dependent upon the international price of a crop. Then, if there are large and long-term swings in this price, a welfare state will also enable redistribution along the temporal axis.

Counterarguments: the overshooting of the welfare state

The above arguments paint a rather rosy picture of the potential for well-designed social policy to enhance economic growth and development. A more balanced view must recognize the realities of the political and economic processes that affect economic growth. According to the arguments we have surveyed, the positive role of the welfare state consists in diminishing the uncertainty associated with change, innovation and openness. In a certain sense, the state's action will in this case always amount to some kind of redistribution. This redistribution should not be designed in such a way that the very incentives for change, innovation and openness are removed. Thus, the question of the proper level and kind of redistribution is a very subtle one and there is no general theory that would predict that democratic political systems would not err on either side.

On the contrary, there are many plausible theories that suggest that redistributive welfare states might expand beyond the point that would be optimal from an efficiency point of view. Perhaps the most convincing of such theories build in one way or another on the notion of *transaction costs* associated with information. If a welfare programme is financed by a general tax but benefits a small but readily identifiable group of people, that group of people has a strong incentive to become informed about the project and lobby the political system for its implementation. As the cost of the programme is borne for a large number of voters, it might well be too burdensome for the average voter-taxpayer to find out about the deadweight loss that the project imposes on the rest of the economy. Assar Lindbeck (1993) offers one representative example of this argument.

Finland as a Nordic case

The experience of a late industrialized country like Finland can illustrate the interplay of economic agents with the state as a moderator. In the middle of the twentieth century Finland was still a relatively backward country, with a GDP per capita level roughly half of that of central European countries like France and Germany. Beginning from the 1930s and going on through the latter half of the century, the country embarked upon a remarkable 'catching up' process in which many of the elements outlined above were discernible. This is all the more interesting since in 1918 the country had experienced a bitter civil war which divided the nation into two camps – the defeated 'red' side and the victorious 'white' side. Furthermore, the very existence of Finland as an independent nation was under threat for most of the century, since the country found herself in a contested geopolitical zone, first between Germany and Russia in the interwar years and then between Soviet and NATO after the Second World War. I have argued elsewhere[3] that the subsequent political will to industrialize may even have benefited from this threat, since it made a free-riding strategy unattractive for all agents: the country could not afford to fail economically.

Anyway, from these premises, the Finnish political system was able to generate a remarkable class compromise in which the powerful working class, as represented by the trade union movement and two strong political parties, accepted a class compromise that did not put into question the basic mechanisms of property rights, capitalist wealth creation and participation in the international economy, but in which the state would use a large part of the economic surplus to undertake direct productive investment and provide welfare services as soon as the economic wealth of the country would permit.

Two early political decisions that paved the way for the subsequent developments were the 'January wedding' of 1940, in which the employers' organizations and the trade unions recognized each other as legitimate and trusted parties, and the fiscal policy measures of the late 1940s, in which the high taxes of the war economy were effectively kept unchanged in order to increase the freedom of the state to support economic growth and the growth of welfare services.

The Finnish developmental state had from the earliest days acquired corporatist characteristics. As such, corporatism was not a new phenomenon. By the 1930s, the state and the main economic actors like the banks and the export industry had been working together, in ways not unlike the experience of the Asian late industrializers. Thus, key economic decisions have been taken in co-operation with organized economic agents. Such corporatist characteristics were enhanced by the war experience.

Anyway, the phase of rapid accumulation of capital from the late 1940s through the 1980s can be seen as a long-term class compromise in which the workers abstained from using their full bargaining power while the state guaranteed a high level of investment and capital accumulation as well as the build-up of basic public services and social security transfers. The policy tools used to generate this outcome included taxation, credit rationing, selective support for investment and a gradual build-up of the welfare state. Thus, the outcome can be interpreted as a long-term agreement in which the workers accepted lower wages and got guarantees that the fruits of these sacrifices would benefit not only the capital-owners. Despite its crudeness, this characterization is quite adequate to depict the Finnish postwar experience.

One important characteristic of the resulting politics of the welfare state has been its close relationship to the needs of labour markets and worklife. The social partners – employers' and employees' organizations – have been closely involved with the state in the design of social policy, and it has then been natural that many social policy programmes and measures have been tailored to encourage labour force participation and boost productivity. A typical pattern of political decision making has been that many initiatives have first been launched by the social partners or voluntary organizations but have subsequently been adopted by the state.

Key examples of this are:

- *Comprehensive education*; after the war, primary schools were vigorously erected all over the country; free education was first confined to the primary and secondary classes, but in the 1970s a free and universal 12-year schooling scheme was introduced.
- *Day care of children*; in 1973, a comprehensive right to day care at subsidized prices was introduced. This encouraged female labour force participation, which in turn, sustained economic growth through the last decades of the twentieth century. This exemplifies the Finnish and Nordic principle according to which people's entitlements may be either universal or related to work but are in general not tied to marriage or family. Thus, women are treated as independent providers of labour.
- *Sickness insurance*; Finland adopted such a scheme late, in 1964, but at the time of its introduction it was one of the most universal of its kind. It was later complemented by the provision of free health services.
- *Occupational pensions*; In addition to a basic pension provision, the social partners initiated a system of occupational pensions in 1962. Even that scheme made it very attractive to participate in the labour market, in comparison to inactivity.

Is there anything to learn for the future?

The growth experience and the associated political regime analysed above was clearly an example of a national solution to the challenge of economic growth. It presupposed that there was a sufficiently well-functioning national political system in place, and many of its policy tools made use of economic measures that were available at a time when the global economy was less integrated. At that time, rationing of investment and interest rates, control of the exchange rate and taxation of national subjects were all part of the policy makers' tool kit. In today's world of market-driven rules of the game, there is less scope for such national growth pacts. However, that there is less scope does not mean that there is no scope. As the analyses surveyed in this article have shown, there is a clear case for using the public sector and its social insurance as a way to get the best out of participation in the global economy.

Notes

1. Sen (1967) has analysed this 'isolation paradox' in an abstract and elegant way.
2. In a similar vein, Rodrik (1997) notes that the extension of the market mechanism has in many countries fostered an anti-market, traditionalist reaction in the political arena.
3. See Vartiainen (1999) in which I argue that a similar mechanism may have worked in some Asian tigers like Korea and Taiwan.

Bibliography

Aghion, P., and Howitt, P. (1998) *Endogenous Growth Theory*. Cambridge, MA: MIT Press.

Azariadis, C., and Drazen, A. (1990) 'Threshold Externalities in Economic Development. *Quarterly Journal of Economics'*, 105, 501–26.

Fernandez, R., and Rodrik, D. (1991) 'Resistance to Reform: Status Quo Bias in the Presence of Individual-Specific Uncertainty', *American Economic Review*, 81, 1147–55.

Lindbeck, A. (1993) 'Overshooting Reform and Retreat of the Welfare State', *Seventh Tinbergen Lecture*. Nederlandsche Bank: Institute for International Economic Studies.

Rodrik, D. (1997) 'The 'Paradoxes' of the Successful State', *European Economic Review*, 41, 411–42.

Rodrik, D. (1998) 'Why Do More Open Economies Have Bigger Governments?', *Journal of Political Economy*, 106, 997–1032.

Sen, A. (1967) 'Isolation, Assurance and the Social Rate of Discount', *Quarterly Journal of Economics*, 81, 112–24.

Sinn, H.-W. (1994) *A Theory of the Welfare State*. Munich: Centre for Economic Studies, University of Munich.

Vartiainen, J. (1999) 'The Economics of Successful State Intervention in Industrial Intervention'. In I. M. Woo-Cumings (ed.), *The Developmental State*. Ithaca: Cornell University Press.

10

'Late Industrializers' and the Development of the Welfare State

Chris Pierson

Introduction

Industrialization has long been recognized as a key component in the emergence and development of state welfare regimes. The classic source in the comparative literature is Wilensky's (1975) *The Welfare State and Equality*. Drawing on the earlier work of Cutright (1965), Aaron (1967) and Pryor (1968), Wilensky concluded that 'economic growth and its demographic and bureaucratic outcomes are the root cause of the general emergence of the welfare state' (1975: p. xiii). According to this account, the origins of the welfare state lay in secular changes associated with the broad process of industrialization and, particularly, the breakdown of traditional forms of social provision and family life. These changes included economic growth (and the greater affluence it generated), growth in population (especially of an aged and urban population), the developed division of labour, the creation of a landless working class (and, subsequently, its political mobilization), the rise of cyclical unemployment, changing patterns of family and community life and (at a somewhat later stage) industry's increasing need of a reliable, healthy and literate workforce. The empirical work of Cutright, upon which Wilensky drew, suggested that 'the degree of social security coverage is most powerfully correlated with its level of economic development' (Cutright 1965: 537). Wilensky's own empirical work led him to conclude that more than 85 per cent of the international variance in social security effort was to be explained by economic development, combined with the dependent effects of the proportion of aged in the population and the age of the social security system. He concluded that 'there is not much variance left to explain' (Wilensky 1975: 22–5, 47).

Industrialization and welfare state growth

Whilst this emphasis upon the exclusive importance of industrialization in the development of welfare states has been widely challenged in the subsequent literature (see, for example, Stephens (1979), O'Connor (1988)), few would contest the centrality of industrialization to the general process through which welfare states emerge. However, what has become clear from later comparative surveys is that there is no straightforward association between the *level* and *duration* of industrialization and the *extent* of welfare state development. Following Uusitalo (1984), we can see that the significance of economic development in explaining *variation* in social policy effort between nations depends very substantially upon the size and diversity of the sample under review. (It may also depend upon the ways in which crucial variables, such as 'welfare effort', are measured; see O'Connor and Brym (1988).) Thus, in samples, which draw upon a very wide range of very differently developed nations (as when for example, contrasting the experience of OECD states with those of Sub-Saharan Africa), economic development emerges as a very powerful indicator of welfare state growth. However, among similarly developed nations (for example, in studies confined to members of the OECD) much less is explained by variation in the level of economic development. In Figure 10.1, for example, the poorest countries (in terms of GDP) also report the lowest proportionate spending on social security (and are concentrated in Sub-Saharan Africa and the poorest parts of South Asia) and the OECD countries (with the interesting exceptions of relative newcomers Mexico, Turkey and Korea) are all in the top half of the spending profile. Yet three of the four most affluent states rank 9th, 10th

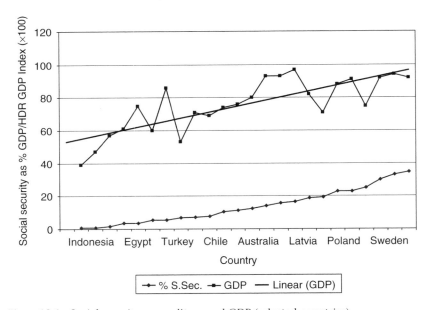

Figure 10.1   Social security expenditure and GDP (selected countries)

and 11th in this listing behind substantially less affluent (and less advanced and less industrialized) states such as Poland and Latvia.

A similar pattern emerges when we consider the relationship between the length of time a nation has been industrialized and the extent of its welfare effort (for the relevant data, see Appendix 1). We have already seen that the age of social security programmes was, for Wilensky, one of the key predictors of a state's welfare effort. Again, at a global level this proves to be true. Most of the early industrializers are amongst the more developed welfare states. Western Europe was (alongside the north-eastern US) the earliest industrializing region and it contains most of the world's 'big' welfare spenders. Those regions that industrialized rather later were correspondingly later in developing their social programmes (in Latin America from the 1930s; in East Asia, with the exception of Japan, from the 1950s). They fall correspondingly into a pattern of 'medium' and 'low' spenders. But there are important exceptions. The US is an obvious outlier, an early industrializer whose welfare 'breakthrough' did not come until the 1930s, was then incomplete (with no provision of comprehensive health care or family allowances) and is still an 'under-spender' in terms of its natural comparators. Similarly the westernmost 'transition economies' of the former Soviet Union reported remarkably high social expenditure levels throughout the 1990s (though, of course, on a global scale their industrialization was long-established and their welfare effort was recorded in terms of what was in several instances a rapidly declining GDP; UNICEF-ICDC (1997)). Still, it remains the case that, at a global level, there is a strong association between the period of industrialization and levels of welfare effort (mediated through the age of social security programmes).

Upon closer inspection, however, a rather more complex general pattern emerges. Crudely, the very first welfare states did not emerge amongst the pioneers of industrialization. Although the periodization of industrialization is complex and contested (see, for example, Rostow (1978), Bairoch (1982), Reynolds (1985)), it is widely accepted that Britain was 'the first industrial nation' and that it was followed somewhat later by the US (though in a regionally quite diverse pattern), Switzerland, Belgium and France. Germany's take-off was a little behind these, though once embarked upon this path, it grew very rapidly. Still, as late as 1913 per capita levels of industrialization were lower in Germany than in not only the UK and the US but also Belgium and Switzerland (Bairoch (1982: 281)). Yet it was Germany under Bismarck that is widely regarded as 'the first welfare state'. Amongst the other welfare innovators were Austria (or rather Austria-Hungary) and Denmark. Yet Austria's (per capita) level of industrialization was consistently lower than that of Germany and well behind the European average (Bairoch 1982: 281). As late as 1870, nearly one-half of Danish national product was derived from agriculture (though as mechanization kicked in over the last quarter of the nineteenth century much of the output was to be found in the co-operative agricultural sector (Johansen 1985: 297; Kuznets 1966: 88–9).

The pattern of subsequent programme adoptions in Europe is complex and there is some disagreement about whether the spread of welfare state programmes is best explained in terms of *prerequisites* (with state welfare initiatives being a response to endogenous national developments) or *diffusion* (a process of international imitation of welfare state innovators). Most states had an indigenous pre-history of state involvement in welfare (often as an aspect of internal security) and of the statutory regulation of labour markets. Yet, as soon as there were extant models to consider, a cottage industry developed in the study of programmes overseas (though this did not necessarily lead to programme adoption as the history of investigative commissions sent from the US to pre-1914 Europe attests (Skocpol 1992, 1995)). There has long been a lively debate about the extent to which second and subsequent adopters were following Germany's example or simply bringing their own internal developments to fruition (on Denmark, for example, see Johansen (1985), Levine (1983)). But whatever was the proximate source of these programme initiatives, it appears that, in the period to 1901, there was a move from less industrialized and more authoritarian regimes (Germany, Austria-Hungary, Denmark, Sweden) towards the more developed and democratic (Belgium, UK, France, Netherlands). In so far as we are concerned with the emergence of the welfare state within the more developed (western and northern) areas of Europe, welfare innovation moves more or less consistently from *less* towards *more* economically developed states (Flora and Heidenheimer 1981: 60–70).

Industrialization, enfranchisement and bureaucracy

Of course, something much more than a change in the technology of production is involved in the process of industrialization which precipitated welfare state innovation, and some have preferred to characterize these developments in terms of the more multidimensional category of 'modernization'. Thus, Hage, Hanneman and Gargan (1989) argue that it is modernization (represented by urbanization and the increasing density of communications) rather than industrialization that best explains patterns of welfare state growth, whilst Flora and Heidenheimer (1981) and de Swaan (1988) draw attention to the independent impact of political organization and state capacity. Although there is some sort of association between the extension of the (male) franchise and the development of social security (both grew apace in Europe between 1880 and 1914), the innovators were not the most extensively enfranchised states but constitutional-dualistic monarchies. Famously, Bismarck's reforms have been seen as a (pre-emptive) response to the threat of working-class mobilization. Just as famously, it has been suggested that liberal reticence about state compulsion was much less developed here than, for example, in France, the US or Britain (see, for example, Rimlinger (1974)). (Indeed, part of the explanation for the strange pattern of US welfare development – a pattern in which early growth through veterans' pensions was allowed to wither away in the early twentieth century – may relate to a mixture of early enfranchisement plus a deliberate strategy to undo state capacity at the Federal level; see Skocpol (1992)). Attention has also been drawn (most notably though certainly not exclusively in the German case) to a pre-existing administrative capacity (and confidence) to deal with the technicalities of mass insurance systems. At the same time, there may be a distinction to be drawn between the (perhaps quite limited) role of an extended franchise in *creating* welfare state programmes (and/or of the attempt to head off working-class political mobilization) and the (perhaps quite different) logic that drives established programme *growth* under democratic imperatives. Here it is worth remembering that, at their origins, the costs of welfare states were quite modest. It was the extension of coverage and levels of entitlement that made them the giants of public expenditure in the second half of the twentieth century (see Pierson (1998)).

The interaction between industrialization, enfranchisement and administrative capacity in the early development of welfare state regimes is neatly captured by Skocpol and Ikenberry:

> The ideas for modern social insurance and welfare policies came from domestic experimentation and transnational communication, and they were put into effect by sets of political executives, civil administrators, and political party leaders who were looking for innovative ways to use existing or readily extendable government administrative capacities to deal with (initially key segments of) the emerging industrial working class. Pioneering social insurance innovations, especially, were not simply responses to the socio-economic dislocation of industrialism; nor were they straightforward concessions to demands by trade unions or working-class-based parties. Rather they are best understood... as sophisticated efforts at anticipatory political incorporation of the industrial working class, coming earlier (on the average) in paternalist, monarchical-bureaucratic regimes that hoped to head off working-class radicalism, and coming slightly later (on the average) in gradually democratizing liberal parliamentary regimes, whose competing political parties hoped to mobilize new working-class voters into their existing political organizations and coalitions. (Skocpol and Ikenberry 1983: 89–90)

Perhaps the one qualification we may now want to add to this gloss is that the classes which reforming politicians and administrators sought to address were rather more diverse than this summary suggests. In their differing ways, both Esping-Andersen (1985) and Baldwin (1990) draw attention to the importance of middle-class and agrarian interests and parties in the early development of Europe's welfare states (in these instances in the Scandinavian countries).

Welfare states and 'late industrializers'

It was Europe's 'late industrializers' which led the process of welfare state innovation, although their example was soon taken up across the more developed states of western and northern Europe. Of course, we have to recognize at once that Europe's 'late industrializers' were, in a global context, amongst the earliest and, in the case of Germany most powerful, industrial nations. (Even in 1860, Bairoch reckoned Germany and Austria-Hungary to lie respectively seventh and eight in the ranking of the world's leading manufacturing countries, though this placed them behind not only the UK, France and the US but also China, India and Russia. (Bairoch 1982: 284).) If the earliest pattern of welfare state adoptions saw a move from less to more developed, in the period between 1908 and 1923, the principal determinant of innovation appears to have been geographical proximity to an existing welfare state rather than the level of industrial development. After 1923, there is a clear tendency for countries to adopt welfare state measures at a lower level in their own economic development (with the notable exception of the US) and, paralleling the pattern of the spread of industrialization, 'late starters' have tended to develop welfare state institutions earlier in their own individual development and under more comprehensive terms of coverage (Alber 1982; Collier and Messick 1975: 1301; Alber cited in Flora 1986: vol. 1, p. xxiv; Kuhnle 1981; Kyo-seong 2001; Schneider 1982). Within regional economies (say in Latin America or East Asia) there is a tendency for welfare state initiatives to be taken earlier in the developmental time of later industrializing states, following regional pioneers which have themselves tended to adopt social security programmes at lower levels of industrialization than those which prevailed in Western Europe when these programmes first emerged. Figure 10.2 shows how these patterns have persisted at a global level for nearly a century.

'The advantages of backwardness'

The modern welfare state was a Western European initiative (though far-flung Anglo-Saxon outposts in New Zealand and Australia had something more than a walk-on part in its early history) and it was the (slightly) later industrializers within Western Europe that led this process (on Australia and New Zealand, see Castles 1985; Castles et al. 1996). In that literature, which deals more narrowly with the economic history of industrialization, it has long been argued that 'late developers' differed significantly from those who had pioneered the industrialization process and that, in some respects, latecomers enjoyed developmental advantages precisely

221

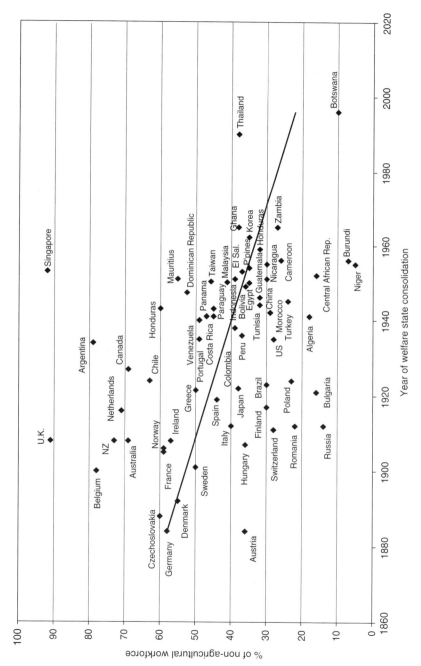

Figure 10.2 Industrialization and consolidation of welfare (global)

because of their lateness. Here the classic source is Gerschenkron's *Economic Backwardness in Historical Perspective* (1962). Marx (among others) was broadly-speaking correct, so Gershenkeron supposed, when he imagined that in the process of industrialization late developers would follow the example of those who had already made the transition to a fully industrialized economy. But he (and others) were wrong if they imagined that later developers would simply follow the path through which early industrializers had reached their goals. In many ways, the definitive industrializing experience of Britain was unique. For perhaps as much as a century, Britain had derived extraordinary advantages from her position as the first industrial nation. In 1860, the UK was responsible for about 37 per cent of Europe's industrial production, that is about one-fifth of total world industrial production (Bairoch 1982: 292). For a time, this gave Britain a colossal economic advantage. But it also embedded certain long-standing weaknesses in the British economy – an over-development of manufacturing for domestic markets, sub-optimal plant size, a reluctance to innovate, and a shortage of capital for industrial investment at home. Though initially 'backward', latecomers were able to exploit their late arrival – adopting proven new technologies that had been developed elsewhere, adapting more appropriate plant sizes and exploiting new ways of funding development. They were able to industrialize rapidly where the pioneers (above all, Britain) had developed slowly. This is part of the story of how the German economy came first to challenge and then to outpace the British. But late developers also generated quite new institutional solutions to the 'problems of backwardness'. Amongst these, Gershenkeron draws particular attention to the much greater role of investment banks (classically in the German experience) and a much more active role for the state (especially in Germany and Russia). This meant that the experience of late industrializers was not just later; it was also qualitatively different from what had gone before.

Looking beyond Europe, we see that later developers did not only industrialize differently. They also tended, as we have seen, to legislate the characteristic suite of welfare state measures when their own industrialization was less developed, with a more extensive role for the state and under more inclusive rules. This was, at least in part, a response to the different institutional and societal framework which late industrialization itself generated (more organized interests especially amongst domestic capital-holders, an earlier concern with the quality of human capital). In response to this experience, it has been suggested (Mkandawire 2001) that the advantages of 'late industrializers' may extend into a series of particular experiences (and opportunities) amongst 'late-developing welfare states'. A much more active social policy, Mkandawire suggests, may have been part of that overall institutional nexus through which later industrializers were able successfully to play 'catch up' with more industrially advanced states. It follows that those regimes which are still pursuing developmental goals should recognize and value the central importance of state-sponsored social welfare as part of a comprehensive strategy for economic development. In the rest of this chapter, I explore the issues this poses for the study of comparative welfare state development.

Late industrialization and welfare: Latin America

Much of the recent discussion of this issue of welfare state development among late industrializers has focused naturally enough upon recent experience in East and Southeast Asia – where this is a very 'live' issue – and, prospectively, upon the opportunities for welfare development in the world's poorer regions, in the less affluent parts of Asia and in Sub-Saharan Africa. But, in fact, we already have a wealth of evidence about this experience from the long-established pattern of welfare state development amongst the 'old' late industrializing nations of Latin America.

Latin America was one of the first areas outside Europe to develop welfare state institutions and it represents, in some senses, a first regional experience of the social policy consequences of 'late' development. Figure 10.3 (plus the material in Appendix 1) gives a clear record of this pattern of welfare state development in Latin America. Carmelo Mesa-Lago, the leading authority on Latin American social security development, identifies three groups of states within the region. A group of regional 'pioneers' (Uruguay, Argentina, Chile, Brazil and Costa Rica) began to develop social insurance schemes as early as the late 1910s and 1920s. Although most of these states had legislated for work injury insurance and some form of pension and sickness-maternity insurance by 1950, the level of coverage was very uneven. Certain privileged groups (especially amongst the armed forces and the civil

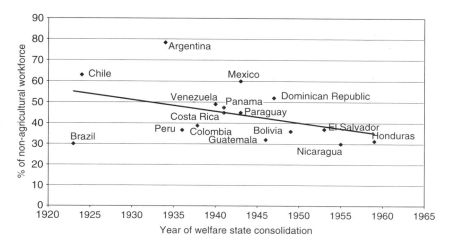

Figure 10.3 Industrialization and consolidation of welfare (Latin America)

service) received preferential treatment in a system that was highly stratified and fragmented. These are generally the only states in Latin America to have introduced unemployment insurance and amongst that half of our sample, which introduced some form of family allowance. As the data on suffrage suggest, many of these initiatives predate a fully democratic period – and the consolidation of democracy in Latin America has in many cases been deeply problematic. The latest Freedom House ratings show most of Latin America falling into a middling range of 'partly free' states, and many of them have had more or less extended experience of authoritarian government within the past twenty years. Somewhat notoriously, Chile's celebrated pension reforms were pushed through under a military dictatorship. In this context, Costa Rica is something of a stable democratic outlier (Freedom House 2002). Evidence also suggests that special interests, often occupationally-based and often within the state apparatus itself (above all, within the armed forces), have been a powerful influence on the patchwork coverage of social insurance programmes in the region.

In a second 'intermediate' group of states (Panama, Mexico, Peru, Colombia, Bolivia, Ecuador, Paraguay and Venezuela), social insurance only really emerged from the 1940s onwards, to some extent under the international influence of the International Labour Organization and the Beveridge Report (Mesa-Lago 1991: 360). These countries tended to introduce social insurance at a lower level of industrialization than the 'pioneers' (in most of them more than half of the economically active population was still involved in agriculture at the point of the 'consolidation' of their social security regimes). An effort was made to avoid the patchwork of different schemes and occupational groupings that had characterized the 'pioneer' states, but levels of coverage were generally much lower. This pattern has persisted, albeit in an attenuated form. At the end of the 1990s, social expenditure as a percentage of GDP averaged 19.4 per cent in the 'pioneer' countries and 11.8 per cent among these 'intermediate countries' (ECLAC 2001).

Finally, 'latecomers' within the region (the Dominican Republic, Guatemala, El Salvador, Nicaragua, Honduras and Haiti) have only really developed their programmes in the 1950s and 1960s. Coverage is still very limited and does not generally extend to either unemployment insurance or family allowances. Average social expenditure as a percentage of GDP in these states is 7.7 per cent. Programme coverage of the economically active population is low and this in societies where large numbers of the poorest work only, if at all and often intermittently, in the informal economy.

What should we make of the Latin American experience? Clearly it fits the pattern of early adoption in later developers, both in global terms (in which 'pioneers' such as Argentina are 'late' developers compared with Europe) and within the region (where the intermediate and latecomer states adopt programmes earlier in their own developmental time than did the region's 'pioneers'). Both these trends are illustrated in Figures 10.1 and 10.2. We can also see, as we might expect, that, for the most part, the longest-established welfare regimes are the biggest spenders, though patterns of expenditure throughout the region actually vary widely (see Appendix 1). Amongst Mesa-Lago's intermediate welfare states, for example, public expenditure as a percentage of GDP in 1999 varied between 6.8 per cent (Peru) and 16.1 per cent (Bolivia). There was also significant variation in the region in those areas of social expenditure which received the greatest effort. Given the lack of coherence or progressivity in pension systems, expenditure on social security (largely pensions expenditure) does the least work of redistribution. In the larger welfare states, social security accounted for a larger part of the growth in expenditure through the 1990s. Later developing welfare states, with a smaller overall budget, tended to put more of their spending effort into health care and primary education – areas which are more progressive in their distributional outcomes. In terms of the European model, Latin American welfare states are radically 'incomplete', with family allowances in place in little more than half the cases and unemployment insurance provided amongst fewer than a third (see Appendix 1). Average social expenditure in the region was 13 per cent at the end of the 1990s. In the most comprehensive survey of recent developments in social expenditure in the region, the Economic Commission for Latin America and the Caribbean (ECLAC) typifies its states generally as 'under-spenders' in terms of welfare effort, especially in terms of the capacity to address poverty. This is within a region which has always been seen to have an unusually unequal distribution of initial incomes and an unusually large informal sector (given its level of economic development)(ECLAC 2001, 2002).

The sense that Latin American states have derived peculiar advantages from 'lateness' requires considerable qualification. We might argue that, *within the region*, later developers have learnt some lessons from the region's pioneers, particularly in terms of consistent coverage of the population and in prioritizing those areas in which social expenditure can be expected to have a distributional impact upon both income inequality and 'life chances' more generally. But, overall, social spending is lower than might be predicted upon the basis of the level of economic development. According to ECLAC, 'around the mid-1990s, public spending as a share of GDP in the Latin American countries was around nine percentage points below the standard that would apply for their output level', with a similar shortfall in tax revenues (2001: 125). Coverage is often patchy and inconsistent. The limited resources that are available are not always directed to maximize either economic efficiency or social equity. (For a critical survey of current forms and levels of social protection, see ECLAC (2002).)

None of this should be particularly surprising, given that one of the leading themes in the discussion of Latin America's economic development has always been its 'dependency'. Indeed, Latin American experience was one of

the principal sources of the first unseating of that orthodoxy on 'modernization' that characterized North American social science in the postwar period
(Harrison 1990). That earlier theory of modernization, drawing on 'classical'
sources in Marx, Durkheim and Weber, had seen development in terms of
a more or less unilinear process in which the underdeveloped would gradually
adopt the technology, institutions and culture of the more developed, carrying
them towards and then across the threshold of modernity. It was largely the
Latin American experience that informed the scepticism of economists such
as André Gunder Frank who in the 1960s depicted the underdevelopment
of Latin America in terms of a hierarchy of nations in twentieth-century
capitalism within which the dominant nations (and multinational corporations) of the already-developed North and West flourished through keeping
emergent economies in a state of dependency (Frank 1967). Dependency
theory has its own complex history, engaged in a debate with its neo-liberal
detractors for the best part of forty years (for a critical evaluation of *both*
sides, see Haggard (1990)). What we can legitimately draw from this ongoing
debate is a recognition that 'lateness' is certainly attended by as many disadvantages as advantages. Without siding unambiguously with the *dependistas*,
we can say that latecoming has been associated with a distinctive repertoire
of developmental policies – at some times with a focus on import substitution,
at others dominated by export-led growth. The existence of an already-
industrialized world and abundant foreign capital (at a price) makes the
matrix of choices facing latecomer states different, creating new and distinctive
opportunities for that rent-seeking behaviour to which states are always
vulnerable. This has led states in Latin America to adopt a range of distinctive
approaches to domestic and international capital, to domestic political
organization and to domestic labour movements (and/or their repression).
There has been plenty of state involvement in Latin American welfare but
this has not always generated outcomes that are more equitable or generous
or efficient than those that have prevailed in an earlier generation of
European welfare states.

Late industrialization and welfare: East and Southeast Asia

Widespread interest amongst western social scientists in the social and
economic development of societies in East and Southeast Asia can be retraced
at least to the classic work of Dore on the organization of the Japanese firm
in the 1970s (Dore 1973). Above all else, western commentators were interested
in the principles and practices that underlay the Japanese 'economic miracle'
of the postwar years. It was the same sorts of concerns that sparked a similar
interest in the rather later successes of the Asian tiger economies (World
Bank 1993). For a long time there was no matching interest in the welfare
regimes of East Asia – at least in part because it was assumed that such
regimes were rudimentary and residual. In fact, the residual nature of East

Asian welfare states sometimes features as one of the aspects of these economies' success, contrasting with the overburdened welfare states of Western Europe. This neglect of welfare developments in East and Southeast Asia has now been rectified. Following the lead of Rose and Shiratori (1986), Gould (1993) and Jones (1993), we now have a wealth of detailed analyses of the varying welfare regimes of East Asia and a series of typologies to match: 'Confucian' (Jones 1993), 'America-Pacific' (Rose and Shiratori 1986), 'hybridized' (Esping-Andersen 1997), 'regulatory' (Goodman *et al.* 1998), 'developmental' (Holliday 2000), 'Bonapartist' (Gough 2001) and 'Japanese-focused East Asian social welfare regime' (Goodman and Peng 1996). East Asia is definitively a region of late industrialization – indeed, it could be said to have had three distinctive waves of late industrialization – and the wealth of material we now have enables us to interrogate claims about the relationship between late industrialization and welfare in the region in some detail.

Japan has a unique place in this story. Compared with Western Europe and North America, Japan is a late industrializer and it is clear that she drew on experience with the enactment of social insurance elsewhere, particularly the occupationally-based reforms of Bismarck's Germany. Within the region, however, Japan was a precocious industrializer and, in part through her experience as an imperial power, an onward exporter of social welfare policies (notably to Korea and Taiwan). Japan's welfare experience reflects her position within the regional and the global economy – and her troubled history. Although investigative commissions were sent to look at experience in Britain, Germany and the US before the end of the nineteenth century and despite the legislative measures of 1911 and 1922, the current Japanese welfare state is largely a product of the post-Second World War period in which the social security regime was re-built under American tutelage. In a pattern seen to be characteristic of the region, Japan subordinated social policy to the logic of nation (re-)building through economic development. By pursuing a (successful) strategy for economic growth built around full (male) unemployment, Japan was able to avoid the social costs that unemployment placed upon less successful economies elsewhere. By encouraging a widely admired system of corporate welfare (and weak unions), it was possible to deflect onto private market actors social costs which were elsewhere met by the public exchequer. This was easier to achieve in a context of highly-fragmented and occupationally-segregated social insurance where there was little or no commitment to use the state as an agent of vertical redistribution. Building upon an already existing network of communal and more especially family social support, Japanese governments were able to keep to a minimum the state's responsibility for personal social services. It was this combination of institutions and practices that persuaded some to speak of the Japanese welfare state (and of later similar developments elsewhere in the region) as 'Confucian', though this is a label, which recent analysts regard with some caution (for a critical review, see White and Goodman 1998). Overall, social expenditure levels in Japan are low (by comparison with other OECD states, even including the US), standing at 14.1 per cent in 1996 (see Appendix 1). Public education and health care spending in Japan is lower (in the later case rather marginally) than in most of its OECD peers. It is in the area of social security (especially non-pension expenditure) that Japan has spent so much less than comparably developed states elsewhere (Jacobs 1998, 2000).

Although Japan is a low spender in OECD terms, it is by some way the largest social welfare spender within the region. It is followed (at what appears to be a declining distance) by two of the original four tiger economies, Taiwan and (South) Korea, whose total social spending (including health care and state education) runs at around 10 per cent of GDP (see Appendix 1; Jacobs 2000: 4). These are both interesting exemplars of the complex relationship between late industrialization and welfare. Although we tend to think of the success of the tiger economies being built upon a strategy of export-led growth, in both countries this was preceded by a period of (successful) growth through import substitution (Haggard 1990). What is crucial here is that both strategies were fashioned by an interventionist 'developmental state', in association with both local and international capital. In both examples, we have an authoritarian state, acting closely with business interests and in a context in which unions were deliberately kept weak where necessary through the use of repressive legislation and force, to fashion a strategy for national economic development. Social welfare was not a priority, but maximization of employment and improvement of the skills base of the economy were. Improving welfare would come from sustained economic growth as, indeed, to a significant degree, it did, as both Korea and Taiwan developed rapidly in the 1960s and 1970s (Lee 1999). In both states (as throughout Southeast Asia) state education was prioritized, with a later and slightly lesser emphasis upon health care. There were pre-emptive moves to improve welfare under authoritarian governments, but promised improvements were not always delivered (as was notoriously the case with Korea's national pension plan which was originally legislated in 1973, but only implemented in 1988 with an expectation that the first full pensions would be paid in 2008; Lee 1999). In both countries, democratization seems to have brought real changes in welfare policy, including improvements to the public health care systems and moves towards employment insurance in Korea and the introduction of national health insurance and moves towards a national pension scheme in Taiwan (Jacobs 2000; Kuhnle and Hort 2000; Lee 1999).

Experience in the two other first-wave tigers was rather different. Before its return to Mainland China in 1997, Hong Kong had a pattern of social welfare that could properly be described as residual. There was a small public assistance programme and a rather larger, but ungenerous system of allowances for the elderly and disabled. Public health care was virtually free but its quality was poor. The state was, however, a major provider of primary and secondary education. Overall social expenditure amounted to little more than 5 per cent of GDP (Jacobs 2000: 92–4). Singapore was different again. A small entrepot city-state economy (with its 'industry' very heavily focused in services), public provision of welfare services in Singapore remains extremely limited. The key welfare institution here is the Central Provident Fund (CPF). Established (under British rule) in 1955, the provident fund is a compulsory savings scheme for employees and employers. Originally envisaged as a means of providing retirement incomes, the scheme has been expanded to include provision for house purchase, education and (highly-regulated) investment. Although heavily state-regulated, the assets of the CPF are not owned by the government and the mandatory contributions go into private accounts. Accordingly, the CPF does virtually no work of redistribution. The fact that so much welfare effort is delivered by a quasi-public system whilst social expenditure is kept extremely low (around 5 per cent of GDP) has made the CPF an object of much interest and admiration by the governments of other advanced industrialized states. (On Singapore's CPF, see Vasoo and Lee 2001.)

Industrialization is a well-established fact in all of the first-wave tiger economies. GDP per capita in Korea now exceeds that in the poorer members of the European Union. In Singapore, it is broadly comparable to the UK at around $23,500 (UNDP 2002). But there is a range of other states in the region, which are at a rather earlier stage in the process of industrialization. These industrializing states, mostly in the south of the region, include Malaysia, Thailand, the Philippines and Indonesia, the regional giant. These states have certain features in common. They are less industrialized and less affluent than their neighbours to the north (though per capita annual incomes vary from around $9,000 in Malaysia to little more than $3,000 in Indonesia: UNDP 2002). In general, business interests are strong and labour organizations weak. Democracy here is less securely consolidated. Corporate welfare is much more limited than in either Japan or Korea. Gough characterises these welfare regimes (with some qualifications) as 'bonapartist', borrowing Baldwin's (1990: 39) definition of a 'bonapartist' social policy as one which is 'used by social elites (as a means) of preserving the status quo, side-stepping the threat of major reform by granting modest concessions to increasingly important but still largely disenfranchised classes'. As was the case in more northerly parts of Asia, social policy and welfare have been seen as part (though very much the subordinate part) of a broader state strategy for national economic development. This helps to explain the continuing emphasis in the region upon the 'investment' elements of public welfare – health care and, above all, education – rather than income maintenance (especially where this might entail an element of redistribution).

Amidst these broad similarities, there are some important differences. Malaysia's social security arrangements reach back into a British colonial past, with a key role for its provident fund (originally established in 1951) whose original remit of providing retirement income has now been expanded to cover home ownership and some medical costs. A system of state occupational injury insurance has been expanded since its inception in 1969, but coverage is still limited and there is no system of unemployment insurance or family benefits. There is a national health service, but its coverage is uneven. Overall, social expenditure is around 8 per cent of GDP (though two thirds of this is made up of spending on education). In the Philippines, the welfare regime is of long standing, dating back to the period of US administration in the 1920s, but much of this was a dead letter or systematically undermined by corruption. A raft of reforms in the early 1990s (on pensions, health care and occupational injury) improved the situation but left large numbers of the population – especially those in the vast informal sector – without coverage. There is no provision for unemployment compensation or family benefits. Social expenditure is around 6 per cent (nearly one half of which is spending on education).

Significant developments in public welfare in Thailand and Indonesia are still more recent. In Thailand, the legislative framework for social security was largely established in 1990 with a long-term timetable for the development of pensions, unemployment benefits and child benefit. This schedule was disrupted by the economic crisis of 1997. The national pensions system will not begin to pay out full pensions before 2014. Health care coverage is limited, with the best cover provided for those in the public services. Overall social expenditure is around 6 per cent but fully two-thirds of this spending goes on education, with less than one per cent being devoted to social security. Indonesia is by some way the largest country in Southeast Asia (with a population in excess of 200 million). Although, its foundational welfare legislation can be retraced to the 1950s, Indonesian social security is extremely limited outside the public sector. Her provident fund has failed to develop into a major financial institution as in Malaysia and Singapore. Agricultural and seasonal workers (still a very significant part of the Indonesian workforce) are wholly excluded from such limited welfare provision as there is. There is no unemployment insurance and no additional financial support for families with children. Indonesia is (with the possible exception of the Philippines) the poorest of the states we have considered. Little more than 3 per cent of its GDP is devoted to social spending with even its educational spend falling well below the regional average.

What general lessons may we draw for the East Asian experience and how do these differ from what we found in Latin America? Clearly, East Asia has its own 'late/pioneer' industrializer in Japan. Although Rostow (1978) dates Japan's initial industrialization from the last years of the nineteenth century, the Second World War had a devastating impact on her productive capacity and she did not recover her prewar position in the world's manufacturing economies until the early 1960s. In the miraculous decade between 1963 and 1973 production grew at a rate of 12 per cent per annum (Bairoch 1982:

302–5). Older industrial powers in Europe, perhaps in the UK more than anywhere else, were acutely aware of the advantages that Japan derived from its particular form of late industrialization. The role of the state in this industrial development, and in particular the record of MITI, was the object of particular awe, as was the enviable record of seemingly harmonious industrial relations and the capacity to run an economy at full employment without unleashing uncontrollable inflationary pressures (see Dore 1973; World Bank 1993; Johnson 1982). Indeed, the closeness of politicians (especially in the ruling LDP) and businessmen was to become a major cause of concern in a later and less successful period for the Japanese economy when corruption was seen to be holding back the process of reform. At the same time, it is clear that lateness did not make Japan an especially 'generous' welfare state. Given its overall level of affluence and the extent of its industrial development, Japan has always stood out within the OECD as an unusually low spender, consistently underspending even the United States. Of course, one of the important issues here is that the welfare state in Japan just does not look like a 'traditional' welfare state of the European kind. This has become something of a commonplace in the literature on Japan's welfare evolution (see, for example, Esping-Andersen 1997; Jacobs 1998).

Many of the same arguments apply to the broader experience of welfare state evolution in East and Southeast Asia. The literature of newly-industrialized countries (NICs) is above all concerned with the rapidly-expanding economies of this region and we have seen that it is possible to draw a distinction between the 'first-wave' tiger economies and those that are coming up (more or less fast) from behind. In all of these cases of late industrialization, the state has been very active in promoting national economic development, through a strategy which exploits the (above all trading) opportunities that are peculiar to a small industrializing economy in a world of already industrialized giants (see Vartiainen 1995; Wade 1995). The economic status of these first tiger states has been transformed but, thus far, changes in their welfare expenditures have been much more modest. Undoubtedly this is to be explained at least in part in terms of what is distinctive about these states and the period and circumstances of their industrialization. (To industrialize in the global economy of the early twenty-first century is just not the same as industrializing in the global economy at the start of the twentieth century.) But we need to exercise some caution before seeing the East Asian welfare state as wholly different from what has gone before or reaching too readily for an explanation in terms of 'culture' (of distinctive 'Asian values' or 'societal Confucianism' or whatever). We need to remember that the 'big' welfare states of Western Europe were quite modest in spending terms at their origins. Many of the newer welfare states of East Asia report spending levels at or below 5 per cent of GDP. Yet these were levels reached in Western Europe often as much as thirty to forty years after the first social security legislation (see Pierson 1998: 107). Similarly, we know that demography plus the age of programmes is a key driver of welfare expenditure (following Wilensky, above), yet the demographic structure of the mature welfare states/industrialized countries is quite different from the NICs of East Asia. The latter are still comparatively 'young' countries whose pensions schemes will not come fully on stream until some time into the century. As we have seen, for most of these societies it is in social security spending (within which age profile plus pension entitlement is the key issue) rather than spending on education and health care that the real lag lies. As a changing demographic profile 'kicks in', these newer industrialized societies will face rapidly increasing pressure on what has always been the most expensive part of the welfare state – provision for the elderly (for details, see World Bank 1994).

If we look at prior experience in Europe (and Latin America) we see also that there is a clear sequential pattern in the adoption of welfare programmes (see Appendix 1). This sequencing is extraordinarily robust, moving through industrial accident insurance and health insurance towards old-age pension provision. Generally speaking, unemployment insurance and family allowances have come later – in the case of the latter often much later. This pattern is largely reproduced in Latin America. (Although many states here lack unemployment insurance, almost all the 'pioneer' states have some such provision.) The sequence can also be seen in East Asia, though here it is radically incomplete. Only Japan has thus far legislated for both unemployment insurance and family allowances. The experience of Korea is particularly interesting in this context. Korea is a late industrializer, which has grown rapidly over the past twenty years to become the world's eleventh largest economy with a per capita income similar to that of Greece and Portugal. It is one of the OECD's lowest welfare spenders, but its social expenditure has grown (from as little one per cent in 1965) to command something like a tenth of a vastly expanded GDP. It now has a more or less comprehensive system of health care insurance, a national pension system (due to mature in 2007) and a system of unemployment insurance (albeit, in keeping with the times, the emphasis is much more upon active labour market measures than compensation for those without jobs). All of this is enough to persuade Kuhnle and Hort (2000: 179) that the East Asian welfare states are following 'the "route to modernity" followed by their developed predecessors in Europe'. We may want to be just a little bit more cautious. History seldom quite repeats itself, either as tragedy or farce. It is likely that, for reasons discussed below, welfare states in eastern Asia are unlikely quite to follow the trajectory of their European predecessors (after all, these forerunners are themselves changing). Nonetheless, many of the pressures – political, economic and societal – that drove the social policy process in an earlier generation of industrializers are likely to re-emerge in however transformed ways for those who are entering upon this path a century later.

Late industrialization: the lessons

We have now had an opportunity to consider, however schematically and briefly, the relationship between late industrialization and welfare in a number of different national and regional contexts and over a time-span of more than a century. What, if any, general conclusions can we draw?

First, it is clear that there are some well-defined trends that persist throughout almost all of the period under review. The (slightly) later industrializers within Europe developed the 'first' welfare states. Thereafter, the trend has been for later industrializing states to introduce welfare measures earlier in their process of economic development and with rather more extensive coverage (the pattern clearly mapped out in Figure 10.2 above). The sequencing in which accidental injury insurance tends to be the first social security measure, followed by health and maternity insurance and then pensions for the old aged and disabled, with unemployment insurance and family allowances coming some way behind is astonishingly robust. So too is the pattern through which initial measures and covered populations are both extended (typically from key industrial workers to other workers, dependents, agricultural workers and the self-employed). Often state actors have a privileged place within these social insurance schemes (with pension arrangements for army officers, civil servants and teachers frequently marking them out from the generality of the population). Almost everywhere we have seen welfare states grow. The ageing of populations which is a part of the demographic transition that industrialization brings is a built-in accelerator of welfare budgets and, whatever the declarations and expectations of politicians, it is the pace of growth rather than growth itself that has been checked over the past thirty years (see Pierson 1998). We have seen that later developers have tended to devote rather more resources to health and education – but this may be in part a reflection of their societal youthfulness. The big historical picture also shows us that, in the area of social insurance at least, policy transfer is not a new phenomenon. Policy emulation goes all the way back to Bismarck and some policy tools have reached practitioners at second or even third hand. (Consider the trajectory of the Bismarckian elements in some of the newer south Asian welfare regimes.) Again, whilst we tend to think of the reforming influence of international financial institutions as quite recent, it is clear that the impact of the ILO, for example, stretches over at least fifty years. Similarly in some regions (above all in East Asia) we can trace clearly the impact of colonial institutions and practices upon subsequent social policy development.

At the same time, there are some ways in which the context of social policy has been qualitatively different for latecomers. Perhaps most importantly, this is because the trajectories of industrialization upon which latecomers have embarked have been different precisely because of the extent of the already-industrialized world (as is clearly the case, for example, with both import-substituting and export-led growth strategies). This gives late developers special opportunities but also presents them with particular problems – the 'opportunities' perhaps being best seen in Southeast Asia, with the 'problems' especially clear in Latin America. Crucially, many of the newer industrialized societies, in part precisely because they have been able to foreshorten the transition to industrialism, face a process of accelerated societal ageing in the near or medium-term future. This is likely to place a severe strain upon their less well-established social policy regimes (see World Bank 1994).

Before we give any further consideration to the special circumstances of late developers, however, we need to address a more generic claim that the integrity of *all* established social welfare regimes is about to be undermined through the supposedly corrosive impact of *globalization*. In some accounts of this process, the creation of a borderless world economy is undermining the capacity of states to manage economic actors and processes within their territories. Increasingly, capital will migrate to those areas which will offer the lowest social costs (or at least the lowest social costs consistent with a requisite level of quiescent skilled labour), forcing developed (and developing) welfare states either to lower their costs/standards or else to face a future of mass unemployment and steady economic decline. Whilst this argument captures something real in the processes of global economic change, as it stands it is unsustainable. It has often been small states with open trading economies (Denmark provides a good example) that have been able to sustain the largest public sectors (a feature pointed out as long ago as 1965; see Cutright (1965)). Indeed, the earliest welfare states themselves emerged in a period of highly open international trading (before 1914). Still more telling is the fact that the low-cost states to which capital (and employment) migrated in the 1960s, 1970s and 1980s have themselves sponsored growing welfare regimes (Taiwan and Korea are excellent examples of this phenomenon). This is absolutely not to say that processes of change in the global economy have no impact upon the range of policy options that are available to states. Rather, it is to insist that these economic changes do not systematically undermine the viability of welfare regimes, old or new. (For a much more extensive discussion of the consequences of globalization for welfare states, see Pierson (1998, 2001) and Garrett (1998).)

At the same time, welfare regimes, whether new or established, are likely to have to change. Amongst these changes we should expect to see a growing role for non-state actors – both domestically and internationally. Indeed, as attention shifts from methods of governing to modes of governance, we should expect that the lines of demarcation between domestic and international will become increasingly blurred. (It requires a colossal exercise of historical forgetfulness to believe that these lines were ever very clear-cut, especially for those who have normally been world history's policy takers.) Aside from families (always the key welfare agents), institutions in civil society – churches, charities, and commercial organizations – have long played a key role in the delivery of welfare. This is as true for long-established welfare states as it is for newcomers. But there is a case for thinking that the more successful late developers may now find themselves copied by more established welfare regimes. Singapore's Central Provident Fund has been much admired by political leaders and policy makers in the West and, in more general terms, the East Asian model of 'regulatory' welfare has been seen as a key element in the reform of state welfare in the developed West (as governments seek to distance themselves from the 'production' of welfare services). Historically, high levels of private spending on tertiary education and high co-payments for health care have been seen as signs of the *under*development of welfare regimes in East Asia – but they may, in fact, anticipate reforms elsewhere. (Having committed itself to reach by 2010 levels of participation in higher education for young people already achieved in Korea, Labour in the UK now finds itself struggling to find a sustainable funding regime, though it seems certain to rely in one form or another upon greater co-funding by students themselves (Mingat 1998; UK Labour Party 2001)). The regulatory welfare state is not unheard of in the older welfare states – indeed, it is a key component of the Australian welfare regime, both in its 'classical' form and in the reforms of superannuation of the last decade (Pierson and Castles 1996) – but it may now assume an increasing role, as states seek to secure adequate retirement incomes for a growing elderly population without the commitment of additional tax resources (which Western publics are reluctant to vote to supply).

In the international arena, late-developing welfare states have always been strongly influenced both by the example of developed welfare states elsewhere (with a debt to both Bismarck and Beveridge) and by the promptings of international agencies. We have already noted the well-established (and ongoing) impact of the ILO – and the UN has a similarly long-standing influence. More recently influential, and authoritatively so when social policy reform has been made a condition of wider financial support, is the impact of the IMF and the World Bank. The history of these interventions is complex and multivalent. Some agencies have always placed a greater weight upon social development (the UN in its various manifestations) and the maintenance of international standards (the ILO). Though to varying effect, the IMF and the World Bank have tended to place greater weight upon the imperatives of economic growth (variously defined and qualified). Recent changes of approach have led to a very public spat between these two agencies, with the World Bank interestingly repositioning itself on the issue of social policy and development. From a stance in which it appeared fully signed up to the 'Washington Consensus' and the market-led thrust of *Averting the Old Age Crisis* (World Bank 1994), the World Bank has moved through its revised advocacy of the developmental state (in the 1997 World

Development Report) to the quite radical(-sounding) advocacy of a renewed focus upon *Attacking Poverty* in the 2000/01 World Development Report (World Bank 2001). For a series of commentaries on these developments, see the *Special Issue* of the *Journal of International Development* (Hubbard 2001). The transition between 1990 and 2000 has been described as a move from a strategy with two-and-a-half legs (labour-intensive growth and human capital with a limited role for safety nets) to three legs (opportunity, empowerment and security). The more recent document gave unprecedented space to the 'voices of the poor', allowing them, to some significant extent, to define for themselves what poverty (as 'pronounced deprivation of well-being') means.

Some have doubted whether the World Bank has the policies to match the rhetoric of *Attacking Poverty*, but it represents, at the very least, an important attitudinal change. However, the World Bank's recognition of a greater range of market failures does not lead straightforwardly to an advocacy of greater state involvement. In contexts in which states are mistrusted or lack efficacy, it places considerable weight upon non-state and community responses or, indeed, upon the competence (and trustworthiness) of (domestic or international) NGOs. Again, the World Bank may not be able fully to specify the mechanisms through which its renewed commitment to democracy may be met, but it is important that it should be signed up to an account of the development process in which the voice of those on the ground is seen to be consequential (not least because there has always been a strong 'development now, democracy later' school among the international financial agencies). Given the importance of the stance of international financial institutions for states that aspire to industrialize (and correspondingly to refashion their domestic social policy) such a shift in focus is highly consequential.

One other development in the approach of the international agencies is of especial importance, not just for late industrializers but also for well-established and yet-to-be industrialized states. This is a shift in focus from welfare *inputs*, especially state welfare inputs, to (societal) welfare *outcomes*. Of course, such a shift is well established in the work of Esping-Andersen (1990) amongst others, and outcomes have always been seen as important if under-theorized, but this change is especially consequential in the case of less-developed welfare regimes. If we contrast East Asian and Latin American welfare regimes, for example, we find that, though the East Asian regimes are often smaller and notoriously non-redistributive, overall welfare outcomes (in terms of the minimization of poverty and the equality of incomes) are often significantly better than in Latin America. In Latin America, many of the longer established welfare states have a Gini inequality index in excess of 50 (although in Peru it is 46 and in Uruguay 42). This contrasts with levels of 25 in Japan, 31.6 in Korea and 32.6 in Taiwan (World Bank 2001). In part, this relates to contrasting patterns of employment and differential patterns of household income in the two regions. It also points to the fact that some types of public expenditure are more equal than others. Generally speaking, expenditure on education and health has a more equalizing effect than expenditure on social security. Evidence from Latin America in the 1990s suggests that the highest-spending welfare states devoted proportionately more of their increase in social expenditure through the decade to pensions, whilst lower spenders (generally the latecomers) devoted more to primary education and health care. In this sense, the expenditure of the lower overall spenders did more 'redistributive work' (ECLAC 2001: 113–44). In considering the records and above all the future opportunities for welfare latecomers, it is important that we capture the whole picture and focus upon what matters most – that is, improving welfare outcomes rather than (just) increasing welfare expenditures.

Nowhere is this more true than in Sub-Saharan Africa, the region of the world in which industrialization and policies for the attainment of real social security seem to have the furthest to travel. We know that Sub-Saharan Africa is the poorest region of the world and that in comparative and absolute terms it may well have become still poorer in the 1990s (World Bank 2001). Average social expenditure in Africa in the mid-1990s was around 4.3 per cent – an average which is greatly inflated by the inclusion of some higher-spending states in northern Africa (see Appendix 1). In 1991, von Braun reported that social security made up as little as one-tenth of government spending in the states of Sub-Saharan Africa. According to Barbone and Sanchez B. (1999), writing of Sub-Saharan Africa a decade later, with very few exceptions.

> formal social security institutions have not been successful in fulfilling their main mission, broad-based coverage of the population. What is more important, it is unlikely that pensions and disability coverage will be extended to the informal sector, which represents the vast majority of the employed population, *within the next generation*. (emphasis added)

In this context, the issue of social security in the region remains much as it was when outlined by von Braun at the start of the 1990s. In the long term, effective social security in Sub-Saharan Africa can probably only be achieved 'as a consequence of, and after, economic growth' (Von Braun 1991: 395). But it is not possible to wait until this economic growth has been achieved before the issue of social insecurity is addressed. Sub-Saharan Africa is poor and still predominantly agricultural. The priority is on reducing absolute levels of insecurity: reducing infant mortality, increasing the security of food supplies, improving sanitation and access to clean water, providing basic education and securing basic health care. In the short run, and given existing levels of public mistrust and limited governing infrastructure, the central state may play only a limited role in these initiatives, with a correspondingly larger role for community- and family-based schemes. These are likely to be based upon an economic growth strategy, which is as much agricultural development as it is industrial. In the longer term, there is an issue of reconciling these sort of community-led measures with a more traditional social security apparatus under the jurisdiction of a competent centralized authority. But 'a sizeable percentage of the children born today in Africa will spend their lives in the traditional or informal sectors, with little hope they will be covered by formal social security arrangements' (Barbone and Sanchez B. 1999). In the short term, the issue is one of finding the most effective means of addressing high levels of absolute insecurity, rather than setting about the construction of a welfare state in its traditional form (of social insurance linked to participation in the formal economy).

All this brings us some considerable distance from our first thoughts about Germany as a late industrializer. This is hardly surprising. Almost everyone (with the exception of the UK, the US and a handful of West European states) has been a late industrializer at some time (and this includes the current industrial giants of Germany and Japan). Narrowing our focus to the more recent period, it clearly makes limited sense to think of Korea and the Congo or even Korea and Indonesia as 'late industrializers' in quite the same way. As we have seen, this does not preclude us from making some fairly robust claims about the similarities that have characterized the process of welfare state growth as societies have industrialized. At the same time, this does leave us with the reality of some quite differing regime types, not just across the globe, but also within regions. This was, of course, one of the key conclusions of Esping-Andersen's (1990) magisterial survey of the *Three Worlds of Welfare Capitalism*, but it is probably as true of states in Latin America, perhaps even of the reform process of recent years. (On the differences in the reform process in Chile, Peru, Colombia and Brazil, for example, see Nitsch and Schwarzer (2000).) 'Lateness' is one very important aspect of welfare state development and historically it has probably helped later industrializing states to achieve more encompassing social policy regimes. But this has always been qualified by the initially subaltern position of such states within the global economy and their generally limited resources. In practice, the optimal future solutions, whether we reach them or not, are likely to be an amalgam of state, market, family and community. For today's late industrializers it is not a matter of playing 'catch up' with much more developed (and much wealthier) regimes elsewhere. Much more is it a challenge to use a wide range of resources and mechanisms in order to deliver the best possible real welfare *outputs*. In fact this will be as much a challenge for the old-established welfare regimes as it is for those whose transition lies some way in the future.

Bibliography

Aaron, H. J. (1967) 'Social Security: International Comparisons'. In O. Eckstein. (ed.), *Studies in the Economics of Income Maintenance*. Washington, DC: The Brookings Institution.

Alber, J. (1982) *Von Armenhaus zum Wohlfahrtsstaat*. Frankfurt (Germany): Campus.

Bairoch, P. (1982) 'International Industrialization Levels from 1750 to 1980', *Journal of European Economic History*, 11, 269–310.

Baldwin, P. (1990) *The Politics of Social Solidarity*. Cambridge: Cambridge University Press.

Barbone, L., and Sanchez B., L.-A. (1999). *Pensions and Social Security in sub-Saharan Africa: Issues and Options*. Washington, DC: World Bank.

Castles, F. (1985) *The Working Class and Welfare*. Wellington, NZ: Allen and Unwin.

Castles, F., Gerritsen, R., and Vowles, J. (1996) *The Great Experiment*. Sydney: Allen and Unwin.

Collier, D., and Messick, R. E. (1975) 'Prerequisites Versus Diffusion: Testing Alternative Explanations of Social Security Adoption', *American Political Science Review*, 69, 1299–1315.

Cutright, P. (1965) 'Political Structure, Economic Development, and National Social Security Programs', *American Journal of Sociology*, 70, 537–50.

De Swaan, A. (1988) *In Care of the State*. Cambridge: Polity Press.

Dore, R. (1973) *British Factory, Japanese Factory*. London: Allen and Unwin.

ECLAC (2001). *Social Expenditure in Latin America: Overview of a Decade in Social Panorama of Latin America 2000–2001*. Santiago: ECLAC.

ECLAC (2002). *Globalization and Social Development*. Santiago: ECLAC.

Esping-Andersen, G. (1985) *Politics Against Markets*. Princeton: Princeton University Press.

Esping-Andersen, G. (1990) *The Three Worlds of Welfare Capitalism*. Oxford: Polity Press.

Esping-Andersen, G. (1997) 'Hybrid or Unique? The Japanese Welfare State between Europe and America', *Journal of European Social Policy*, 7, 79–89.

Flora, P. (1986). *Growth to Limits*. Berlin: De Gruyter.

Flora, P., and Heidenheimer, A. J. (1981). *The Development of Welfare States in Europe and America*. New Brunswick: Transaction.

Frank, A. G. (1967) *Capitalism and Underdevelopment in Latin America*. New York: Monthly Review Press.

Freedom House (2002). *Freedom in the World: Country Ratings 1972–73 to 2001–2*. London: Freedom House.

Garrett, G. (1998) *Partisan Politics in the Global Economy*. Cambridge: Cambridge University Press.

Gerschenkron, A. (1962) *Economic Backwardness in Historical Perspective*. Cambridge, MA: Harvard University Press.

Goodman, R., and Peng, I. (1996) 'The East Asian Welfare States'. In G. Esping-Andersen (ed.), *Welfare States in Transition* (pp. 192–224). London: Sage.

Goodman, R., White, G., and Kwon, H.-J. (1998). *The East Asian Welfare Regime Model: Welfare Orientalism and the State*. London: Routledge.

Gough, I. (2000). *Welfare Regimes in East Asia*. Bath: University of Bath.

Gough, I. (2001) 'Globalization and Regional Welfare Regimes', *Global Social Policy*, 1, 163–89.

Gould, A. (1993) *Capitalist Welfare Systems*. London: Longman.

Hage, J., Hanneman, R., and Gargan, E. T. (1989) *State Responsiveness and State Activism*. London: Unwin Hyman.

Haggard, S. (1990) *Pathways from the Periphery*. New York: Cornell University Press.

Harrison, D. (1990) *The Sociology of Modernization and Development*. London: Routledge.

Holliday, I. (2000) 'Productivist Welfare Capitalism: Social Policy in East Asia', *Political Studies*, 48, 706–23.

Hubbard, M. (2001) 'Attacking Poverty – a strategic dilemma for the World Bank', *Journal of International Development*, 13(3), 293–8.

Jacobs, D. (1998) *Social Welfare Systems in East Asia: a Comparative Analysis including Private Welfare*. London: LSE, Centre for Analysis of Social Exclusion.

Jacobs, D. (2000) 'Low Social Expenditures on Social Welfare: Do East Asian Countries Have a Secret?' *International Journal of Social Welfare*, 9, 2–16.

Johansen, L. N. (1985) 'Denmark'. In P. Flora (ed.), *Limits to Growth*. Berlin: De Gruyter.

Jones, C. (1993) 'The Pacific Challenge: Confucian Welfare States', *New Perspectives on the Welfare State in Europe*. London: Routledge.

Kuhnle, S. (1981) 'The Growth of Social Insurance Programs in Scandinavia'. In P. Flora and A. J. Heidenheimer (eds), *The Development of Welfare States in Europe and America* New Brunswick: Transaction.

Kuhnle, S., and Hort, S. E. (2000) 'The Coming of East and South-East Asian Welfare States', *Journal of European Social Policy*, 10, 162–84.

Kuznets, S. (1966) *Modern Economic Growth: Rate, Structure, and Spread*. New Haven: Yale University Press.

Kyo-seong, K. (2001) 'Determinants of the Timing of Social Insurance Legislation among 18 OECD Countries', *International Journal of Social Welfare*, 10, 2–13.

Lee, H. K. (1999) 'Globalization and the Emerging Welfare State – the Experience of South Korea', *International Journal of Social Welfare*, 8, 23–37.

Levine, D. (1983) 'Social Democrats, Socialism, and Social Insurance: Germany and Denmark, 1918–1933'. In R. F. Tomasson (ed.), *The Welfare State 1883–1983: Comparative Social Research*. London: Jai Press.

Mesa-Lago, C. (1991) 'Social Security in Latin America and the Caribbean'. In E. Ahmad, *et al*. (ed.), *Social Security in Developing Countries*. Oxford: Oxford University Press.

Mingat, A. (1998) 'The Strategy Used by High-Performing Asian Economies in Education', *World Development*, 26, 695–715.

Mkandawire, T. (2001) *Social Policy in a Development Context*. Geneva: UNRISD.

Nitsch, M., and Schwarzer, H. (2000) 'Recent Developments in Financing Social Security in Latin America', *Issues in Social Protection*. Geneva: ILO.

O'Connor, J. (1988) 'Convergence or Divergence? Change in Welfare Effort in OECD Countries, 1960–1980', *European Journal of Political Research*, 16, 277–99.

O'Connor, J., and Brym, R. J. (1988) 'Public Welfare Expenditure in OECD Countries: Towards a Reconciliation of Inconsistent Findings', *British Journal of Sociology*, 39, 47–68.

Pierson, C. (1998) *Beyond the Welfare State?* Cambridge: Polity.

Pierson, C. (2001) *Hard Choices*. Cambridge: Polity.

Pierson, C. and Castles, F. (1996) 'A New Convergence? Recent Policy Developments in the UK, Australia and New Zealand', *Policy and Politics*, 24(3) 233–45.

Pryor, F. L. (1968) *Public Expenditures in Communist and Capitalist Nations*. Homewood, IL: Irwin.

Ramesh, M., and Asher, M. G. (2000) *Welfare Capitalism in Southeast Asia: Social Security, Health and Education Policies*. New York: Macmillan.

Reynolds, L. G. (1985) *Economic Growth in the Third World 1850–1980*. New Haven: Yale University Press.

Rimlinger, G. V. (1974) *Welfare Policy and Industrialization in Europe, America and Russia.* London: Wiley.

Rose, R., and Shiratori, R. (1986) *The Welfare State East and West*. New York: Oxford University Press.

Rostow, W. W. (1978) *The World Economy: History and Prospect*. London: University of Texas Press.

Schneider, S. K. (1982) 'The Sequential Development of Social Programs in Eighteen Welfare States', *Comparative Social Research*, 5, 195–219.

Skocpol, T. (1992) *Protecting Soldiers and Mothers: the Political Origins of Social Policy in the US*. Cambridge, MA: Harvard University Press.

Skocpol, T. (1995) *Social Policy in the US*. New Haven: Princeton University Press.

Skocpol, T., and Ikenberry, J. (1983) 'The Political Formation of the American Welfare State'. In R. F. Tomasson (ed.), *Comparative Social Research: the Welfare State 1883–1983*. Greenwich, CT: Jai Press.

Stephens, J. (1979) *The Transition from Capitalism to Socialism*. London: Macmillan.

UK Labour Party (2001) *General Election Manifesto: 2001*. London: Labour Party.

UNDP (2002) *Human Development Report 2002: Deepening Democracy in a Fragmented World*. Washington, DC: UNDP.

UNICEF-ICDC (1997) *Children at Risk in Eastern and Central Europe*. Florence: UNICEF.

Uusitalo, H. (1984) 'Comparative Research on the Determinants of the Welfare State: the State of the Art', *European Journal of Political Research*, 12, 403–22.

Vartiainen, J. (1995) 'The State and Structural Change: What can be Learnt from the Successful Late Industrializers?' In H.-J. Chang and R. Rowthorn (eds), *The Role of the State in Economic Change*. Oxford: Oxford University Press.

Vasoo, S., and Lee, J. (2001) 'Singapore: Social Development, Housing and the Central Provident Fund', *International Journal of Social Welfare*, 10, 276–83.

Von Braun, J. (1991) 'Social Security in Sub-Saharan Africa'. In E. Ahmad *et al.* (ed.), *Social Security in Developing Countries*. Oxford: Oxford University Press.

Wade, R. (1995) 'Resolving the State–Market Dilemma in East Asia'. In H.-J. Chang and R. Rowthorn (eds), *The Role of the State in Economic Change*. Oxford: Oxford University Press.

White, G., and Goodman, R. (1998) 'Welfare Orientalism and the Search for an East Asian Model'. In R. Goodman, G. White and H.-J. Kwon (eds), *The East Asian Welfare Model – Welfare Orientalism and the State*. London: Routledge.

Wilensky, H. (1975) *The Welfare State and Equality*. Berkeley: University of California Press.

World Bank (1993) *The East Asian Miracle*. Oxford: Oxford University Press.

World Bank (1994) *Averting the Old Age Crisis: Policies to Protect the Old and Promote Growth*. New York: Oxford University Press.

World Bank (2001) *World Development Report 2000/1: Attacking Poverty*. Washington, DC: World Bank.

World Bank (2002) *World Development Indicators 2002*. Washington, DC: World Bank.

242

Appendix 1: First Introduction of Social Insurance Programmes, Universal Suffrage and Current Social Expenditure (as % GDP, 1996)

OECD COUNTRIES

Country	Work injury	Sickness and Maternity	Old age, dis., death	Unemployment ins.	Family allowances	Universal suffrage	Social exp. (% GDP)
Australia	Fr. 1902	1944	1908	1944	1941	1902	15.7
Austria	1887	1888	1909	1920	1948	1918	26.2
Belgium	1903	1894	1900	1920	1930	1948	27.1
Canada	Fr. 1908	1984	1927	1940	1944	1950	15.7
Czech Republic	1887	1888	1906	1991	1945	1920	18.8
Denmark	1898	1892	1891	1907	1952	1915	33.0
Finland	1895	1963	1937	1917	1948	1906	32.3
France	1898	1928	1910	1905	1932	1944	30.1
Germany	1884	1883	1889	1927	1954	1918	29.7
Greece	1914	1922	1934	1945	1958	1952	22.7
Iceland	1925	1936	1909	1956	1946	1915	18.6
Ireland	1897	1911	1908	1911	1945	1928	17.8
Italy	1898	1912	1919	1919	1937	1945	23.7
Japan	1911	1922	1941	1947	1971	1947	14.1
Korea	1953	1963	1973	—	—	1948	5.6
Luxembourg	1902	1901	1911	1921	1947	1919	25.2
Mexico	1943	1943	1943	—	—	1947	3.7
Netherlands	1901	1931	1919	1916	1939	1919	26.7
New Zealand	1908	1938	1898	1930	1926	1893	19.2
Norway	1894	1909	1936	1906	1946	1913	28.5
Poland	1984	1920	1927	1924	1947	1918	25.1
Portugal	1913	1935	1935	1975	1942	1976	19.0
Slovak Republic	1887	1888	1906	1991	1945	1920	20.9
Spain	1900	1929/42	1919	1919	1938	1931	22.8
Sweden	1901	1891	1913	1934	1947	1921	34.7
Switzerland	1911	1911	1946	1924	1952	1971	25.9
Turkey	1945	1945/50	1949	—	—	1930	7.1
UK	1897	1911	1908	1911	1945	1928	22.8
USA	Fr. 1908	—	1935	1935	—	1920	16.5

LATIN AMERICA

Country	Work injury	Sickness and maternity	Old age, dis., death	Unemployment ins.	Family allowances	Universal suffrage	Social exp. (% GDP)
Argentina	1915	1934/74	1944	1967	1957	1947	12.4
Bolivia	1924	1949	1956	—	1953	1952	7.0
Brazil	1919	1923	1923	1965	1941	1934	12.2
Chile	1916	1924	1924	1937	1937	1949	11.3
Colombia	1915	1938	1946	—	1957	1954	6.1
Costa Rica	1925	1941	1941	—	1974	1942	13.0

Dominican							
Republic	1932	1947	1947	—	—	1942	2.5
Ecuador	1921	1935	1928	1951	—	1967	2.0
El Salvador	1949	1949	1953	—	—	1950	3.6
Guatemala	1947	1946	1969	—	—	1965	(4.2)
Haiti	1951	1951	1965	—	—	1967	—
Honduras	1959	1959	1959	—	—	1955	(7.4)
Mexico	1943	1943	1943	—	—	1955	3.7
Nicaragua	1945	1955	1955	—	1982	1955	9.1
Panama	1916	1941	1941	—	—	1946	11.3
Paraguay	1927	1943	1943	—	(1993)	1961	(7.4)
Peru	1911	1936	1936	—	—	1955	(6.8)
Uruguay	1914	1958	1829–1934	1934	1943	1932	22.4
Venezuela	1923	1940	1940	1940	(1940)	1946	(8.6)

EAST ASIA

Country	Work injury	Sickness and maternity	Old age, dis., death	Unemployment ins.	Family allowances	Universal suffrage	Social exp. (% GDP)
China	1951	1951	1951	1986	—	1949	3.6
Hong Kong	1971	1971	1971	1977		1971	(5.5)
Indonesia	1939	1957	1951	—	—	1945	1.7
Japan	1911	1922	1941	1947	1971	1947	14.1
Korea	1953	1963	1973	—	—	1948	5.6
Malaysia	1929	1951	1951	—	—	1957	2.9
Philippines	1974	1954	1954	—	—	1937	—
Singapore	1933	1983	1953	—	—	1947	3.3
Taiwan	1929	1950	1950	1968	—	1947	(11.1)
Thailand	1972	1990	1990	1990	1990	1932	1.9

'TRANSITION ECONOMIES'

Country	Work injury	Sickness and maternity	Old age, dis., death	Unemployment ins.	Family allowances	Universal suffrage	Social exp. (% GDP)
Albania	1947	1947	1947	1993	1993	1920	10.9
Armenia	1955	1912	1956	1921	1944	1921	—
Belarus	1939	1955	1956	1921	1944	1919	17.4
Bulgaria	1924	1918	1924	1925	1942	1944	13.2
Czech Rep.	1887	1888	1906	1991	1945	1920	18.8
Estonia	1924	1924	1924	1991	1922	1918	17.1
Georgia	1955	1955	1956	1991	N.D.	1921	—
Hungary	1907	1891	1928	1957	1938	1918	22.3
Kazakhstan	1955	(1995)	1956	n.d.	n.d.	1993	13.6
Moldova	1955	N.D.	1956	1992	1944	1993	15.5

'TRANSITION ECONOMIES' (Continued)

Country	Work injury	Sickness and maternity	Old age, dis., death	Unemployment ins.	Family allowances	Universal suffrage	Social exp. (% GDP)
Kyrgyz Rep.	1922	1922	1922	1921	1944	1918	—
Latvia	1927	1924	1922	1991	1990	1918	19.2
Lithuania	1991	1925	1925	1919	1991	1921	14.7
Poland	1984	1920	1927	1924	1947	1918	25.1
Romania	1912	1912	1912	1991	1944	1946	12.4
Russia	1903	1912	1922	1921	1944	1918	10.4
Serbia/ Montenegro	1922	1922	1922	1927		1949	—
Slovak Rep.	1887	1888	1906	1991	1945	1920	20.9
Slovenia	1922	1922	1922	1927	1949	1945	(29.5)
Turkmenistan	1955	1955	1956	1991	N.D.	1927	29.0
Ukraine	1912	1912	1922	1921	1944	1919	19.8
Uzbekistan	1955	1955	1956	1991	N.D.	1938	—

AFRICA

Country	Work injury	Sickness and maternity	Old age, dis., death	Unemployment ins.	Family allowances	Universal suffrage	Social exp. (% GDP)
Algeria	1919	1949	1949	1994	1941	1962	7.6
Benin	1952	1952	1970	—	1955	1956	2.2
Botswana	1936	—	1996	—	—	1965	2.7
Burundi	1949	1984	1956	—	1971	1961	2.2
Cameroon	1944	1956	1969	—	1956	1956	2.2
Cape Verde	1960	1976	1957	—	1957	1975	5.0
Central African Republic	1935	1952	1963	—	1956	1986	1.9
Congo	1935	1952	1962	—	1949	1963	4.2
Egypt	1936	1964	1950	1959	—	1956	5.4
Ethiopia	1963	—	1963	—	—	1955	3.7
Ghana	1940	—	1965	—	—	1955	3.1
Guinea	1932	1960	1958	—	1956	1958	—
Kenya	1946	1966	1965	—	—	1963	2.0
Madagascar	1925	1952	1969	—	1956	1959	1.3
Mali	1932	1952	1961	—	1955	1956	3.1
Mauritania	1932	1952	1965	—	1955	1961	0.8
Mauritius	1931	—	1951	—	1961	1956	6.0
Morocco	1927	1959	1959	—	1942	1963	3.4
Mozambique				—		1975	4.7
Namibia				—		1989	3.9
Niger	1960	1952	1967	—	1955	1948	1.9
Nigeria	1942	1961	1961	—	—	1958	1.0
Senegal	1932	1952	1975	—	1955	1945	4.3
Seychelles	1970	1979	1971	—	—	1948	11.6

Togo	1964	1956	1968	—	1956	1945	2.8
Tunisia	1921	1960	1960	1982	1944	1959	7.7
Zambia	1929	1973	1965	—	—	1962	2.5
AFRICA							**4.3**

Methodological note: Figure 10.1 displays social security as a percentage of GDP plus the UNDP's GDP index (on a scale of 0–1 multiplied by 100). Material in Figures 10.2 and 10.3 and Appendix One are drawn from the following sources: United Nations Development Programme (2002). World Bank (2002), CD-ROM. Additional data (always in parenthesis) has been drawn from the following sources: ECLAC (2001); M. Ramesh with M. G. Asher (2000); Didier Jacobs (2000); I. Gough (2000); S. Kuhnle and S. E. O. Hort (2000). Methodologies vary (sometimes significantly) in the collection and notification of this data. These should not, however, mislead us in identifying the main variations in public expenditure trends across our wide range of examples. In establishing the date for 'consolidation' of welfare states, I follow Kuhnle and Hort (2000), using the year in which the second key social insurance measure was legislated.

11
The Role of Social Policy in Economic Development: Some Theoretical Reflections and Lessons from East Asia

Ha-joon Chang

Introduction

During the heady days of neo-liberal counter-revolution in the 1980s, the World Bank and the IMF prided themselves on not wasting their time on 'soft' things like social policy in designing their 'structural adjustment programmes'. In the older, hardcore version of neo-liberal orthodoxy that had prevailed until the early 1990s, diverting resources to social policy, which softens the blow of the adjustment on the weaker sections of the society, was regarded as buying short-run palliatives at the cost of long-term productive development, since it would only slow down the necessary 'adjustments'. Many people remember how strongly this line of thinking was pursued during the 1980s. This was pursued to the point of producing a call for 'adjustment with a human face' by those who did not completely reject the need for structural adjustment programmes but were deeply concerned by what they saw as unnecessary human suffering caused by such programmes in their unadulterated forms (Cornia *et al.* 1987).

However, in the face of the continued economic crises in many developing countries throughout the 1990s, and the failures of the neo-liberal 'adjustment' and 'reform' programmes to resolve such crises (many would in fact say that these programmes were one of the contributory factors of these crises), even the World Bank and the IMF are now beginning to pay serious attention to social policy. (Mkandawire (2001) provides an illuminating review of this shift). They now acknowledge that developing countries may need a 'social safety net' to catch those who fall through the cracks in the process of economic 'reform' based on their programmes. This shift in the attitudes of the part of the Bretton Woods institutions was, for example, manifest in the IMF programmes adopted in the East Asian countries after the 1997 financial crises (Korea, Thailand, and Indonesia), where the Fund and the Bank placed an unprecedented emphasis on building 'social safety network' devices.

The attention to social policy by the Bank and the Fund is most welcome. It is a positive development that they are now considering the broader social consequences of their economic policies. However, there still exists a fundamental limit to their understanding of social policy. As UNRISD has pointed out in a series of recent publications, the Bank and Fund still view social policy as an essentially residual category of 'safety nets', and not as an essential ingredient in developmental strategy (Mkandawire (2001) succinctly summarizes the UNRISD view).

However, social policy, if it is well designed, can be much more than a safety net and can make a significant contribution to productive development (for further details, see Chang (2002: ch. 3). Cost-effective public provision of health and education can bring about improvements in the quality of the labour force that can, in turn, raise efficiency and accelerate productivity growth. Social welfare institutions reduce social tensions and enhance the legitimacy of the political system, thus providing a more stable environment for long-term investment. Smoothing of consumption patterns through devices such as unemployment benefit can even contribute to dampening the business cycle, which stabilizes the macroeconomy and thus encourages investment.

The present chapter aims to elaborate on how social policy can be – and indeed needs to be – an integral part of a dynamic developmental strategy, using the East Asian development experience as an example.

The choice of East Asia as an exemplar in this context may sound somewhat surprising, because traditionally East Asia has been regarded as 'social-policy-free zone'. Indeed, in the days before the Asian financial crisis, the apparent absence of social policy in the East Asian countries was often brandished by many free market economists as proof that countries do best when they concentrate on economic policy and ignore social policy. However, as we shall show later, this is a fundamentally mistaken characterization of the East Asian developmental experience. The East Asian countries have used many policies and institutions to address 'social' problems. The reason why many people think they have not used social policy is because many of the policies and institutions that they used in order to address 'social' problems were *not* ones that are usually defined as 'social policy' in the narrow sense. For this reason, considering the East Asian experience can open up some new horizons in the discussion of the role of social policy in economic development.

The importance of 'hidden' or 'surrogate' social policies in East Asian developmental experience makes it necessary for us to engage in a theoretical discussion as to the validity of the customary distinction between economic policy and social policy before we look at the empirical evidence.

Economic policy versus social policy: a false dichotomy?

As I have also implicitly accepted in my discussion in the introductory section, it is customary to distinguish economic policy from social policy. However, I would argue that in the final instance there can be no meaningful distinction between economic policy and social policy. What is the reason for making this assertion?

The separation of economic policy and social policy implicitly assumes that it is possible to objectively define an economic sphere that should (and does) operate according to some 'scientific' economic logic and a social sphere where we may want to (but are normally advised, by those 'hard-nosed' economists, not to) override the economic logic with 'ethical' considerations (such as better income distribution, employment creation, protection of human rights, and so on) despite the 'inefficiencies' that such action is going to create.

This dichotomy is a useful fiction at one level, which I also use for some purposes. However, I think that it unduly constrains and ultimately misleads our research and policy agendas. I say this because I believe that, in the final analysis, there can never be such a thing as an objectively definable economic sphere, neatly separable from other ('social' or whatever) spheres of life.

People usually assume that what goes on in the market belongs to the economic sphere and the rest is properly placed in the social sphere. However, a market can be defined only with reference to the rights and the obligations of its (legitimate) participants, which in turn are products of various (conscious and unconscious) political decisions, and not some 'scientific' law of economics. In other words, as Polanyi (1957) has so clearly shown, the market itself is a political (and social) construct, and therefore there cannot be such a thing as a neatly separable domain of 'market' that is free from 'politics' or 'social concerns' in the final analysis (this point is further developed in Chang (2001)).

To begin with, all markets are based on institutions that regulate who can participate. For example, laws may stipulate that certain types of individuals (such as slaves or foreigners) cannot own (certain types of) property or that children may own property, but cannot exercise full property rights until they reach a certain age. Banking laws or pension laws may limit the range of assets that banks or pension funds own and therefore limit the range of asset markets that they can enter. Child labour laws, immigration laws, and laws regulating professional qualification (e.g., doctors, lawyers) dictate who can participate (or not) in particular labour markets. Company laws and industrial licensing rules will decide who can participate in the product market, while stock market listing rules and brokerage regulations determine who can participate in the stock market.

Secondly, there are institutions which determine the legitimate objects of market exchange (and, by implication, of ownership). In most countries, there are laws illegalising transactions in things such as addictive drugs, 'indecent' publications, human organs, or firearms (although different societies have different views on what count as, say, addictive drugs or indecent publications). Laws on slavery, child labour, and immigration will stipulate, respectively, that human beings, labour service of children, and labour service of illegal immigrant may not be legitimate objects of exchange.

Thirdly, even when the legitimate participants in and the legitimate objects of exchange have been stipulated, we need institutions that define what exactly each agent's rights and obligations are in which areas. So, for example, zoning laws, environmental regulations (for example, regarding pollution or noise), fire regulations, and so on, define how property rights in land can be exercised (such as what kinds of building can be built where). For another example, the laws regarding health, safety, and grievance resolution in workplaces will define the rights and the obligations of the workers and the employers.

Fourthly, there are numerous institutions that regulate the process of exchange itself. For example, there are rules regarding fraud, breach of contract, default, bankruptcy, and other disruptions in the exchange process, which are backed up by the police, the court system, and other legal institutions. Consumer laws and liability laws, for another example, will stipulate when and how buyers of unsatisfactory or faulty products may annul the act of purchase and/or claim compensation from the sellers. Social conventions (e.g., those regarding fairness and probity) or codes of conduct issued by trade associations (e.g., bankers' associations or industry associations) may also influence the way in which economic agents behave in economic transactions.

All of the above-mentioned 'regulations' that define the boundaries of the market (and thus of the 'economic' sphere) are products of complex interaction between political bargaining, moral values, and technical considerations. And as the political bargains and moral values change, the legitimate boundary for the 'economic' and 'social' also changes.

Historically, what is regarded as the legitimate boundary of the economic sphere has changed tremendously. There are many things that used to be perfectly legitimate objects of monetary transaction which are no longer regarded as such. Public offices, the rights to collect taxes (tax-farming that was widely used among the European countries up to the eighteenth century), human beings (as in the slave trade), the labour service of children (as in child labour), and so on were perfectly legal and politically legitimate objects of exchange in all societies in the past, but they are not so in many societies now (at least explicitly).

Many institutions defining the boundary of the 'economic' sphere that we take for granted today had been greeted with outrage when they were first introduced. Although the languages used differed across cases, essentially their detractors saw those institutions that re-drew the boundary of the 'economic' sphere as an unwarranted imposition of 'social' concerns on the sacrosanct 'economic' domain. Let us illustrate this point with a number of examples (further details can be found in Chang (2000; 2002: ch. 3)).

The most striking example in this regard is the institution of self-ownership. This institution was obviously an anathema to slave-owners, and during the Civil War, even many non-slave-owning Americans in the Southern states were willing to go to war in objection to the introduction of such an institution, which they perceived as a grave threat to their states' economic (and by extension, political) freedom.[1]

The attempt to regulate, not to speak of banning, child labour was initially greeted with outrage by many people. For example, in the UK, in the debate surrounding the 1819 Cotton Factories Regulation Act, which banned the employment of children under the age of 9 and restricted children's working hours, some members of the House of Lords argued that child labour should not be regulated because 'labour ought to be free' (Blaug 1958).[2]

People showed even stronger reactions when the first attempts to introduce maximum working hours for adults (especially adult males) were made in the now-advanced countries during the late nineteenth and the early twentieth centuries. For example, in 1905, the US Supreme Court declared in the famous *Lochner* vs *New York* case that a ten-hour act for the bakers introduced by the New York state was unconstitutional because it 'deprived the baker of the liberty of working as long as they wished' (Garraty and Carnes 2000: 607).

When central banking was first introduced, the influential nineteenth-century British political thinker Herbert Spencer objected to it on the grounds that it would encourage excessive risk-taking, since if the financial system got into trouble, imprudent lenders as well as deserving ones will be rescued by the central bank. He succinctly argued: '(t)he ultimate result of shielding man from the effects of folly is to people the world with fools'.[3]

Likewise, when limited liability was first introduced, many people regarded it as being a deviation from a sensible economic principle. Commenting on late nineteenth-century Britain, Rosenberg and Birdzell (1986) document how even decades after the full-scale introduction of the principle of limited liability (although limited liability had been occasionally granted by royal charters, it was generalised only in 1855), small businessmen 'who, being actively in charge of a business as well as its owner, sought to limit responsibility for its debts by the device of incorporation' were still frowned upon (200).

The examples could go on, but the point that emerges from these discussions is the following (further examples can be found in Chang (2002: ch. 3)). We seem to use the term 'economic policy' as a shorthand for a policy whose underlying structure of rights and obligations is relatively uncontested (or, more likely, should not be contested according to the point of view of the person making the particular distinction) and 'social policy' as a shorthand for a policy whose underlying structure of rights and obligations is more contested.

So, for example, regulation of child labour may be regarded as a 'social policy' in countries where the priority of the rights of the children not to toil and to be educated over the employer's right to hire anyone they like is not widely accepted, but in countries where such a priority is clearly accepted, it will be regarded as one of the routine 'economic' policies.

Given our discussion to this point, we can say that accepting the very dichotomy between economic policy and social policy is in effect equivalent to accepting the (often implicit) political and social values underlying the particular demarcation of these two spheres that exists in the status quo. Unless we start by denying this dichotomy, those who want to implement policies that aim to modify the existing rights structure (usually the 'progressives') will always be at a disadvantage in the debate, because they are always portrayed as the 'softies' who have no stomach for 'hard economics'. Bearing this point in mind, let us now consider the role of social policy in East Asian development.

Social policy in East Asian development: an unconventional view

Social policy in East Asia: some misunderstood facts

As I have mentioned in the introduction, the conventional wisdom has regarded East Asia as a 'social-policy-free zone'. And in the days before the Asian crisis, when many schools of thought had tried to use the East Asian economies as the vindication of their particular theories, many right-wing theorists argued that the economic success of the East Asian countries proves that countries do well when they concentrate on economic policy and do not waste valuable resources on social policy, which is likely to have a negative impact on economic growth.

There are at least three problems with this view – that is, even when ignoring the problems with the assumption that 'social' policy is harmful for 'economic' growth, a point that is increasingly disputed by even many mainstream economists (for example see Rodrik (1999); for a discussion from a non-mainstream point of view, see Chang and Rowthorn (1995)).

The first problem with the view that East Asia achieved its successful economic development despite, or rather because of, the absence of social policy is that there have actually been many more social policies in the East Asian countries than conventional wisdom has hitherto suggested.

It may be true that these countries may not have introduced many social policies in the narrow sense of the term – that is, 'welfare-state'-style policies, such as public health care, free education, unemployment benefit, state pensions, and income support. However, even then there were some important examples of social policy in the narrow sense among these countries. For example, Korea has had income support and public works programmes for the very poor (although the coverage was relatively limited), while Singapore had a strong state pension system based on a compulsory saving scheme (the Provident Fund).

Moreover, if we define social policies more broadly to include not simply 'welfare-state' policies but to include all policies (and institutions) that address 'social' problems (poverty, income inequality, workers' rights, human rights, etc.), we begin to see that a wide range of social policies have been used in the East Asian countries (the following details are from Chang (1998)). The most important example in this regard is land reform. Japan, Taipei (China), and Korea all instituted comprehensive land reform measures in the early post-Second World-War years, involving the redistribution of land, land ownership ceilings, and restrictions on the terms of tenancy. Other countries in the region – for example, the Philippines – also instituted some limited land reform measures, albeit with relatively limited success. Governments of countries like Malaysia and Thailand provided supports to the schemes for opening up new lands in order to ease the pressure for land redistribution.

Labour movements were often brutally suppressed in many East Asian countries, but even these countries have made some efforts to incorporate working-class interests in policy making. Even countries such as Korea and Singapore, which have been notorious for adopting a harsh policy towards union movements, have co-opted some sections of the union leadership (for example, by appointing some union leaders to government posts). They also provided some degree of protective measures for the ordinary workers (such as, cover for industrial accidents, legal priority for wage claims over other claims in case of enterprise bankruptcy).

Hong Kong and Singapore also placed an emphasis on providing extensive public housing, thereby easing the tension over the most contentious political issue in these land-constrained city-states. Other countries have also run public housing programmes, but these have not been as extensive or as successful as those of Hong Kong and Singapore. However, it needs to be pointed out that these measures were implemented after a period of political unrest over the issue – in Hong Kong, there were even housing-related riots in the early postwar years (more on this later).

In the case of Malaysia, the income gap between the politically dominant Malay community and the economically better off, but politically weaker Chinese community was seen as the major threat to national cohesion. Following the infamous race riot of the late 1960s, the Malaysian government implemented the NEP (New Economic Policy) programme that included measures intended to reduce the economic gap between the two ethnic communities. The measures included quotas on entry into higher education, quotas on enterprise share ownership, and the establishment of a range of public enterprises, which kept certain industries away from Chinese interests. Government supports for small-scale agriculture can also be interpreted as a measure of ethnic redistribution, given the predominance of the Malay community in the sector. While there have been many problems with these measures of ethnic redistribution, it will be hard to deny that without these measures the Malaysian society is likely to have experienced greater political unrest.

To sum up, there were many more social policies in East Asia than is typically believed, if we define social policy more broadly than usual (which equates it with 'welfare-state' type of policies). There have been land reforms, some protection of labour, public housing programmes, and even inter-ethnic income redistribution.

The second problem with the conventional view regarding the role of social policy in East Asian development is that many 'social problems' were addressed by policies and institutions that would not be classified as 'social policies' or 'social welfare institutions' even in the broader sense of the term that we have used in the preceding paragraphs.

In countries like Japan and Korea, the corporate welfare system (including not just the famous lifetime employment system but also matters such as housing and health provision or educational subsidies for the employees' children) has played an important role in 'buying' industrial peace in large firms. And it has to be pointed out that corporate welfare schemes were strongly encouraged, if not legislated, by the governments of these countries.

Some regulatory measures, which are regarded by some outsiders as 'unfair' hidden trade protection measures were, at least in their inception, mainly motivated by concerns for income distribution and social cohesion. The most important example in this regard is the protection of certain 'losers' in the economic development process such as small farmers (through agricultural trade protection and/or restrictions on farmland ownership) and small shopkeepers (through the 'Large Store' Law in Japan and through urban planning in Korea). These were people who were neither qualified enough to get a job in the modern manufacturing sector nor entitled to much social protection measures due to the poorly-developed welfare state (for further discussion see Chang (1996), Kusano (1992); and Upham (1996) for details on the Japanese retail sector protection).

Even policies aimed at vigorously restraining luxury consumption in the earliest phases of development which were adopted by the governments of some East Asian countries – notably Japan and Korea, but also Taipei (China) – can be understood as a social policy in the broader sense. These governments controlled luxury consumption not only because they thought it would reduce the overall level of savings and the foreign exchanges available for importing capital goods, but also because they regarded conspicuous luxury consumption as damaging for social cohesion through its 'demonstration effect' (for further details, see Chang (1997)).

Thus seen, the functions that are usually associated with social policies in other countries – helping the weak (e.g., small farmers, small shopkeepers), providing industrial, and in general social, peace and so on – have been served in the East Asian countries by policies and institutions which are not normally classified as 'social policy' or 'social welfare institutions'. These have included corporate welfare system, 'protective regulations' in favour of certain 'losers' in the economic development process (e.g., farmers and small shopkeepers), and luxury consumption control.

Last but not least, the conventional view on the role of social policy in the economic development of East Asia is based upon the misconception that the East Asian countries did not *need to* have strong social policies (which, as we have pointed out, is not true) because they did not have many 'social' problems that had to be addressed. In this view, the East Asian countries are seen as low-conflict societies thanks to historical factors such as egalitarian income distribution, ethnic homogeneity, or even an inherently less conflict-oriented 'Asian' culture.

However, the truth is that social peace in East Asia is in fact a relatively new thing (see Chang (1998) for a further discussion). Between the end of the Second World War and the 1970s, East Asia was arguably the most conflict-ridden part of the world. The Chinese Communist revolution, the Vietnam War, and the Korean War (despite arguably one of the most homogeneous populations in the world) are some of the best-known incidences of violent conflict in the region – but the list of less well-known conflicts in the East Asian countries is a lengthy one.

Despite its recent reputation as a country of industrial peace, in the 1950s and the early 1960s, Japan lost more working days per worker in industrial strikes than did UK or France, not to speak of West Germany or Sweden which were known for industrial peace in those days. For example, during the period 1955–59, Japan lost 254 working days per 1,000 employees whereas the UK and France lost respectively 220 and 180 days. During the period 1960–64, Japan lost 177 days per 1,000 employees but the UK and France lost respectively 146 days and 197 days (Table 11.1).

There was a riot in Taiwan in 1947 by the 'Taiwanese' (descendants of the immigrants from the mainland during the previous few centuries) against

Table 11.1 Number of working days lost in industrial disputes, 1955–80 (per 1,000 employees)

	1955–59	1960–64	1965–69	1970–74	1975–80
Japan	254	177	107	151	69
USA	615	301	513	539	389
UK	220	146	175	624	521
France	180	197	163	201	195
Italy	433	932	1,204	1,404	1,434
West Germany	47	23	7	55	41
Sweden	19	6	38	69	222

Source: Koike (1987).

the 'Mainlanders' (those who were parts of the Kuomintang, or the Nationalist Party, government that took Taiwan over from Japan after the latter's defeat in the Second World War), who the former saw as alien invaders. Indonesia's 1965 military coup ended up in a civil war that was arguably one of the bloodiest in the twentieth century, with millions of deaths. There were armed Communist insurgencies in Malaysia, Singapore, and Thailand until the 1970s, and in the Philippines it still continues. There was a race riot in Malaysia in 1969. Hong Kong had a famous housing riot in the late 1960s. Korea was world-famous for its leftist student demonstrations throughout the 1980s. And so on.

These examples show that, until the 1970s at least, the East Asian societies had been highly conflict-ridden societies. Social peace is a relatively recent thing in these countries. And the recent events in Indonesia show how much fragile some of such social peace has been in fact. It was only because of a range of social policies (combined with political repression in some cases, of course) that the East Asian countries could hold their societies together and maintain social peace better than other developing countries have done during the last two decades.

So to summarize the discussion in this section up to now, East Asia has not been a 'social-policy-free zone' as it is often portrayed to be, not least because there were various policies and institutions which played the role that 'social policy' in the narrow, conventional sense played in other countries. Moreover, it is important to recognize that the East Asian countries did not start their postwar economic development as 'low-conflict' societies, as it is often believed to have been the case. The region has seen more than its share of war, armed insurgencies, military coups, and riots of various kinds (e.g., ethnic, housing-related, etc.). The social cohesion they have subsequently achieved during the last two or three decades has been deliberately manufactured through an active use of social policy in both the narrow and the broad senses of the term.

Social policy and economic development in East Asia

In the above I have shown, contrary to the popular perception, how social policy, broadly defined, has been crucial in generating social cohesion in the East Asian countries. In the analysis below, I would like to argue that such social cohesion positively contributed in generating rapid economic growth and development in the East Asian economies.

The importance of political stability and industrial peace in assuring the potential investors of the feasibility of long-term investments is widely known. Therefore, it does not need much elaboration here why social policy, in both the narrow and the broader senses, has been useful in promoting an environment conducive to long-term investment by generating greater social cohesion and social peace in the East Asian countries.

Less widely acknowledged is the importance of policies and institutions that give the workers their long-term employment security (although not security in their current job) through encouraging technological progress, another key to economic growth. This point is probably best illustrated by the Japanese institution of the lifetime employment guarantee (large firms in Korea offered similar guarantees, but they were never as comprehensive, widespread, and deeply embedded in corporate culture as in the case of their Japanese counterparts).

Since the late 1950s, in the face of agitation by Communist unions and concerned with high job turnover, Japanese firms started granting employment security to the core workforce (roughly two-thirds of the workers in the large enterprises and one-third of the workers in smaller firms) by offering them what is commonly known as 'lifetime employment'. Here it is important to note that lifetime employment is a practice that was only recently started, and not a remnant of old feudal culture, as some people believe.

Through this 'institutional innovation' of lifetime employment, the Japanese firms were able to make their workers more readily accept the introduction of new technologies with less labour demand and involving reorganization of the shopfloor. It is no coincidence that Japan and Sweden, which provided such security through a comprehensive welfare state and an 'active labour market policy' (involving training and relocation subsidies to displaced workers), are two of the most robotized economies in the world. This contrasts starkly with the experience of Britain in the 1960s and the 1970s, where the absence of mechanisms to provide employment security drove the unions into defensive obstructionism, which made it very difficult for the firms to introduce new technologies, which in turn seriously damaged the economy's international competitiveness.

Thus seen, the East Asian developmental experience shows the importance of social policy, or, more broadly, the institutions and the policies that enhance social cohesion, in encouraging capital accumulation and technological progress – the two main sources of economic development. Contrary to the conventional wisdom, East Asia does *not* prove that a neglect of social policy is compatible with – not to mention being conducive to – economic development.

The future of 'social policy' in East Asia

The policies and institutions that had enhanced social cohesion in various East Asian countries have come under increasing strain recently as a result of changing national and international circumstances.

First of all, the rise of neo-liberal ideology on a worldwide scale generated increasing opinions both inside and outside the East Asian countries that supported radical deregulation. Secondly, the very economic success of the countries in the region generated pressures from the European countries, and especially the USA, to open up their markets, including the deregulation of the retail sector that was perceived as a covert protectionist mechanism. Thirdly, with economic success also came growing domestic constituencies calling for liberalization and opening-up: certain sections of business clamouring for freedom from state intervention; upper-middle-class people who wanted the American salary scale and lifestyle; and some radical intellectuals who (mistakenly) believed greater market forces would weaken the power of unwieldy big business; and so on.

Some measures, such as the protection of the small retailers, are regarded as covert protectionist measures that are unacceptable in the new era of globalization. Other measures – for example, ceilings on the ownership of farmland (imposed in some countries after the early postwar land reform) and restrictions on large retail stores – are criticized for increasing inefficiencies in the farming and the retail sectors. Still some other measures, such as ethnic quotas, are attacked from both inside and outside as being inefficient and unfair. Institutions like the corporate welfare system are, in my view correctly, criticized for privileging certain workers over others.

As a result, there have been calls for greater liberalization and for the dismantling of corporate and other institutions that the East Asian countries have used to enhance social cohesion. And in countries like Korea, which has been subject to a radical policy and institutional overhaul after the recent financial crisis, moves have been made towards the dismantling of traditional, segmented 'social policies' in the broader sense and towards a more universal, citizenship-based welfare system.

On one level, such moves are to be welcomed, because they have the potential of instituting a more egalitarian welfare system. However, there are clear limits to such an approach.

To begin with, in the general push towards a small government and given the history of anti-welfare-statism in the country (see below), the universalistic welfare provisions recently introduced in countries like Korea are more of a minimalist 'safety net'-type provision, rather than, say, a Swedish-style fully-fledged welfare state. The limitations of the 'safety net' approach are testified to by the sharp increase in income inequality and poverty in these countries after the 1997 crisis (although probably not all such increases would have been preventable even with a generous welfare state, given the severity of the crisis). However, the more serious problem with the suggestion that the East Asian countries should dismantle 'inefficient' and 'unfair' policies and institutions that protect certain group of people in favour of a more universalistic (if minimal) social welfare provision is that it obscures the bigger picture.

What the East Asian countries have been 'buying' with these sometimes (but not always) inefficient and sometimes unfair institutions are social cohesion and political peace, which have been the foundational stones of their prosperity, as I have pointed out above. It may be possible to increase the 'efficiency' of the Asian economies by abolishing many of the abovementioned 'social' policies and institutions. However, in the longer run, this will increase social tension and political unrest, and may ultimately damage their prosperity by shaking both investors' confidence and the workers' willingness to accept technological changes. Let us elaborate this point in some more detail by using the example of the notoriously 'inefficient' and 'unfair' protection of farmers and small shopkeepers in Japan and Korea (for further details see Chang 1996).

It is true that many of the policies and institutions that are intended to protect the 'losers' in the developmental process, such as the farmers and the small shopkeepers in Japan and Korea, have been costly, and are perhaps becoming more so, in relative terms. For example, on some estimates, a farreaching deregulation (including opening up to foreign competition) of these protected sectors will bring about unemployment rates of above 10 per cent, which implies that there has been a significant 'over-manning' and thus inefficiency in these sectors (Eatwell 1995). On the basis of these kinds of estimates, many commentators suggest that it will be actually less costly to withdraw the protective regulations for them and use the resources released by the resulting efficiency gains to pay off the small farmers or the small shopkeepers, either in the form of continuous income supports or in the form of 'severance payments'.

The problem with this argument is that Japan and Korea simply do not have the political basis and the ideological inclination for such a dramatic transition towards a European-style 'welfarist' regime.

Historically, as 'frontier states' in the Cold War, the sort of social democratic coalition that can back a fully-fledged welfare state could not develop in these countries. In Korea, no party with strong links with labour unions or with a social democratic leaning was allowed. Even in Japan where there Communist, Socialist, and Social Democratic parties existed, they remained more or less in permanent opposition since the late 1950s in the presence of the grand right-wing coalition constructed around the Liberal Democratic Party (itself a product of a merger between two right-wing parties, the Liberal Party and the Democratic Party), which has been the government, mostly alone and occasionally in coalition with other parties, continuously (except for a few years during the 1990s) since its foundation in 1958.

It is from such right-wing dominance in politics that a strong tradition of anti-welfare-statism has developed in Japan and Korea (as in the case of many other East Asian countries). The policy makers and the citizens of these countries do not seem to be willing to accept that people can claim income without 'working', however socially unproductive they may be (e.g., self-employment in low-productivity retail shops). And for the same reason, the governments of Japan and Korea are averse to the idea of expanding income support much beyond the minimal level that is given to the very poor – even if this can be shown to be less costly than maintaining the 'expensive' protection of the weaker sectors. Another complication is that many of those who work in the protected sectors are self-employed and do not want to 'retire', partly because they do not have the qualification to be employed in the modern sectors but partly because they seem to derive intrinsic values from 'being one's own boss'.

Given all of the political and ideological obstacles, it is highly unlikely that a new political coalition can be built in the short to medium run in the East Asian countries that will support a high-tax regime that can finance a generous welfare state. Yet this is not to say that things have not been changing.

Japan has slowly but surely expanded its welfare state over the last couple of decades, not least because of the dramatic aging of its society. Similarly, Korea has gradually expanded welfare provision over the last decade or so. This was, initially, because of the increasing dissolution of traditional family and community support networks with the progress of economic development and more recently because of the need to fill the vacuum left behind by the dismantling of many corporate welfare institutions following the recent financial crisis.

Nevertheless, these changes have been slow and gradual because of anti-welfarist political coalition and ideologies, which has in effect meant an increasing failure to address the 'social' problems. Unless a new system can be established that can address the 'social' problems at least as effectively as the old system, the long-term prosperity of these countries may be compromised.

Conclusion

My chapter started by observing that the increasing attention to social policy that the World Bank and the IMF, traditionally the scourges of social policy, have been paying in the recent past is far too narrow and misleading. They see social policy only as a 'safety net' that can be used to catch those who fall through the cracks during the process of absolutely necessary and generally beneficial 'reforms'. They do not see it as a crucial, or even beneficial, component of a dynamic developmental process.

The developmental experience of East Asia shows that this new orthodox view on social policy is seriously mistaken. Conventionally, many commentators have attributed the economic success of East Asia to a single-minded pursuit of economic growth and the neglect of 'social' problems. The implication is, of course, that 'social' problems will be taken care of through 'trickle down', if you have rapid economic growth.

In this chapter, I have shown how the East Asian countries have used a wide range of policies and institutions that address 'social' problems and how these have contributed to generating high investment and rapid technological progress through various channels. The reason why East Asia appears on first examination to be a 'social-policy-free zone' is only because many of these policies and institutions do not comfortably conform to the conventional idea of social policy – namely, some version of welfare-statism as defined by today's advanced industrial countries. Theoretical points were also made to show why the definition of 'social policy' should be expanded beyond this narrow definition.

More importantly, we should remember that, as highly conflict-ridden countries up until the 1970s, the East Asian countries had to find ways to reduce social conflict and enhance social cohesion, and they worked hard at it. The fact that the current popular image of the East Asian countries is those of societies which inherited historically low levels of inequality, low conflict, and a conformist culture is the very proof of their success in deploying policies and institutions that address social problems and enhance social cohesion.

The role of social policy in the economic development of East Asia, and the theoretical considerations that form the backdrop of our discussion of it in this chapter, must have challenged some theoretical concepts and empirical 'facts' that have been taken for granted by many people. I do not claim that my theoretical positions and empirical interpretations advanced in this chapter are necessarily the correct ones, but I hope they at least support a call for some serious re-thinking on the role of social policy in economic development.

Notes

1. It is well known that slavery was a key issue behind the American Civil War. However, it is less well known that this was not the only cause of the war. Another important cause was the disagreement over trade policy, where the South wanted free trade with Britain (so that they could buy higher-quality British manufacturing products) and where the North wanted protection of their newly-emerging manufacturing industries. Some would argue that the 'tariff' issue was in a way more important than the slavery issue in the sense that at least at the beginning of the war, Lincoln, who although he objected to slavery, thought the blacks racially inferior and regarded the abolition of slavery only as a theoretical possibility in a distant future, was quite willing to compromise on the slavery issue (he openly said that he did not want to impose slave emancipation upon Southern states that did not want it). However, no compromise was even proposed seriously on the tariff issue. See Chang (2002) for further details.

2. In chapters 10 and 15 of his *Capital, Volume 1*, Karl Marx provides a classic documentation and an illuminating discussion of the child labour issue at the time of first regulation on it in Britain. See Marx (1976).

3. As quoted in Kindleberger (1996). The original source is Spencer (1891) 'State Tampering with Money Banks', *Essays: Scientific, Political, and Speculative*, 3, 354.

Bibliography

Blaug, M. (1958) 'The Classical Economists and the Factory Acts: a Re-examination', *Quarterly Journal of Economics*, 72, 211–26.

Chang, H.-J. (1996) *Understanding the Recent Regulatory Change in Japan and Korea*. Washington, DC: Economic Development Institute, World Bank.

Chang, H.-J. (1997) *Luxury Consumption and Economic Development*. Geneva: UNCTAD.

Chang, H.-J. (1998) 'The Role of Institutions in Asian Development', *Asian Development Review*, 16, 64–95.

Chang, H.-J. (2000) 'The Hazard of Moral Hazard – Untangling the Asian Crisis', *World Development*, 28, 775–88.

Chang, H.-J. (2001) *Breaking the Mould – an Institutionalist Political Economy Alternative to the Neo-Liberal Theory of the Market and the State*. Geneva: UNRISD.

Chang, H.-J. (2002) *Kicking Away the Ladder? – Policies and Institutions for Economic Development in Historical Perspective*. London: Anthem Press.

Chang, H.-J., and Rowthorn, R. (1995) 'Role of the State in Economic Change: Entrepreneurship and Conflict Management'. In H.-J. Chang and R. Rowthorn (eds), *The Role of the State in Economic Change*. Oxford: Clarendon Press.

Cornia, G., Jolly, R., and Stewart, F. (1987) *Adjustment with a Human Face*. Oxford: Clarendon Press.

Eatwell, J. (1995) *Disguised Unemployment: the G7 Experience*. Cambridge: Trinity College.

Garraty, J., and Carnes, M. (2000) *The American Nation: a History of the United States*. New York: Addison-Wesley-Longman.

Kindleberger, C. (1996) *Manias, Panics, and Crashes*. London: Macmillan.

Koike, K. (1987) 'Human Resource Development'. In K. Yamamura and Y. Tasuba (eds), *The Political Economy of Japan*. Stanford: Stanford University Press.

Kusano, A. (1992) *The Large-Scale Retail Store Law: the Structure of Economic Regulation*. Tokyo: Nihon Keizai Shimbunsha.

Marx, K. (1976) *Capital*. London: Penguin Books.

Mkandawire, T. (2001) *Social Policy in a Development Context*. Geneva: UNRISD.

Polanyi, K. (1957) *The Great Transformation*. Boston: Beacon Press.

Rodrik, D. (1999) 'Institutions for High-Quality Growth: What They Are and How to Acquire Them', *IMF Conference on Second-Generation Reform*. Washington, DC: IMF.

Rosenberg, N., and Birdzell, L. (1986) *How the West Grew Rich*. London: IB Tauris & Co Ltd.

Spencer, H. (1891) 'State Tampering with Money Banks'. *Essays: Scientific, Political, and Speculative*, 3, 354.

Upham, F. (1996) 'Retail Convergence: the Structural Impediments Initiative and the Regulation of the Japanese Retail Industry'. In S. Berger and R. Dore (eds), *National Diversity and Global Capitalism*. New York: Cornell University Press.

12

The Economic Crisis and the Politics of Welfare Reform in Korea

Huck-ju Kwon

Introduction

While many OECD countries have tried to reduce the size of their government and social spending in particular, the welfare states in East Asia have expanded the scope and commanded an increasing bulk of their public financing. The governments in this region have begun to take active responsibility for social welfare in recent years (Eto 2001; Goodman *et al.* 1998; Kuhnle and Hort 2000; Kwon 2001). This trend has been further strengthened after the Asian economic crisis of 1997–98. In particular, Korea, one of the victims of the crisis, has witnessed the rapid expansion of the welfare state since the economic crisis. The Employment Insurance Programme has been extended to small-scale workplaces to cover the newly unemployed amidst the economic crisis. Emergency public works programmes have been implemented to create jobs for the low-skilled workers who would otherwise have been unemployed with no social protection. The Korean government has also introduced a new income support programme for the poor. This programme, the Minimum Living Standard Guarantee (MLSG), will give benefits to those below the poverty line, which has increased to a much higher level than previously defined. It also aims to cover the wider population of the poor. The health care system was also reformed during the period 1998–2000. A quasi-governmental agency was set up to manage integrated National Health Insurance, and the functional division of health care professionals, notably between physicians and pharmacists, was redefined. The question arising from this observation is why Korea has extended its welfare state, at a time when neo-liberal ideology has been predominant in public policy discourse in Korea and abroad.

A prima facie account for such policy responses could be a 'crisis-and-response' theory, based on the explanation that the economic crisis increased the demand for social welfare and that the Korean government, in response, extended the welfare programmes to alleviate the hardship of its people. This explanation would be consistent with the IMF policy recommendation, which advised the Korean government to improve its social safety net in order to carry out structural reforms. This explanation is true to a large extent, but it also raises to further questions. First, the policy strengthening the welfare state was not the only option to choose in order to overcome an economic crisis. A number of Latin American countries resorted to authoritarian politics to contain popular demand instead of adopting welfare policies when they were faced with economic crisis (Stallings 1999). Some European countries, such as the UK, implemented austere policies when they were faced with economic recessions in the 1970s and 1980s. We need to look into the political and economic context in which Korea chose the welfare option rather than other options. Secondly, the 'crisis-and-response' theory cannot explain why some of the welfare reforms that were not directly related to economic restructuring took place. The reforms in some areas of social policy tackled long-term structural issues rather than short-term requirements arising from the economic crisis. There was also a major shift in the policy approach to public assistance, which used to be like that of the poor law. Under the newly introduced income support programme, the MLSG, those whose income falls below the poverty line can claim income support as their social right, and the state is obliged to provide such support. The poverty line, which used to be defined in terms of absolute poverty, has been raised to a level near to relative poverty. This was a change in principle.

Welfare reforms since the economic crisis cannot be fully explained by the crisis-and-response theory, since reforms have been carried out beyond the functional minima required by the economic crisis. To answer the question as to why Korea attempted to carry out the reform towards a more comprehensive welfare state in the wake of the economic crisis, it is necessary to look into the politics of welfare reform in Korea, in which two different advocacy coalitions have competed for the policy paradigm since the 1960s. 'Advocacy coalition', here, refers to the group of actors from various public and private organizations who share a set of beliefs and who seek to realise their common goals over time (Sabatier 1986). Of course, an advocacy coalition cannot spring up simply because some political actors, policy experts and concerned citizens share a belief system and policy goals. An advocacy coalition needs a closer network of contact, co-operation and organisational structure, although this is often informal.

This chapter will examine the way in which those advocacy coalitions competed with each other and achieved success or failed to produce the policy output they pursued. It will examine political strategies of advocacy coalitions from an historical-institutional perspective, which will enable us to look into the institutional dynamics in which individual actors as well as groups of political actors interact with each other (Hall 1986; Steinmo and Thelen 1992). I will argue that, after the long period when economic-pragmatists exercised a strong influence in policy making, the advocacy coalition of the welfare-idealists was able to grab the effective point of decision amidst the economic crisis of 1997–98, which had altered the course of political competition and to a great extent changed the socioeconomic conditions in Korea. Once the welfare-idealists had gained the strategic advantage over the economic-pragmatists, they were able to produce the policy outputs that had eluded them for the previous four decades. Before we move to the politics of reforms in social policy, it is necessary to look at the social impact of the economic crisis, since it set the context of the politics of welfare reform since 1997.

Economic crisis and its social impacts

Although the economic crisis of 1997–98 pushed the Korean economy near to collapse, Korea managed to emerge from the crisis rather well compared to other Asian economies hit by the crisis by implementing a series of structural reforms. Those reforms dealt with a wide range of economic and social issues ranging from government bureaucracy, corporate governance, and the financial market, to the labour market. Most of the reform programmes were in line with the IMF directives (Ministry of Economy and Finance 1998), and some commentators like Cummings argued that the IMF directives were harsher than was necessary. He contended that the IMF was instrumental in allowing the US to regain its strategic leadership in East Asia (Cummings 1998: 45), since some of the reform programmes had unsuccessfully been pressed by the US government before the crisis (Chung 2000). Nevertheless the Korean government vigorously carried out structural reform programmes, partly because a successful structural reform would enhance foreign investors' confidence in the Korean economy, which would in turn persuade them to return to Korea. The Korean government also saw most of the reform programmes as necessary for the economy and already overdue. For example, a legislative package aiming at the labour market reform was blocked by the opposition parties at the first attempt in 1997 and was toned down at the second attempt in 1998 (Koo 2000).

Some years after the economic crisis, it is still controversial whether those reform programmes have produced their intended outcomes (Islam and Chowdhury 2000; Park 2000b). It is, however, certainly true that the economic crisis of 1997–98 and subsequent reforms have had a significant social impact. It is worth noting, *inter alia*, three immediate impacts of the economic crisis, which subsequently set the context of the politics of welfare reform. In terms of political impact, first, the economic crisis altered the course of the presidential election, which took place at the end of 1997. In this election, the long-time opposition leader Kim Dae-jung was elected to the presidency. During the campaign prior to the emergence of the economic crisis, the governing candidate was leading the race, while Kim Dae-jung was struggling to mend his broken promise that he would retire from politics after his defeat in the 1993 presidential election. His support remained confined to his strongholds, leaving him to trail the front-runner. As the economic crisis unfolded, he successfully presented himself as a national leader who could deal with this unprecedented crisis, and this ensured his electoral success.[1] To be sure, one cannot argue that the economic crisis was the only important factor deciding the electoral outcome. Many other factors should be taken into account, such as the construction of a coalition between the opposition parties, and defection from the governing parties. All these events, however, unfolded against the background of the economic crisis, which discredited the governing party and devastated the prospects of its candidate. In the end, the 1997 presidential election produced a victory for the opposition. The transition of political power to the opposition, in turn, changed the political dynamics between political actors and advocacy coalitions in public policy making, including that of social policy, although the constitutional configuration remained the same.

Secondly, the Korean bureaucrats were blamed for much of the failure of economic management. Although there are two strands of explanations, they both pointed a finger of blame at the bureaucrats for the mismanagement of the economy (Weiss 1999). The neo-liberal view, which the IMF and the World Bank shared, argued that too much state intervention and opportunistic behaviour had resulted in political favouritism and a lack of competitiveness, which in turn undermined international investors' confidence in the Korean economy. The second view contended that the crisis had taken place due to the weakening of the regulatory role of the state (Chang 1998). Running up to the economic crisis of 1997–98, the bureaucrats in the economic ministries failed to monitor the rapid increase of short-term loans from foreign lenders, which was an immediate cause of the economic crisis. What also undermined the credibility of the bureaucrats was their initial response to the crisis. According to Kim's study (2000), which observed the behaviour of senior officials running up to the economic crisis, senior officials in the economic ministries were complacent about the possibility of economic crisis, and too arrogant to listen to different views when there were already clear signs of an imminent crisis. They denied that Korea would ask the IMF to bail out until the US Treasury Secretary refused publicly to provide a bilateral loan to Korea.

Lastly, the reform package following the IMF bail-out resulted in a great number of people being made unemployed. The IMF advised the Korean government that interest rates should be maintained at a high level to avoid capital flight. The interest rate even reached 22 per cent at one point in 1998. Since Korean firms traditionally maintained a high debt-to-equity ratio, they were vulnerable to this sharp rise in interest rates. Indeed, a great number of firms went into default during 1998. This inevitably resulted in the sharp rise of unemployment. The labour market reform was, however, the most direct cause of unemployment. Considering that the main purpose of the labour market reform was to make the labour market more flexible, the sharp rise in unemployment was, at least in the short term, inevitable. The reform had two strands of programmes. One was to allow firms to lay off workers easily, while the other legalized the private agencies to supply labour for other business on a contract basis.

The labour market reform had an immediate impact as shown in Table 12.1. Considering that the Korean economy had slowed down from 1996, the fact that the unemployment rate was kept at a low level before the crisis showed that the labour market did not indeed have much flexibility.

In February 1999 the official unemployment rate rose to 8.6 per cent. There were, *inter alia*, three important characteristics in this massive unemployment. First, the unemployment rate among young people was very high and the sheer number of young unemployed people was also massive. In 1998, the number of the unemployed aged 15–34 was about 781,000, which was about 53.9 per cent of all the unemployed. The majority of these were new graduates from high schools and colleges. The Korean government was concerned about the worst-case scenario that militant students and college graduates would organise mass demonstrations, sparking off protests from trade unions, the urban poor and many others.[2] Secondly, the sharp rise of unemployment left no safe haven. Before 1998, full employment was maintained among the male working population aged over 35. The male unemployment rate went up to 6 per cent in all age groups between 35 and 59. Considering that a great number of people among these were the main breadwinners in households, the social impact was much higher than the figure suggests. For example, the increase in crime and divorce in 1998 was markedly higher than in previous years.[3] Thirdly, there have also been noticeable changes in employment status (see Table 12.2). The proportion of regular workers was considerably reduced while the proportion of the temporary and daily workers increased. For temporary and daily workers,

Table 12.1   The trend of unemployment in Korea (percentages)

Year	Participation	Unemployment	Male	Female
1990	60.0	2.4	2.9	1.8
1991	60.6	2.3	2.5	1.9
1992	60.9	2.4	2.6	2.1
1993	61.1	2.8	3.2	2.2
1994	61.7	2.4	2.7	1.9
1995	62.0	2.0	2.3	1.7
1996	62.0	2.0	2.3	1.6
1997	62.2	2.6	2.8	2.3
1998	60.7	6.8	7.6	5.6
1999	60.5	6.3	7.1	5.1

Source: Ministry of Labour, *Yearbook of Labour Statistics* (1996, 1999, 2000).

Table 12.2   Changes in employment status (percentages)

	1995	1996	1997	1998	1999
Regular workers	58.1	56.6	54.1	53.0	48.3
Temporary workers	27.7	29.5	31.6	32.8	33.4
Daily workers	14.2	13.8	14.3	14.2	18.3

Source: Ministry of Labour (2000).

employment security is fragile in addition to the low level of compensation. Of course, this trend had already emerged some time before the labour market reform, but reform measures such as the legalization of private agencies that provide temporary workers made it irreversible.

The sharp rise in unemployment and its characteristics created considerable pressure for the Korean government to act quickly. It is also worth noting that there was a sweeping change in the public perception of the role of the state in social welfare during this period. According to the survey research conducted twice – in May 1997 and in October 1998 – 83 per cent of the respondents replied that the state was responsible for citizens' social welfare in 1998, whereas 49 per cent responded in that way in 1997 (Shin and Rose 1998; Shin 1997).[4] Taken together, these social impacts of the economic crisis set the context of the politics of welfare reform, to which we now turn.

The emergence of the welfare-idealists and the welfare reform

In my previous work (Kwon 1997), I argued that in the history of the contemporary Korean welfare state, economic development was the over-whelming concern, taking priority over social protection. For instance, Industrial Accident Insurance was chosen as the first social welfare programme by the Park Chung Hee government (in office 1961–79) in 1962. This programme was regarded as an essential requirement for a country embarking upon an ambitious economic development plan. In the case of National Health Insurance, industrial workers employed in big businesses were the first group of people to be protected while the more vulnerable were left unprotected. It was also clearly shown that economic growth was being given overwhelming priority in policy making when the National Pension Programme was first considered in 1973. The National Pension Programme was seen as an effective measure for mobilizing the capital much needed for economic development. In this policy paradigm, the economic-pragmatists had dominated social policy making until the economic crisis of 1997–98. The economic-pragmatists included bureaucrats in the economic ministries, and policy experts in the government think-tanks, notably the Korea Development Institute (Park 1975). Of course, most of the incumbents of the presidency strongly supported the economic-pragmatists' approach since they wanted to enhance their weak political legitimacy through economic performance (Kwon 1999).[5] Given the authoritarian institutional setting in which the president occupied the most effective point of decision, it was very difficult for different voices to be heard in policy making.

There were, of course, policy experts and bureaucrats who adopted what I have called a welfare-idealist approach. These were a group of people who were mainly concerned with issues like social citizenship and social protection. The Committee for Social Security was a case in point. It was an advisory committee for the Minister of Health and Welfare in the 1960s and 1970s, and it played an important role in introducing Industrial Accident Insurance in the early 1960s, but its role in policy making became marginalized soon after. Its proposal for National Health Insurance was rejected since it was unable to incorporate its welfare-idealist approach into the prevailing policy paradigm. President Park did not give any opportunity for the Committee for Social Security to put forward its case when he considered the National Pension Programme in 1973. The Committee for Social Security was abolished in 1980 when it made a strong case for the reform of National Health Insurance against the policy being advanced by the economic-pragmatists. Some bureaucrats, such as those in the Ministry of Health and Welfare and academics specializing in social policy, took this view but they were unable to form an effective advocacy coalition.

In a nutshell, the economic-pragmatists – including the presidents – dominated social-policy making, because they were well positioned in the institutional configuration, whereas the welfare-idealists were unable to form an effective policy coalition. In other words, the debates on social policy were scarcely conducted on an equal footing. This situation changed dramatically after the economic crisis.

Unemployment policy and the tripartite committee

In February 1998 amid the economic crisis, the President-elect Kim Dae-jung convened a tripartite committee to carry out an urgent labour market reform based upon a social consensus. This was a kind of corporatist committee, which included delegates from the government, the Korean Federation of Business, the Korean Federation of Trade Unions and the Korean Confederation of Trade Unions. What made this committee special was not only that it made employers and employees talk to each other, but that it brought two hostile national trade unions together to represent diverse views of labour. The President-elect Kim should get credit for this, since it was his political ability which brought the trade unions into the tripartite committee. In the end, the committee was able to sign a social pact on 98 measures, including the revision of the Labour Standard Law and social policy programmes for unemployment. From the point of the Korean Confederation of Trade Unions, which had been the subject of harsh treatment from the previous government, it was also an opportunity to put forward its case for labour market reform, which was seen as inevitable.

They also expected that President-elect Kim Dae-jung's policy toward labour would be different from that of the previous government (Park 2000a: 165), and they successfully pressed the government to legalize the schoolteachers' trade unions, which had long been opposed by the Ministries of Education and Labour. What is worth noting here is that in this body of decision-making, the economic-pragmatists such as bureaucrats in the economic ministries, policy experts in the government think-tanks and notably the outgoing president Kim Young-sam, played virtually no part. In contrast, trade unions, whose influence on policy making had previously been marginal at best, were able to push through social policy measures to protect the unemployed when they accepted the labour market reform.

After assuming office the Kim Dae-jung government carried through the labour market reform based on the 'social consensus'. The unemployment rate rose sharply after the reform, as seen in Table 12.1. As agreed in the tripartite committee, the Korean government introduced a package of social policies, the 'Master Plan for Tackling Unemployment', to deal with unemployment and protect those made redundant. First, the Korean government extended the Employment Insurance Programme to cover those previously outside the programme and loosened its eligibility requirement for unemployment benefits to take up people who were made unemployed. Although a great number of people benefited from the change, this effort was not, however, very effective in helping the unemployed previously working in small-scale workplaces and informal sectors, since the Employment Insurance Programme only covered the large-scale workplaces. Nor could relaxing the rules for eligibility be effective, since most of the unemployed had not paid contributions to the Employment Insurance Programme. At the introduction of the Employment Insurance in 1995, one needed to contribute for at least a year to be eligible for unemployment benefits (Yoo 1995). This minimum period of contribution was reduced to six months in 1998, but nevertheless it was necessary to pay a premium first. In others words, the Employment Insurance Programme was still of no use for the unemployed who had not previously paid unemployment contributions (Table 12.3). Other social assistance programmes, such as the Public Assistance Programme, did not play much of a role, since the Korean government maintained its strict means-test system.

Secondly, the Public Works Projects were launched and targeted at those people who were outside the Employment Insurance Programme and the Public Assistance Programme.[6] In other words, this programme was for those unemployed who were ineligible for unemployment benefits and at the same time not poor enough to get public assistance benefits. It did not, however, mean that this group of people did not need help. They were not eligible for public assistance benefits, simply because the means-testing of

Table 12.3   Unemployment benefit recipients within the Employment Insurance Programme (percentages)

Year	Recipients/ the unemployed	Recipients/the unemployed with prior job experiences
1997	2.4	4.1
First half 1998	5.6	6.1
Second half 1998	9.6	10.3
1999	10.5	11.2

Source: Hwang (2000: 10).

Table 12.4   Applications and selection for the Public Works Projects

Year	1st 1998	2nd 1998	1st 1999	2nd 1999	1st 2000	2nd 2000
No. of Applications	133,000	435,000	1,156,000	784,000	716,000	427,000
No. of those selected	77,000 (57.9%)	273,000 (62.7%)	832,000 (71.9%)	607,000 (77.4%)	543,000 (75.8%)	252,000 (59.0%)

Source: MoGH (1999) *The Progress Report of the Public Works Projects*; http:n4000–01.mogaha.go. kr:3374/work/ (February 2001).

the Public Assistance Programme was very strict in Korea. In fact, the World Bank also recommended that the Public Works Projects should fill this gap, and President Kim Dae-jung could not ignore this constituency, since he was able to take a grip of power in the 1997 election on the basis of the support from the low-income groups as well as people from the south west of the country. President Kim needed to continue the Public Works Projects because of his unsuccessful efforts to gain a majority at the general election scheduled for April 2000.

To target the right people, the Korean government set up the guidelines for the selection of applicants for the public works projects since the number of available jobs in the projects was small compared to the number of applicants (see Table 12.4). According to these guidelines, there are a number of criteria by which each applicant's situation is evaluated. For instance, the main breadwinners of the household, those aged between thirty to fifty, and the disabled would get a more favourable review than others. In contrast, those who had previously participated in the public works projects would have some disadvantage. (People who participated in the projects in three consecutive periods would be disqualified for the next period.) The evaluation is then quantified, and those who have more points according to the criteria will be selected for the Public Works Projects. There are also certain people who would not be allowed to apply for the Public Works Projects: the recipients of unemployment benefits, pensioners within the National Pension Programme and people whose spouses are earning incomes. In order to check all these details, the local officials have access to the 'Work-net', which is a collection of data for the labour force, compiled by the Ministry of Labour. Since a phase of the Public Works Projects lasts for three months, people need to apply for the work every three months.

The Public Works Projects provided jobs for those who otherwise would have lost their source of income. As shown in Table 12.5, the amount of expenditure devoted to the Public Works Projects was higher than for any other social assistance programme in Korean history. The total number of participants varied in each phase of the year; for example, in 1999 the Public Works Projects provided on average 400,000 jobs at a certain point in time, which accounted for 2 per cent of the reduction in unemployment rate. Since the jobs within the Public Works Projects have been assigned on the basis of means-testing, there have been equalizing impacts on income distribution, as the preliminary assessment reported by the World Bank research suggests (Atinc 2000).

The whole package of programmes under the 'Master Plan for Tackling Unemployment' accounted for 10 per cent of Korean government expenditure. The total outlay of the government in the social policy area rose by 22.1 per cent from 1997 to 1998 and 28.3 per cent from 1998 to 1999.[7]

Despite such effective participation in policy making as in the case of unemployment policy, the Employees–Employers–Government Committee began to falter after the country began to emerge from the emergency situation. The participants in the committee were often unable to get their house in order to carry out the reform measures – an essential requirement for honouring the compromise. As for the government, the Kim Dae-jung government was in a minority in the National Assembly, and the opposition Grand National Party often prevented the Kim government from carrying through the compromise made in the tripartite committee after the worst situation had gone. As for the trade unions, on many occasions unions on the shopfloor did not follow the national union's policy. This was particularly

Table 12.5 Implementation of the Public Works Projects in Korea

Year	No. of participants[1]	Expenditure[2]
1998	350,000	0.71
1999	1,439,000	1.62
2000	795,000	0.89

[1] total in all phases in each year. A phase lasts three months.
[2] as percentage of government expenditure.
Source: Ministry of Public Administration and Local Autonomy (1999), 'Implementation of Public Work Projects', mimeo; http: n4000–01.mogaha. go.kr: 3374/work/ (February 2001).

the case regarding the Korean Confederation of Trade Unions, since it did not institutionalize the national structure, due to its short period of existence as legalized unions (Park 2000a: 171). For this reason, the unions became uncompromisingly hard in negotiating with the government, and they often walked away from the negotiating table. Given such weakness, the committee's main agenda were not social policy issues but labour market reform and corporate governance. In short, the tripartite committee lost its effectiveness in policy making soon after its initial success.

The Minimum Living Standard Guarantee and the welfare-idealists

The advocacy coalition of the welfare-idealists, which was mainly concerned with social protection, emerged as an influential force during the process of policy making for the Minimum Living Standard Guarantee (MLSG). This advocacy coalition clearly took the stance of pursuing the idea of citizenship rights rather than economic concerns. It included activists from social pressure groups, academics, political advisers to the president in the Presidential Office, and some of the National Assemblymen. They successfully pushed the bill through the National Assembly and the MSLG was implemented from October 2000. What is the underlying logic for this success of the new emerging welfare-idealists?

As discussed in the previous section, it became clear during the economic crisis that there was a gap in income maintenance policy in Korea. The Public Assistance Programme introduced in 1961 (implemented from 1965) was based on the idea of poor relief, and provided cash or in-kind support to the poor as officially defined, depending upon the recipients' situation. In 1997, people receiving benefits from the Public Assistance Programme amounted to 3.1 per cent of the population (Ministry of Health and Welfare 2000). The level of cash benefits was estimated at half of the official poverty line defined in absolute terms (Kwon 2001), and it had a strict means-test provision. For this reason, the Public Assistance Programme was a mere relief and not sufficient to prevent people from falling below the poverty line. The Public Assistance Programme also had a 'demographic test', in which those aged between 18 and 65 were automatically disqualified from cash benefits. They were regarded as having earning ability and not deserving income support. During the time of economic growth, some of them managed to find sources of modest income, either from jobs or from family members or relatives. During the period of economic crisis, those private incomes became harder to secure since there were fewer jobs available for them and family help did not come as often as before. The Public Works Projects were intended to help these people, but could not help all those in need.

The MLSG was aimed to address these two issues. First, it changed the concept of poverty from an absolute to a relative one. This means that those who were previously not qualified would now be entitled to it, since the poverty line had risen significantly. It also means that the level of benefits would increase, because the MLSG would guarantee a living standard equal to the relative poverty line. Secondly, the MLSG abolished the 'demographic test' and would provide benefits to those aged between 18 and 65 if their income fell below the poverty line. There are, however, conditions that require these people to participate in job training programmes, public works projects or community services. These are similar conditions to those 'welfare-to-work' programmes adopted in other countries. In a nutshell, the MLSG recognized the social rights of citizens to a minimum living standard.

This was an obvious shift in policy paradigm regarding the social policy in general and income maintenance in particular. The welfare-idealists played an important role in this development and, more importantly, institutional dynamics in Korean politics worked to their advantage. The Citizens' Coalition for Participatory Democracy played the pivotal role in this process. When it convened a conference on poverty in 1995, the MLSG was regarded as a mere idealist proposal. There were also a small number of National Assemblymen sympathetic to the reform, but there was no concerted effort to put the reform on the legislative agenda. The Kim Yong-Sam government (in office 1993–98) did not pay attention to this meeting, which demanded the reform of the Public Assistance Programme.

During the economic crisis, the Citizens' Coalition for Participatory Democracy began to step up its efforts to introduce the MLSG. The change of government opened up various access points to policy making for the Citizens' Coalition for Participatory Democracy. In 1998 it began to organize the welfare-idealists in order to push their agenda effectively. The Citizens' Coalition for Participatory Democracy established an ad hoc committee with other pressure groups while it lobbied a number of the National Assemblymen (Ahn 2000: 6). A social policy academic and a veteran civil activist spearheaded this ad hoc committee.[8] They found a small number of the National Assemblymen sympathetic to the idea from both the governing Democratic Party and the opposition Grand National Party. Although the

Table 12.6 'Welfare-to-work' programmes within the MLSG

Programmes	Activities
Job placement	Regular consultation with job placement agencies
Job training	Participation in training programmes according to need and capability
Fostering business	• Self-employed programmes • Co-operative programmes
Public works projects	Participation in the public works projects
Community services	Contributing to the community and maintaining work ethic
Counselling	Problem solving and maintaining work ethic

Source: Ministry of Health and Welfare (2000), *Planning the MLSG for 2001*.

number of those National Assemblymen was small, the cross-party support they offered was instrumental in getting the bill into the National Assembly. These Assemblymen proposed a bill to the Health and Welfare Committee of the National Assembly December 1998. Up to this point in time, however, the bill did not go further beyond the committee floor at the National Assembly. Most Assemblymen did not pay much attention to the bill. Bureaucrats in the Ministry of Health and Welfare were sceptical about the bill, since they thought that the delivery system for an income support programme such as the MLSG was not in place (Lee 2000: 146). The economic ministries were also not enthusiastic about the proposal, since it would cost a great deal of money, certainly more than the Public Assistance Programme.

The big breakthrough came from the presidential office. President Kim Dae-jung had led a minority government, and managed to establish a coalition with the third party in the National Assembly. His coalition was always fragile against the main opposition, the Grand National Party. President Kim found it hard to pass his reform bills through the National Assembly. From the beginning of 1999, he focused on the general election scheduled for April 2000. Winning an overall majority in the National Assembly was an absolute priority in his political strategy in the medium term. President Kim aimed at the low-income class to pull out political support for his government. In August 1999, he launched a new policy initiative, the so-called 'Productive Welfare', in his address on National Liberation Day. This new idea, influenced by the 'Third Way' as indicated by the presidential office, placed an emphasis on the role that welfare could play in promoting economic productivity (Presidential Office 1999).

Whereas 'Productive Welfare' was for political rhetoric, a subtler political manoeuvre was planned by President Kim even before he launch this new idea. In June 1999, he appointed a university professor with long experience in social pressure groups as his political adviser at the presidential office. He also appointed a Protestant minister with experience in social movements to be chairman of the policy committee of the Democratic Party.[9] After their appointments, they maintained a close link with a number of social pressure groups, which later ran a strong civil campaign for 'de-listing' a number of political parties' candidates from the parties' official line-up for the general election.[10] The de-listing camp accused a number of candidates of involvement with the authoritarian government and corruption in the past. This dealt a severe blow – mainly to candidates of the opposition Grand National Party. The majority targeted by the campaign lost at the general election, which took place in April 2000.

From the point of those who pressed for the MLSG, the appointment of sympathetic figures to these two key posts provided strong allies within the decision-making process. President Kim also appointed a former bureaucrat to be Minister of Health and Welfare, who had been dismissed because of his welfare-idealist view under the Chun government (in office 1980–87). In other words, it completed the link of the advocacy coalition for the MLSG. In June 1999, President Kim made it clear that he would introduce the MLSG. In August 1999, the MLSG bill was proposed at a plenary session of the National Assembly, and it was passed with a number of opposition members backing it as well as the governing party. In this process, the economic-pragmatists at the Ministry of Finance and Economy, the Ministry of Health and Welfare and government think-tanks such as the Korea Development Institute did not voice explicit opposition. This was mainly because the MLSG was seen as being the president's programme. Of course, some parts of the media, especially those critical to the Kim government, noted their concerns, but they were unable to derail the MLSG.

Reform of the National Health Insurance and its financial crisis

National Health Insurance, which has covered the whole population from 1988, has been subjected to intense policy debates. When it was introduced in 1977, it only covered employees in large-scale workplaces with 500 people. In 1978 government employees and private schoolteachers became compulsory members and the number of people covered reached 20.49 per cent of the population (see Table 12.7). Thereafter the National Health Insurance scheme was rapidly extended to smaller workplaces. However, those who had no recognized employers, for example, farmers, the self-employed, informal sector employees, the retired and the unemployed, remained outside the scheme. This was partly because of the contribution arrangements under which the employers and employees each paid half of the contributions to National Health Insurance. (In 1980, the average contribution rate was 1.9 per cent of wages and 2.62 percent of wages 1999).[11] The groups of people mentioned above did not have employers who would have paid half of their contributions. The government was not prepared to pay the equivalent of the employers' share for those without formal employers. There were also other reasons for this, as Mills (1985: 80) explained: 'Social Insurance

Table 12.7 Coverage of National Health Insurance, 1977–89 (percentage of the whole population)

	Industrial	Public	Occupational	Regional	Others	Total
1977	10.33	—	—	—	—	10.33
1978	10.34	10.15	—	—	—	20.49
1981	18.70	10.27	0.06	0.47	0.19	29.69
1984	28.75	10.11	2.02	0.97	0.53	42.38
1987	36.01	10.50	3.17	0.76	0.69	51.13
1988	38.76	9.67	2.58	16.15	0.64	67.8
1989	38.96	10.55	0.00	44.69	0.00	94.2

Note: Percentage of members and their families respectively.
Source: National Health Insurance Agency (1990).

schemes are concentrated in the industrial sector in developing countries, not least because wages and profits are high enough for compulsory levies to be paid, and the structure of wage employment makes collection of the levies feasible.' National Health Insurance is a typical example of this observation. In short, the Korean governments took an economic-pragmatist approach during this period, because they did not have enough public money to pay for those without employers nor a well-organized administrative structure to manage a unified health insurance programme. Such an approach, however, left a large section of the population outside the programme, most of whom belonged to low-income groups. These groups of people felt stigmatized as they had to pay much more for their treatment than the National Health Insurance patients, who paid only 30 per cent of the fees.

Throughout the 1980s, National Health Insurance was extended to the self-employed and in 1988 covered the whole population as the government pledged to pay half of the contribution for those without employers. This change of policy was brought about after the first contested election for the presidency in 1987. Despite the universal coverage, National Health Insurance was not integrated in a single national health fund, but it comprised more than 300 financially (and administratively) separate funds that collected contributions and paid hospitals and doctors for treatment on a fee-for-services basis. People who were newly covered by National Health Insurance formed their own health funds (Regional Health Funds), whereas the existing members maintained their own (Governmental and Industrial Health Funds). This made the extension of National Health Insurance easier, since the exiting members' funds did not have to transfer financially to new ones, but the redistribution effects of National Health Insurance were very limited, as it only took place within fragmented health funds.

The welfare-idealists challenged the idea of a separate management system. They argued that the separation of funds made the pooling of health risks narrower and redistributive effects limited. They also argued that health funds for the low-income groups would not be financially viable. In fact, the health funds for farmers and urban residents who did not have employee status, such as the self-employed, urban informal workers and the retired, were financially in difficult positions (see Table 12.8). Throughout the 1980s the welfare-idealists argued for an integrated National Health Insurance Fund without much success. In contrast, the economic-pragmatists maintained that redistribution is not the main goal of National Health Insurance. They also pointed out that the rich self-employed would most benefit from the integration due to the deficiency of the tax system in Korea. For example, practising lawyers, doctors and wealthy shopowners tend to under-report their income, and pay less taxes and social insurance contribution than they should.[12] Most wage and salary owners, their employers and their trade unions shared this view.

Table 12.8 The current accounts of health insurance funds (before transfer; billion won)

	1991	*1992*	*1993*	*1994*	*1995*	*1996*	*1997*	*1998*	*1999*
Governmental	87.7	72.9	68.5	70.5	60.0	52.1	−142.9	−296.6	35.6
Industrial	340.3	435.1	436.2	479.2	440.2	280.8	11.0	−172.3	−411.0
Regional	345.8	289.1	226.5	183.8	19.0	−186.1	−118.7	−114.5	−366.8

Governmental: health insurance fund for public employees and private school teachers.
Industrial: health insurance funds for wage and salary workers.
Regional: health insurance for those without officially defined employers.
Source: *National Health Insurance Statistical Yearbook*.

In 1980, the Committee for Social Security put forward a policy proposal that would integrate all health insurance funds into one national health insurance fund. The then minister of Health and Social Affairs backed the proposal based on policy advice from his staff, who had a welfare-idealist viewpoint (Kim 1992). The Korean Federation of Business and Industries and the Korean Chamber of Commerce made it clear that they would oppose the proposal. In contrast, the Korean Federation of Trade Unions supported the idea. However, this proposal was rejected by the presidential office, which feared that the integration would lead the state to take direct financial responsibility for National Health Insurance. After the intervention from the presidential office, the minister discarded the idea of integration and was dismissed after a while. It was also reported that a couple of bureaucrats at the Ministry of Health and Social Affairs were forced to resign by the presidential office due to their welfare-idealist views. The Committee for Social Security, a stronghold for the welfare-idealists, was also dismantled (Kim 1992: 62). The authoritarian government did not tolerate the welfare-idealists, who seemed be at odds with government policy.

The same debate took place in 1989 with a different institutional setting. After winning the first contested presidential election in 1987, President Roh Tae-woo (in office 1988–93) lost his majority in the National Assembly at the general election in April 1988. The election result produced an unprecedented confrontation between the president and the National Assembly. Three opposition parties managed to form an alliance, and they pressed the Roh government hard on many occasions. Regarding social policy, the alliance successfully passed the integration bill for National Health Insurance in March 1989. An integrated National Health Insurance Fund would allow financial transfer from one group to the others according to their risk. Most interested parties and social groups joined the debate, but the president vetoed the bill, fearing that he would lose the support of the middle classes (Kwon 1999: 67). The Roh government, however, allow limited financial transfers between health insurance funds from 1991.

During the course of this debate, it was clear that the welfare-idealists were unable to form a strong advocacy coalition to carry out their proposal. More importantly, however, the previous presidents who occupied the most effective point of decision did not support the welfare-idealists' view. In contrast to such experiences in the 1980s, the welfare-idealists in the 1990s tried to establish an advocacy coalition in connection with opposition parties, trade unions and religious groups. While the welfare-idealists in the 1980s were a small number of social policy academics and welfare bureaucrats and lacked in organizing skills, the new breed in the 1990s were prepared to take actions such as demonstrations, legal disputes with the government and union strikes – whatever was necessary to pursue health care reform. Many of them had had experience in the students' movement while in campus or the union movement at shopfloor level in the 1980s. In 1994, the Korean Confederation of Trade Unions and the Citizens' Coalition for Participatory Democracy spearheaded the formation of a Coalition for the Integration of National Health Insurance, which included 77 social pressure groups and maintained close contact with the opposition parties (Lee 2000: 86).

The economic crisis and the government change in 1997–98 provided a timely opportunity for the welfare-idealists to achieve their policy. Politicians of the Democratic Party, trade unionists, activists from social pressure groups and some academics managed to form a strong advocacy coalition during this period. They successfully put forward the idea of the integration of National Health Insurance as part of the agenda of the abovementioned tripartite committee. They also took an active role in the Transition Committee for the New Government, which decided on the integration as one of the new government policies. As in the case of the MLSG, the bureaucrats in the government were unsure whether they could make their objections in public (Lee 2000: 122–3). President Kim Dae-jung showed his intention clearly when he appointed a former bureaucrat who was dismissed by the Chun government for his welfare-idealist views to be the Minster of Health and Welfare. Lee (2000) pointed out that it was like a military operation when the welfare-idealists tried to push through the National Health Insurance integration bill. He argued that they made the same mistake of not giving their opponents due opportunity to express their views, exactly as the economic-pragmatists had done in the 1980s. A newly established agency began to administer the integrated National Health Insurance from July 2000.

As well as reforming National Health Insurance, the Kim Dae-jung government introduced another health care reform, which redefined the functional division between physicians and pharmacists. For many years, pharmacists had been allowed to prescribe and sell medicines to their customers without physicians' prescriptions. At the same time, patients could buy medicines from hospitals where they received prescriptions from physicians. This was a marriage of convenience, since clinics and hospitals were few and far between when Korea was poor. In fact, pharmacists played a role similar to that of general practitioners. This system led pharmacists and physicians alike to prescribe medicines beyond medical necessity. Long after Korea managed to have a reasonable number of clinics and hospitals, this system remained in operation until 2000. The Kim Dae-jung government redefined the roles of physicians and pharmacists: physicians were to prescribe and pharmacists were to deliver. It is, however, worth noting that this redefinition policy was already planned under the previous government. Nevertheless, the Kim government showed more vigour in implementing this reform than its predecessor, and the public identified it as part of the Kim government's agenda.

This reform led to a series of strikes by doctors and trainee doctors throughout the second half of 2000. Pharmacists were in support of the reform, but were not entirely happy about it. Citizens had to suffer a number of disruptions in the health care system, and did not show strong support for the reform. It is also worth remembering that President Kim had failed to win an overall majority in the general election in April 2000 despite all of his efforts. He had to establish a coalition with smaller parties, but his coalition commanded a majority of only one seat in the National Assembly. His mandate for reform became precarious and evaporated quickly. In order to carry through the reform, the Kim government increased health care fees by almost 60 per cent to calm down doctors and trainee doctors.[13] In March 2001, the chief executive of National Health Insurance announced that the system of National Health Insurance would be financially bankrupt in one month's time unless the government provided the extra funding. He attributed this to the increase of payment for treatment after the implementation of redefinition policy. This announcement led to a national outcry and the Kim government lost a great deal of its political support, which had already become fragile. In this reform, active members of the advocacy coalition of the welfare-idealists, such as the Citizens' Coalition for Participatory Democracy, strongly supported the government's reform policy. President Kim and the welfare-idealists became subject to strong criticisms from various sections of the public. One prominent ally of President Kim publicly criticized him by saying that the president had lost his sense of political balance and leaned too much toward left-wing social pressure groups (Lee 2001). The Korean Bar Association issued a statement that President Kim had relied too much on populism instead of the rule of law. President Kim sacked the Minister of Health and Welfare twice following the reform. The advocacy coalition for welfare-idealists was also in retreat after this setback.

Conclusion

Since the economic crisis of 1997–98, Korea has witnessed a rapid expansion of the welfare state following a series of reforms. This essay has examined the reform policies in income maintenance programmes for the unemployed and the poor and in the public health care system, including the reform of National

Health Insurance and the policy of redefining health professionals' work. These reforms went beyond the functional minima necessary to cope with those social problems caused by the immediate impact of the economic crisis. This essay has paid particular attention to the advocacy coalition of the welfare-idealists, who were the driving force behind the reforms. Of course, the economic crisis changed the socioeconomic conditions so that no one could be sure of avoiding unemployment. This in turn changed attitudes toward social solidarity and the role of the state in social welfare. The economic crisis has also altered the course of political struggle for the presidency, which resulted in 1997 in the victory of the opposition party for the first time in the Korean history. At this historical juncture, the advocacy coalition of the welfare-idealists successfully seized a number of strategic points of decision-making, including the office of president. This was an illuminating contrast with the situation of the welfare-idealists in the past, who were small in numbers, scattered in the different ministries and universities and unable to form an effective advocacy coalition. The economic-pragmatists who dominated social policy making in the developmental era did not give due opportunity to this group of people. The present-day welfare-idealists who share the same beliefs are different from their predecessors. They were prepared to take to the street, initiate legal disputes with the government, and interfere with unionists strike and were also able to implementing a strategic plan in pursing their policy.

More importantly, however, President Kim needed the support of the welfare-idealists in order to carry out structural reforms, and to win the general election. This ultimately provided the advocacy coalition of the welfare-idealists with the strategic edge to produce their preferred policy outputs. The Employment Insurance Programme became more comprehensive, the MLSG institutionally acknowledged social rights for the less well-off to live with a decent income, and the integration of National Health Insurance paved the way for broader risk-pooling and redistribution. Having achieved these policy outputs, the welfare-idealists and President Kim suffered from the setbacks regarding the redefinition policy for health professionals. The failure to win the general election in April 2000 also manifested the thrust of reform beginning to lose its momentum. Nevertheless, the welfare reform undertaken during the last two years cannot be easily reversed, although some fine-tuning will be necessary.

Notes

1. Before the economic crisis hit the country, Kim Dae-jung was placed second (*Joongang Daily*, 21 July 1997) but he led the opinion poll on 24 November (*Joongang Daily*, 24 November 1997).
2. Interview with a senior officer at the Presidential Office, May 1998.

3. Crime increased by 11 per cent in 1998 compared to 6.3 per cent in 1997 and the level of divorces was up by 25 per cent in 1998 compared to 0.9 per cent in the previous year: National Statistical Office (2000); *Yearbook of Demographic Dynamics* Seoul: NSO.
4. This work was recited from Shin (2000).
5. It is certainly true that President Chun (in office 1980–88) lacked in political legitimacy since he took power through the military coup. Although President Roh (in office 1988–93) was elected in a democratic contest, he also suffered, though to a lesser extent, from weak legitimacy since he took part in the military coup in 1980.
6. There are four categories of work. First, infrastructure-maintaining projects include cultivating forests, building small public facilities and repairing public utilities. These are types of work that have been, by and large, considered for some time before by the local authorities but postponed due to their low priority and budget constraints. Secondly, the Public Works Projects provide a workforce for social service and charity organizations such as community centres and welfare institutions. This sort of work includes a variety of jobs, such as maintaining the facilities of those institutions and teaching children in after-school classes. Thirdly, there is environment-cleaning work, which includes roadside cleaning and rubbish collection. Lastly, there are information-technology-related projects, which are targeted at the young, and computer-literate people. These projects provide timely help for many central ministries and local authorities, which have a great deal of backlog in digitalizing their databases.
7. The figures are calculated from the *Korea Statistical Yearbook, 2000*, based on the current price.
8. They are Dr Moon Jin-young at Sogan University and Catholic Minister Song Kyong-yong.
9. They are Kim, Sung-jae and Lee, Jae-jung.
10. The Presidential Office strongly denied that they were behind the de-listing campaign, but many commentators believed otherwise (*Joongang Daily*, 28 June 1999).
11. Wages here means not actual take-home pay but 35 bands of Standard Monthly Wage.
12. This is, of course, the case in most countries, but in Korea the proportion of those who are defined as self-employed and informal sector workers by the tax authority is very large, more than 40 per cent.
13. Increase in health care fees took place four times: July 2000 (9.2 per cent), August 2000 (6.5 per cent), September 2000 (6.5 per cent) and January 2001 (6.5 per cent).

Bibliography

Ahn, B.-Y. (2000) 'The Legislative Process of the Minimum Living Standard Guarantee', *Review of Public Administration*, 38, 1–50 (in Korean).

Atinc, T. M. (2000) *Coping with Crises: Social Policy and the Poor in East Asia*. Washington: World Bank/ASEM(Asia-Europe Meeting).

Chang, H.-J. (1998) 'Korea: the Misunderstood Crisis', *World Development*, 26, 1555–61.

Chung, C.-Y. (2000) 'Political Economy of the Financial Crisis and the Logic of Policy: What is Happening?', *Economy and Society*, Spring: XX, 66–89 (in Korean).

Cummings, B. (1998) 'The Korean Crisis and the End of "Late" Development', *New Left Review*, 231, 43–72.

Eto, M. (2001) 'Public Involvement in Social Policy Reforms: Lessons from Japan's Elderly-Care Insurance Scheme', *Journal of Social Policy*, 30, 17–36.

Goodman, R., White, G., and Kwon, H.-J. (1998) *The East Asian Welfare Regime Model: Welfare Orientalism and the State*. London: Routledge.

Hall, P. (1986) *Governing the Economy: the Politics of State Intervention in Britain and France*. New York: Oxford University Press.

Hwang, D.-S. (2000) *Evaluating Unemployment Benefits and Future Direction*. Seoul: Korea Labour Institute.

Islam, I., and Chowdhury, A. (2000) *The Political Economy of East Asia: Post-Crisis Debates*. Oxford: Oxford University Press.

Kim, H.-H. (2000) 'An Analysis of Senior Officials' Policy Making Behaviour with Respect to the Economic Crisis', *Journal of Korean Association of Public Administration*, 34, XX(4), 41–58 (in Korean).

Kim, J.-K. (1992) 'Policy Debates on National Health Insurance in Korea'. Unpublished PhD Dissertation, Sung Kyun Kwan University (in Korean).

Koo, H. (2000) 'The Dilemmas of Empowered Labour in Korea: Korean Workers in the Face of Global Capitalism', *Asian Survey*, 40, 227–50.

Kuhnle, S., and Hort, S. E. (2000) 'The Coming of East and South-East Asian Welfare States', *Journal of European Social Policy*, 10, 162–84.

Kwon, H.-J. (1997) 'Beyond European Welfare Regimes: Comparative Perspectives on East Asian Welfare Systems', *Journal of Social Policy*, 26, 467–84.

Kwon, H.-J. (1999) *The Welfare State in Korea: the Politics of Legitimization*. London: Macmillan.

Kwon, H.-J. (2001) 'Globalization Unemployment and Policy Responses in Korea: Repositioning the State?', *Global Social Policy*, 1, 215–34.

Lee, H.-Y. (2000) 'A comparative analysis of participants in policy makings: Kim Yong-sam and Kim Dae-jung governments'. Unpublished PhD Dissertation, Sung Kyun Kwan University (in Korean).

Lee, J.-C. (2001) 'Interview', *Joongang Monthly*, 126–39 (in Korean).

Mills, A. (1985) 'Economic Aspects of Health Insurance'. In A. Mills and K. Lee (eds), *The Economics of Health in Developing Countries*. Oxford: Oxford University Press.

Ministry of Economy and Finance (1998) *Economy White Paper*. Seoul: Ministry of Economy and Finance.

Ministry of Health and Welfare (2000) *Planning the MLSG for 2001*. Korea: MHW.

National Statistical Office (2000) *Yearbook of Demographic Dynamics*. Seoul: NSO.

Park, C.-K. (1975) *Social Security in Korea: an Approach to Socio-economic Development*. Seoul: KDI (in Korean).

Park, D. (2000a) 'The Social Consensus Politics in Korea and its Weakness', *Korean Political Science Journal*, 34, 161–77 (in Korean).

Park, S.-I. (2000b) 'Labour Market Policy and Social Safety Net in Korea: One Year After Crisis', *Korean Policy Studies Review*, 9, 291–318 (in Korean).

Presidential Office (1999) *Generative Welfare for the New Millennium*. Seoul: Presidential Office.

Sabatier, P. (1986) 'Top-Down and Bottom-up Approach to Implementation Research: a Critical Analysis and Suggested Synthesis', *Journal of Public Policy*, 6, 21–48.

Shin, D. C. and Rose, R. (1997) 'Koreans Evaluate Democracy: a New Korean Barometer Survey', *Studies in Public Policy*, XX, SSP no. 292.

Shin, D. C., and Rose, R. (1998) 'Responding to Economic Crisis: the 1998 New Korea Barometer Survey', *Studies in Public Policy*, XX, SSP no. 311.

Shin, D. M. (2000) 'Financial Crisis and Social Security: the Paradox of the Republic of Korea', *International Social Security Review*, 53, 83–107.

Stallings, B. (1999) 'Politics and Economic Crisis: a Comparative Study of Chile, Peru and Columbia'. In J. Nelson (ed.), *Economic Crisis and Policy Change: the Politics of Adjustment in the Third World*. Princeton: Princeton University Press.

Steinmo, S., and Thelen, K. (1992) 'Historical Institutionalism in Comparative Politics'. In S. Steinmo, K. Thelen and F. Longstreth (eds), *Structuring Politics: Historical Institutionalism in Contemporary Analysis*. Cambridge: Cambridge University Press.

Weiss, L. (1999) 'State Power and the Asian Crisis', *New Political Economy*, 4, 317–42.

Yoo, G.-S. (1995) *The Employment Insurance Programme and the Active Labour Market Policy*. Seoul: Korea Labour Institute (in Korean).

13
Social Policy in Indian Development

Jayati Ghosh

Introduction

The recognition that social policy is not just the outcome of simple welfare considerations, but rather a key instrument in the process of development, which works in association with economic policy as part of a broader strategy, is an important step towards working out mechanisms for its greater spread and effectiveness. However, in order to ground social policy more firmly within development strategy and work out the links between it and more straightforward macroeconomic policy, it is necessary to be aware of the political economy contexts within which both sets of policy are developed and evolve. In this chapter, an attempt is made to analyse the nature of social policy in the recent Indian development experience, to ask why it has taken these specific forms and patterns, to consider its achievements and limitations, and to probe how it can be transformed into a more effective instrument for equitable and sustainable development.

What is social policy all about?

In essence, social policy – or, rather, the complex web of related policies, schemes and institutions that are concerned with the social conditions of economic activity – reflects the broad social contract between capital and labour. In developing economies this refers to the social contract between capital and labour specifically for the management of the development project. The latter in turn has been defined, for much of the past half-century, as the project of increasing material welfare for most of the citizenry through economic development, using the agency of the nation-state. For many developing countries, including India, this project remains partially or largely unfulfilled – although this state of incompletion still has not prevented it from being very nearly abandoned in several instances.

It is increasingly evident that social policy has a significance that goes beyond even the valid concerns about basic equity and minimal living standards, which form part of the social and economic rights of citizens. In fact, it can play a major role in the capitalist development project, at several levels. At the most basic level, social policies of different types are crucial to the state's capacity to 'manage' modernization, and along with it the huge economic and social shocks that are necessarily generated. Thus, for example, social policies of affirmative action in parts of Southeast Asia (as in Malaysia) have been essential to maintaining ethnic harmony during periods when existing income inequalities and social imbalances across groups within the aggregate population would be otherwise accentuated by economic growth patterns. Similarly, when overenthusiastic and possibly insensitive developmental projects overturn existing local communities or destroy material cultures without satisfactory replacement, social policy can become the basic instrument for rehabilitation and renewed social integration. The massive human shifts (geographic, economic, social) that most development projects entail are potentially sources of much conflict, and often social policy is the most effective means of containing such conflict – or at least keeping it within levels that do not destabilize society or derail the development project itself.

The second important, and related, role of social policy is of course that of legitimization – not only of the state, but also of the development project itself. This need for legitimization arises both for the long-run process and in terms of short-run crisis management. Thus, over the long run, or planning horizon, it is especially important in growth trajectories that rely on high investment and savings rates, thereby suppressing current consumption in favour of high growth for greater future consumption, and which therefore imply sacrifices typically made by workers and peasants. In such a scenario, social policy that is directed towards providing basic needs and social services to those who are otherwise deprived of the gains from economic growth in terms of increased current consumption, would be not just important but even necessary in ensuring social stability and continuity of the process itself.

In so far as the growth process also generates or entails cyclical volatility in growth or incomes, or has a tendency towards periodic crises of whatever sort, social policy can also serve as a cushion for dampening the worst social effects of crisis, which in turn can contribute to the feasibility and sustainability of the entire process. For example, sudden and severe economic contractions causing sharp peaks of unemployment may be socially easier to tolerate if some forms of unemployment compensation or benefit are provided. Even when the shocks stem from natural rather than economic causes (such as earthquakes or cyclones), social policies in the form of, say, public insurance schemes or micro credit schemes can cushion the worst effects of such shocks, in addition to direct relief. Such strategies have macroeconomic consequences as well: thus, it is now accepted that economies with a large public sector presence (in terms of share of GDP or employment) have more muted business cycles or tend to suffer less extreme recessions.

The fourth crucial role of social policy is in terms of affecting the conditions of labour such that there is an increase in the aggregate social productivity of labour, rather than simply increases in labour productivity in particular sectors which reflect different technological choices. It is now widely recognized that the universal provision of good education and basic health services is an important condition for raising aggregate labour productivity levels. But even other aspects of social policy – such as working conditions, access to other public services, and so on – play important roles in this regard. It is even being accepted that the latter can in turn influence technological choices themselves, and nudge growth trajectories towards 'high road' paths rather than 'low road' strategies which are chiefly dependent upon cheap labour.

In capitalist economies which are quite closely integrated with international markets or which rely on export markets as an engine of growth, social policy has played a very important but largely unsung role in terms of underwriting a significant part of labour costs for private capital and therefore providing employers with greater flexibility and contributing to their external competitive strength. For example, (but not exclusively) in some countries of East Asia, the publicly assisted provision of cheap food to the urban population, along with basic housing, cheap and adequate public transport, basic public health and education services, and so on, effectively meant that substantial portions of the wage basket were at least partly provided by the state. This in turn meant that wages paid by private employers could be correspondingly lower, since basic needs were already to a significant extent taken care of, and this gave such employers a major competitive edge in export markets.

In addition to being an integral part of the economic growth process, social policy also evolves with this process, and changes depending upon how the development process impacts upon different classes and groups. In other words, both the economic policy and the social policy patterns, even when they appear to be unchanging in a statutory sense, are actually quite dynamic and intertwined with the political economy configurations, which also constantly evolve (Ghosh 1995). In case this sounds excessively complicated, consider this example: Certain types of industrialization strategy generate particular types of employment – for example, a small-scale engineering industry may grow based on supply and demand linkages emanating from a large publicly funded railway expansion programme. Such increases in employment in turn generate demands for certain types of social policy, such as the provision of housing, health and education facilities for workers' families, and so on. This in turn can create not just greater political voice for such groups but also more productive workforces which in turn encourage the demand for certain types of technological change in products and processes, which in turn again leads to pressure for certain types of public investment which could incorporate such technological innovation.

In contrast to such a positive dynamic process, consider a different pattern of industrialization in which relatively few new jobs are generated, but the profits from such economic activity are quite high. The shift in income distribution will not only shift demand in favour of certain types of non-mass consumption goods, but will also increase the political and lobbying power of capital in various ways. This in turn can influence state policy to encourage fiscal patterns (whether in the form of taxation, direct spending, or subsidies), which further accentuate the income and employment inequalities, and so on. Or they can involve the expansion of certain types of employment, effectively creating or enlarging certain classes such as the urban middle classes, which can then become important in terms of political voice and the ability to influence economic policy decisions as well as to demand certain social policy measures which largely benefit these groups only.

It thus emerges that while social policy is both a desirable and a necessary concomitant of the development process, its existence and form in each social context cannot be taken for granted, but rather depends upon political economy configurations which influence both its extent and its evolution. This is clearly evident from the Indian experience, which shows both the clear need for effective social policy and the relative inadequacy of what has been provided by the state in terms of meeting the basic objectives of the nationalist developmental project. It is argued in this essay that the relative inadequacy of social policy in India during the post-independence period is one important reason why the development project itself has remained incomplete and unsatisfactory in terms of fulfilling the basic requirements of the majority of citizens. These issues are discussed in more detail below.

The Indian development experience in the second half of the twentieth century

The post-independence development experience of India has always excited much interest, not least because, while India is one of the poorest countries in the world in terms of per capita income, it is also the world's largest liberal democracy. Furthermore, it has managed to retain this political system, however inadequate and flawed, while many democratic experiments in other countries have foundered and, not infrequently, collapsed. This raises the obvious question: to what extent has this influenced the nature of social policy in India? Have the pressures on the state that result from democratic functioning meant that the state pays greater attention to particular types of social policy, and which social groups or classes have they benefited? Why has democracy itself not resulted in greater attention to the provision of basic goods and minimally acceptable levels of public services for all citizens?

These issues are further complicated by the fact that India has not only a system of liberal democracy but also a federal polity, in which a substantial number of the concerns which are particularly important from the perspective of social policy (land reforms, education, health, rural infrastructure) are either specifically 'state government subjects' or are concurrently under both state and central governments. This in turn means that the different political groupings in different state governments can have significant implications for both social policy and its effects. This partly explains why there is so much regional variation in terms of major demographic, economic and social variables across states. There is a further dynamic as well, in that certain types of social policy, as discussed above, have ripple and process effects which affect the various classes in society directly, but also determine their desire and appetite for further public intervention. This point is elaborated below, when the specific experience of some states is considered. But first it is necessary to provide a brief review of the development experience in general.

At the time of independence from colonial rule in the mid-twentieth century, there was broad social consensus in India about the role of the state as a crucial player in the development process. State-led capitalism and state intervention in various ways were seen as essential instruments in the development of a relatively autonomous Indian capitalism, displacing metropolitan capital from the pre-eminent position it had occupied in the colonial economy. The economic policy regime that was erected in the 1950s had its roots in the nationalist freedom struggle, which emphasized that freedom meant freedom not only from political control, but also from external economic domination. It was felt that this could not be ensured without giving the state in independent India a major role in building up infrastructure, expanding and strengthening the productive base of the economy, setting up new financial institutions and regulating and co-ordinating economic activity. This was recognized to be necessary for building capitalism itself, though some no doubt entertained the fond hope that all this would add up to an eventual transition to socialism.

However, there were a number of features of India's post-independence growth strategy that structurally limited the potential of the economic system to expand in a sustainable manner. Many of these features, which stemmed from the political economy of class configurations at the time, contributed in turn to the specific manner in which the development process unfolded and to the limitations of social policy in accelerating the process of development. The most significant such feature was the inability of the Indian state in general to address the most basic form of inequality in the country – that concerning the ownership and control over land. Despite the overt declarations regarding the need for land reforms and for curbing the concentration of economic power, relatively little was done to attack or redress asset and income inequality. Similarly, while some monopolistic practices were curbed, private asset concentration in the industrial sector was never really challenged. In fact, state intervention became yet another mechanism for existing monopolists to consolidate their positions.

One consequence of the associated persistence of asset and income inequality was that there were definite limits to the expansion of the market for mass consumption goods in the country (Bharadwaj 1994). This in turn meant that employment and income growth in the private sector was limited. The absence of any radical land redistribution meant that the domestic market, especially for manufactured goods, remained socially narrowly based. It also meant that the growth of agricultural output, though far greater than in the colonial period, remained well below potential levels.

Under these circumstances, continuous growth in state spending became essential for the growth of the market since it was the key element in whatever overall dynamics the system displayed. Further, given the strength and assertiveness of the domestic industrial capitalists, the government was not in a position to discipline them to the extent required to launch a mercantilist strategy that sought to use cheap labour resources as the base for a thrust into the international market for manufactured mass consumption goods (Amsden 1989; Wade 1990).[1] This meant that the stimulus for growth had to be internal, even though the autonomous expansion of the domestic market was constrained by the inequality of asset distribution.

The central government provided domestic capitalists with a large 'once-and-for-all' market for manufactures by widening and intensifying import protection and encouraging import-substituting industrialization. It then sought to expand that market through its own current and capital expenditures (Chakravarty 1987). Simultaneously, it supported the domestic capitalist class by investing in crucial infrastructure sectors. Like many other Asian newly industrializing countries, control of financial intermediation was seen as key to the process of development, and therefore the Indian government also concerned itself with channelizing household savings to finance private investment through the creation of a number of industrial development banks (Chandra 1988).

For the first two decades after Independence, this strategy did pay dividends in terms of economic growth. Rates of industrial growth were creditable by international standards, the country built up a diversified industrial base, and the public sector expanded rapidly. As a consequence, public economic activity was able to continue to provide crucial infrastructure services, industrial raw materials and capital goods to sustain industrial growth even when the foreign exchange available to import these commodities was limited. However, because this strategy did not involve a widening of the mass market in any significant way, it proved to be unsustainable beyond a point. By the mid-1960s, the 'once-and-for-all' stimulus offered by import substitution was exhausted. Further, the ability of the state to continue to serve as the engine of growth through its own expenditure was undermined by its inability to raise adequate resources through taxation and other means. This reflected not only the state's inability to discipline the domestic elites in a manner necessary for rapid industrialization, but also the fact that this lack of discipline involved explicit and implicit subsidisation of private investor's activities.

The consequence of this was that by the late 1960s, aggregate growth decelerated. The growth revival of the 1980s was once again based on increasing state expenditure, this time relying on the rapid (and ultimately unviable) accumulation of public external debt and on an import boom, which allowed the consumerist aspirations of the growing middle class to be at least partially satisfied. This process in turn was halted by the balance of payments crisis of 1990–91, which heralded the onset of a more systematic neo-liberal economic programme, involving wide-ranging deregulation, liberalization of many activities and the reduction of overt state involvement in a number of crucial economic areas.

Over the 1990s, the Indian economy experienced rates of growth averaging between 5 and 6 per cent, and very substantial increases in income accruing to a small minority of the population, which have fuelled the increases in market demand. Essentially the last two decades of the twentieth century marked the emergence of a slightly different macroeconomic strategy, which was openly based on the demand stimulus emanating from certain sections of capital and what could be called a 'labour aristocracy' comprising middle-class professional groups and more skilled workers. While this demand was necessarily highly import-intensive, the very fact that it could be fulfilled because of the combination of deregulation and import liberalization meant a short-lived boom in certain consumer goods sectors. However, by the turn of the decade (and the century) it was already evident that the limits to this type of expansion had also been exhausted, and the growth process decelerated once again.[2]

The economies of South Asia – and especially India – are often portrayed in comparative discussion as among the 'success stories' of the developing world in the period since the early 1990s. The sense that the Indian economy performed relatively well during this period may simply reflect the much more depressing or chaotic experiences in the rest of the developing world, with the spectacular financial crises in several of the most important and hitherto dynamic late industrializers in East Asia and Latin America, and the continuing stagnation or even decline in much of the rest of the South. Compared to this, the Indian economy was largely stable and was also spared the type of extreme crisis that became almost a typical feature of emerging markets elsewhere. But the picture of improved performance is a misleading one at many levels, since in fact the Indian economy experienced economic growth that was actually less impressive than what was achieved in the preceding decade. Further, the growth process was characterized by low employment generation, greater income inequality and the persistence of poverty. In other words, despite some very apparent successes in certain sectors or pockets, on the whole the process of global economic integration did little to cause a dramatic improvement in the material conditions of most of the population, and added to the greater vulnerability and insecurity of the economies in the region.

Thus, the rate of growth of aggregate GDP in constant prices was between 5.5 per cent and 5.8 per cent in each five-year period since 1980, and the process of accelerated liberalization of trade and capital markets did not lead to any change from this overall pattern. Further, while investment ratios increased slightly (as share of GDP) this reflected the long-term secular trend, and in fact the rate of increase decelerated compared to earlier periods. More significantly, the period since 1990 was marked by very low rates of employment generation. Rural employment in the period 1993–94 to 1999–2000 grew at the very low annual rate of less than 0.6 per cent per annum, lower than any previous period in post-Independence history, and well below (infact, only one-third) of the rate of growth of rural population. Urban employment growth, at 2.3 per cent per annum, was also well below that of earlier periods, and employment in the formal sector stagnated.[3]

Other indicators point to disturbing changes in patterns of consumption. For example, per capita food grain consumption declined from 476 grams per day in 1990 to only 418 grams per day in 2001.[4] The National Sample Survey data also suggest that even aggregate calorific consumption per capita declined from just over 2,200 calories per day in 1987–88 to around 2,150 in 1999–2000. Given the aggregate growth rates and the evidence of improved lifestyles among a minority, this points to a substantially worsening income distribution, which is also confirmed by the survey data. While the evidence on poverty has been muddied by changes in the procedure of data collection, which have made the recent survey data non-comparable with earlier estimates, overall indicators suggest that while the incidence of head-count poverty had been declining from the mid-1970s to 1990, subsequently that decline has been slowed or halted (Sen 2002). Meanwhile, declining capital expenditure by the government has been associated with more infrastructure bottlenecks and worsening provision of basic public services.

The major positive feature which is frequently cited, that of the overall stability of the growth process compared to the 'boom-and-bust' cycles in other emerging markets, reflects the relatively limited extent of capital account liberalization over much of the period, and the fact that the Indian economy was never really chosen as a favourite of international financial markets over this period. In other words, because it did not receive large inflows of speculative capital, it did not suffer from large outflows either. Meanwhile, stability in the balance of payments was imparted by the substantial inflows of workers' remittances from temporary migrant workers in the Gulf and other regions.

The less than satisfactory performance during the decade of economic liberalization was not just the result of the nature of integration with the global economy. It also reflected the continuing contradictions in Indian political economy that have been so crucial in inhibiting economic growth and reducing the wider spread of its benefits across all the citizenry, over most of the second half of the twentieth century.

There were at least four such mutually reinforcing and interrelated political economy contradictions (Patnaik 1998). First, the state has had to simultaneously fulfil two different roles that have turned out to be incompatible in the long run. On the one hand it has had to maintain growing expenditure, in particular investment expenditure, in order to keep the domestic market expanding. At the same time, however, the state exchequer has been the medium through which large-scale transfers have been made to the capitalist and proto-capitalist groups, so that the state effectively became the most important instrument for primary accumulation by the domestic bourgeoisie in its various manifestations. This has occurred through various mechanisms such as tolerance of fairly widespread and growing tax evasion, actual reduction in tax rates and incidence, a variety of subsidies and transfers, lucrative contracts and government procurement policies, and most recently even through the privatization of public assets. This contradiction between these two different roles of the state has been necessarily manifested in the government's worsening fiscal position. Since in such circumstances the continued increases in public expenditure which would be required to sustain domestic demand would only be possible through increased borrowing, there are obvious limits on the process over time. So the effort to combine political legitimacy with economic dynamism created contradictions that could not be resolved within the existing parameters of macroeconomic strategy.

The second contradiction lay in a point already mentioned above: the inability of the state to impose a minimum measure of 'discipline' and 'respect for law' among the capitalists, without which no capitalist system can be tenable. Disregard for the laws of the land, including especially those relating to taxes and also other laws which affected the economic functioning of the system, was an important component of capitalist primary accumulation in the post-independence Indian experience. This absence of a collective discipline in turn meant that a successful transition could not be made from an explicitly interventionist regime to an alternative viable capitalist regime with state intervention of a different and less overt kind. Thus, as already noted, the states of countries like Japan and South Korea were also strongly interventionist, but these were forms of interventionism based on close collaboration between the state and capital, which also simultaneously promoted fairly rigorous discipline among the capitalists. However, in India because the domestic capitalist class as a whole proved manifestly incapable of submitting to or imposing upon itself a similar degree of discipline, such an alternative state-supported capitalist regime could not emerge. This is why the only feasible alternative to the earlier *dirigisme* was seen to be a process of deregulation and liberalization that also involved exposing the economy to the caprices of international capital, and reduced its ability to withstand shocks.

The third contradiction had its roots in the social and cultural ambience of a developing country like India. Metropolitan capitalism, which is characterized by continuous product innovation, has experienced the phenomenon of newer goods constantly entering the market and even creating new lifestyles, whereas most developing countries have not only less dynamic innovative capacity because of fewer resources being devoted to such innovation, but also more narrow markets which cannot benefit from economies of scale to the same degree. This creates an imbalance between the possibilities of domestic production and the patterns of demand emanating from the relatively affluent sections of society who account for much of the growth of potential demand for consumer goods. The international demonstration effect has been a powerful instrument in the hands of metropolitan capital in its efforts to prise open the markets of developing countries in general, and India has been no exception to this phenomenon.

The fourth contradiction reflected the political economy configurations in India throughout this period, which implied a high level of social tolerance for high and growing asset inequality, persistent poverty and low levels of human development among a vast section of the population, especially in the rural areas. Two striking features of this pattern of development, even in the more dynamic phases, have been the growing rural–urban divide in terms of per capita incomes, and the inadequacy of productive employment generation relative to the expansion in population. The same sociopolitical forces which allowed such features to persist and become accentuated, also meant that social policy which ensured the provision of basic needs to the entire population was never a priority, nor were provisions which focused on improved work conditions in most workplaces. These issues are considered in more detail below.

Social policy in the Indian development process

Political theorists may be tempted to draw insights from the rather haphazard pattern of social policy implementation in India, finding in its very lack of direction and vision some association with the chaotic democratic polity within which it occurred, and the variegated demands which were sought to be fulfilled at different points of time. Most social policy provisioning has not been universal in terms of its actual effects, even when it has been declared as such. Rather, it has been directed to specific (and restricted) target groups. And almost always, these groups included those with sufficient political voice, such as urban organized workers or, increasingly during the 1990s, particular caste groupings. There have also been much-trumpeted attempts to include (in however limited a fashion) a small proportion of those who naturally appear to be 'deserving', such as households under the poverty line, women from lower-income groups, and so on. However, because such provisioning, whether in terms of protective legislation or in terms of actual resource transfers, has been extremely limited relative to the scale of requirement, it has meant that social policy has not been a basic instrument of development strategy in the manner outlined in the previous section. Rather, it has emerged essentially in the form of ad hoc responses to particular demands emanating from groups that (at least temporarily) have acquired some degree of political voice.

Nevertheless, it is also true that the overall development strategy, however flawed it was in terms of low social development and the lack of fulfilment of basic needs, did at least meet some of the functions of social policy mentioned above. Thus, in very broad terms, the management of at least some of the social effects of modernization was achieved in that the most destabilizing effects were avoided. Similarly, the legitimization of and indeed the social acceptance of the suppression of current consumption on the part of workers and peasants, was also achieved; however, as pointed out above, the same was not true of the capitalist class and the elites who were unwilling to accept the economic discipline necessary for a sustained path of aggregate development. It is also true that the growing size of the public sector served as a cushion against very sharp fluctuations in aggregate economic activity. However, in a longer-term sense the economic regime and associated social policy failed miserably in raising aggregate social labour productivity and reducing the employment slack in the system, or in underwriting labour costs for employers, including exporters.

The more significant forms of social policy in the Indian context have included: agrarian reform; food procurement and distribution; education; employment creation through public works; affirmative action in the form of reservation for public services employment and educational institutions; anti-poverty programmes directed towards small asset creation or micro credit; changes in forms and structures of governance through decentralization and some devolution of resources (Isaac and Franke 2000). Some of these are considered in more detail below. It should be remembered that other aspects of social policy that have been significant elsewhere have been missing. Thus, the substantial public provision of basic housing and of basic health services, that were cornerstones of social policy in East Asia (Singh 1995), has been absent in the Indian case in almost all of the states. Similarly, there has been very little in the form of social insurance programmes.

Land reforms

Under the Indian Constitution, land reforms are placed under the purview of the state governments. This means that there have been very wide variations in their incidence, extent and effectiveness. It would be fair to say that, by and large, the record in this regard is not all that impressive, and certainly there has been no substantial transformation of landholding patterns and agrarian relations across the country through government action, comparable to that which has occurred in some countries of East Asia such as Japan, South Korea and Taiwan China (Bandyopadhyay 1986). However, over time, there have been changes across the country, and particularly in certain states, which have changed the agrarian landscape to some extent. Thus, in the 1950s the worst forms of absentee landlordism were done away with, most dramatically in the Zamindari Abolition Act of 1952 in Uttar Pradesh, but by and large the monopoly of land remained intact in most of rural India. There have been two significant experiences of more substantive land reform: in the state of Kerala in the 1950s and 1960s, and in the state of West Bengal in the 1980s. It is worth noting that in both cases, the attempts at changing land relations were initiated by left-oriented governments who had come to power on just such an explicit programme. In Kerala, the focus was dominantly on land redistribution and improving the conditions of agricultural labourers. In West Bengal, the main focus was on stabilizing the conditions of tenants by formalizing and registering their contracts, to reduce eviction and other forms of harassment, and specifying limits on the rent shares that could be extracted (a fairly drastic reduction from the prevailing one-third rent share to one-quarter). In both states, the process of land reform was accompanied or followed by other social measures that reflected both the impetus from the state governments in question, and the demands emanating from ordinary people as part of the very dynamic set in motion by the initial agrarian reform. In both cases there were also some initial improvements in agricultural productivity: thus, West Bengal experienced the highest rate of growth of agriculture of all of the states of India over the 1980s, and the 'agrarian impasse' of the state was seen to have been overcome (Lieten 1992). However, the other ripple effects that could be anticipated – in terms of wider internal markets for domestic production, generally improved infrastructure conditions, and so on – were much more limited, largely because meaningful agrarian reform itself was so limited in the other parts of the country.

The absence of any radical land redistribution across most of the country meant that the domestic market, especially for manufactured goods, remained socially narrowly based. It also meant that the growth of agricultural output in the aggregate, though far greater than in the colonial period, remained well below its potential. Such growth as did occur was largely confined to a relatively narrow stratum of landlords-turned-capitalists and sections of rich peasants who had improved their economic status. And the large mass of peasantry, faced with insecure conditions of tenure and often obtaining a small share in the outputs they produced, had neither the means nor the incentive to invest. The prospect of increasing productivity and incomes in rural India (which was home to the majority of its population) in order to stimulate domestic demand was therefore restricted.

For the past decade or more, land reforms and other interventions for institutional change have been almost forgotten in the Indian policy debate.

Even the plan documents, which earlier at least paid lip service to the idea of land reform, have recently abandoned even the pretence of concern over such reform. Indeed, insofar as such changes are talked of at all, they are usually along the lines of furthering the corporatization of agriculture, increasing plantation-type organizational structures, and so on. However, land reforms – or institutional changes of various sorts – remain crucial to the sustainable expansion of agricultural growth and productivity in the various regions of India, and are precisely the types of social policy that would play significant roles in terms of furthering the development project. These need not necessarily be land reforms in the classic sense of land redistribution, but can encompass a range of measures which would vary according to the specific requirements of different regions and states.

In many parts of India at present, not only does smallholder agriculture dominate in both ownership and occupancy of land, but also tenurial patterns are still such as to deny security of tenure or viability of holdings. Similarly, credit and marketing arrangements are often monopolistic or monopsonistic in character, and are skewed against the interests of small and marginal cultivators. Fragmentation of holdings, even very small ones, makes cultivation more difficult, less viable, and discourages certain types of investment such as in sustainable irrigation practices. In some areas, control over water has become possibly even more important than control over land, and this also remains highly unequal. Therefore, new patterns of institutional change must be thought of which will incorporate these changing conditions and different regional contexts. The notion of 'land reform', far from being forgotten, must therefore be widened and expanded to cover a range of measures for institutional change in agriculture, which will make for viable smallholder cultivation.

Food procurement and distribution

The original objectives of India's public food management system were threefold: to maintain a reasonable degree of price stability; to provide some producer incentives to cultivators by ensuring that prices remained above estimated costs; and to provide a degree of food security to consumers (Krishnaji 1990). The system rested on the twin pillars of public procurement with minimum support prices provided at farm gate for a range of major crops, and public distribution organized at the state level through a network of Fair Price Shops providing some food items at subsidized prices. Of course, the system was never completely successful, either in terms of its spread, or in terms of fully achieving its basic objectives. Public food grain procurement remained confined largely to certain established 'surplus' states (such as Punjab, Haryana, Uttar Pradesh and Andhra Pradesh) without stretching its regional purview. In terms of food distribution for consumers, most of the rural population (except in some states such as Kerala and

Andhra Pradesh) did not have access to Fair Price Shops and the rationing system. And the attempt at universal provision, in a context of inadequate resources being allocated for the purpose, inevitably meant that many of those requiring cheaper food were in fact the ones who did not have access. Nevertheless, over the 1970s and 1980s, the network did certainly expand in physical terms and Indian food and agricultural prices were certainly more stable than world market prices for such commodities.

However, in the 1990s the system came under increasing pressure – and even under attack – as various measures aimed at first targeting access to the Public Distribution System to only those officially defined as 'poor' and then at reducing the subsidy offered to other consumers, undermined the consumer network. These measures, which were supposed to reduce the food subsidy, had precisely the opposite effect of increasing it, because they led to declining off-take (sales) from the Fair Price Shops (Swaminathan 2000). Because procurement levels did not decline but rather increased, this led to the growth of stocks held by the public system, and therefore to higher carrying costs of holding all this excess food grain. In the early years of the twenty-first century, the level of publicly held food stocks reached around 64 million tonnes, compared to the buffer norms of 16–24 million tonnes.[5] However, cultivators have been under greater pressure, and increasingly have felt inadequately served by the public system, because they have had to cope with rising input prices, as various explicit and implicit agricultural subsidies are reduced, at the same time as trade liberalization has exposed them to import competition from highly subsidized production in the developed countries.

All this has been taking place in a context of the overall deterioration of per capita availability of food grain. Unlike the previous decades since Independence, the 1990s witnessed no trend increase in per capita availability of food grain, and in recent years the situation has deteriorated even relative to the levels achieved thirty years earlier. In fact, per capita cereals availability in 2001, at 417 grams per day, was the lowest it had been since 1975, which was itself an outstandingly bad year. Per capita calorie consumption also declined over this period, as mentioned above. Clearly, therefore, while the food procurement and distribution system played a positive but limited social role especially in the 1970s and 1980s, since the early 1990s it has been undermined to the point where it is almost on the verge of being dismantled and replaced with entirely private operations.[6]

Employment and public works

The inability to generate such employment, thus improving aggregate productivity of labour in the Indian economy rather than just in a few chosen sectors, has been the most obvious symptom of the failure of the Indian economic development process over the post-independence decades

(Bhalla 1991; Jha 1997), along with the persistence of widespread absolute poverty and the slow rate of improvement in human development indicators. This is not just a problem of welfare, since it represents a huge waste of human resources that are crucial to building the economy, and suggests that Indian growth could have been both faster and more equitable if only the enormous labour reserves had been productively utilized.

One of the major disappointments of the neo-liberal adjustment strategy in India in the 1990s was the inadequate generation of employment. In this period, the rate of employment generation was below both the rate of growth of output and the increase in the labour force. It could be argued that this reflected increases in labour productivity which are to be valued. However, the persistence of widespread overt unemployment along with disguised unemployment in fact not only represents a huge waste of resources; it has also emerged as perhaps the most significant problem, leading directly and indirectly to a host of other social tensions.

In the rural areas, aggregate employment grew at around 0.6 per cent per annum over the decade – that is, around one-third of the rate of growth of the labour force during the same period. There was an increase in agricultural self-employment, reflecting the shift away from non-agriculture, and also, in large part, caused by a distress-induced increase in female unpaid family work. Regular employment declined and the casualization of wage employment continued to increase. All this manifested the effects of the overall neo-liberal economic strategy, which affected rural employment in the following ways: actual declines in government spending on infrastructure (as a share of GDP) and on rural development (in absolute terms) in the central budgets; reduced central government transfers to state governments, which have thereby been forced to cut back on their own spending; diminished real expenditure on rural employment and anti-poverty schemes; declines in public infrastructural and energy investments which affect the rural areas; reduced spread and rise in prices of the public distribution system for food; cuts in social expenditure areas such as education, health and sanitation; financial liberalization measures which have effectively reduced the availability of credit to priority sectors including agriculture and small scale industries.

Even in the urban areas, the rate of employment generation in the 1990s was dramatically lower, at only 1.52 per cent, less than half the growth rate of previous periods. Total organized sector employment increased by less than one per cent per annum.[7] The trend was towards an increase in casual employment and a trend decline in regular employment for both men and women. For men, the increase in casual employment was largely at the cost of regular employment. For women, on the other hand, both casual and regular work appear to have increased after the reforms in the urban areas, but casual contracts have dominated. This is part of a wider process of the feminization of work observed in all developing countries, which has also been associated with employers' greater preference for female employees largely because of the lower wages and inferior working conditions associated with such employment.

Thus, employment in the formal sector fell in both rural and urban areas, and was not adequately compensated in quantitative terms by the more insecure and typically lower paid employment opportunities in the non-formal sectors of the economy. This created two related effects. Since the overwhelming majority of the workers in India are in the unorganized sector where wage incomes are not indexed to inflation, they are disproportionately affected by inflation and especially by the rise of food prices – and this proportion of population increased over the 1990s. Thus, not only are the employment conditions faced by most of the labour force more volatile and insecure, the wages that emerge from such contracts are also less certain to command basic necessities for working class and peasant households. Second, the very insecurity of employment, especially in urban areas, has created pressures for secondary activities that could add to the household income and has also caused increased resentment of those with significantly higher standards of living.

It is in this context of low employment generation in the system as a whole, that the inadequacy of social policy in the form of employment creation through public works must be judged. Clearly, this is a macroeconomic context that cries out for substantial expansion of public involvement in the process of employment generation, especially in the more recent period when recession and under-utilized capacity have characterized the Indian macro economy. The obvious solution would be to use public works, in both rural and urban areas, as a means of employment creation as well as to build and maintain crucial physical infrastructure assets or even to provide basic public services which are currently provided very inadequately.

Unfortunately, such public-works-led employment generation has been far below the potential of what could be feasibly achieved, even within the broad fiscal constraints of the government. The 1980s marked something of an exception to this phenomenon, especially in terms of rural employment expansion. An important feature of rural employment generation over the 1980s was the diversification of employment away from agriculture and primary activities, towards secondary and service-sector employment. In general this was a positive feature, especially as it was accompanied by an overall growth of rural employment in most regions of the country and was also associated with a trend decline in the incidence of rural poverty. There is now significant evidence that the main dynamic source of rural employment generation over the period from the mid-1970s to the late 1980s was the external agency of the state rather than forces internal to the rural economy.[8] Indeed, the role of dynamic agriculture as a stimulus was significant only in states such as Punjab and Haryana, where agricultural incomes had crossed a minimum threshold and where further increases in agricultural output were accompanied by labour displacement rather than greater labour absorption. Outside this limited region, the pull was provided mainly by external – that is, governmental – stimuli.

The 1980s was a period when, along with a rapid increase in all sorts of subsidies and transfers to households from government, there was a very large increase in expenditure on the rural sector by both state and central governments. More generally, throughout the period political developments tended to give rural interests greater power and they were able to command an improvement in the historically low share of government expenditure benefiting rural areas. Although this improvement in share should not be exaggerated, an indication may be the fact that nearly 60 per cent of all new government jobs created during the decade accrued to rural areas.[9] By 1987–88, nearly two-thirds of the regular non-agricultural employees in rural areas were employed by the government, which accounted for four-fifths of such regular job creation during that decade.

Thus, the total quantum of increased flow of public resources into rural areas must have been significant. This flow of resources took two predominant forms. There was, first, a fairly large expansion of 'rural development' schemes with an explicit redistributive concern. This included not only the various rural employment and IRDP (Integrated Rural Development Programmes), but also a plethora of special schemes for a variety of identifiable 'target' groups. These programmes were definitely less than entirely successful: they spawned a large bureaucracy and they became a focal point for the politics of 'distributive coalitions'. Yet, even though the intended beneficiaries were often short-changed because of such leakages, these programmes still represented a fairly massive net transfer to rural areas.

The second avenue by which resources flowed from government to rural areas was through the greater accessibility of the rural elites to the varied benefits of government expenditure. In part, this was a result of greater mobility due to better transport infrastructure. But it was also related to the politics of that time: as governments changed frequently (particularly at the state level) more new favours, not just jobs, but also various types of agencies and contracts, had to be distributed more often, and the rural areas got a greater than normal share in such largesse. The resulting flow of resources and the consequent generation of rural demand led to growing opportunities for diversification of the self-employed from agriculture to non-agriculture. Of course, the direct access to government permanent employment and also to many other resources was largely confined to the better-off and more powerful groups in rural society, to whom such incomes were more lucrative than agriculture. Further, such access to better employment or other resources was dominantly accorded to male workers rather than to women workers.

However, over the 1990s, as seen above, several of the public policies which had contributed to more employment and less poverty in the rural areas in the earlier decade were reversed (Sen and Jha 2001). Direct rural employment programmes of both central and state governments have declined in terms of scope, number of workdays generated and number of workers able to benefit from such programmes. In the macroeconomic situation prevailing at the turn of the century, this was more than just an obvious failure. The economy was characterized by low unemployment equilibrium, with *ex ante* savings greater than *ex ante* investment, as expressed in a number of variables: foreign exchange reserves well above the level required by the import requirement and the need to protect the balance of payments from runs of short-term capital flows; excess holding of public food grain stocks at more than four times the desired level; high level of unemployment of labour, both open and disguised; excess capacity in industry. The apparent inability of the government, in such a context, to increase the fiscal allocation and extend the implementation of a large-scale programme of public works, despite the recommendations of a number of economists and popular demands for this, is a manifestation of the changed political economy context in which such evident problems and their solutions can be ignored, essentially because foreign investors and domestic large capital are not seen to require it.

Education

The slow improvements in literacy and education for both men and women remain major failures of the Indian development process. Article 45 of the Directive Principles of State Policy of the Indian Constitution, formulated in 1949, declared that 'The State shall endeavour to provide, within a period of ten years from the commencement of this Constitution, for free and compulsory education for all children until the age of fourteen years.' Despite this commitment, India still contains the largest number of illiterate people in the world, and also the largest number of illiterate women.[10] The progress of improvement in literacy has been very slow, literacy among females remains substantially below that for males, and even at the present time, nearly half of the female population of the country remains illiterate. Furthermore, female literacy rates are much lower (usually between 50 and 70 per cent) among Scheduled Tribes and Scheduled Castes, as well as among certain minority groups.

This reflects the fact that education has unfortunately not been a priority of government policy, or a major instrument of social policy, in India over the past five decades (Dreze and Sen 1999; The Probe Team 1999). Public spending on education, at around 3 per cent of GDP, has been approximately half the international norm of 6 per cent, and many multiples less than the ratio in some of the East and Southeast Asian countries. The consequent denial of education to all citizens is not only a failure in terms of human rights, but also a failure in terms of future possibilities for development, as is widely recognized.

Over the 1990s, the Total Literacy Campaigns and various Adult Literacy Missions attempted to rectify the gap in terms of adult literacy, with varying degrees of success in different states. The attempt was to establish district-level literacy committees with active people's participation, with follow-up schemes for providing access to reading material relevant for newly literates. There is no doubt that this has led to some improvement in the rate of increase of literacy in the past decade, but there are still very significant state-wide variations. This is once again because education remains dominantly a 'state government subject'. Certain states, such as Kerala, with a longer history of literacy and education movements as well as a different level of political awareness of the need for such emphasis, have performed much better in this respect and have literacy levels approaching those of developed countries despite the much lower per capita income.

School enrolment ratios showed a significant increase across India from the mid-1980s onwards, although there is a substantial amount of evidence from micro studies and other surveys that these are typically overestimates. However, even the NSS shows a substantial increase in 'participation in education' for the age-group 6–11 years and 11–14 years in 1999–2000 compared to the earlier large surveys of 1987–88 and 1993–94, and the increases were greater for girls than for boys over this period. However, even with these data there is need for caution in interpretation. While the 'usual status' category (which shows the response to the question 'What do you usually do over the course of a year?') indicates a substantial increase in education for these age-groups, the daily status and weekly status categories show a much lower level of participation in education, especially among girls. This suggests that even when children, especially girls, are formally registered in schools and therefore feel that is their usual activity, they may not be attending regularly for a variety of reasons. Similarly, drop-out rates remain high, and tend to be much higher for girls than for boys.

A number of schemes for increasing access to primary education have been introduced by both central and state governments in India over the 1990s. Most of these schemes have been foreign-aid-driven, in that the major source of funding for such programmes has come from foreign bilateral and multilateral donors. These include the District Primary Education Project (DPEP) which is spread across most states, the Shiksha Karmi and Lok Jumbish projects in Rajasthan, the CEC in West Bengal, and also schemes in Maharashtra and Madhya Pradesh. Many of these schemes include in their primary aims, the reduction of gender disparity in access to schooling, and have accordingly introduced certain changes in the education system. The only danger is that, in a context of reduced public spending on education as a whole, such schemes may involve a diversion of overall resources from the public education system to NGO-led schemes, which may be detrimental to the basic cause of ensuring equal access to education for all.

Affirmative action

The basic form of affirmative action as public policy in India has been in the form of reservations for government jobs and in public educational institutions for certain social groups defined as underprivileged. There have been no attempts to force or encourage private-sector reservation of a similar type. For most of the post-independence period, such reservation was confined to the Scheduled Castes and Scheduled Tribes, usually at just over one-fifth of the total jobs/seats available. In the later 1980s, reservation was also introduced for social groups defined as 'Other Backward Classes', which were essentially socially lower castes who had achieved levels of political and economic voice far greater than their perceived social positions. These new reservations, which effectively meant that just above half the positions would be reserved, led to urban middle-class outrage and protests at the time that they were introduced. Ironically, however, soon after the introduction of such new reservations, a freeze on new employment at central government level and for most state governments, effectively meant that such reservations became irrelevant. However, they did make some difference in terms of access to institutions of higher education for students from such groups.

Overall, such affirmative action has had relatively little impact on the broader socioeconomic position of the population belonging to the defined social groups. Nevertheless, it must be acknowledged that such social policy has a long gestation period in terms of effects, and that it should be situated within a more evolutionary perspective on social dynamics, within which it can clearly play a positive role.

Conclusion

It has been argued in this chapter that social policy in India, while achieving some limited successes in terms of management of the contradictions and instabilities emerging from the development process, has nevertheless been inadequate in terms of the basic functions defined at the start of this chapter. Furthermore, the recent changes in social policy and public intervention that have been associated in India with the 'globalization' phase of neo-liberal economic reform, may have actually undermined some of the gains that were achieved earlier. This is because recent macroeconomic tendencies have been associated with greater inequality and fragility of incomes, which has, in turn, certain important social implications.

Thus, the process of economic liberalization along with the pattern of government spending has been associated with a multiplication of the real incomes of richer groups. Financial liberalization has involved an explosion in financial sector activities and incomes in this sector. Increasingly, professional incomes in finance approach the levels in developed countries, even while real wages in the rest of the economy stagnate and general employment becomes more precarious. Other white-collar services, and related incomes from activities such as construction, trade, advertising and so on which feed on the boom in consumption of higher-income groups, have also increased dramatically. Trade liberalization has brought growing access to a much wider range of consumption goods and international brand names to the Indian upper and middle classes. The apparently insatiable hunger for imported goods is evident from the fact that non-oil imports have continued to increase hugely, despite the ongoing recession in domestic manufacturing industry.

Along with this, there has been a cultural revolution of the sort described above, which is also fed by the emergence of satellite television and huge increases in the advertising budgets of companies operating in the Indian market. This has greatly increased the role of the demonstration effect in the consumption patterns of Indian upper- and middle-income groups. And this 'cultural revolution' has been associated with a much more open display of conspicuous consumption than was traditionally prevalent in Indian society. The implications of the spread of such communications, and the effects of postmodern advertising trends in rural India in particular, have been inadequately studied.

In the large metropolises and cities of the country, such a tendency towards open display of wealth and conspicuous consumption has been a feature that has been more and more evident over the past two decades. But observers have also noted this tendency in rural India, in forms that were not previously so obvious, and found in it a reflection of the reduced interaction between the various rural classes, and a diminished concern on the part of rural elites towards the poorer sections, that used to mark the more paternalistic relations of the past. As social relations fragment and become more contractual, they also lose the few elements of cohesiveness that make location-specific communities functional.

It does not take a great deal of sociological insight to realize that this combination of greater material insecurity in terms of both lower real incomes and more precarious employment opportunities for a very large section of the population, combined with the explosion of conspicuous consumption on the part of a relatively small but highly visible minority, may have very adverse social and political consequences. These consequences tend to be exacerbated by the cultural influences that come across as hegemonic, and which increasingly determine the aspirations of the youth in particular. Thus, as mentioned above, there is a premium not only on the joys of material consumption, but also on individualism, the greater proliferation of the idea that success (which essentially is measured in terms of material advancement) reflects individual talent and achievement rather than any wider social processes, and that it can often be achieved only in competition with one's peers. The alienation that comes from the lack of such success – or even from success which is deemed to be inadequate given the ambition – can only too easily be directed towards any apparent or potential competitor in such a system, or even to those who are not in competition but simply represent a group that can be attacked with relative ease. The current streak of venom that is being directed towards various minority groups can be seen as one expression of this trend. So the inability to confront those who are actually benefiting from the system, or even the lack of desire to do so given that they still have the power to distribute some amount of material largesse, means that they cannot be the objects of any aggressive vent for frustration. Rather, the outlet is increasingly found in terms of growing antagonism, increasingly finding violent expression, towards other categories of people who are nearer home, closer in terms of lifestyle and more susceptible to such attack. It is worth noting that often these groups are already among the most disadvantaged and materially weak sections of society.

Thus, increasingly, the pattern of economic growth as well as the inability of extant social policy to ameliorate or reduce the consequent inequalities, has therefore meant that the management of social tensions has become an even more difficult task for the Indian state. In such a context, the need for sensitive and proactive social policy is, at present, an even more pressing need than at any time in the past.

Notes

1. This was in marked contrast, for example, to the South Korean case, where the ability of the state to exercise control and regulate the behaviour of large private capital turned out to be crucial in that country's rapid industrialization.
2. The nature of this recent growth and its important attributes are discussed in much more detail in Chandrasekhar and Ghosh (2002).
3. The only positive feature in employment patterns was the decline in educated unemployment, largely related to the expansion of IT-enabled services in metropolitan and other urban areas. However, while this feature, along with that of software development, has received much international attention, it is still too insignificant in the aggregate economy to make much of a dent: Chandrasekhar (2000).
4. Of course, it has been argued that this can represent a positive diversification of consumption away from foodgrain that is associated with higher living standards. But it is usually the case that aggregate foodgrain consumption does not decline because of indirect consumption of grain (for example, through meat and poultry products that require feed). In any case, the overall decline in calorific consumption (covering all food products) suggests that the optimistic conclusion may not be valid.

5. This in turn has meant increases in the food subsidy bill of the public exchequer, even though it has been associated bizarrely with a decline in the actual amount of grain sold by the Public Distribution System. By the year 2001, just the carrying cost of food grain stocks exceeded the Central Government's total expenditure on Agriculture, Rural Development and Irrigation & Flood Control.
6. However, recent recommendations of a committee to the Government of India have argued for a substantial expansion of the procurement and distribution system, increasing the spread of procurement operations and doing away with targeting in favour of a universal system: High-Level Committee on Long Term Grain Policy (2002).
7. Of course, there have been some recent increases in educated employment opportunities, mainly resulting from the rapid expansion of the IT-enabled services. However, while these have led to declines in the rates of open educated unemployment, they have not been sufficient to make any real dent in aggregate employment conditions.
8. This argument is elaborated upon in Sen and Ghosh (1993) and subsequently in Ghosh (1999).
9. Moreover, NSS data suggest that, despite a low average contribution of only around 5 per cent of total rural employment, the government's contribution was around a fifth when it came to either total rural non-agricultural employment in 1987–88 or the *increments* in total rural employment between 1977–78 and 1987–88.
10. The Census of India 2002 indicates that only around 74 per cent of men and 54 per cent of women are literate – even when a very low standard definition of literacy is used.

Bibliography

Amsden, A. H. (1989) *Asia's Next Giant: South Korea and Late Industrialisation*. New York: Oxford University Press.

Bandyopadhyay, D. (1986) 'Land reforms in India: an Analysis', *Economic and Political Weekly*, 21, A50–A56.

Bhalla, S. (1991) *Report of the Study Group on Employment Generation*. New Delhi: National Commission on Rural Labour (Government of India).

Bharadwaj, K. (1994) *Accumulation, Exchange and Development*. New Delhi: Sage Publications.

Chakravarty, S. (1987) *Development Planning: the Indian Experience*. Delhi: Oxford University Press.

Chandra, N. K. (1988) *The Retarded Economies*. Bombay: Sameeksha Trust and Oxford University Press.

Chandrasekhar, C. P. (2000) 'Information Technology and the Developing Countries: an Indian Case Study', *Human Development Report 2001*. New York: UNDP.

Chandrasekhar, C. P., and Ghosh, J. (2002) *The Market That Failed: a Decade of Neoliberal Economic Reforms in India*. New Delhi: Leftword Books.

Dreze, J., and Sen, A. (1999) *India: Economic Development and Social Opportunity*. New Delhi: Oxford University Press.

Ghosh, J. (1995) 'State Involvement in the Macroeconomy'. In P. Patnaik (ed.), *Themes in Indian Economics: Macroeconomics*. New Delhi: Oxford University Press.

Ghosh, J. (1999) *Trends in Economic Participation and Poverty of Women in the Asia-Pacific Region*. Bangkok: UN-ESCAP.

High-Level Committee on Long Term Grain Policy (2002) *Report of High-Level Committee on Long Term Grain Policy.* New Delhi: Ministry of Finance, Government of India.

Isaac, T. M. T., and Franke, R. (2000) *Local Democracy and Development: People's Campaign for Decentralised Planning in Kerala.* New Delhi: Leftword Books.

Jha, P. (1997) *Agricultural Labour in India.* New Delhi: Vikas Publishing House.

Krishnaji, N. (1990) 'Agricultural Price Policy: a Survey with Reference to India Foodgrain Economy', *Economic and Political Weekly,* 25, A-54.

Lieten, G. K. (1992) *Continuity and Change in Rural West Bengal.* New Delhi: Sage Publications.

Patnaik, P. (1998) *Whatever Happened to Imperialism?* New Delhi: Tulika Books.

Sen, A. (2002) 'Agriculture, Employment and Poverty: Recent Trends in Rural India'. In V. K. Ramachandran and M. Swaminathan (eds), *Agrarian Studies: Essays on Agrarian Relations in Less-Developed Countries.* New Delhi: Tulika Books.

Sen, A., and Ghosh, J. (1993) *Trends in Rural Employment and the Poverty–Employment Linkage.* ILO–ARTEP Working Paper. Geneva: ILO.

Sen, A., and Jha, P. (2001) *Rural Employment: Patterns and Trends form the National Sample Survey.* New Delhi: CESP, JNU.

Singh, A. (1995) *How did East Asia grow so fast? Slow progress towards an analytical consensus.* UNCTAD Discussion Paper. Geneva: UNCTAD.

Swaminathan, M. (2000) *Weakening Welfare: the Public Distribution of Food in India.* New Delhi: Leftword Books.

The Probe Team (1999) *Public Report on Basic Education in India.* New Delhi: Oxford University Press.

Wade, R. (1990) *Governing the Market: Economic Theory and the Role of Government in East Asian Industrialisation.* Princeton: Princeton University Press.

14

Historical Trajectories of Social Policy in Post-Colonial Africa: The Case of Zambia

Guy Mhone

Introduction

As Zambia enters the twenty-first century, it finds social protection, economic development and democracy elusive after about seventy years of colonial rule and about forty years of independent rule. And this in spite of being endowed with a rich mineral resource that had been exploited for more than a century, and in spite of the honourable social and economic development intentions of various governments since the colonial period to the present. This chapter attempts to explore how social policy has evolved in Zambia with the aim of identifying the constraints that have militated against the attainment of its goals to protect and advance the welfare of vulnerable groups in particular, and that of the populace in general.

Not only has the country failed to align social policy to economic policy, but it has also been unable to articulate and execute an adequate social policy regime, while economic development has proved elusive. The issue is not so much that various governments have been unable to see the wisdom or desirability of developing comprehensive social policy and economic development policy regimes, but that even when they have been able to do so with a fair amount of coherence and fanfare, the results have been dismal. The question then is why this has been the case. As will be shown below, it would be too much to expect policy makers during the colonial era to have attempted to live up to the imperatives of social and economic development in the same way that these objectives became to be understood subsequently. Indeed, during the colonial period the interests of the majority were seen to be secondary and relatively immaterial, except in so far as they facilitated the needs of the colonizing minority and settlers. The difficulty arises with respect to the post-independence period, during which time various regimes made strong pronouncements and commitments to both social and economic development in various policy documents, and at times, with the support of various external donor agencies, all of which came to no avail in terms of practical outcomes. It is this inability to actualize desirable or declared social policy objectives in Zambia that we seek to explore.

Government attention is generally focused on the formulation of social policy measures for the formal part of the economy and polity, while the non-formal rural/traditional and urban/informal sectors in which a large proportion if not the majority of the population in Southern Africa resides also has substitute versions of similar forms of social provisioning. A major problem historically has been that government policy has not only been preoccupied with social and economic policy in the formal sector, where it has only addressed the needs of the minority of the population, but it has also tended to ignore social developments in the non-formal sectors, let alone attempted to interrogate the nature of social provisioning in the given country as a whole.

Implications for social policy

In developing countries such as those in Africa, social policy has to be linked to economic policy. The two policy regimes have to be complementary and mutually reinforcing. Within this context, social and economic policies have to reflect the relative contributions of government, households, the individual, and the private sector. The relative roles and contributions of the foregoing parties to meeting social and economic needs should be expected to change over time as the economy's gross domestic product increases. It will be affected by the nature of the political regimes. In a socialist polity, the major forms of social protection would be assumed by the state. In a mixed economy, the relative roles of the various sources of social protection will depend upon the ideological orientation prevailing in government, the class structure and nature of class coalitions, the dimensions of social needs, the level of development of the economy, and the historical legacies in the given country. In a country with major historical economic and social inequities and with relatively low levels of income, and extensive poverty among the majority of its population, the question arises as to whether social and economic policies predicated on a minimalist state and the market as the major allocative mechanism can address the prevailing social and economic backlogs.

A strong case can be made for African countries to embark upon proactive state policies in both the economic and social spheres, especially if the two have to be designed in a mutually complementary and supportive manner. Essentially, not only are comprehensive social and economic policies needed, but so is a comprehensive and integrated approach to both social and economic policies.

First and foremost there is a need for proactive measures to promote an inclusive growth path which should ultimately entail economic and social development as generally understood – that is, a growth process that entails the upliftment of the standard of living of the poorest members of the society in a sustainable manner over the long term. Since market forces have so far failed to resolve past inequities and since they also tend to reinforce inherited socioeconomic legacies, deliberate measures by the state aimed at transforming the economy and empowering the majority of the population are needed. An inclusive growth path results in a number of eventualities that are important for social policy. First, it reduces the number of people that are indigent from among those that are unemployed and from among the working poor. Secondly, improved incomes among the foregoing groups imply that households to which they belong are likely to benefit in that a proportion of the resulting incomes is likely to be directed toward support for member's dependents (those below the age of 15 years and retirees). Thirdly, an inclusive growth path means that as the incomes of individuals and households increase, more income is spent on services such as education, housing, water, energy, transport and so on, in a manner that partly reduces the obligations of the state. Fourthly, a broadened economic base leads to a broadened tax base, which potentially increases the capacity of the state to raise revenues and thus provides for social needs, at the same time that the social demands on the state are being reduced as inclusive development materializes.

The economic strategy implied by the foregoing needs to be complemented by a comprehensive social policy framework. Social policy in this context needs to be devised in manner that complements inclusive development. First, social policy needs to provide a minimum floor of social protection that can be justified on humanitarian and constitutional grounds. Such a minimum floor in part represents an investment in human resources in that it prevents social disintegration among those that are excluded and marginalized, thereby preserving social and political peace, and in that it allows for the conservation of social capital and individual human capital which provides a basis for future development. Secondly, social policy needs to be designed such that it can institutionalize the social wage by providing a minimum of services to allow individuals to engage in employment more productively. Such services may include subsidized transport, housing, health, education, and utilities. Some such services may be targeted at women to release them of household chores and reproductive roles so that they can, like men, maximize their participation in wage employment and income generating activities. Thirdly, social policy needs to address temporary destituteness caused by unemployment, again for humanitarian reasons and in order to preserve human capital. Finally, social policy needs to be targeted at ensuring that those who cannot take care of themselves either because they are old, disabled, young or disengaged from their households and communities, are provided for in a socially acceptable manner.

An appropriate regime that combines social assistance and social insurance would have to be located within an overall social and economic policy framework that promotes inclusive development. Generally, as the economy expands and as household incomes increase, the burden for social protection can be progressively transferred to households and the private sector without necessarily negating the minimum protection regime guaranteed by the state as described above. As other observers have argued, it is necessary at the microeconomic level that policy measures are put in place to empower individuals and households with asset entitlements, income-generating opportunities and capabilities that can allow them to meaningfully participate in economic activities and to provide some social services for themselves, thereby liberating them as human agents. At the macroeconomic level it is necessary that the state provides for an enabling and facilitative environment for inclusive economic development at the same time that it provides for a social safety net to mitigate structural and conjunctural forms of poverty, inequality and vulnerability, while it also facilitates meaningful economic participation.

Nature of the problem

In undertaking a historical review of the evolution of social policy it is necessary to underline some of the structural features of the social policy landscape, which have evolved and persisted over time in a country like Zambia. First, the population has been increasing over the past century, and while gross domestic product has increased appreciably in some periods, the general trend in recent decades has been for per capita incomes to decrease. Second, formal employment has been decreasing in recent years, while non-formal activities have been expanding laterally, trapping increasing numbers of individuals and households in survivalist economic activities that are below the poverty line. As a consequence, social deprivation has been increasing while the capacity of households, the state, and the economy to support the population in terms of provision of employment- and income-generating opportunities and social service provisioning has been declining. HIV/AIDS has exacerbated the problem by negatively impacting on the population, the demographic composition, and on economic growth. The Jobs for Africa Country Report (ILO/UNDP 2000: 4) notes that 'one of the major characteristics of the demographic situation in the country is that it depicts a youthful population, high but declining rate of population growth, high but declining fertility rates, high but stabilizing infant mortality rate, decreasing life expectancy and uneven spatial distribution of the population'.

As matters currently stand in Zambia, all the categories of social need, with the exception perhaps of the working poor, have been increasing in recent years, albeit at a slowing pace. Over the past 40 years or so, Zambia has not been able to realize the goal of economic development, nor has it been able to reduce poverty. Interestingly, during this period inequalities have increased primarily as a result of the compression of incomes at the top of the socio-economic ladder. In Zambia, while conjunctural factors have worsened the social situation, it is clear that there are structural factors at work that have persisted in paralysing the link between social development and economic development, and in worsening the situation at the same time. These structural factors are historical in nature and pose major challenges to present regimes in terms of social policy formulation and implementation.

Zambia inherited a monocultural economy dependent upon copper. The modern economy was grafted onto the primarily traditional subsistence economy with the primary purpose of exploiting copper for export and not with the intention of transforming the economy as whole. The economy subsequently evolved, dominated by an enclave modern sector that had weak links to the traditional primarily rural economy. The fundamental problem that has confronted Zambia historically has been that an economy evolved that did not have the imperative to transform the totality of Zambian society by absorbing the majority of the labour force into modern-based dynamic and productive activities. Indeed, an economy evolved that tended to marginalize and exclude the majority of the populace. This was not seen to be a major problem during the colonial era since the marginal and gradual inclusion of the local labour force into modern activities was indeed a professed aim of social engineering during this era. This legacy has, however, posed a major difficulty for post-independence policy makers whose declared aim has been to transform the economy so that it would be inclusive of the majority, while also ensuring that the economy was diversified enough to guarantee sustainable increases in income and social welfare for all its citizens.

Essentially the social policy problem had two facets. At one end the excluded rural population which was in the majority until the time of independence, continued to wallow in poverty as it remained excluded and marginalized and as the rural economy degenerated through policy neglect and declining terms of trade vis-à-vis the urban economy. At the other end, the urban population was expanding phenomenally as a consequence of rural to urban migration, while labour absorption into productive and dynamic activities in the urban sector was not keeping pace with the rate of rural to urban migration, thereby generating an informal and peripheral economy characterized by poverty and survivalist activities.

Thus while the colonial state was not by intent or design capable of addressing the plight of the rural majority, the post-independence state, even if committed to total upliftment of the majority of the population in both rural and urban areas, failed to live up to its declared intentions. Thus, when, following the international recession of the mid-1970s, the Zambian economy begun to degenerate in a secular manner, from which it has not been able to recover until this day, social welfare deteriorated precipitously in both formal and non-formal sectors, and in both rural and urban areas. Within this context, formal social security provisions have systematically decreased in significance, especially following the adoption of stabilization and structural adjustment measures, and individuals and households have resorted to various non-formal adaptive mechanisms as a substitute for the declining social provisioning by the state. This situation has been exacerbated by the advent of the HIV/AIDS pandemic. It is in the foregoing structural context, entailing the failure to resolve a legacy of enclave development, that the trajectory of social policy failure in Zambia should be viewed and analysed.

As will be shown, throughout this period while conjunctural factors changed the economic and social scene, yielding various policy stances with respect to economic and social policy, the inherited structural predicament was that of an economy unable to precipitate an inclusive development path while its social obligations continued to expand. What is difficult to explain is the fact that from 1964 onwards, the various governments of Zambia methodically churned out development plans and policy documents that articulately and meticulously spelt out the economic and social objectives and strategies needed to address the constraints of the inherited situation so as to precipitate an appropriate development path that would result in desired social and economic outcomes. However, these governments failed to transform this inherited reality in practice. In the process, and subsequently, Zambia finds itself in a major predicament instead. One view on the nature of the dilemma confronting Zambia is expressed by Nyirenda, who has undertaken a review of planning, social policy and the delivery of social services in Zambia in both colonial and post-independence periods. Nyirenda observes that:

> While colonial era service provision was characterized by the phenomenon of imposition, post-independence services are a product of foreign recipes and borrowed tools. A common factor in both eras is the fact that the majority of social services are either rejected by their potential consumers or where they have been used, they have tended to produce counter-productive results.   (Nyirenda 1975: p. x)

Following a review and an analysis of social policy and the delivery of social services in both colonial and postcolonial periods Nyirenda concludes as follows:

> A major finding of the study is that a wide gap exists between planning approaches and social service delivery mechanisms on the one hand and the Zambian way of life on the other. This is a troublesome paradox in a country where both the national leadership and the lead value are committed to the ideal of improving the welfare of all citizens. On the basis of this finding, a humanistic approach to service provision is offered as

an alternative to current approaches: using the country's philosophy of Zambian Humanism as its value premise.   (Nyirenda 1975: p. xi)

In this chapter we contend that the reliance on this interpretation of the nature of the problem is rather narrow and superficial, and as subsequent events demonstrated, Zambia's attempt to implement the philosophy of humanism during what we have labelled Phase 3 below, while successful to some degree as the price of the key commodity, copper, remained high thereby propelling economic growth and an increase in resources accruing to the state, subsequently did not yield sustainable results in social welfare. The major problem in Zambia as in the rest of Africa has been the inability to address the structural features of underdevelopment and poverty, which have also been exacerbated by various conjunctural factors (such as drought, threats of destabilization by South Africa during the apartheid era, and the HIV/AIDS epidemic).

The continuation and persistence of structural poverty is the underlying feature of the social and economic problem in Zambia, as in the rest of Africa. Various regimes over time have failed to address this problem through appropriate mutually reinforcing economic and social policies and, at times, the policies adopted have exacerbated the problem in spite of the well-meaning intentions of the policy makers. Nonetheless, it is much easier with hindsight to recognize the nature of the problem than to explain why it is that various governments have failed to resolve it.

The trajectory of social policy in Zambia may be divided into the following phases:

- **Phase 1**: Social policy during the pre-colonial period;
- **Phase 2**: Social policy during the period when Zambia was a British Protectorate;
- **Phase 3**: Social policy during the period when the country was part of the Federation of Rhodesia and Nyasaland;
- **Phase 4**: Social policy during the transitional period from 1964 to 1969;
- **Phase 5**: Social policy during the Era of Zambian Humanism, from 1969 to 1975;
- **Phase 6**: The Post Recession Era from 1975 to the present.

Below we discuss the characteristic features of social policy in each of the foregoing phases.

Phase 1: the pre-colonial period

It is well known that social protection in pre-colonial Zambian society, as in the rest of Africa, was fundamentally based on principles pertaining to the importance of collective responsibility, mutuality and reciprocity in which prime importance was placed upon individuals as social beings rather than as atomized entities. The first president of independent Zambia, President Kenneth Kaunda, contended that:

> There is no doubt at all that the greatest blessing bestowed on Africa, if one can generalize, is that we have always had a gift for Man enjoying the fellowship of Man simply because he is Man. This is at the heart of our traditional culture. (Kaunda 1968: 5)

Kaunda went further to characterize traditional African society as a 'mutual aid society', since it was organized to satisfy the basic human needs of all its members and, therefore, individualism was discouraged. It is not necessary to go into much detail regarding the nature of pre-colonial Zambian society other than to observe that the claims made by Kaunda are to a large extent tenable, but need to be qualified by the fact that some of the communities were hierarchical, that the communities lived close to subsistence with all that such livelihoods entail in terms of vulnerability to external shocks such as disease and drought, and warfare, and that standards of living were low and lifespans were short. It is to be accepted nonetheless that extreme destitution among members of a given community was not condoned or tolerated, and everything would be done to ensure that individuals were well taken care of within the existing means available.

No matter how static or imperfect the above system was in comparison to modern social support systems, it was in place to one degree or another prior to colonialism, but was to be disrupted subsequently without a viable – let alone, desirable – substitute being put in its place. This was particularly the case in urban areas. Not even the attempt by the first President of Zambia, Dr Kaunda, to reassert and reinstate the idealized version of rural support systems in the form of what he referred to as Zambian Humanism, could succeed in finding an appropriate and effective social support regime for both rural and urban areas in Zambia once it had been disrupted and disoriented.

With the onset of colonialism, dominant ruling groups simply ignored existing traditional social support systems and relegated them to adaptive mechanisms, which had to continually contend with emerging modern social and economic forces in both urban and rural areas. There was no conscious attempt during the colonial period and after the attainment of Independence to seize upon traditional support systems as stepping-stones for the development of new support systems. This indeterminacy between a beleaguered and collapsing traditional social support system and an inadequate and inappropriate fragmented modern social welfare system has yet to be resolved even to this day. Indeed, the strain has become even more accentuated with the failure to revive the economy and as poverty has increased, while the HIV/AIDS epidemic has further compromised the situation.

The advent of colonialisms resulted in at least two major eventualities. First, it disrupted the relatively static existence of African communities in Zambia, while simultaneously constraining their ability to live the way they had done traditionally. Secondly, colonialism, by imposition and through domination, grafted a new society predicated on different values and norms, but this was a society which was more dynamic and promising of higher standards of living. The nature of the developments henceforth were such that traditional societies in Zambia were thrown into disequilibrium and were compelled to adjust to the new reality without being completely absorbed into it, thereby leading to progressive unravelling of pre-colonial society even if it struggled to maintain a semblance of its traditional basis of social organization and values as a mutual aid society of sorts in the face of disruptive modern developments. In 1929, the Ministry of Native Affairs observed that:

> As natives became more travelled and more enlightened they naturally tend to become more independent and detribalized. The spirit of communal responsibility and cooperation, which belonged to the tribal system is weakening.   (quoted in Mhone 1982: 70)

The emerging modern society was in turn riddled with its own contradictions such that it was not able to fully substitute for the traditional norms of social protection, which were being progressively disrupted. Indeed, in its wake, the relative disparities in standards of living and the higher seemingly greater opportunities for self-advancement promised by the modern economy gave rise to labour migration from rural to urban areas which until this day has yet to diminish, resulting in new demands for social services in urban areas that subsequent governments could not fulfil.

Phase 2: Northern Rhodesia as a British Protectorate-social policy through managed paternalism

Commenting on the care of the poor in colonial Africa, Iliffe observes that:

> The institutions created to assist the poor during the colonial period generally embodied the traditions, preconceptions, concerns and circumstances of the foreigners who devised them. They were, therefore, diverse: independent Africa was to inherit a welfare system of baffling fragmentation and complexity. Partly for that reason, but more because the needy were so numerous, institutions cared for only a minority of poor Africans. Most continued to survive either by the care of their families or by their own efforts.   (Iliffe 1987: 193)

This observation is apt and relevant to the Zambian situation. During the colonial period, social policy developed partly in an ad hoc manner, partly in a planned manner to accommodate the needs of emerging capitalism and its associated modern economy, and partly as a consequence of particular exigencies. Underlying the emerging approach to social policy was the general unquestioned assumption that the majority of the Africans were to be resident in rural villages, and that only a small proportion as needed would be absorbed into modern employment and hence reside in urban areas. Social policy was thus palliative, tentative and marginal in nature, and was not predicated on the eventual total absorption of Africans into the new social reality dominated by capitalism and modern forms of social organization.

Zambia's integration into the world economy began as a British Protectorate. The notion of being a protectorate in effect meant that the British were administering the country on behalf of the local people with the understanding that at some future undetermined date the country would revert back to being controlled and run by the indigenous peoples themselves. This was a paternalistic, seemingly benign, form of colonial rule, which was predicated on British tutelage, implying the need to gradually impart to Zambians education and training and exposure to 'western civilization' such that in the course of time they would finally 'mature' to rule themselves. This approach to ruling and managing Africans was formally entrenched in the 1930 Passfield Amendment, which reiterated the principle of Native Paramouncy, stated thus:

> The interest of the African natives must be paramount and that if and when those interests and the interests of the immigrant should conflict the former should prevail. (quoted in Mhone 1982: 71)

In colonial Zambia, then, social policy was characterized by a number of features arising from the very nature of the country being treated as a protectorate. Social policy was based on western notions of delivery and was differentiated such that resident whites or Europeans, as they were commonly referred to, were provided with social services they would normally expect in Britain, while little systematic thought was given as to how to determine and manage the social services to be provided to Africans that were being brought into the ambit of the modern economy. In this latter aspect there were two differentiated needs – those pertaining to Africans in mining towns, and those pertaining to Africans in non-mining urban and rural modern settings. The mines had much leeway in determining and developing their own approach to social policy provisioning, while the state and missionary agencies assumed responsibility for social provisioning in non-mining urban and modern rural settings. The doctrine on Native Paramouncy was interpreted by the dominant colonial administrators to mean that the interests of the settler Europeans and those of Africans were to be pursued separately as long as they did not constrain each other. In practice, of course, the interests of the dominant group, the settlers, were paramount. For instance, Gelfand traces the development of social policy toward settlers during the early days of colonization and notes that, generally, as the number of settlers increased ways of taxing Europeans to raise revenues for various services were instituted while, simultaneously, decentralized forms of managing districts were established for the management of their affairs. A major problem related to the increase in the number of poor whites, particularly Afrikaners, who were . . .

> extremely poor . . . and lived in mud huts and very often were not able to afford the necessities of life. Their diet was mainly one of meal, pumpkin and other vegetables, and their dwellings were unsuited to the climate and not provided with conveniences.   (Gelfand 1961: 238)

This early report noted that the poor whites 'raised new problems for the Administration'. In general, as the numbers of European settlers increased, they began to demand increased social services such as education, health, housing and sanitation, all of which were systematically provided over time so that by the time of the Second World War European settlers were well catered for in terms of social services. With respect to Africans Gelfand (1961: 247) notes, for instance:

> The first educational measure adopted by administration was in 1905, when it was decided to spend the residue of the hut tax . . . The money was to be used to provide schools, improve villages, set up African hospitals, prevent disease, construct roads and for other purposes of benefit to the Africans. In May the following year Corydon made arrangements for the control of this Trust Fund, which was to remain in the hands of the Administration.

Thus while Europeans were given some measure of control with respect to social policy and every effort was made to meet their needs as their number increased, the approach with respect to Africans was marginal and gradual and guided with the Europeans in full control over the affairs of what they referred to as 'the native'. Nonetheless, within this context, a rational approach to social provisioning was attempted. Gelfand describes an interesting illustration at the beginning of the nineteenth century whereby the first school established for Africans in Mongu required that the pupils pay to go to the school. A subsequent principal changed the policies so that the education was free, and required that the students take three years of education which entailed both technical and general aspects of education, but which required that pupils pay for learning English. The pupils were further exempted from paying the hut tax. In general it was decided that the Africans needed to receive three years of education and no age limit was stipulated.

A number of Native Trust Funds were established during this early period for purposes of development, but the bulk of the funds went to administration in form of salaries for chiefs and officers. Thus, in 1943 out of a total expenditure of £3,412, £2,384 was spent on administration. The balance of the amount comprising £1,028, 'a handsome sum for a Native Treasury' was spent on development and maintenance comprising maintenance of wells, school buildings, court houses, wagon roads, dams, repairs to African wagons, repairs to dams, etc. In one trust about half was spent on development. The expenditures included the following: maintenance of roads, schools, dams and wells, rural postal services, building and agricultural schemes, schools in new areas, fruit farming and new schools. Nonetheless, it should be noted that given the needs among Africans, these expenditures were quite marginal in nature and only benefited a small number.

During this same period, the mines were systematically, but gradually providing housing, social services, sanitation, allowances for repatriation to the villages, education and what were generally known as welfare facilities that provided entertainment and leisure for Africans.

During the colonial period, the approach to social policy was paternalistic, managed and minimalist. In what could be labelled as the first phase of colonial rule, extending from the time of colonization right up to the Second World War, the aim was to ensure that Africans were brought into the urban setting as temporary residents while ensuring that there was minimal disruption to traditional rural societies. One committee observed as follows that:

> the African is born into a position within which that group which it takes for granted, it never occurs to him that he many attain a higher position which means that he has a very restricted range of wants. For his monetary wants probably not much than tax and bride price he comes to the urban areas...But money does not interest him. The rural migrant worker who intends to go back is therefore not only much less responsive to normal incentives than the detribalized man but is also mainly responsible for the large turnover so evident in African labour. (quoted in Baldwin 1966: 185)

Thus only minimal social service provisioning was envisioned for urban Africans, including those in the mines, during this period. However, this approach to social policy and economic management of African workers proved unmanageable since on the one hand, due to autonomous and induced factors such as various control measures and policies to compel Africans to offer themselves as cheap labour in urban areas and on mines in particular, African communities were being disrupted to such an extent that migration from rural to urban areas was beginning to escalate each year.

A compromise approach was arrived at which entailed the need to preserve the integrity of rural life, while ensuring that the African was to be gradually socialized into the industrialization process. But even within this context tremendous strides were made in the provision of such services as education. Thus, between 1925 and 1952 immediately after the Second World War the number of government schools increased from 355 to over 6,000; the number of private schools increased from 42 to over 1,000; and total expenditures on education increased from £10,000 to £311,529.

Phase 3: the Federation of Rhodesia and Nyasaland – the settler-dominated partnership of the rider and the horse

The period between the Second World War and the advent of majority rule and independence was dominated by the experiment in European-dominated rule in the context of the Federation of Rhodesia of Nyasaland, which began in 1953. The Federation was perceived by the dominant settler and expatriate colonial group to be based on an enlightened form of partnership based upon European custodianship and guidance, which, in the eyes of the Africans, was seen to be no more than a disguised form of domination. It was often characterized by Africans as similar to the partnership between a rider (the European) and the horse (the African). The major development in the approach to social policy was the recognition of the fact that the African was no longer a mere temporary sojourner in the modern environment. Not only did both the British and the settlers accept that the proportion of Africans that would be living permanently in the urban or modern setting would be increasing, but it was also increasingly accepted that it was a matter of time before Africans or the elite among them became equal partners in the emerging society of Rhodesia and Nyasaland. The resulting policy was one of 'balanced stabilization' in which the migrant worker was expected to have a rural childhood, long service in an industrial occupation and early retirement in middle age to peasant life (H. Heisler, quoted in Nyirenda 1975: 122).

This recognition meant, on the one hand, that social policy had to accommodate and facilitate such permanence, especially for the potential and existing working African class which was the primary preoccupation with respect to social policy during the earlier period, and, on the other hand, it meant that a class of Africans not directly involved in formal employment and their families would also be residing in the urban or modern environment and be needing social services. This latter group would consist of recent migrants who intended to stay in urban and rural formal sectors; individuals making a living in the informal sectors; retirees not wishing to return to their villages; the disabled; the unemployed, and so on. There was a general belief among the dominant group that, eventually, the Africans would return to their home village. Thus, permanence of residence in urban areas was often understood to mean continuous living and working in urban areas with short visits to the village as needed until one was ready to retire or no longer needed in the urban areas, following which one was expected to return 'home'. The earlier period had been characterized by the majority of the Africans working in urban areas for short periods and frequently returning to their villages, even if the proportion staying in towns steadily increased over time. With this acceptance of permanent residence as a major trend, the dominant group was intent on ensuring that urban migration was 'orderly', implying that it be properly controlled and regulated, and that undue demands were not placed on government, especially with respect to the provision of social services.

The Federation of Rhodesia and Nyasaland entailed decentralization of social policy for Africans in particular. The 'band-aid' approach to social policy proceeded, but with a conscious attempt to understand the dynamics of social change entailed by modernization. Thus the Rhodes–Livingstone Institute (established in Lusaka) undertook seminal studies aimed at interrogating social change in Central Africa (the current Zambia, Malawi and Zimbabwe) with the aim of informing the debate on social policy and wage determination. Thus, for instance, in 1957 and 1958 comparative studies on standards of living among Africans were undertaken which 'revealed the existence in certain households of a considerable adverse difference between costs at a minimum standard and income from wages' (Bettison 1970). Bettison went on to comment as follows regarding this evolving phenomenon:

> The phenomenon is clearly not the making of any one single government, nor does it reflect a dereliction of duty on the part of any official. Rather must it be viewed as the outcome of certain pressures, beliefs and attitudes that appear in a given type of socio-economic system at a particular time in its development.
>
> In the absence of alternative sources of income, the gap between costs at a minimum standard and income from wages will lead to an actual standard of living below that defined as minimum. The question will need to be answered: 'How then does such as person or household actually come out and continue to do so for a considerable number of years?' It is tentatively suggested that increasing rates of pulmonary tuberculosis in Southern Rhodesia, of increasing numbers of under and malnourished children at the out-patients departments of some Northern Rhodesia hospitals, and similar phenomena, are pointers to the fact that many persons living in poverty do not maintain a standard commensurate with the minimum for human needs over a considerable duration of time. (Bettison 1970)

Outside of the fairly progressive social engineering that was taking place in the copperbelt mines to accommodate a permanent labour force, not much transpired in terms of social policy during the period of the Federation of

Rhodesia and Nyasaland. In the non-mining parts of the country there was a slow, but progressive expansion and improvement in social services such as health, sanitation and housing, but not on any significant scale. On the mines, the more liberal Rhodesia Selection Trust pioneered innovative ways of providing for permanent African workers with differentiated occupations, while the Anglo American Corporation, which controlled the other mines that had South African roots, tended to pursue fairly conservative social policies on its mines.

The period of the Federation of Rhodesia and Nyasaland saw the pursuit of a policy of accommodating the needs of a permanent labour force, at least for as long as the Africans worked for the mines, and of advancing Africans into higher occupations and eventually substituting African workers for white workers. Thus social centres, known as 'welfare centres', were strategically established in the African townships, replete with entertainment facilities such as sports and games, restaurants, cinemas, libraries, swimming pools, beer halls, bars and social welfare and training clubs. Most of these centres had nominal fees and cost recovery pricing for commodities, but they were also subsidized by the mines, especially with respect to infrastructure. There was indeed a time when education in the mines was compulsory and health facilities were accessible. All this was undertaken in an environment that placed a high premium on planning of townships, sanitation, and preventative primary care. Also, African workers were vertically differentiated according to occupational status as well, while ensuring that workers in the lowest occupations still had access to essential social services. Indeed, in terms of modern social welfare, the mines were exemplary within the context of their controlled and paternalistic environment. By the time of independence in 1964, destitution in the mines and their related municipalities, which took advantage of the economic rents from the mines was unheard of. Nonetheless, the rest of the country outside of the mines and their immediate municipalities was essentially lagging behind. In fact around the mining towns, which consisted of mining townships and municipalities, informal settlements with all their attendant social ills were expanding, but these were generally ignored by authorities.

Phase 4: the euphoria of independence, the economic boom and social policy – the transitional period, 1964 to 1969

The advent of independence brought with it the end of the colonial order and its paternalistic modes of control and regulation. The social agenda changed as well from one that was based on racial considerations to a non-racial one, and from one that tended to selectively cater to special groups, particularly in urban areas, to one based on principles of inclusivity. Progressively as well the autonomy of the mines in providing social services was eroded as the state took on the task of centrally controlling expenditures and provision of social services. A major consequence of the dawn of independence was the explosion of those social demands that had been ignored during the colonial era – either due to racial considerations, or due to the fact that the environment was controlled. In addition, the emerging trend towards increasing population and urban to rural migration also had the effect of accentuating the demand for social services. Lastly, a year after Zambian independence, the minority government of Southern Rhodesia declared independence from Britain, precipitating a near-war-like situation in Southern Africa in which the new white-controlled country of Rhodesia, together with the then apartheid regime of South Africa, coalesced, pitted against the insurgent liberation movements and their main host countries, Zambia and Tanzania.

The first major policy initiative following the attainment of independence was the formulation of the Transitional Development Plan (1965 to 1966), which had the following overall objective:

All future planning will involve, directly or indirectly, a deliberate guidance of the whole economy. The present plan, while still mainly concerned with government capital expenditure, is more tied to the overall development objectives and reflects the beginning of full government coordination of all its parts   (Government of the Republic of Zambia, 1965).

Specific objectives were identified as the following:

- To provide adequate standards of defence and administration because of neglect of these functions by previous administrations;
- To rapidly expand post-primary education to help solve Zambia's severe shortage of skills then and in subsequent periods;
- And to greatly expand agricultural production and related to this, to extend the spread of economic activity into the rural areas of the line of rail.

The Transitional Plan reflected on these early years of independence and their implications for social policy, with particular reference to health, as follows:

Three separate sets of considerations explain why it was not possible to the time when the Transitional Plan was being prepared either to work out a comprehensive health strategy for Zambia or to identify assurance projects which would without question contribute to the achievement of basic health policy aims. There was of course first the fact that health had for a decade been a non-territorial 'subject' directed and administered from Salisbury [the capital of the then white controlled Federation of Rhodesia and Nyasaland]...Under that regime health policy was very much orientated along racial lines...

And in the last years of the Federation when money was short – health services came to be looked upon as something on which money could be saved...

[Second], having taken over in such generally unfavourable circumstances the new Health Ministry was confronted, almost at once, with an extraordinarily sharp increase in the demand for services at the two main hospitals... Given the inherent difficulties of administering a health service properly in a country with a population as widely dispersed as Zambia's, the burden of these additional strains should not be underestimated...

The third reason is that it has been realized for some time that the claims of education, national security and the key sectors were going to have priority during the first phase of development after independence... Once the quite exceptional and partially non-recurring claims of sectors like defence and education have been met, it will be sectors like health and housing, which have priority. In the meantime, these departments must, wherever possible, get along as best they can.   (Government of the Republic of Zambia 1965)

The plan went on to note that 'all this should explain – and justify – a certain "stitch and patch" quality about the health programme as approved under the Transitional Plan'. Thus Zambia's major social policy priority after independence was education. In the health sector a hierarchical system of health provision was stipulated which favoured the two large urban hospitals, and facilities along 'the line of rail', essentially the urban areas, but which was generally biased against rural areas. But, the government, aware of the disparities, noted as follows:

An arrangement of this kind is easy to describe in schematic terms. It is, of course much harder to judge where exactly the emphasis should come. In general, however, and for good reason, Government policy leans towards a strengthening of facilities at the base of the pyramid and towards correcting the present glaring disparity between facilities available along the line of rail and in the rural areas. With the limits set by costs and the availability of doctors, the aim is – and must be – to make 'normal' medical treatment geographically and even locally accessible to all.   (Government of the Republic of Zambia 1965)

With respect to housing, the Transitional Development Plan noted the problems posed by the increasing rate of urbanization on the one hand, which placed Zambia, with about 25 per cent of its population in urban areas at the time, as one of the most urbanized countries in Africa (Kenya and Tanzania were estimated to have 7 per cent and 4 per cent rates of urbanization), and the dispersed nature of the population, on the other hand:

Thus Zambia must face the problems of urban concentration. Outside of the main towns and off the line of rail, the problems are the reverse. They are the problems thrown up by the geographical dispersal of population over thinly-populated areas. Housing and Local Government policy in Zambia has evolved basically with these two quite opposite phenomena in mind – with preventing urban overcrowding and the development of slums on the one hand, and with knitting together widely dispersed communities on the other. (Government of the Republic of Zambia 1965)

Accordingly, the Plan allocated fairly significant amounts of money toward a balanced programme of housing development aimed at meeting the emerging needs in both urban and rural areas. The policy was to give repayable loans to urban areas and grants to rural authorities for housing construction and development of sanitation and electricity grids. In this manner it was hoped:

To even out the disparities between more and less well-favoured areas and thus to bring them closer together. But the same policy is even more strikingly reflected if the ministry's financial treatment of urban and rural local authorities is set against each other. For, whereas, in the case of the urban authorities almost 90 percent of the money which the ministry will make available during the plan period will be in the form of loans, the lending proportion in the case of rural authorities will be less than 25 percent. The rest of the money, which the ministry makes available to the rural authorities will be in the form of grants. (Government of the Republic of Zambia 1965)

The Plan went on, further, to note that 'this policy of subsidizing more remote areas of the country on the part of the ministry (of Housing and Social Development), is of course only another reflection of the Government's general policy of developing rural areas which has been noted elsewhere and which is reflected throughout the Transitional Plan' (Government of the Republic of Zambia 1965). This approach was seen to reflect 'a new search on the part of the country's first popular government to find a proper relationship between the centre and the rural areas'. The government was anxious not to encourage rural to urban migration, especially in a manner that would deplete rural areas of key human resources and stifle imitative and development in these areas. At the same time it noted that it could not overly emphasize rural areas such that skilled personnel migrated from the centre to rural areas. The writers of the Plan were alert enough to identify this predicament as a major problem, which would continue to haunt the nation in the future:

More generally the country is so young – and its population 'scattered' so exceptionally – that it is difficult to foresee the way in which local community and provincial life is going to be related to national life and how they should be encouraged. The only certain thing, perhaps, is that these problems – particularly the problem of 'dispersal' but also the opposite problem of urban overcrowding – will continue to pose themselves long after the Transitional Plan has been successfully implemented (and despite the fact that its successful implementation will ease the pressures). (Government of the Republic of Zambia 1965)

The above comments in the Transitional Plan have been cited at length, first, because they demonstrate the normative intentions of the new government in aiming at an inclusive social policy; secondly, because they show that the government was from the outset well aware of the social deficits and exacerbating trends with which it was confronted with; and thirdly, because they show that the government was not unduly optimistic about resolving the emerging social policy dilemma. We noted earlier that in a developing country, social policy is only one aspect of a broader development problem that requires an economic policy counterpart. Here, it may be noted that the Transitional Plan observed that a normal development agenda could not be pursued under the new circumstances precipitated by the unilateral declaration of independence by the minority regime in Rhodesia and by the belligerent stance taken by apartheid South Africa toward the newly independent majority ruled countries, especially Tanzania and Zambia which were harbouring liberation movements and were viewed as progressives.

Education, housing and health were major components of social policy during the early years. Other aspects of social policy are summarized by Dixon (1987) as consisting of the following during the early socialist-oriented period:

- A Department of Social Welfare provided probation, public assistance and child care, but with the major expectation that extended family responsibility would be the major form of child support and care;
- Urban local authorities and mining townships provided recreational facilities;
- The Community Development Department provided women's clubs, literacy clubs and basic facilities such as housing and roads;
- Voluntary organizations provided recreational training, health and child welfare;
- And the National Provident Fund was established which catered for almost all formal sector workers including agricultural workers.

In areas of social policy in which government had a mandate, centralized control was emerging to be a major factor.

The Transitional Plan (1965 to 1966) was followed by the first National Development Plan (1966 to 1970). Over this period, government sought to pursue the following objectives: balanced growth; a leading role for the public sector in developing economic and social infrastructure; and the need to de-link from the settler-dominated countries of Rhodesia, Mozambique, South Africa, and Angola. Thus while in the Transitional Plan 56 per cent of development expenditures went to social infrastructure (with 21 per cent and 23 per cent allocated to economic infrastructure and productive investment) the First National Development Plan allocated 34 per cent to social infrastructure and 30 per cent to economic infrastructure and 34 per cent to productive investment (Dresang 1970). However, the actual implementation of the plan deviated from what had been initially postulated primarily due to the exigencies of the emerging tensions in Southern Africa. Increased amounts of actual expenditures were spent on economic infrastructure aimed at diversifying sources of oil (by building a pipeline to Dar es Salaam) and transportation routes to the sea away from dependence on routes passing through Rhodesia, Mozambique, South Africa and Angola.

Further developments affecting both economic and social policy began in 1968 with the Mulungushi Declaration, which introduced an all-embracing nationalization of major economic activities in Zambia and the promulgation of Zambian Humanism in 1969 as the guiding ideology of government. As these new initiatives were beginning, Zambia had not made any major dent on its social policy deficits nor on the need for economic restructuring toward diversification and inclusive growth. Reflecting on these early developments in planning in Zambia, Dresang concluded as follows:

> It is a cruel irony those states (that)need the advantages of efficiency and coordination that accrue from planning for balanced growth are those states that are least capable of planning rationally and implementing efficiently and effectively.   (Dresang 1970)

Phase 5: indigenizing social policy through Zambian Humanism

The social policy implications of the Mulungushi Declaration and the new philosophy of Zambian Humanism were contained in the statement issued by Dr Kaunda, the first President of Zambia, titled 'Zambia's Guidelines for the Next Decade', which, as the ILO noted, substantively articulated a basic needs approach to social and economic policy. The main elements were summarized by the ILO (1981) as the following:

> The opportunity and ability for all to earn an income, in cash or kind, to meet their family needs for food, shelter, clothing and other basic goods; access for all within reasonable distance to health, education, clean water, a reliable bus service; agricultural extension and community services to

provide support for households and communities; above all, an end to malnutrition of children, so the next generation grows up in full health and strength.

The above guidelines appeared feasible given that the prices of the major commodity, copper, were high and the country's economy was on an upswing, hence the observation in the Transitional Development Plan that finance was not a constraint. These conditions, and the accompanying optimism in anticipated social and economic policy, were not to last long. The international recession, which began in the mid-1970s, had a major destabilizing effect upon the Zambian economy. This was exacerbated by escalating war in Zimbabwe and difficulties Zambia was facing in finding alternative transportation routes for its exports and imports, both of which were quite critical for the economy. But, as the ILO (1981) observed: 'Also, and perhaps of comparable importance, domestic distortions of priorities within Zambia have meant that goals and plans for broad-based development and rural advance have not been carried into action'.

The ILO notes that, in spite of the commendable efforts the country had begun with at the attainment of independence, the international recession, which led to drastic falls in the price and output of copper, the mainstay of the economy, reasserted long-standing underlying tendencies whereby: 'The urban sector and large scale modern industry have increasingly pre-empted the lion's share of resources pledged in plans of rural revival, employment creation and basic needs for all' (ILO 1981). Between 1974 and 1979/80 gross domestic product declined by 52 per cent; private consumption declined by 21 per cent; government recurrent expenditure declined by 25 per cent and government capital expenditure declined by 65 per cent. By 1980 not only was expenditure on social services drastically reduced, except perhaps for that on education and health, but the greater proportion of this expenditure went to personal emoluments with less than 3 per cent being spent on programme related expenses (Dixon 1987).

By the end of the 1970s the social situation, while not particularly desperate, had not improved significantly for the majority of the people, as indicated by the following indicators cited by the ILO in 1981:

- The population had increased markedly, to about 6 million people compared to a population of about 4.3 million ten years earlier;
- The life expectancy was estimated at about 48 years;
- The infant mortality and child mortality rates were estimated to be 140 and 197 per thousand respectively;
- Unemployment was relatively low and so was informal-sector employment;
- Income distribution was such that the poorest 40 per cent only received about 8 per cent of total income while the richest 5 per cent received 35 per cent of total income;

- About 60 per cent of the households were estimated to be living below the basic minimum threshold;
- Daily calorific intake was estimated to be about 87 per cent of requirements;
- Third degree and moderate malnutrition of children under 5 years of age was estimated to be about 40 per cent in rural areas;
- Only 40 per cent of rural households had access to clean water;
- 81 per cent of households could access a health facility within 12 kilometres;
- While more than 80 per cent of households in urban areas had access to relatively decent housing, less than half this percentage had similar access in rural areas;
- While adult literacy rates were below 50 per cent, enrolments of school-going children were high at more than 80 per cent, while progression rates were very low.
- Overall half of the households were estimated to be poor or very poor.

Thus, in 1981 the ILO's Basic Needs Mission concluded as follows:

> Zambia's economic prospects are thus extremely serious – more serious than at any time since independence. Already the mass of the population is under considerable pressure in terms of meeting their basic needs for food, every day consumption goods, medicines, basic services and transportation. Effective action to meeting these basic needs is thus urgently required.

The social and economic situation was never to recover fully from this setback. Indeed, the situation progressively deteriorated right up to the present. Following the recession the capacity of government to articulate coherent economic and social policies, or let alone implement them declined precipitously, while the social situation continued to deteriorate in spite of brief respites of economic growth and the adoption of ancillary or palliative social policy measures as advocated by multilateral donors such as the World Bank.

Phase 6: the post-recession era from 1975 to the present

Between 1975 and 1990, the government stubbornly stuck to its so-called socialist policies based on control over the main activities in the economy and price control of basic commodities, and relatively free provisions of social services such as health and education. As the years progressed, however, it became clear that both the economy and the provision of social services were unsustainable. Nationalized industries continued to drain public expenditures as they failed to perform profitably. Meanwhile prices of basic commodities such as mealie meal (the basic staple), cooking oil, beer, bread, salt and other similar basic goods continued to be controlled resulting in pervasive shortages of these commodities and yielding a black market in basic goods. All of the basic goods virtually disappeared from formal shops (mainly state-owned) and could only be bought through black marketeers at extremely inflated prices. Meanwhile, the government continued to insist on selling basic goods at prices that were below the cost of production, seemingly oblivious to the impact of the black market. Essentially, those that had connections and who could stand in queues early in the mornings, and for long hours, could manage to buy basic goods at controlled prices and then proceed to sell the same goods at black market prices. The free for all services began to deteriorate as the government was unable to maintain the quality of services especially their related infrastructure. The shortage of foreign exchange, also exacerbated the many problems that continued to plague the economy. For more than a decade, the government continued to run an economy that was basically degenerating without any intention of wanting to reverse or change its policies.

By the end of the 1980s, as both the domestic and external debts increased phenomenally, and as access to basic goods and services became increasingly difficult and cumbersome, it was clear that a change in policy direction was needed. Meanwhile, pressures for democratization were also mounting as the citizenry began to question the one-party system of government that had been in effect for more than two decades. This, of course, coincided with the collapse of the Soviet Bloc and the increased call for worldwide democratization. At the beginning of the 1990s a combination of internal lobbying among the elite, and external pressures from the World Bank and the IMF, led to the eventual adoption of structural adjustment and stabilization programmes under the tutelage of the Bretton Woods institutions. Over the decade of the 1990s Zambia attempted to implement standard economic reforms, but the economic situation, although improved, has had little impact on the social situation. Most recently, Zambia has embarked on the HIPC-associated initiative on debt relief, which is accompanied by the formulation of a poverty reduction strategy programme (PRSP). These initiatives have yet to make any major dent on the deteriorating economic and social trends in Zambia.

The stabilization and structural adjustment programmes reinstated the role of the market, rather than the state, as the major mechanism for allocating resources. This actually ejected the agenda for economic and social inclusion as a conscious state policy stance, leaving the outcomes to market forces. Essentially, as many commentators had observed, the return to a laissez-faire market regime merely restored the market-driven enclave and dependent economic tendencies that had been dominant since the colonial period and which had been inherited at independence. Thus in fact reinstatement of the market regime without the guidance of the state merely reinforced the marginalization of the majority of the labour force and households which had been inherited from the colonial period and which subsequent experiments in social and economic policies had failed to reverse substantively. And by rolling back the state such that its role is restricted to merely overseeing the economy and not guiding it towards desired outcomes, the state has been stripped of its ability to embark on developmental economic and social policy measures. In effect, the state has been weakened at the very time that poverty is escalating and the economic dualism is deepening.

The nature of the deterioration in social indicators over the period is easily seen from the following data:

- Population growth has continued to grow at a rate of about 2.3 per cent per year while growth in gross domestic product declined at the rate of about 2 per cent per year in 1995, and in 1998 picking up to a positive growth rate of 2 per cent per year in 1999.
- Life expectancy at birth, which was estimated to be about 48 years in 1979, had fallen to about 45 years in 1995 and 39 years by 1999, mostly due to the HIV/AIDS epidemic;
- Infant mortality had increased from 110 per thousand births in 1995 to 114 by 1999, while child mortality stood at 187 per thousand births in 1999;
- School enrolments had fallen from over 80 per cent in the 1970s to below 75 per cent by 1995;
- By 1995 unemployment rates in the urban areas of Lusaka and the Copperbelt were estimated to be as high as 29 per cent and 26 per cent, with higher rates among female youth (about 75 per cent for those between the ages of 12 and 19) and youth generally;
- In 1996 levels of poverty were estimated to be about 83 per cent in rural areas and 46 per cent in urban areas while levels of extreme poverty were estimated at 68 per cent and 27 per cent in rural and urban areas respectively.

Conclusion: lessons from the Zambian experience

By the turn of the twenty-first century, about forty years after attaining independence, it is clear that Zambia is a country under siege economically, and is very much unable to address its social agenda. Over all these years the country has been unable to resolve its inherited dilemma. The country was colonized in a manner that evolved an enclave formal economy dependent upon copper exports. Social policy was initially a controlled exercise that catered to the need of the settler class and the small proportion of Africans that were needed to service the newly developing economy, its administrative apparatus, and induced secondary and tertiary sectors. The rest of the population, which was in the majority, was seen as residual and relatively redundant to this new economy. Social and economic policies were predicated on the needs of the emerging formal economy – and not on the needs of the majority of population.

Thus, in spite of pronounced intentions to embark on broad-based inclusive development in which social policy and economic policy mutually interacted in a self-reinforcing manner, the actual outcomes have been exclusionary and circumscribed, even during times when finance was not a constraint. It may be noted that the clearest articulation of the broad-based development and integration of social and economic policy occurred just as the country was experiencing a boom, yet the outcomes were contrary to the declared intentions. The onset of the recession in the mid-1970s merely revealed the social and economic weaknesses that underlay the system. Indeed there had been enough warnings from a number of analysts regarding the need for careful management of the economic rents arising from the boom (Baldwin 1966) and dependence upon copper (Mhone 1982), but while such warnings were reflected in successive Development Plans, the actual implementation of the policies fell far short of expectations. In part the problems lay with the intransigence of the bureaucracy which increasingly became self-serving; in part, it was due to various biases and distortions in market indicators induced by well-meaning but poorly implemented economic and social policies; and in part it was due to policy implementation failures that progressively compounded the situation.

In the event, Zambian social policy remained an ambiguous appendage to economic policy even if major gains had been made in the provision of education and health during the decade and a half of independence. The onset of the recession in the mid-1970s and the HIV/AIDS epidemic from the early 1990s onwards has resulted in the reversal of many of the gains that had been made especially with respect to quality of services, even if the numbers having access to various social services such as health and education have remained relatively high. The scourge of HIV/AIDS has made Zambia one of the most affected countries in Africa, placing an additional strain on the health system and poverty being experienced by many households. Thus the country has been unable to achieve an inclusive, broad-based growth path, and its social indicators have deteriorated.

The clarity of vision in economic and social policy that characterized the early years of independence has been dissipated in the wake of an opportunistic ruling elite and collapsing bureaucracy. Reporting on a World Bank meeting with government officials and donor agencies a press release issued by the World Bank as recently as 2000 notes as follows:

> Taking cognizance of the very high levels of poverty in Zambia, the delegates expressed the need to focus government development strategy firmly on poverty reduction. It was also noted that the most effective way to achieve sustained poverty reduction is through broad-based economic growth and diversification from copper into other productive services.

To this end the Government informed the meeting that it is working on a Long Term Development Vision to cover the period up to 2025, which would address these issues. The Government is also working on a Poverty Reduction Strategy Paper, which will cover the first three years of the Vision. Both the Vision and PRSP will be prepared in a participatory manner. While commending the Government on programme and strategy formulation, delegates stressed the need for increased government focus on implementation of agreed upon programmes in order to improve results.

This meeting was attended by all the major multilateral and bilateral donors in Zambia.

Now the above recognition is one that the government has articulated on a number of occasions since the Transitional Development Plan, but which the government has been unable to achieve. Interestingly, the donors refer to the need for a development plan, which the government intends to deliver in form of the long-term vision, when government has been shorn of all the instruments and capacity to implement a development plan by the very nature of stabilization and structural adjustment programmes that have been adopted. Indeed the very policies advocated by the Bretton Woods institutions do not allow for a conscious approach to 'guiding' the economy towards the mooted diversification and broad-based outcomes. Rather, it is expected that the market will realize those outcomes once appropriate macroeconomic fundamentals are in place.

Finally, the government and the donors do not indicate what the role of a PRSP would be, and how it will differ or complement the long-term development vision being embarked upon. The present policy thrust recommends a passive role for government, at the precise time when a proactive role is needed to reverse the deteriorating and economic and social situation. Current trends in Zambia reinforce the enclave growth accompanied by an evolutionary deterioration of the social situation for the majority of the population so that social policy is not only de-linked from economic policy which is supposed to take its own market-driven path as the enabling environment is 'improved' through stabilization and structural adjustment measures, but is also increasingly seen as a residual de-linked from the economic sphere. Thus, both development reinforcing social welfare and socially sensitive economic policy making are precluded by the current policy stance, hence vitiating the possibility of promoting a virtuous interaction between social and economic policy directed at precipitating an inclusive growth path that would improve both economic growth and social welfare, thereby realizing economic development, as understood in its classic sense.

The case of Zambia throws into sharp relief the problems confronting enclave economies that have a legacy of colonialism, and the difficulties of arriving at a policy regime that combines economic and social policy in a manner that is mutually reinforcing to underpin an inclusive development path. One aspect of this problem concerns the diagnosis of the economic and social predicament of such countries; another concerns the design of appropriate economic and social strategies to address the inherited problems, including the relative roles of the state and the market; and lastly another relates to the political economy and governance requirements for an appropriate strategy. These and similar issues need to be further interrogated for a country like Zambia if an appropriate and desirable social policy regime is to be arrived at.

This case study on Zambia provides lessons for a country such as South Africa, which is in its early stages of embarking on economic and social transformation. South Africa is now approaching the end of the first decade of the transition to democracy, and, already, there is concern that the pace at which various social and economic policies that are being implemented and impacting upon the majority of the population which bore the brunt of previous policies of exclusion, marginalization and exploitation is rather slow.

Historically, in South Africa access to social services was unfortunately also skewed in favour of the privileged households. Thus access to education, housing, transport, health, water, and sanitation for instance generally depended upon one's race, gender and location. Generally, the relative status of a household as determined by employment status and income on the basis of their race or gender would also tend to influence their relative access to social services and amenities. Historical inequities in the provisions of and access to social services and amenities are well known. By 1996, for instance, while only 28 per cent of Africans had access to piped water in a dwelling almost 100 per cent of whites had similar access; and while 34 per cent of African household heads said that they had access to a flush or chemical toilet, almost all whites had access to such facilities. Generally about 97 per cent of whites and 75 per cent of Africans had access to safe tap water.

For a middle-income country, levels of poverty in South Africa are relatively quite high. When all the relevant measures of social and economic deprivation are taken into account the rate of poverty (which measures levels of absolute poverty) was about 45 per cent in 2000 (UNDP 2000). The percentage of the population living in poverty differed markedly by province as follows: Northern Province – 78 per cent; Eastern Cape – 74 per cent; Mpumalanga – 64 per cent; Kwa Zulu Natal – 63 per cent; Northwest – 61 per cent Northern Cape – 58 per cent, Free State – 54 per cent; Gauteng – 32 per cent; and Western Cape – 29 per cent. Overall an estimated 18 million persons out of a population of about 42 million lived in absolute poverty. Levels of poverty were generally higher in rural (71 per cent) areas than in urban areas and much higher among Africans (61 per cent) than among whites (1 per cent). Poverty also has a gender dimension with 60 per cent of female-headed households as compared to 30 per cent of male-headed households living in absolute poverty. That a significant number of South Africans lived in poverty or were highly vulnerable to being poor was also reasserted by the Poverty and Inequality Report (May 1998).

The socioeconomic disparities outlined above, underpinned by political relations of domination and subjugation, and an economic system which excluded and marginalized the majority from partaking of the opportunities it offered, were the motive force behind the struggle for democratization, which ushered in the democratic dispensation of 1994. The new government has been intent on ensuring that within the resources available, the backlog of social needs would be addressed. A major instrument in this respect was the reprioritization of the budget in order to address the various disparities on the basis of race, gender, and province. A major aim in this respect has been the need to ensure that basic needs were met. Thus, as noted in the Human Development Report 2000 (UNDP 2000), government proceeded to reprioritise it as follows:

- 46 per cent of the total education budget was spent on basic education;
- 29 per cent of the total health budget was spent on basic health care, with free health care being provided for pregnant women and children under six years of age;
- 2 million people were given access to safe water;
- Half a million houses had been built;
- A land restitution programme was initiated although at a slow pace given the legal procedures required to process the various claims.

The new government had initially articulated its agenda for socioeconomic transformation in the Reconstruction and Development Programme, which was an ambitious and comprehensive programme for socioeconomic reform. But two years into the democratic dispensation the government felt obligated to subordinate its ambitious programme of socioeconomic transformation to the imperatives of a stabilization programme, which restricted the degree to which government could proactively pursue a social reform and developmental agenda. Government argued that this was the best way to ensure that a more sustainable basis for both economic growth and social progress could be promoted. But four years since the adoption of the economic reform and stabilization programme, both the social progress and the economic resuscitation have been elusive, with the backlog of socioeconomic needs expanding.

A number of reasons are given for the fundamental shift in policy approach from the pre-1994 developmental state-led agenda to the post-1996 market-based approach to both social and economic policy, among which are the following. First, there is a strong belief in government that the current globalized environment requires that the market be relied upon as the major instrument for allocating resources. Secondly, stabilization requirements with respect to fiscal and monetary policy are seen as necessary if sustainable growth is to be achieved. Thirdly, it is expected that by restricting the role of the state and indeed by rolling it back resources can be diverted from what may be seen as unproductive consumption to more productive uses which will contribute to the resuscitation of the economy; in addition, it is expected that such a withdrawal and restriction of the state would act as a signal to foreign investors that the government is committed to free enterprise, and, as such, will encourage them to invest in the country.

The future direction of social policy in South Africa still remains to be seen. However, the government recently appointed a Committee to examine this particular issue and to make recommendations on possible policies that could be adopted to address the plight of those experiencing persistent social deficits. The post-1994 government has been formally committed to eradicating – or at least reducing – the social deficit backlog by addressing the social and economic needs of the majority. These intentions by the new government were well articulated in the Reconstruction and Development Programme and have been translated, to one degree or another, into a number of policies and initiatives in the various government departments at national, provincial and local levels.

But, as noted earlier, and as shown above, the social and economic deficits and backlogs are intimately intertwined. On the one hand the dimensions of the social backlogs is amplified by the inability of the economy to precipitate an inclusive growth path able to absorb the previously and historically excluded majority, while, by this same token, government finds itself unable to muster the resources needed to address the persistent and emerging social needs. On top of all this, globalization, economic liberalization and the HIV/AIDS epidemic continue to exacerbate the situation. Thus, the country is being called upon to consider the need for a comprehensive social policy at the same time that it has to embark on an economic strategy that would begin to uplift the majority of the people more directly than through trickle-down effects implicit in the current macroeconomic stance. This is a major challenge that the socioeconomic legacy has bequeathed to the current government and polity, and it is a challenge that is becoming increasingly imperative to address. This is also a challenge that continues to haunt many African countries other than Zambia and South Africa that have been independent, but have yet to address and resolve the legacy of colonialism, even after more than four decades of independence.

Bibliography

Baldwin, R. E. (1966) *Economic Development and Export Growth: a Study of Northern Rhodesia, 1920 to 1960*. Berkeley: University of California Press.

Bettison, D. G. (1970) *The Poverty Datum Line in Central Africa, Human Development in British Central Africa*. Manchester: Manchester University Press.

Dixon, J. (1987) *Social Welfare in Africa*. New York: Croom Helm.

Dresang, D. L. (1970) 'Bureaucracy and Development in Zambia', paper presented at the 13th Annual Meeting of the African Studies Association.

Gelfand, M. (1961) *Northern Rhodesia in the Days of the Charter: a Medical and Social Study 1878 to 1924*. Oxford: Basil Blackwell.

Government of the Republic of Zambia (1965) *An Outline of the Transitional National Development Plan*. Lusaka: Government of the Republic of Zambia.

Iliffe, J. (1987) *The African Poor: a History*. Cambridge: Cambridge University Press,.

ILO (1981) *Zambia: Basic Needs in an Economy Under Pressure, Jobs and Skills Programme for Africa*. Addis Ababa: ILO.

ILO/UNDP (2000) *Jobs for Africa: Poverty Reduction Employment Strategies for Africa (JFA-PRESA)*. Geneva and New York: ILO.

Kaunda, K. D. (1968) *Humanism in Zambia and a Guide to its Implementation*. Lusaka: Government Printer.

May, J. (1998) *Poverty and Inequality in South Africa*. South Africa: The International Ministerial Committee for Poverty and Inequality.

Mhone, G. C. Z. (1982) *The Political Economy of a Dual Labour Market in Africa: the Copper Industry and Dependence in Zambia 1929 to 1969*. New Jersey: Associated University Presses/Fairleigh Dickinson University Press.

Nyirenda, V. G. (1975) 'Social Change and Social Policy in a Developing Country: The Case of Zambia'. Unpublished PhD, University of California.

UNDP (2000) *Human Development Report 2000*. New York: UNDP.

World Bank (2000) *Zambia: Partnership Renewed for Growth and Poverty Reduction*. Washington, DC: World Bank.

Index